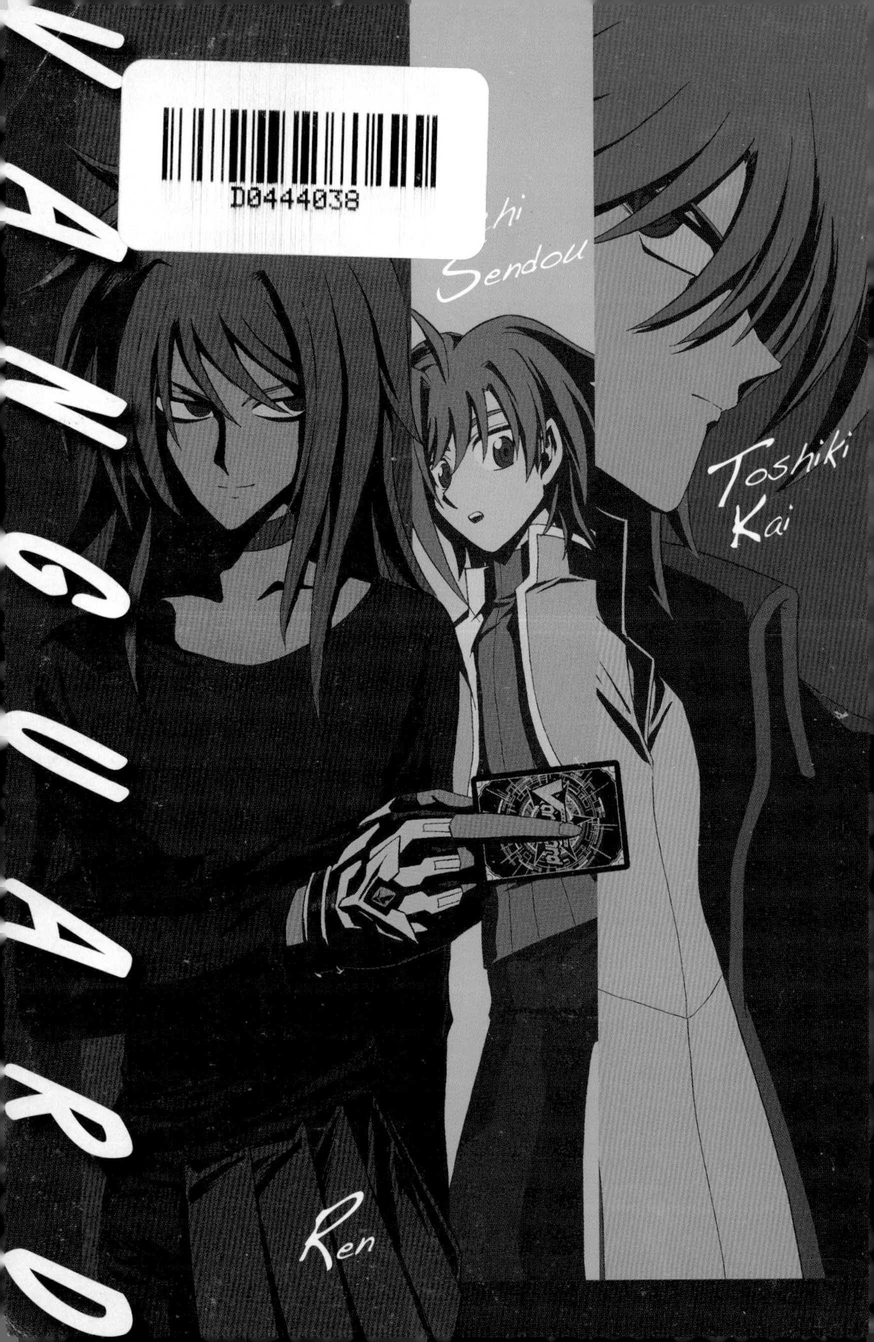
VANGUARD
Sendou
Toshiki
Kai
Ren

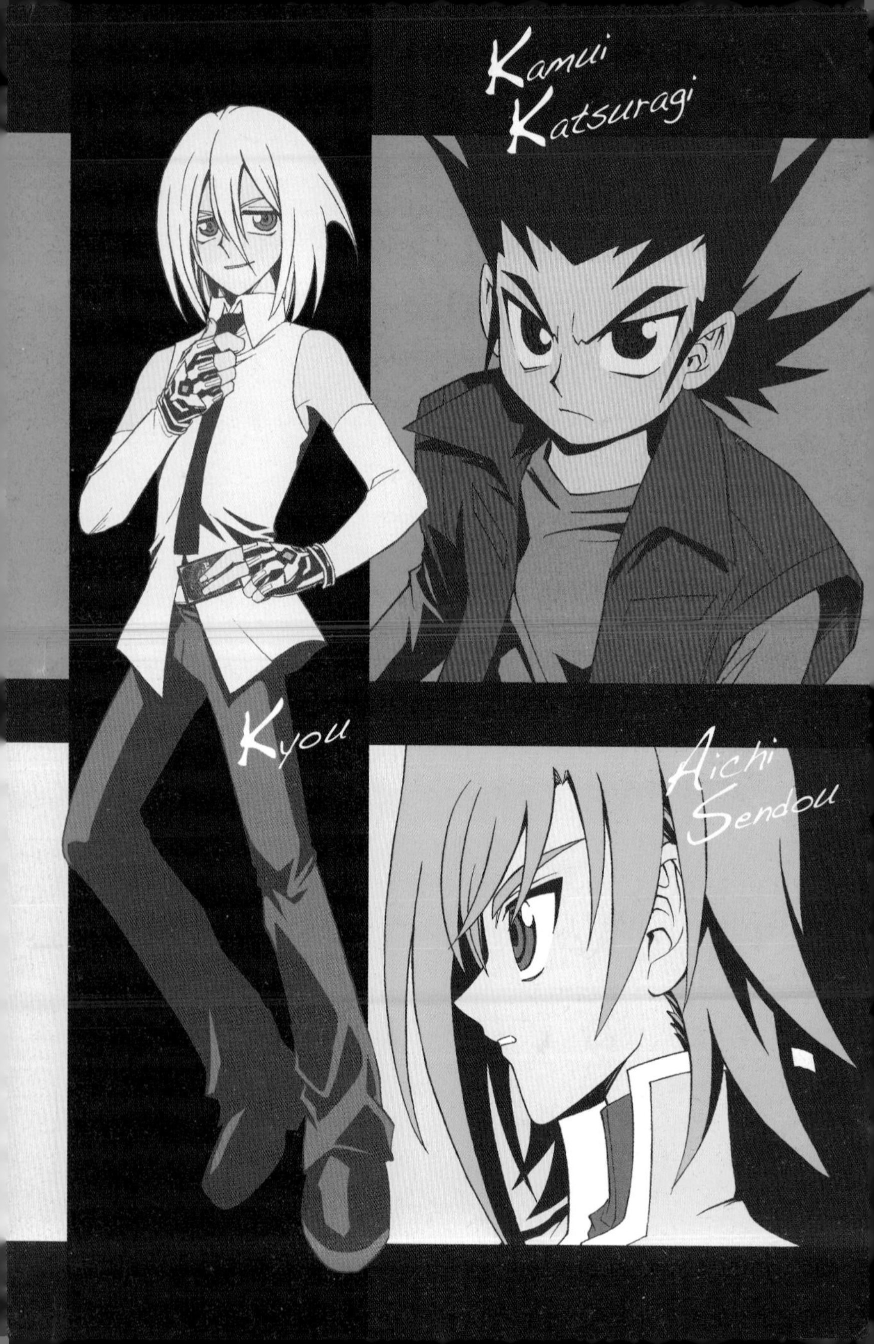
Kamui Katsuragi
Aichi Sendou
Kyou

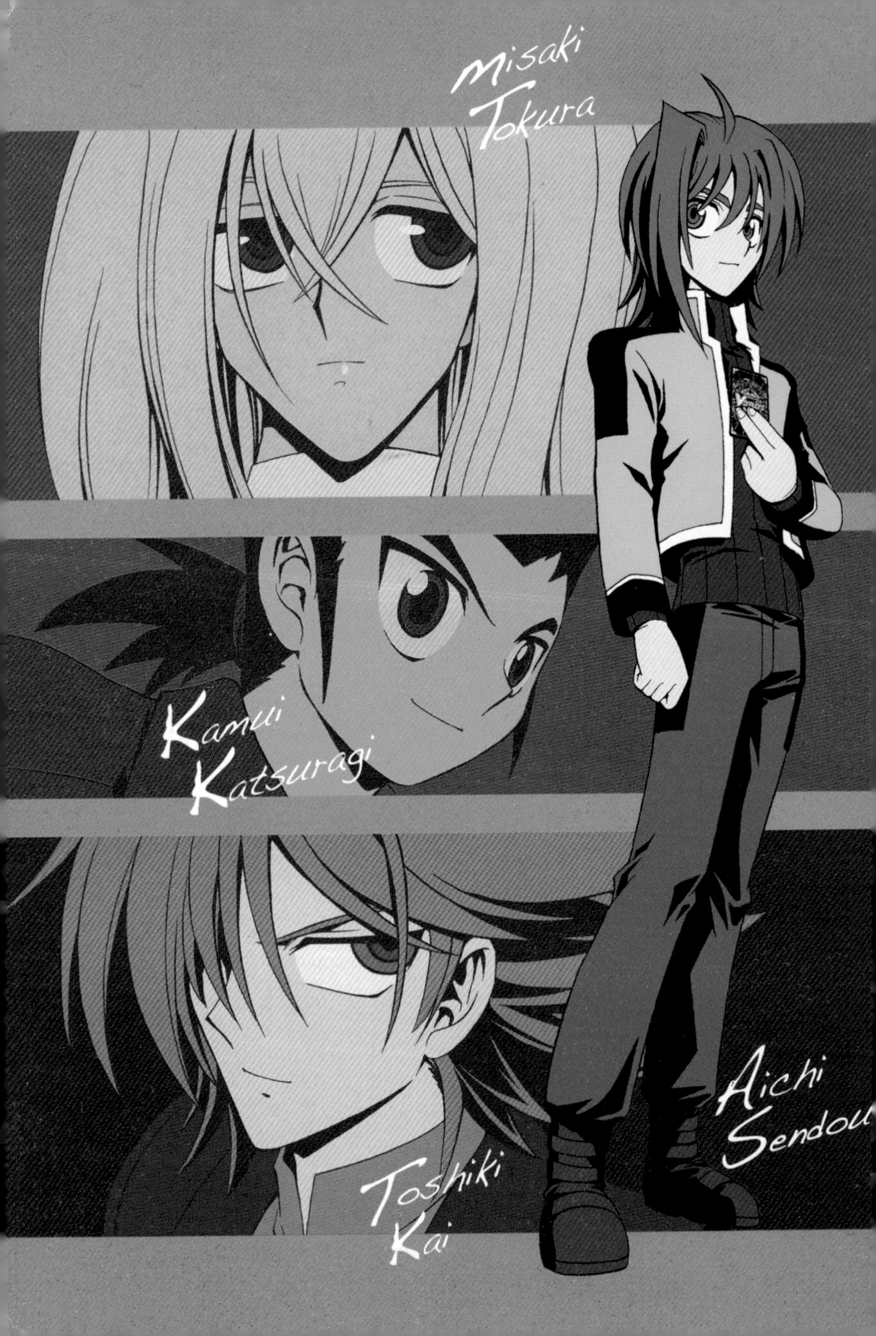
Misaki Tokura
Aichi Sendou
Kamui Katsuragi
Toshiki Kai

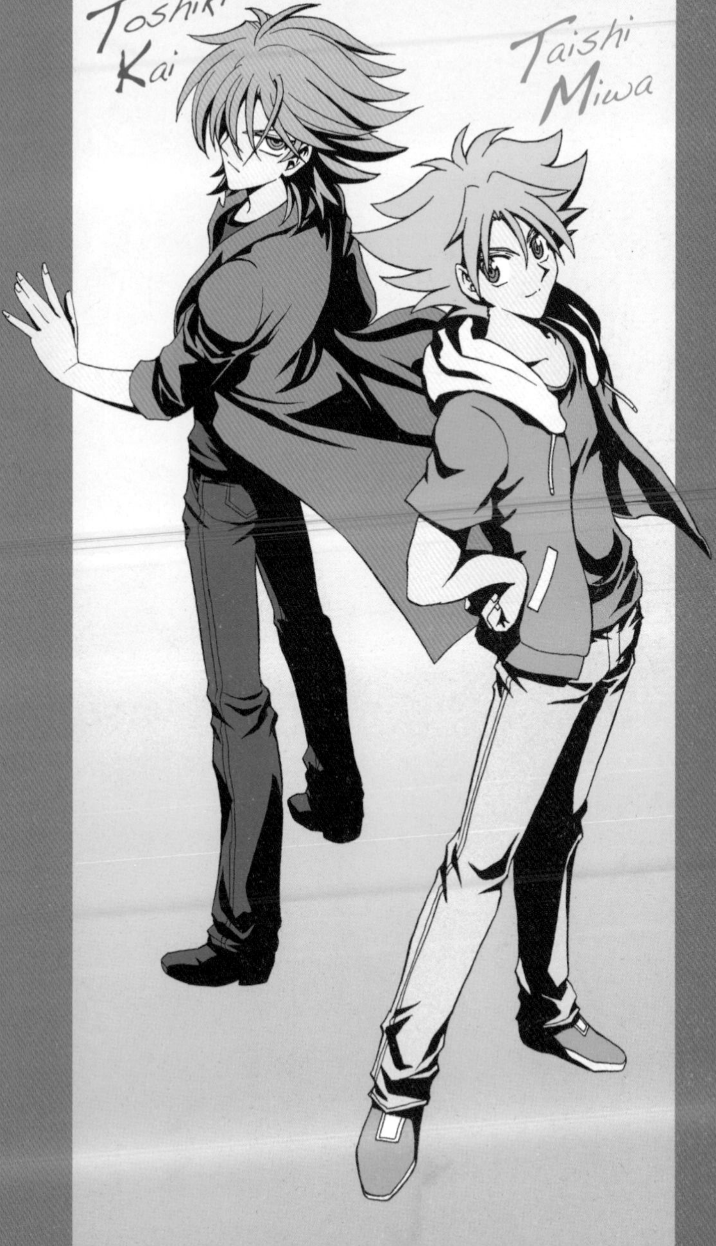
Toshiki Kai
Taishi Miwa

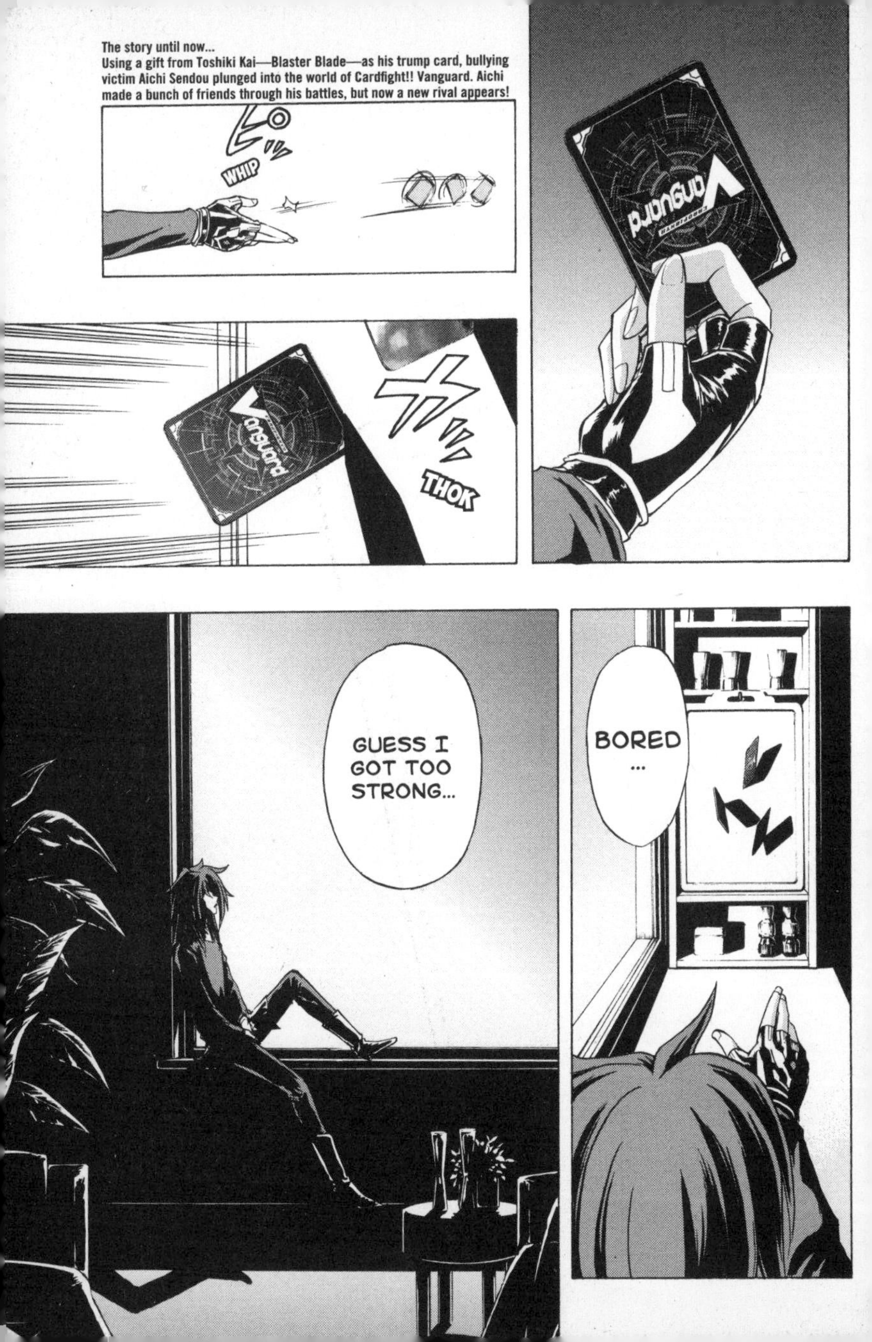
The story until now...
Using a gift from Toshiki Kai—Blaster Blade—as his trump card, bullying victim Aichi Sendou plunged into the world of Cardfight!! Vanguard. Aichi made a bunch of friends through his battles, but now a new rival appears!
WHIP
THOK
BORED...
GUESS I GOT TOO STRONG...

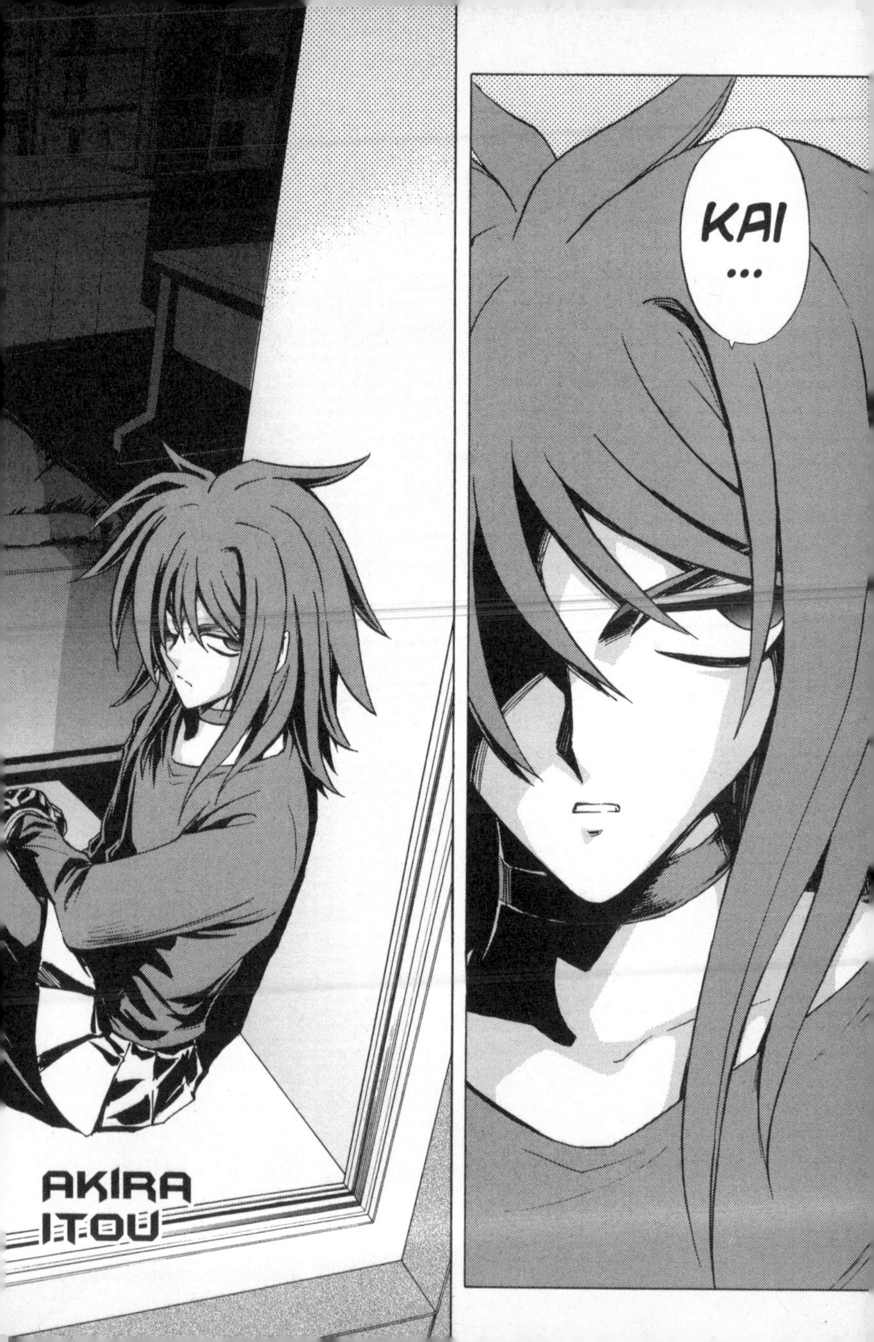
KAI ...
AKIRA ITOU

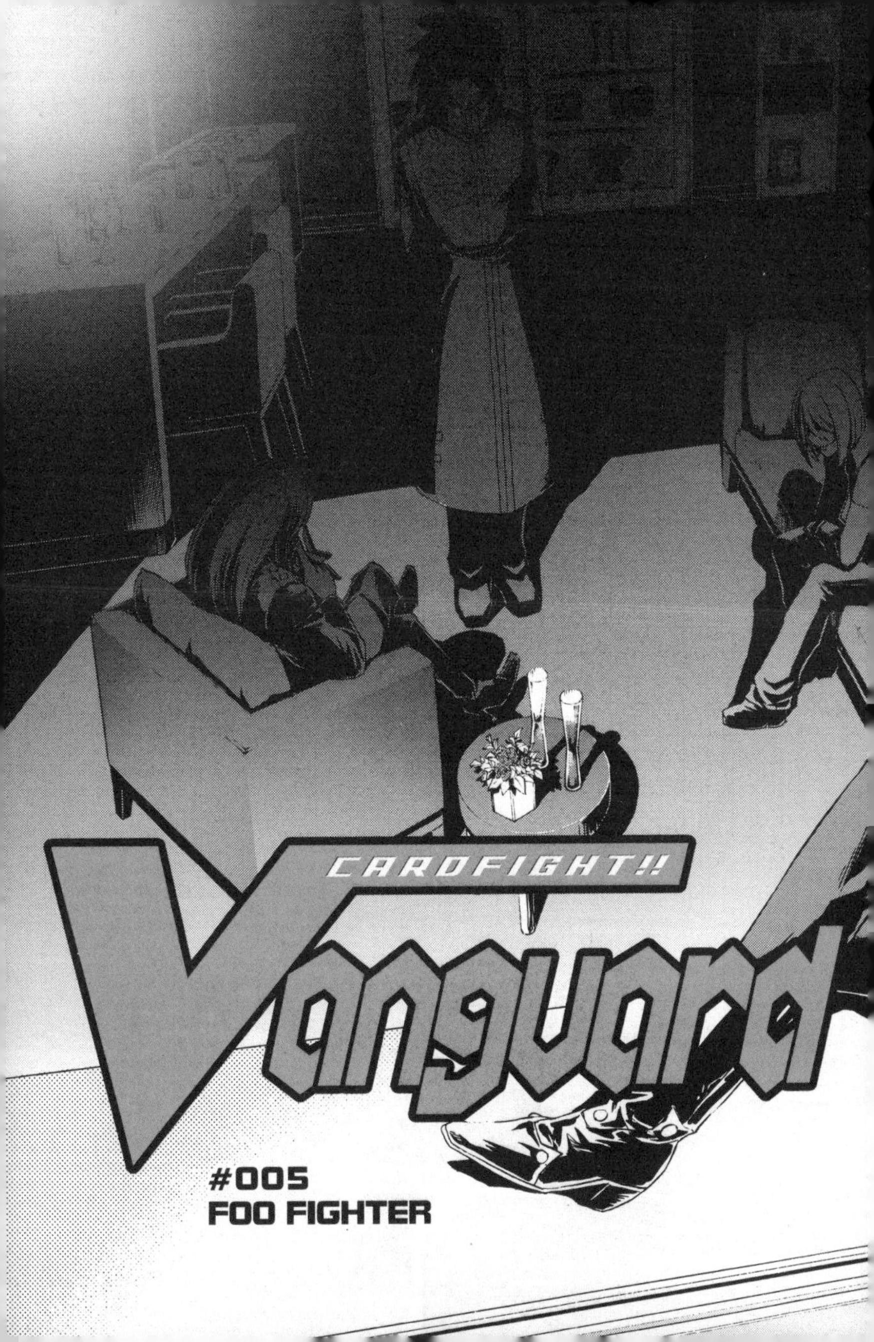
CARDFIGHT!!
Vanguard
#005
FOO FIGHTER

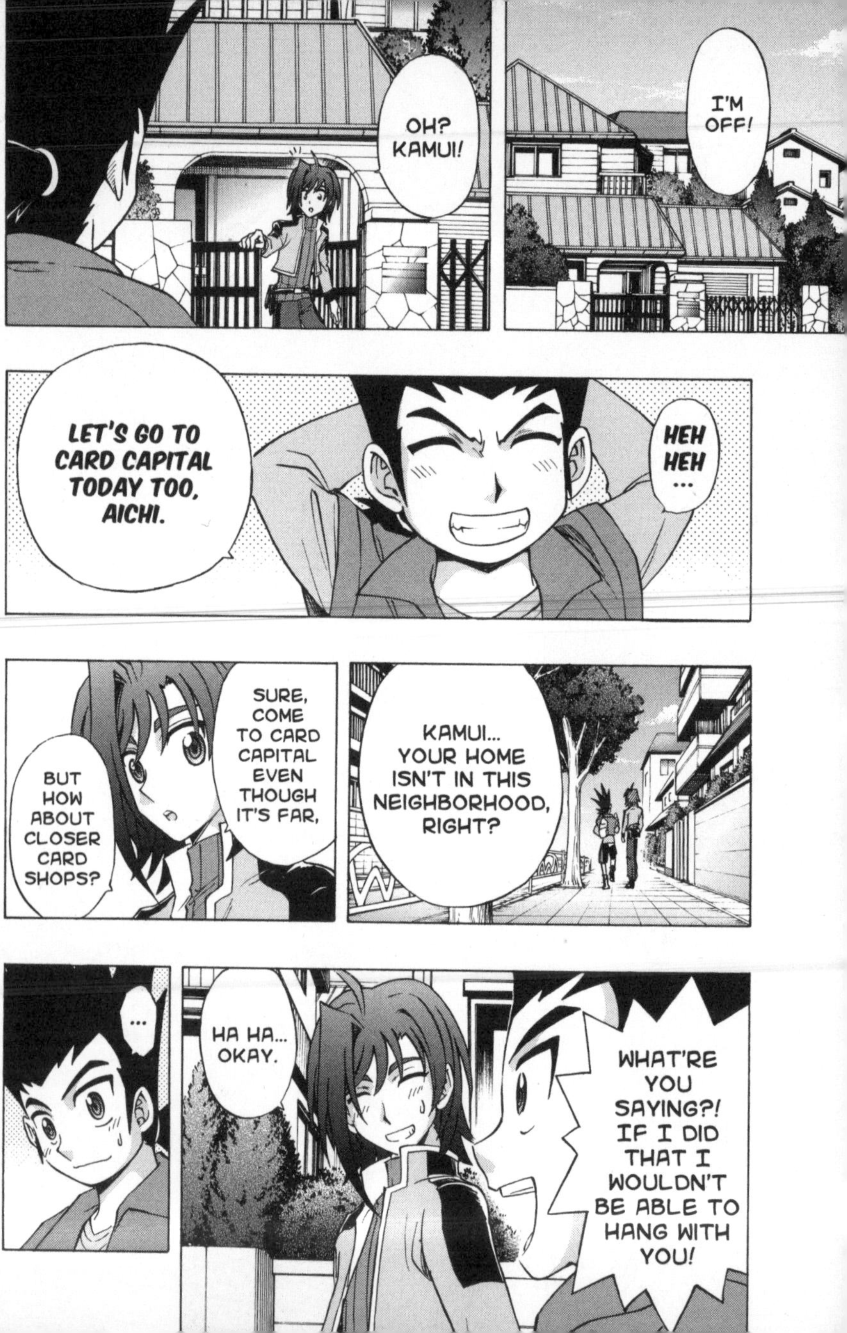
I'M OFF!
OH? KAMUI!
HEH HEH ...
LET'S GO TO CARD CAPITAL TODAY TOO, AICHI.
KAMUI... YOUR HOME ISN'T IN THIS NEIGHBORHOOD, RIGHT?
SURE, COME TO CARD CAPITAL EVEN THOUGH IT'S FAR,
BUT HOW ABOUT CLOSER CARD SHOPS?
WHAT'RE YOU SAYING?! IF I DID THAT I WOULDN'T BE ABLE TO HANG WITH YOU!
HA HA... OKAY.
...

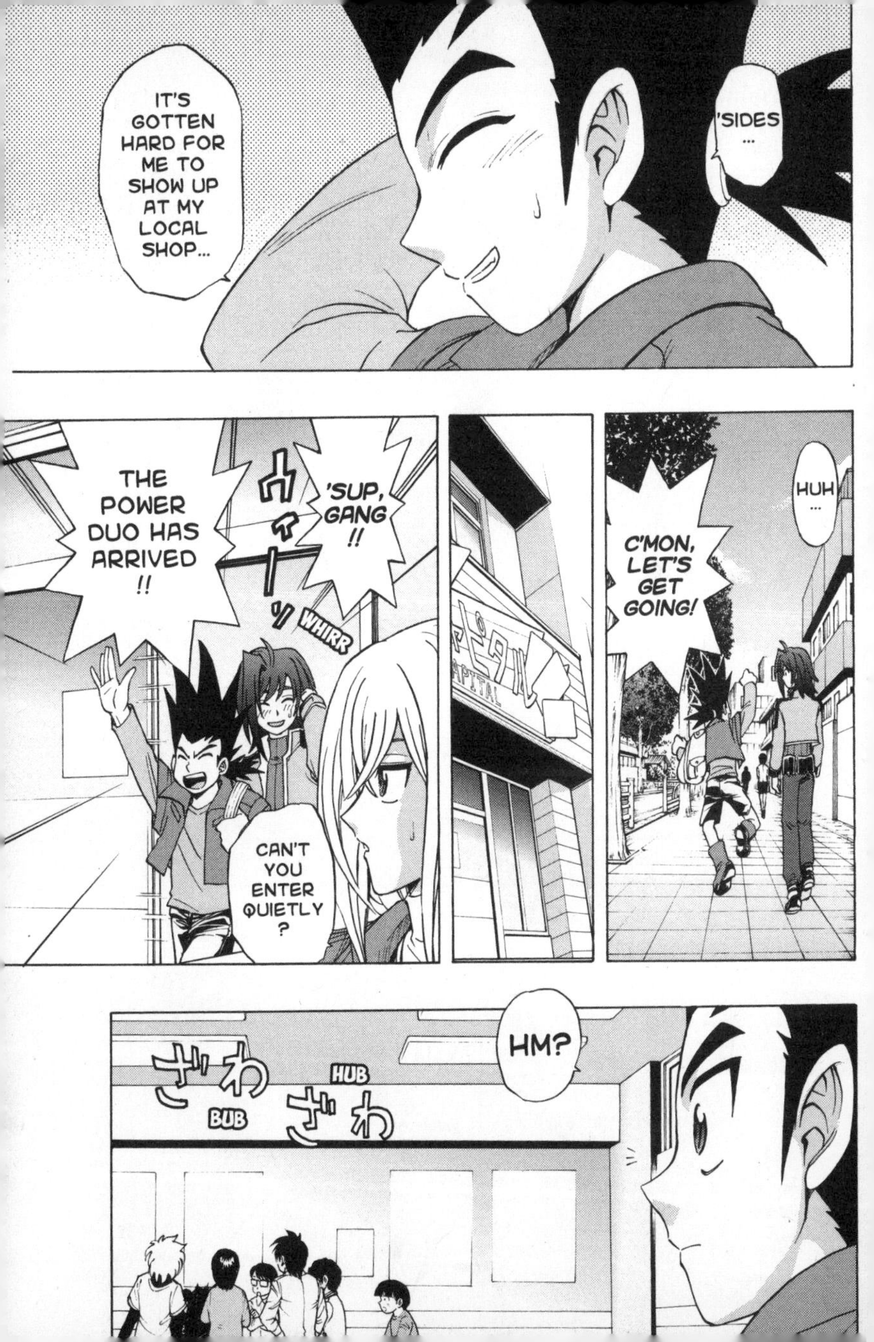
'SIDES...
IT'S GOTTEN HARD FOR ME TO SHOW UP AT MY LOCAL SHOP...
HUH...
C'MON, LET'S GET GOING!
'SUP, GANG!!
ウィーッ
WHIRR
THE POWER DUO HAS ARRIVED!!
CAN'T YOU ENTER QUIETLY?
HM?
ざわざわ
HUB BUB

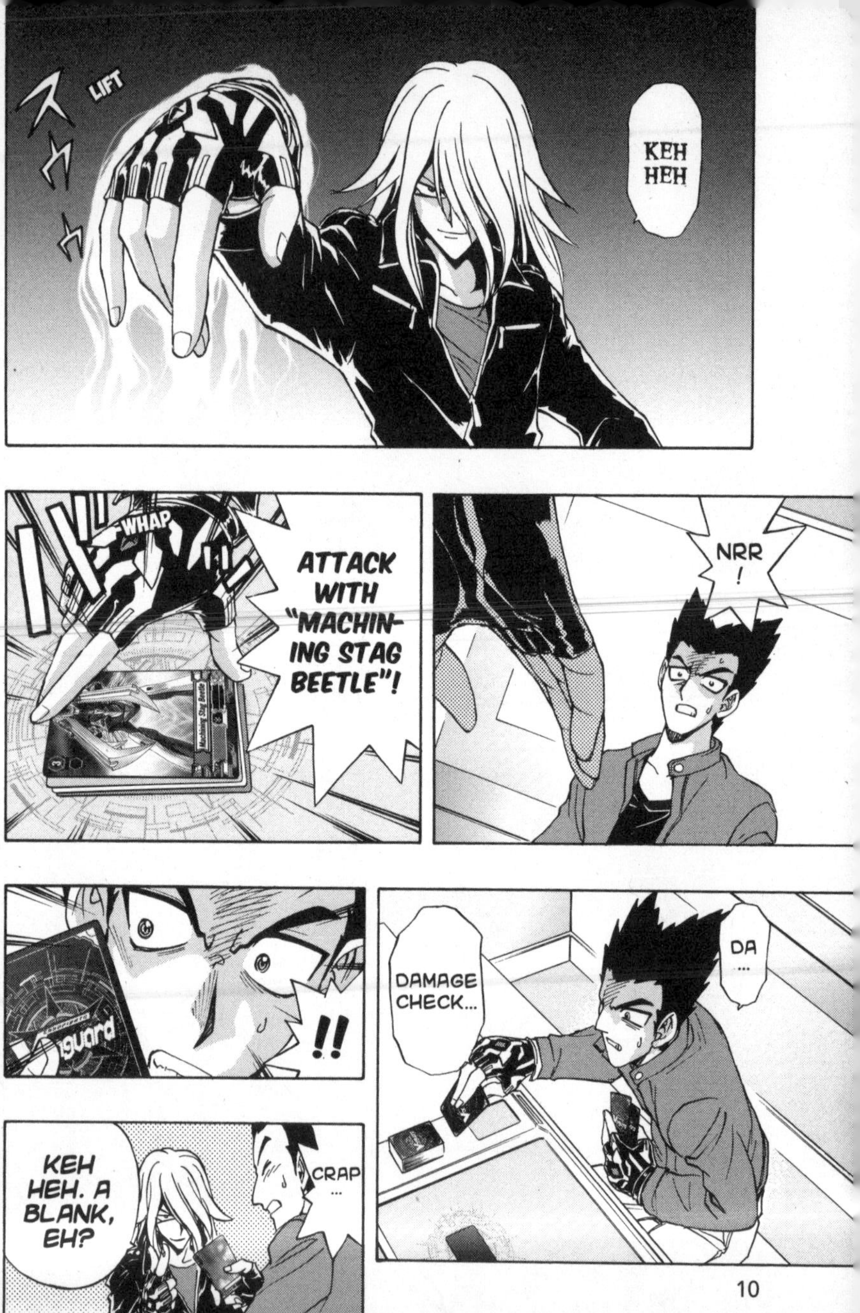
KEH HEH
LIFT
NRR!
WHAP
ATTACK WITH "MACHINING STAG BEETLE"!
DA...
DAMAGE CHECK...
!!
CRAP...
KEH HEH. A BLANK, EH?

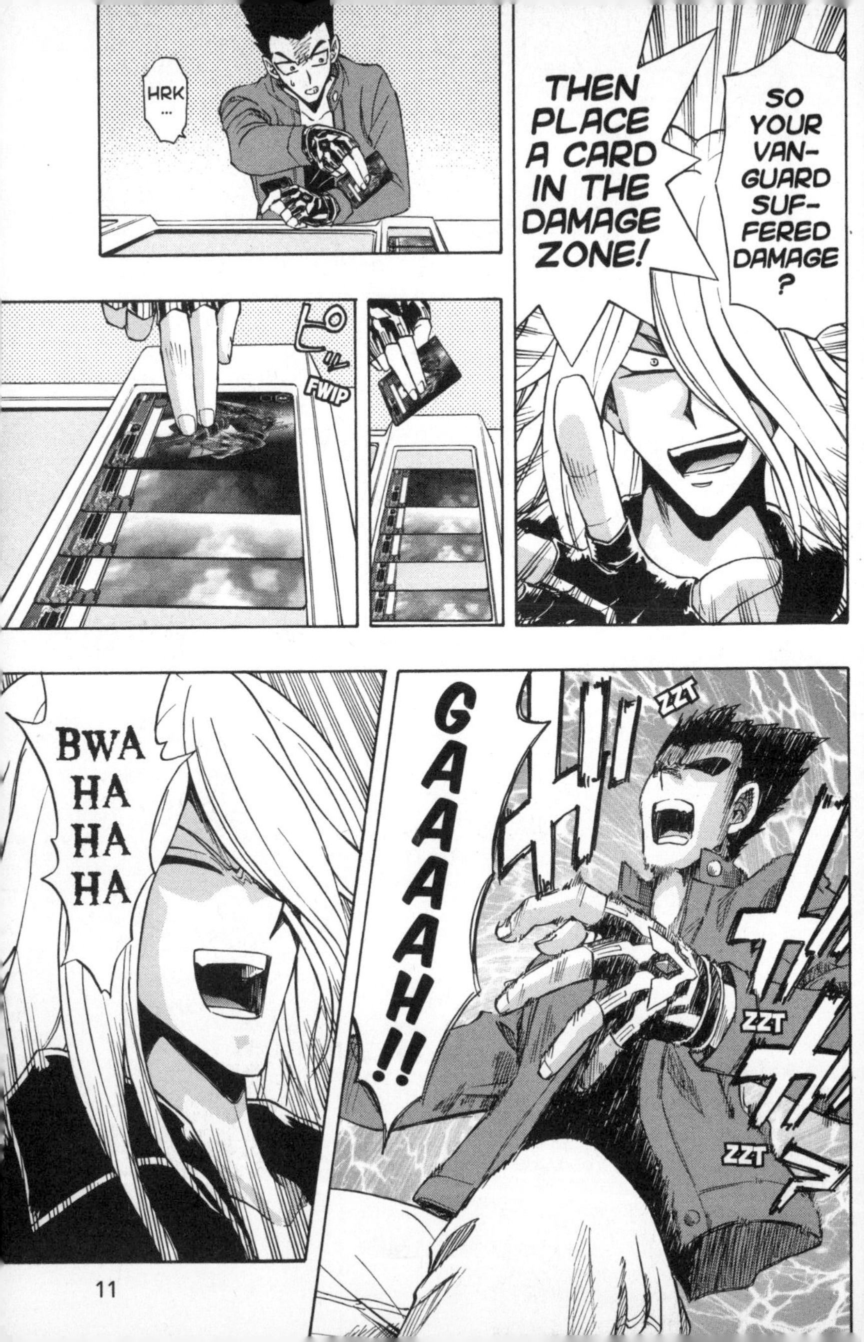
SO YOUR VAN-GUARD SUF-FERED DAMAGE?
THEN PLACE A CARD IN THE DAMAGE ZONE!
HRK...
FWIP
GAAAAAH!!
ZZT
ZZT
ZZT
BWA HA HA HA HA

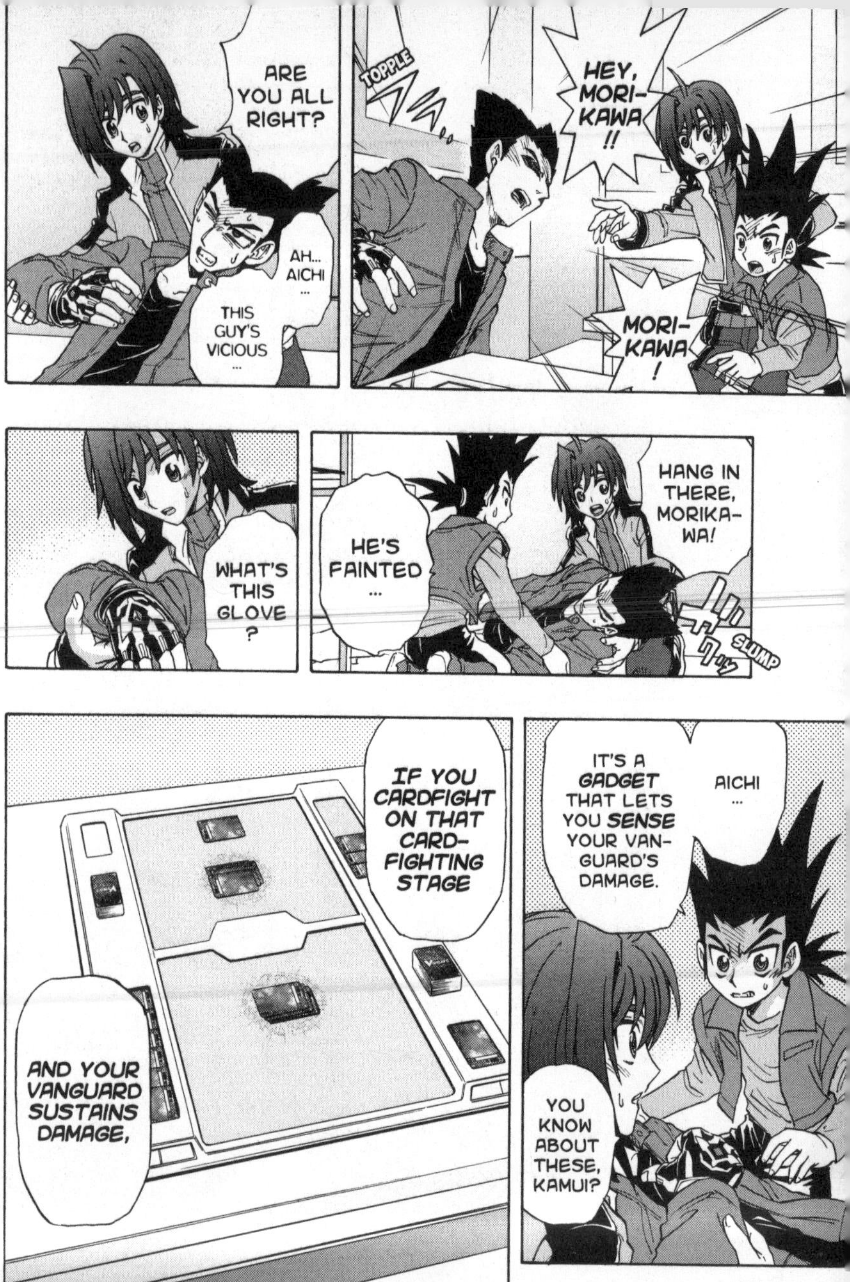
TOPPLE
HEY, MORI-KAWA!!
MORI-KAWA!
ARE YOU ALL RIGHT?
AH... AICHI ...
THIS GUY'S VICIOUS ...
HANG IN THERE, MORIKA-WA!
HE'S FAINTED ...
SLUMP
WHAT'S THIS GLOVE ?
AICHI ...
IT'S A GADGET THAT LETS YOU SENSE YOUR VAN-GUARD'S DAMAGE.
YOU KNOW ABOUT THESE, KAMUI?
IF YOU CARDFIGHT ON THAT CARD-FIGHTING STAGE
AND YOUR VANGUARD SUSTAINS DAMAGE,

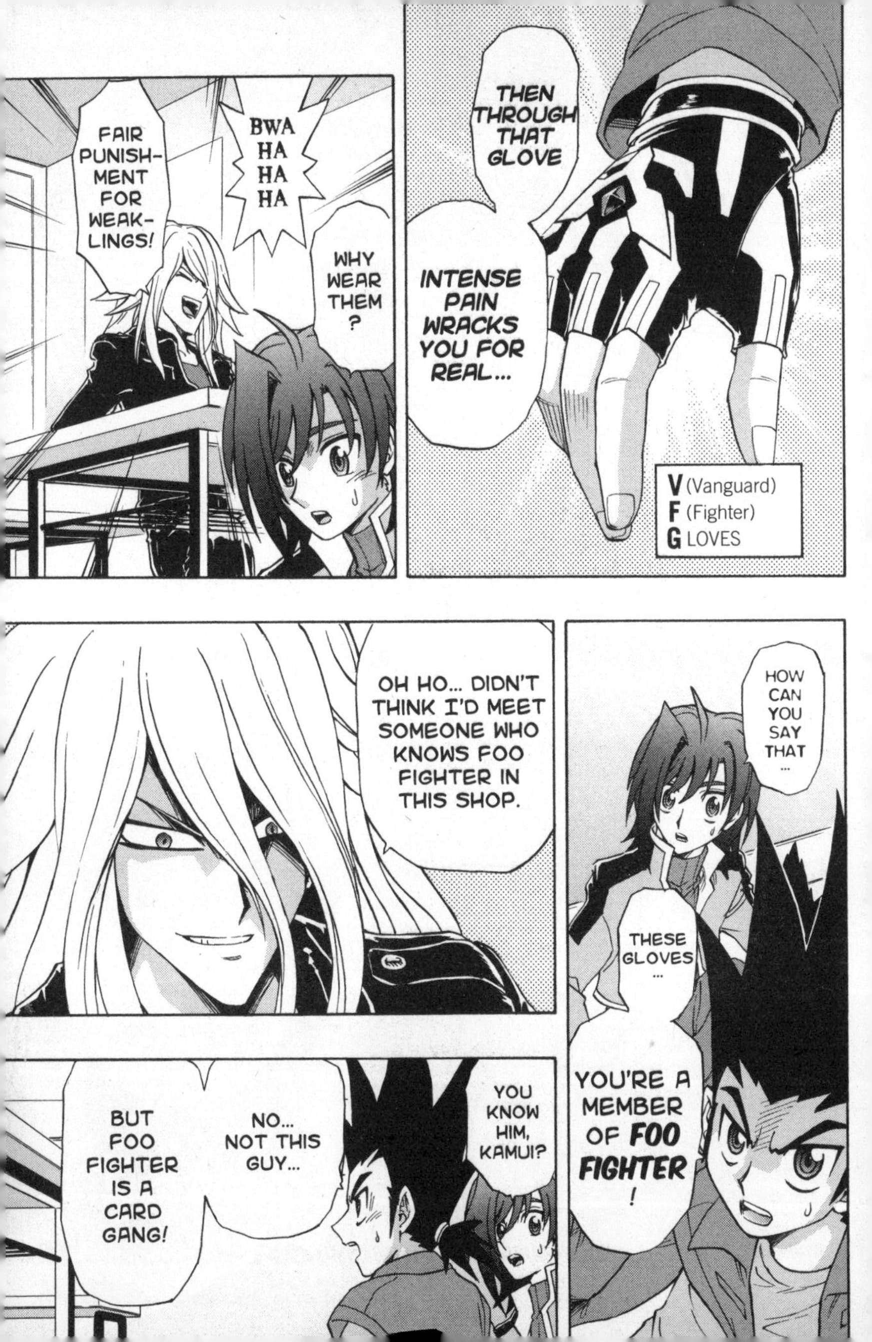
THEN THROUGH THAT GLOVE
INTENSE PAIN WRACKS YOU FOR REAL...
V (Vanguard) F (Fighter) G LOVES
WHY WEAR THEM?
BWA HA HA HA
FAIR PUNISHMENT FOR WEAKLINGS!
HOW CAN YOU SAY THAT...
THESE GLOVES...
YOU'RE A MEMBER OF FOO FIGHTER!
OH HO... DIDN'T THINK I'D MEET SOMEONE WHO KNOWS FOO FIGHTER IN THIS SHOP.
YOU KNOW HIM, KAMUI?
NO... NOT THIS GUY...
BUT FOO FIGHTER IS A CARD GANG!

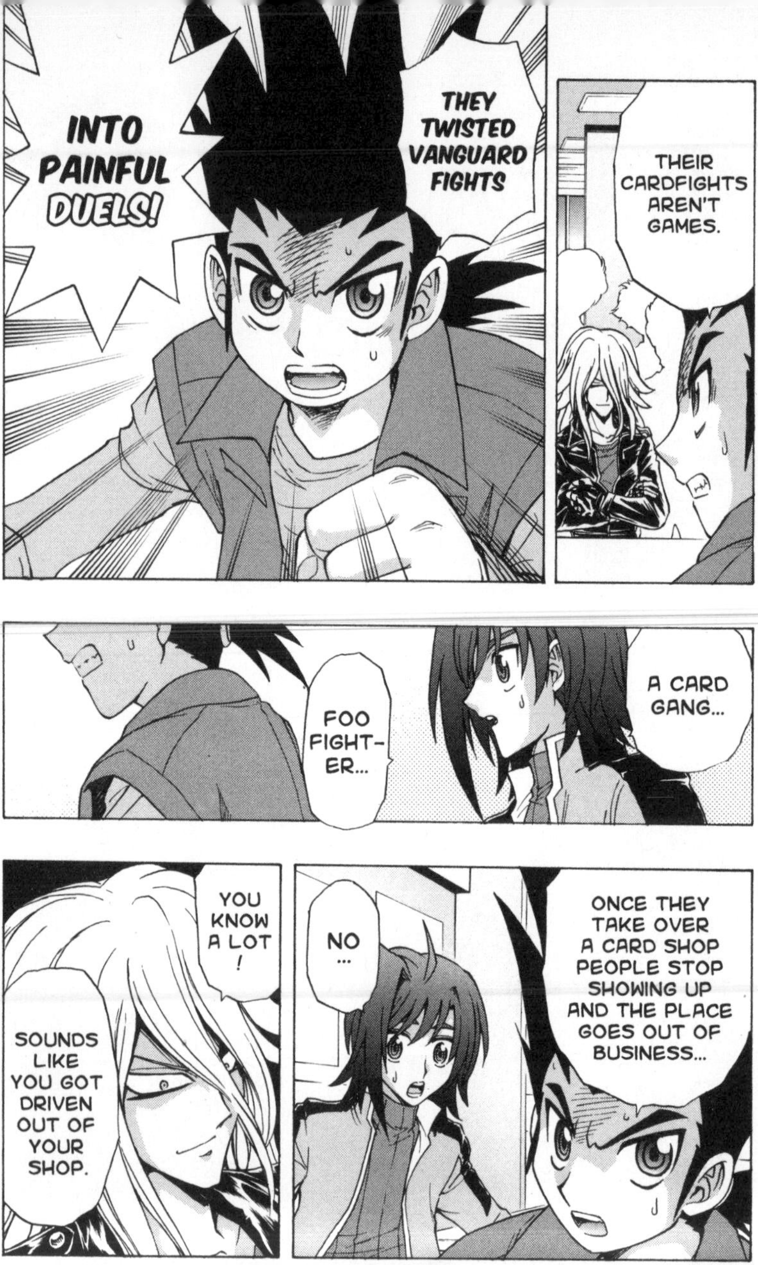
THEIR CARDFIGHTS AREN'T GAMES.
THEY TWISTED VANGUARD FIGHTS
INTO PAINFUL DUELS!
A CARD GANG...
FOO FIGHTER...
ONCE THEY TAKE OVER A CARD SHOP PEOPLE STOP SHOWING UP AND THE PLACE GOES OUT OF BUSINESS...
NO ...
YOU KNOW A LOT!
SOUNDS LIKE YOU GOT DRIVEN OUT OF YOUR SHOP.

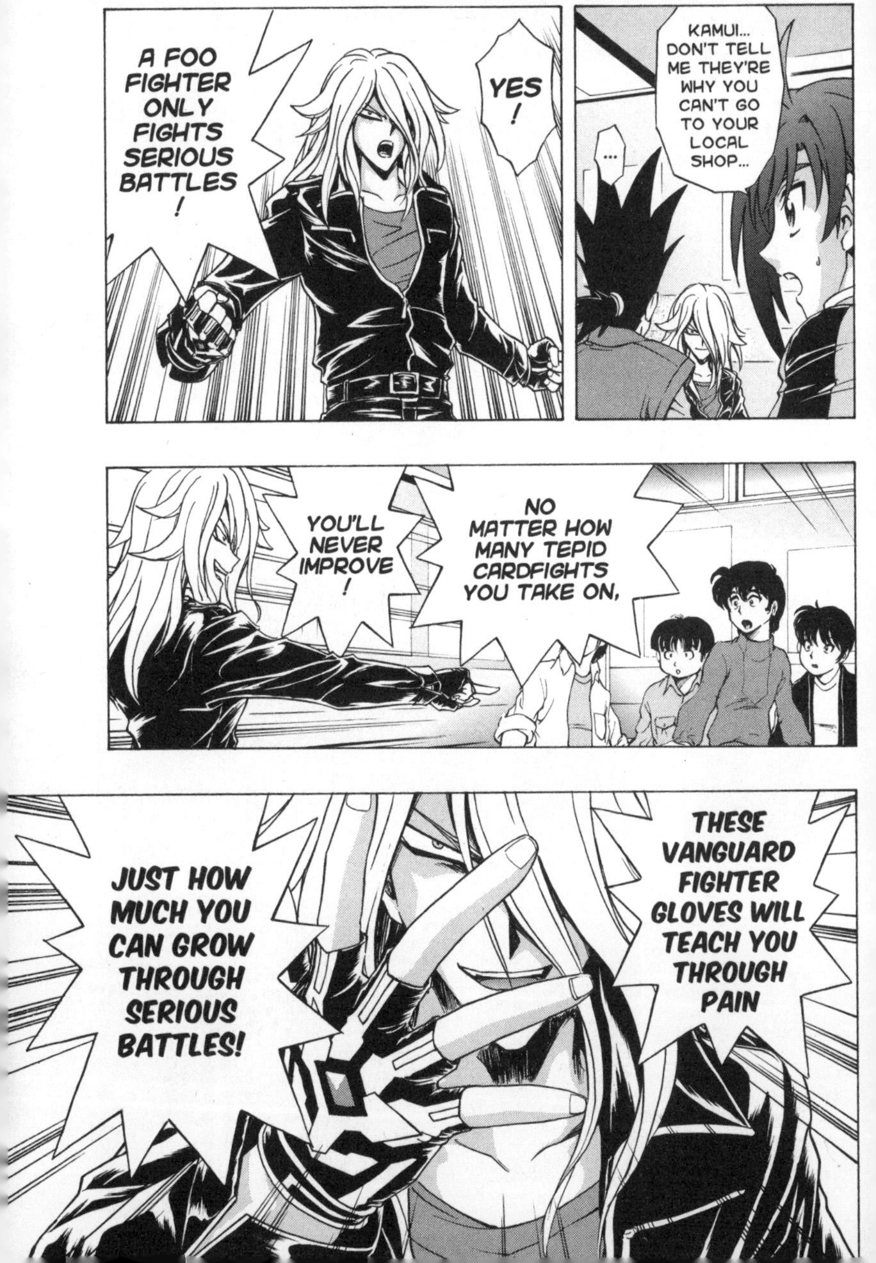
KAMUI... DON'T TELL ME THEY'RE WHY YOU CAN'T GO TO YOUR LOCAL SHOP...
...
YES!
A FOO FIGHTER ONLY FIGHTS SERIOUS BATTLES!
NO MATTER HOW MANY TEPID CARDFIGHTS YOU TAKE ON,
YOU'LL NEVER IMPROVE!
THESE VANGUARD FIGHTER GLOVES WILL TEACH YOU THROUGH PAIN
JUST HOW MUCH YOU CAN GROW THROUGH SERIOUS BATTLES!

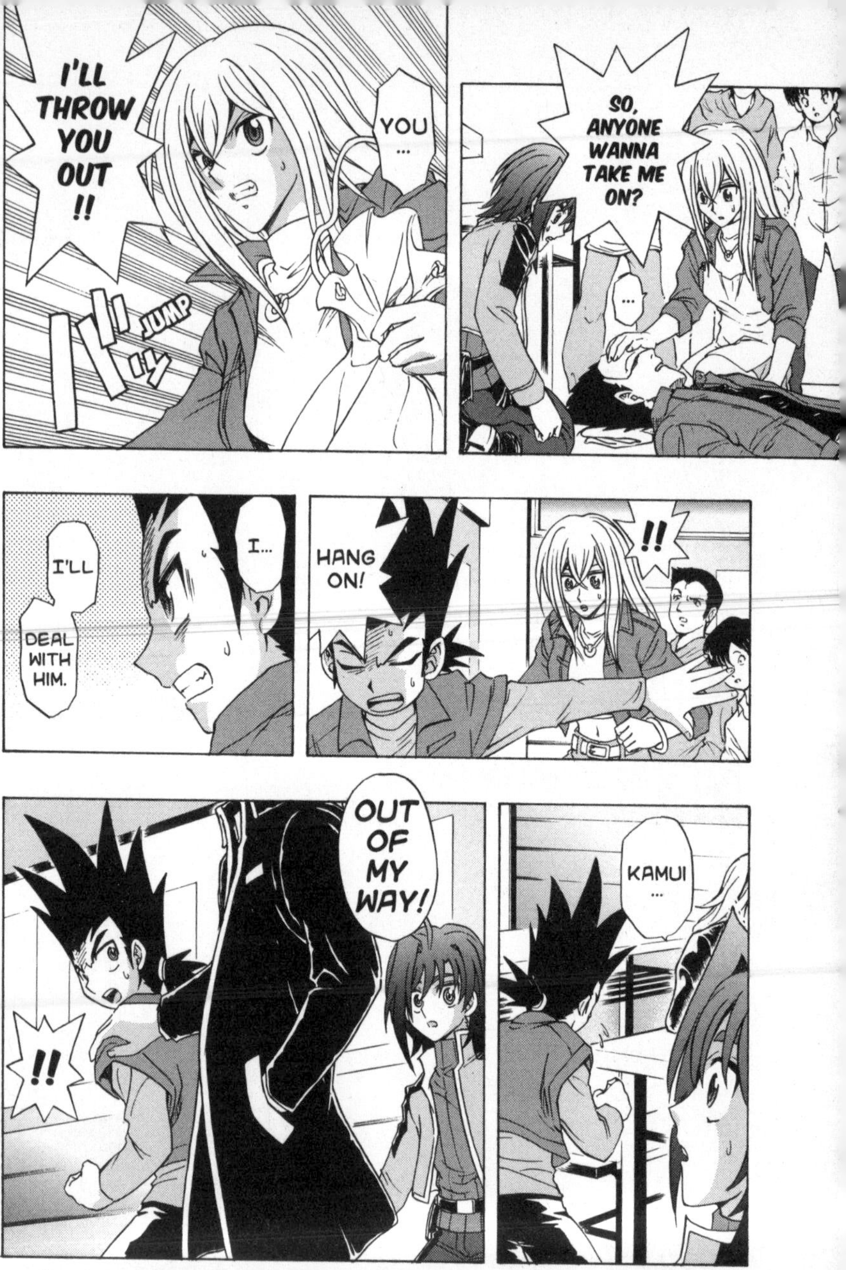
SO, ANYONE WANNA TAKE ME ON?
...
YOU ...
I'LL THROW YOU OUT !!
JUMP
!!
HANG ON!
I...
I'LL DEAL WITH HIM.
KAMUI ...
OUT OF MY WAY!
!!

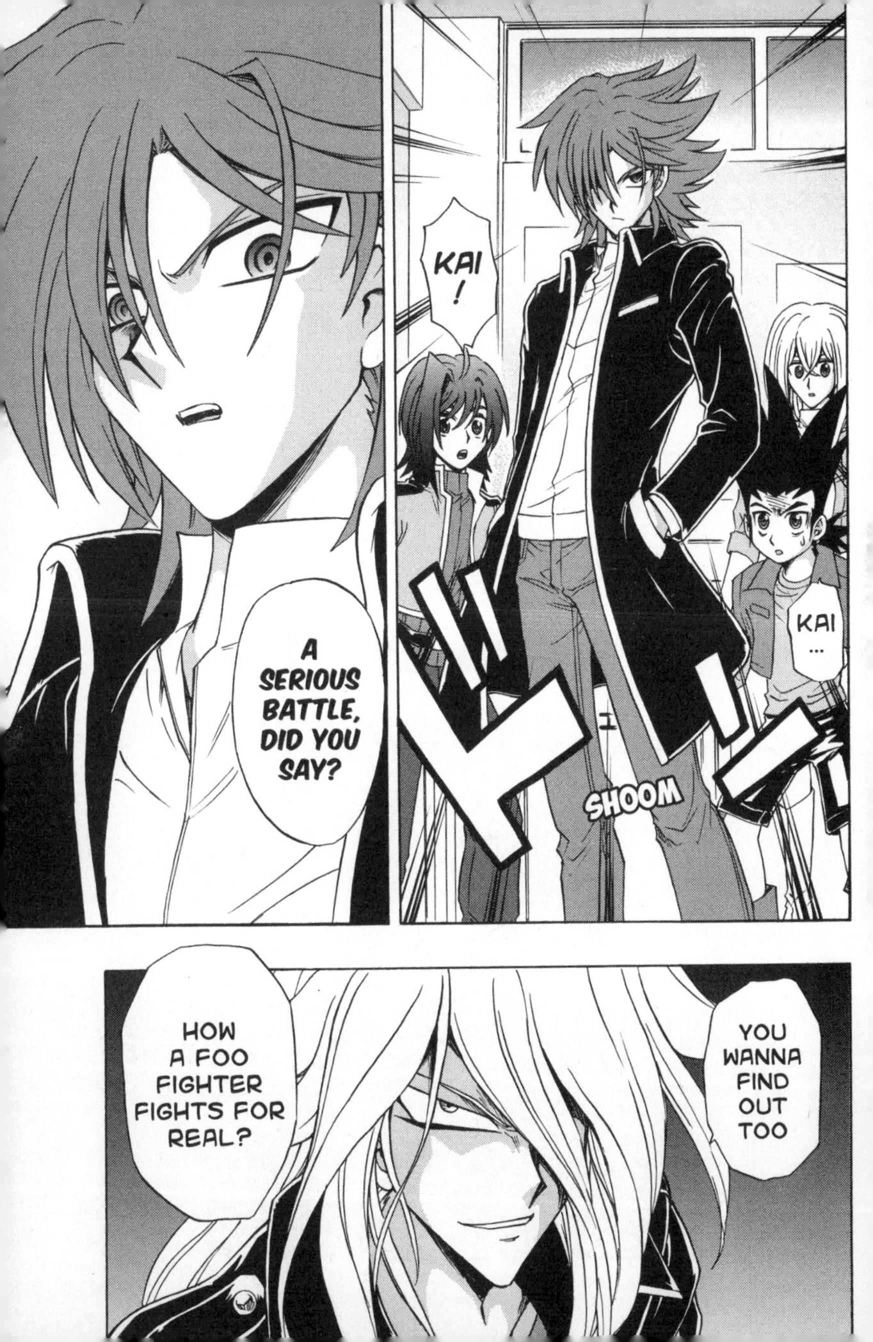
KAI!
KAI...
SHOOM
A SERIOUS BATTLE, DID YOU SAY?
YOU WANNA FIND OUT TOO
HOW A FOO FIGHTER FIGHTS FOR REAL?

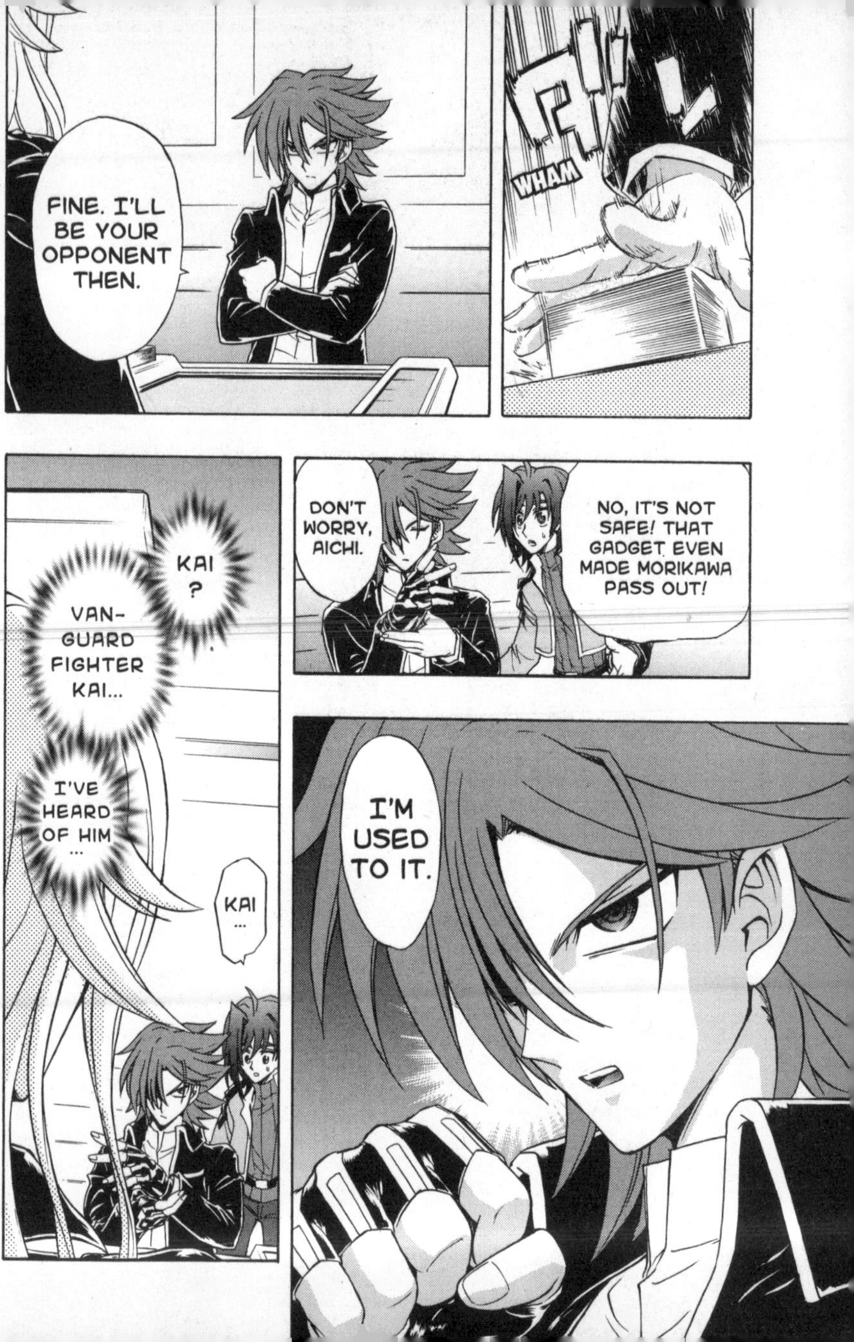
WHAM
FINE. I'LL BE YOUR OPPONENT THEN.
NO, IT'S NOT SAFE! THAT GADGET EVEN MADE MORIKAWA PASS OUT!
DON'T WORRY, AICHI.
I'M USED TO IT.
KAI?
VAN-GUARD FIGHTER KAI...
I'VE HEARD OF HIM...
KAI...

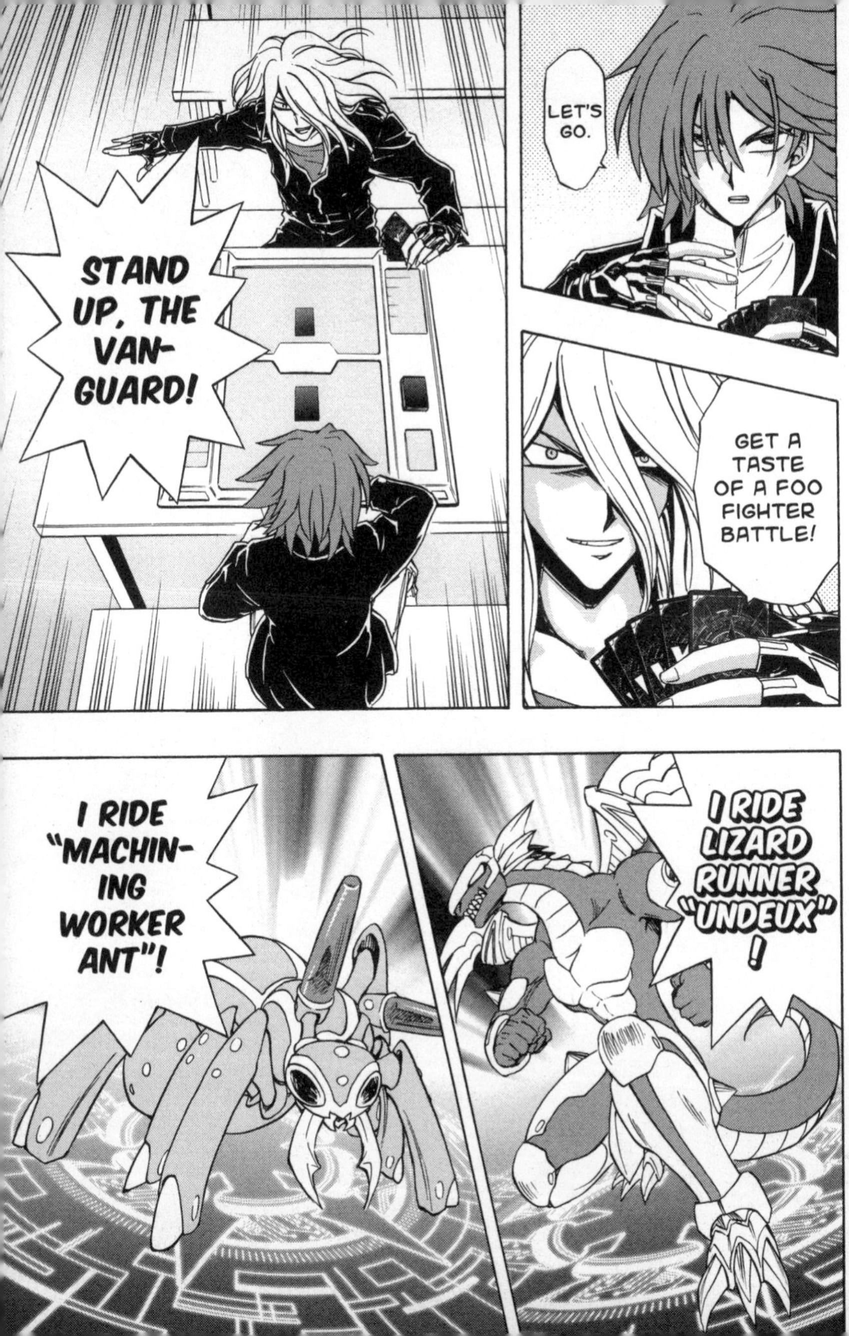
LET'S GO.
GET A TASTE OF A FOO FIGHTER BATTLE!
STAND UP, THE VAN-GUARD!
I RIDE LIZARD RUNNER "UNDEUX"!
I RIDE "MACHIN-ING WORKER ANT"!

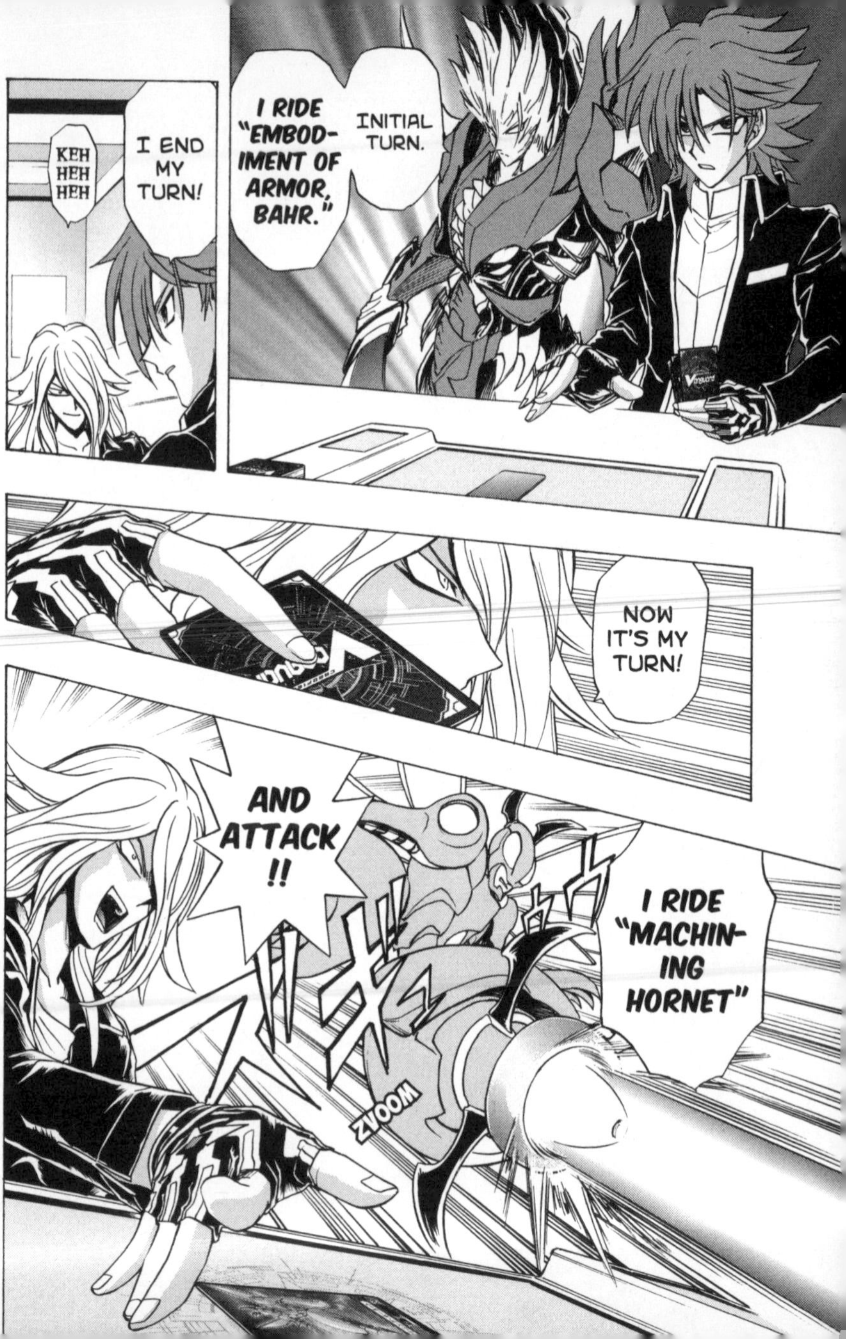
INITIAL TURN.
I RIDE "EMBODIMENT OF ARMOR, BAHR."
I END MY TURN!
KEH HEH HEH
NOW IT'S MY TURN!
I RIDE "MACHINING HORNET"
AND ATTACK!!
ZVOOM

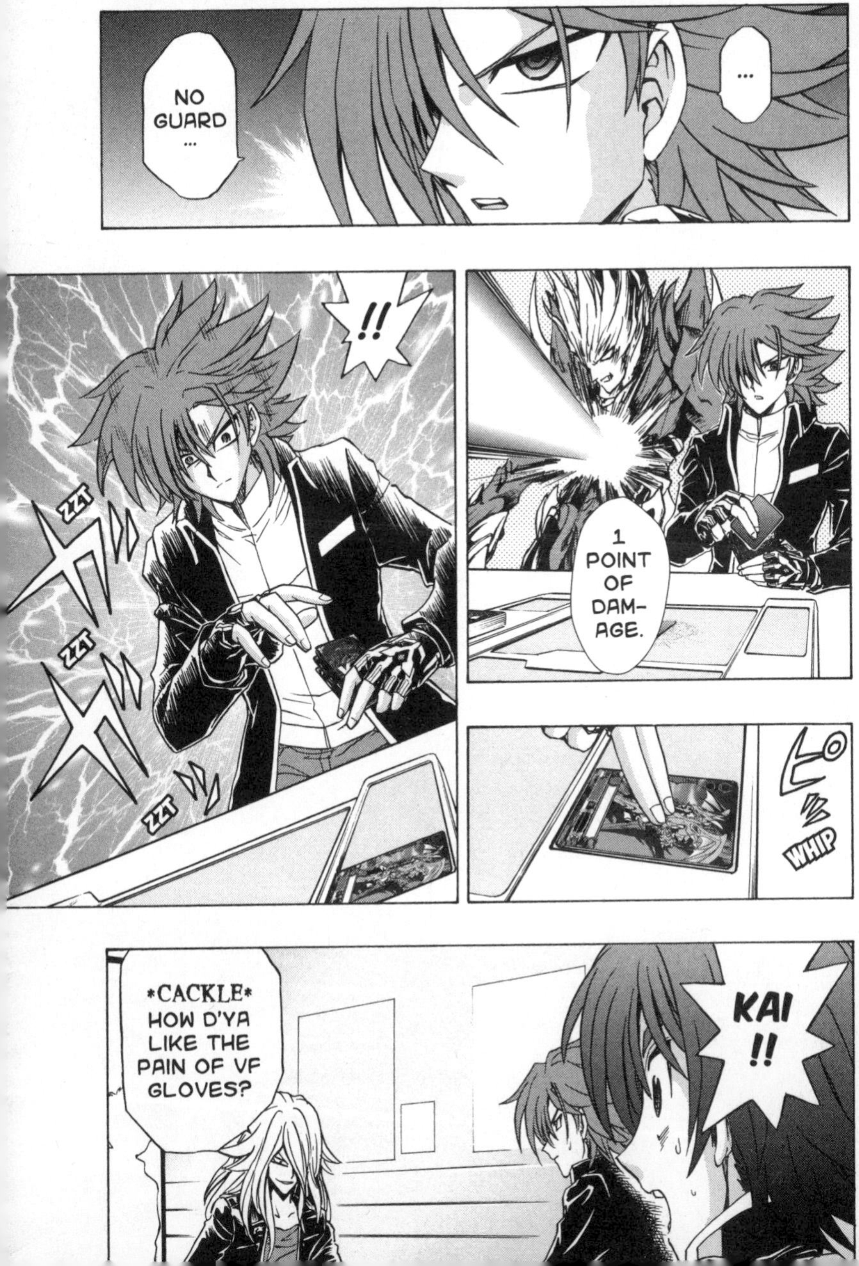
...
NO GUARD ...
1 POINT OF DAM-AGE.
WHIP
!!
ZZT
ZZT
ZZT
KAI !!
CACKLE HOW D'YA LIKE THE PAIN OF VF GLOVES?

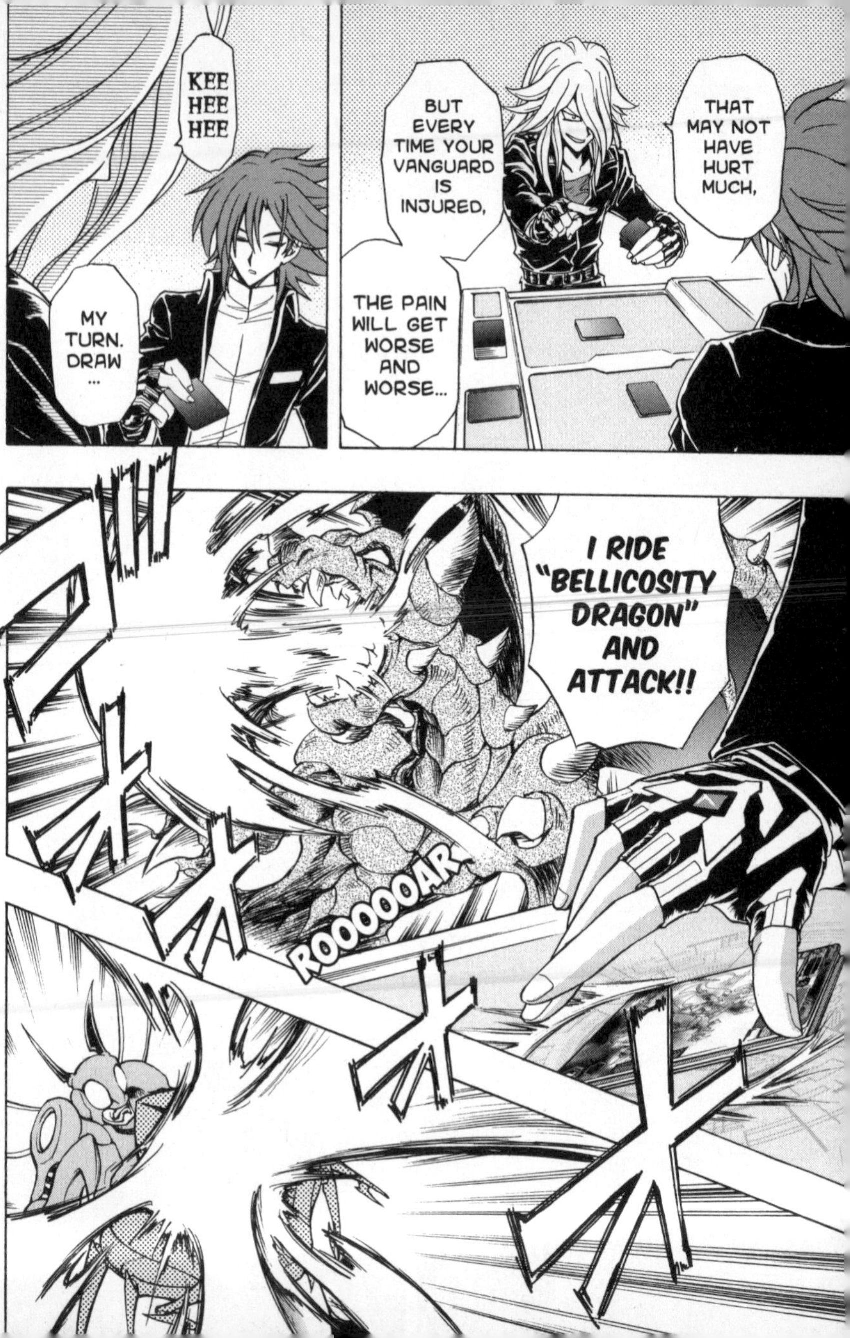
THAT MAY NOT HAVE HURT MUCH,
BUT EVERY TIME YOUR VANGUARD IS INJURED,
THE PAIN WILL GET WORSE AND WORSE...
KEE HEE HEE
MY TURN. DRAW ...
I RIDE "BELLICOSITY DRAGON" AND ATTACK!!
ROOOOOAR

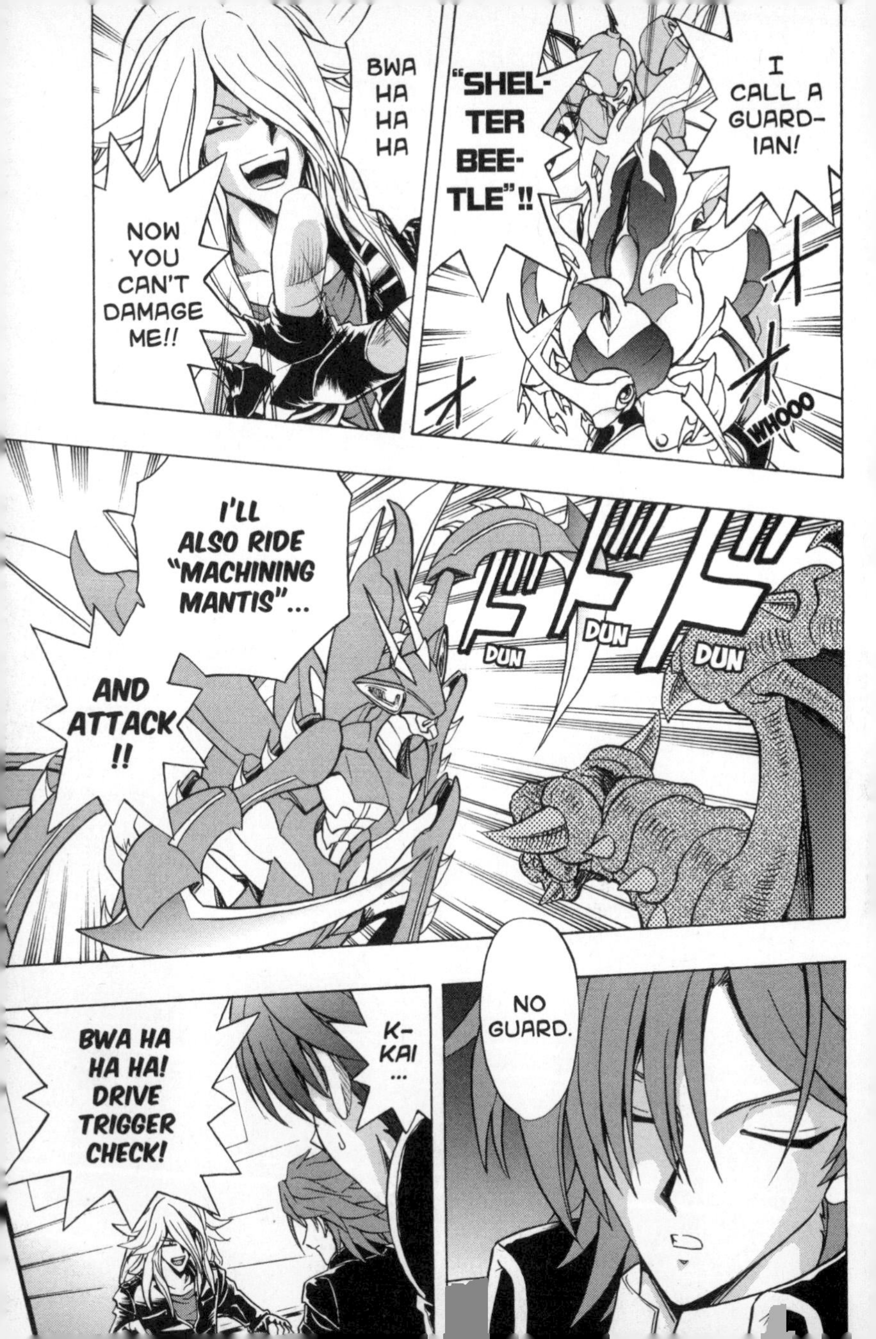
I CALL A GUARD-IAN!
"SHEL-TER BEE-TLE"!!
WHOOO
BWA HA HA HA
NOW YOU CAN'T DAMAGE ME!!
DUN
DUN
DUN
I'LL ALSO RIDE "MACHINING MANTIS"...
AND ATTACK!!
NO GUARD.
K-KAI...
BWA HA HA HA! DRIVE TRIGGER CHECK!

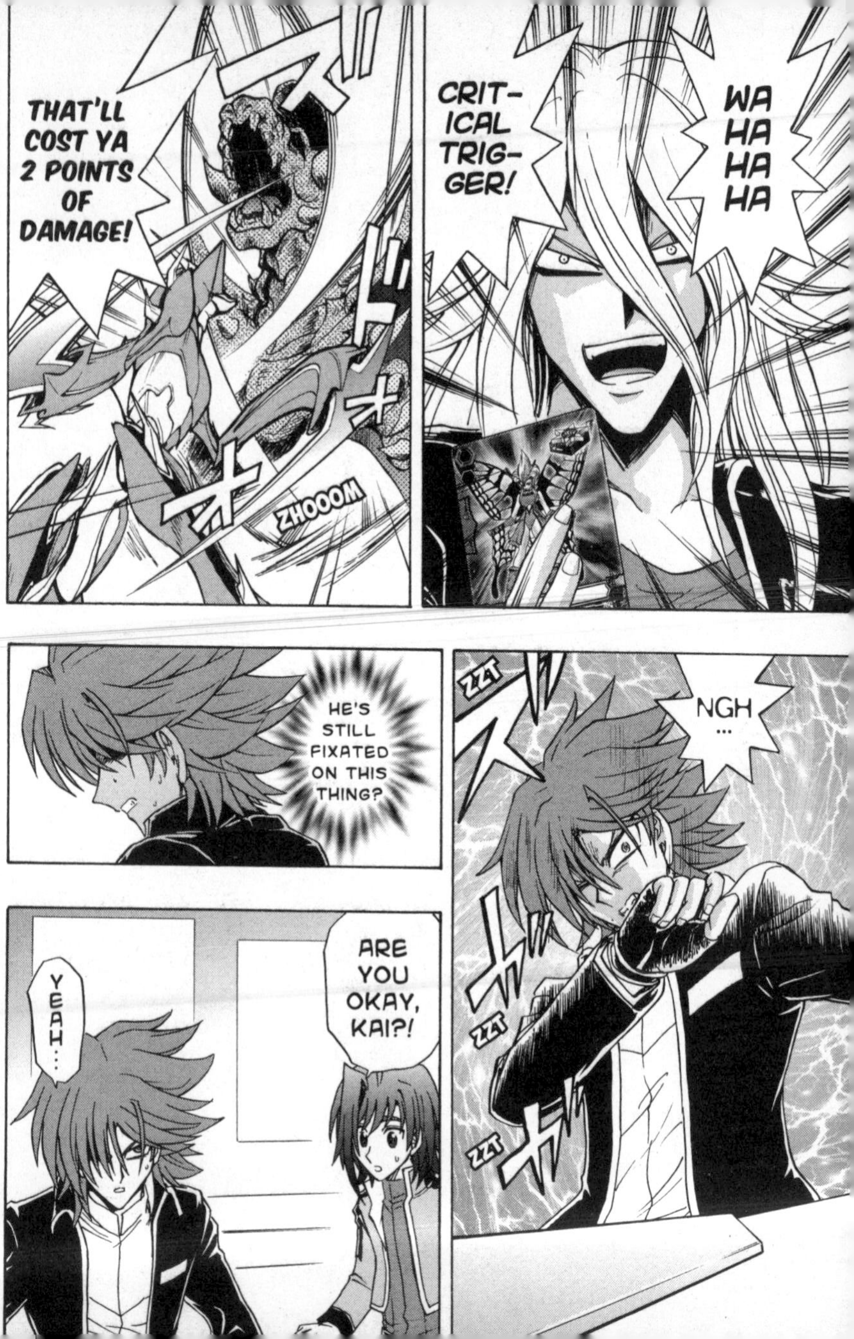
WA HA HA HA
CRIT-ICAL TRIG-GER!
THAT'LL COST YA 2 POINTS OF DAMAGE!
ZHOOOM
NGH ...
ZZAT
ZZAT
ZZAT
HE'S STILL FIXATED ON THIS THING?
ARE YOU OKAY, KAI?!
YEAH...

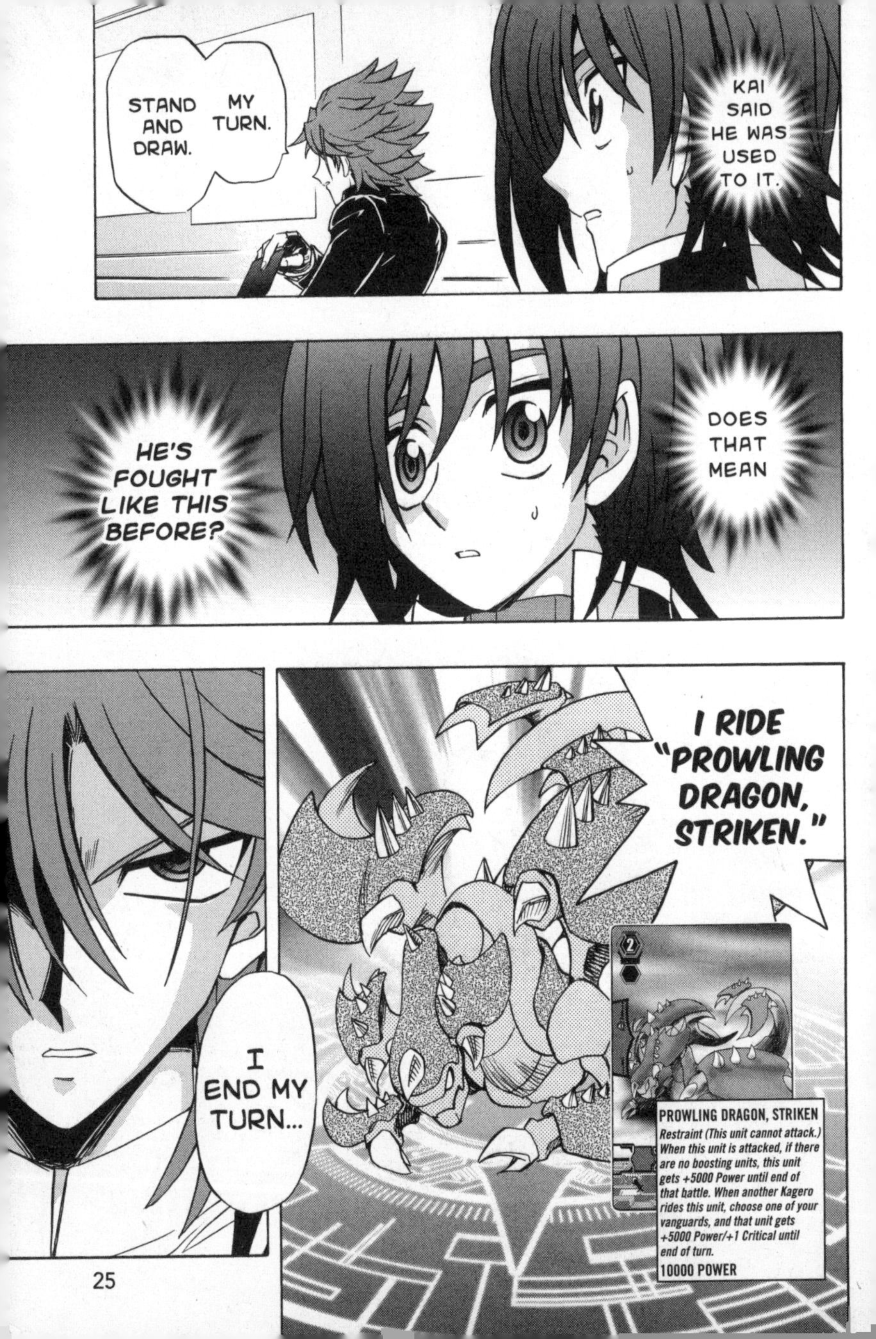
KAI SAID HE WAS USED TO IT.
MY TURN.
STAND AND DRAW.
DOES THAT MEAN
HE'S FOUGHT LIKE THIS BEFORE?
I RIDE "PROWLING DRAGON, STRIKEN."
2
PROWLING DRAGON, STRIKEN
Restraint (This unit cannot attack.) When this unit is attacked, if there are no boosting units, this unit gets +5000 Power until end of that battle. When another Kagero rides this unit, choose one of your vanguards, and that unit gets +5000 Power/+1 Critical until end of turn.
10000 POWER
I END MY TURN...

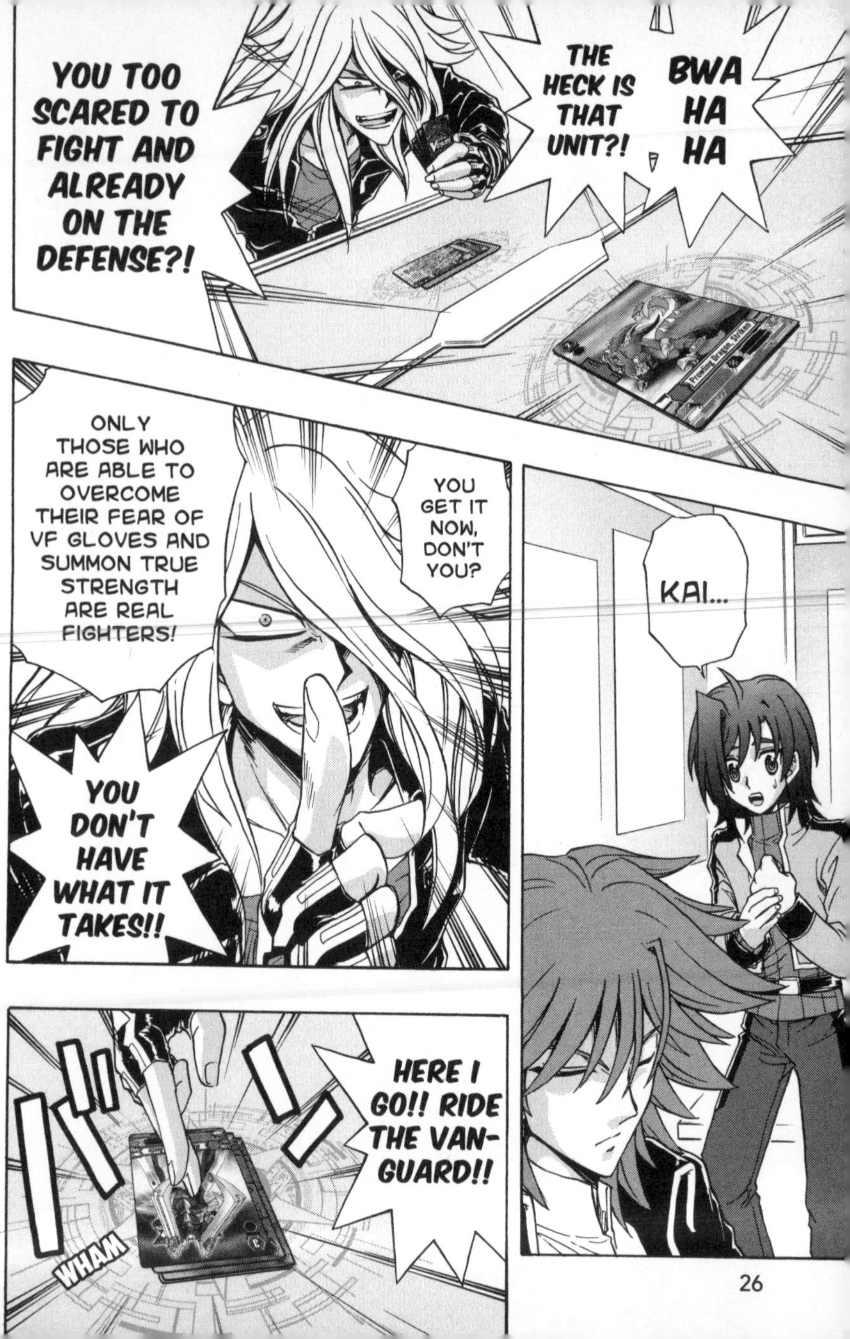
BWA HA HA
THE HECK IS THAT UNIT?!
YOU TOO SCARED TO FIGHT AND ALREADY ON THE DEFENSE?!
Prowling Dragon, Striken
KAI...
YOU GET IT NOW, DON'T YOU?
ONLY THOSE WHO ARE ABLE TO OVERCOME THEIR FEAR OF VF GLOVES AND SUMMON TRUE STRENGTH ARE REAL FIGHTERS!
YOU DON'T HAVE WHAT IT TAKES!!
HERE I GO!! RIDE THE VAN-GUARD!!
WHAM

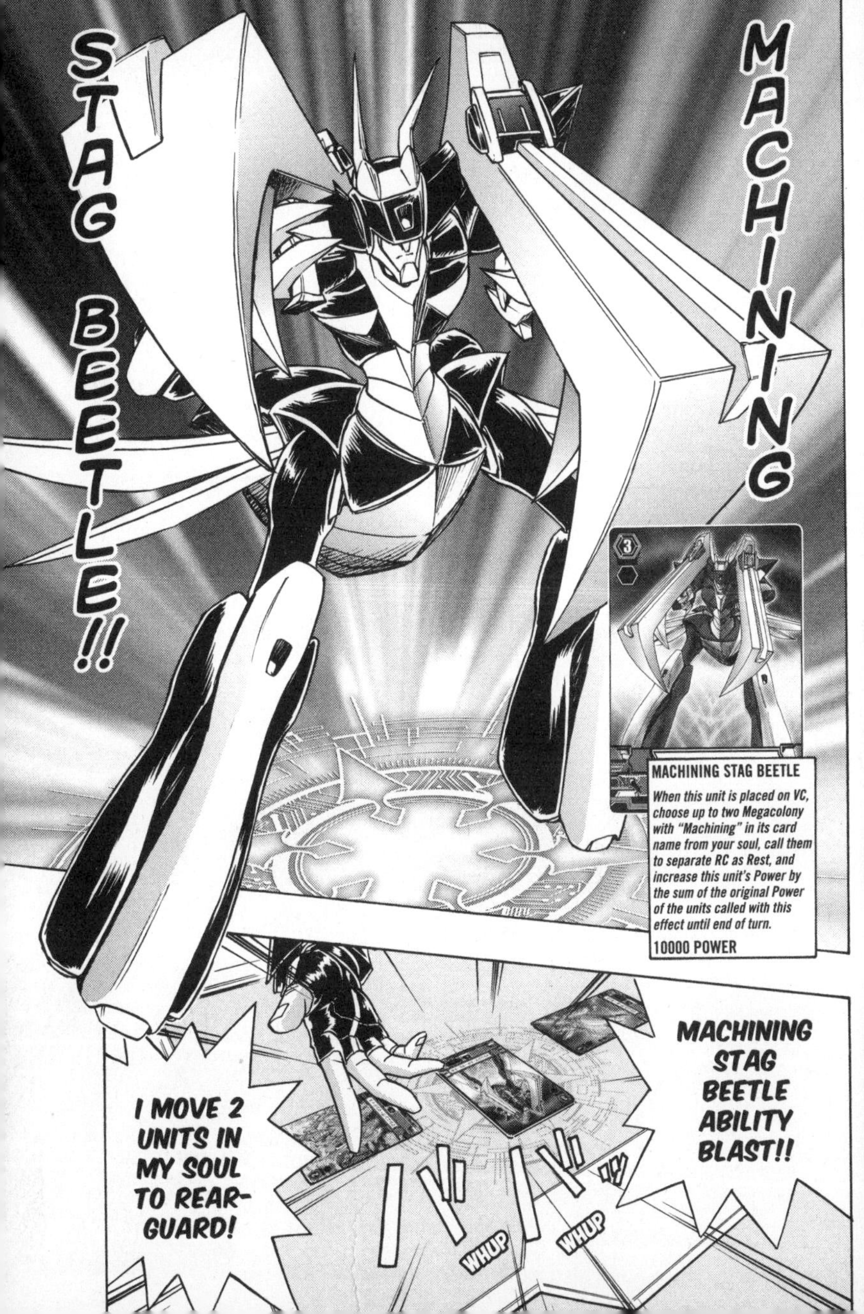
MACHINING
STAG BEETLE!!
MACHINING STAG BEETLE
When this unit is placed on VC, choose up to two Megacolony with "Machining" in its card name from your soul, call them to separate RC as Rest, and increase this unit's Power by the sum of the original Power of the units called with this effect until end of turn.
10000 POWER
MACHINING STAG BEETLE ABILITY BLAST!!
I MOVE 2 UNITS IN MY SOUL TO REAR-GUARD!
WHUP
WHUP

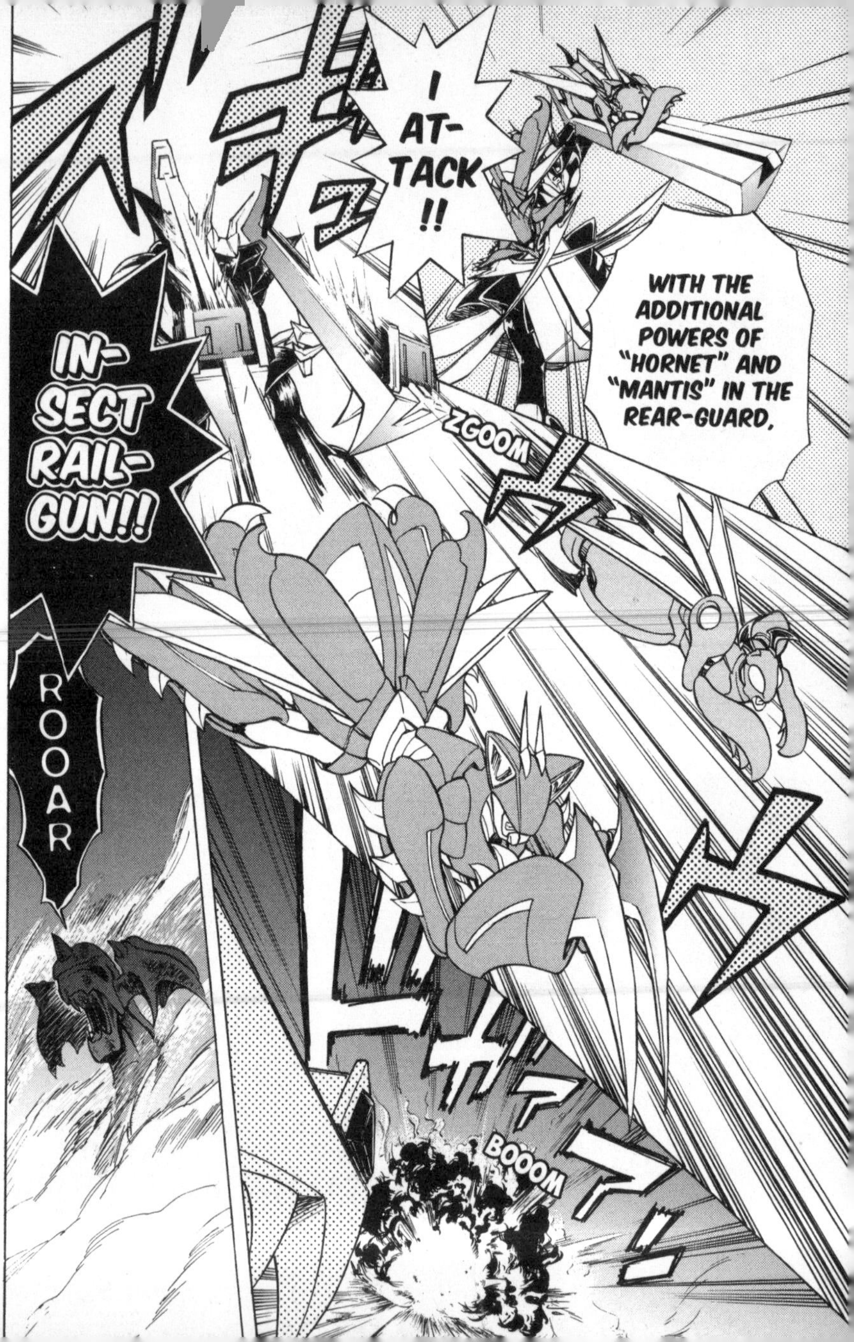
WITH THE ADDITIONAL POWERS OF "HORNET" AND "MANTIS" IN THE REAR-GUARD,
I AT-TACK!!
ZGOOM
IN-SECT RAIL-GUN!!
ROOAR
BOOOM

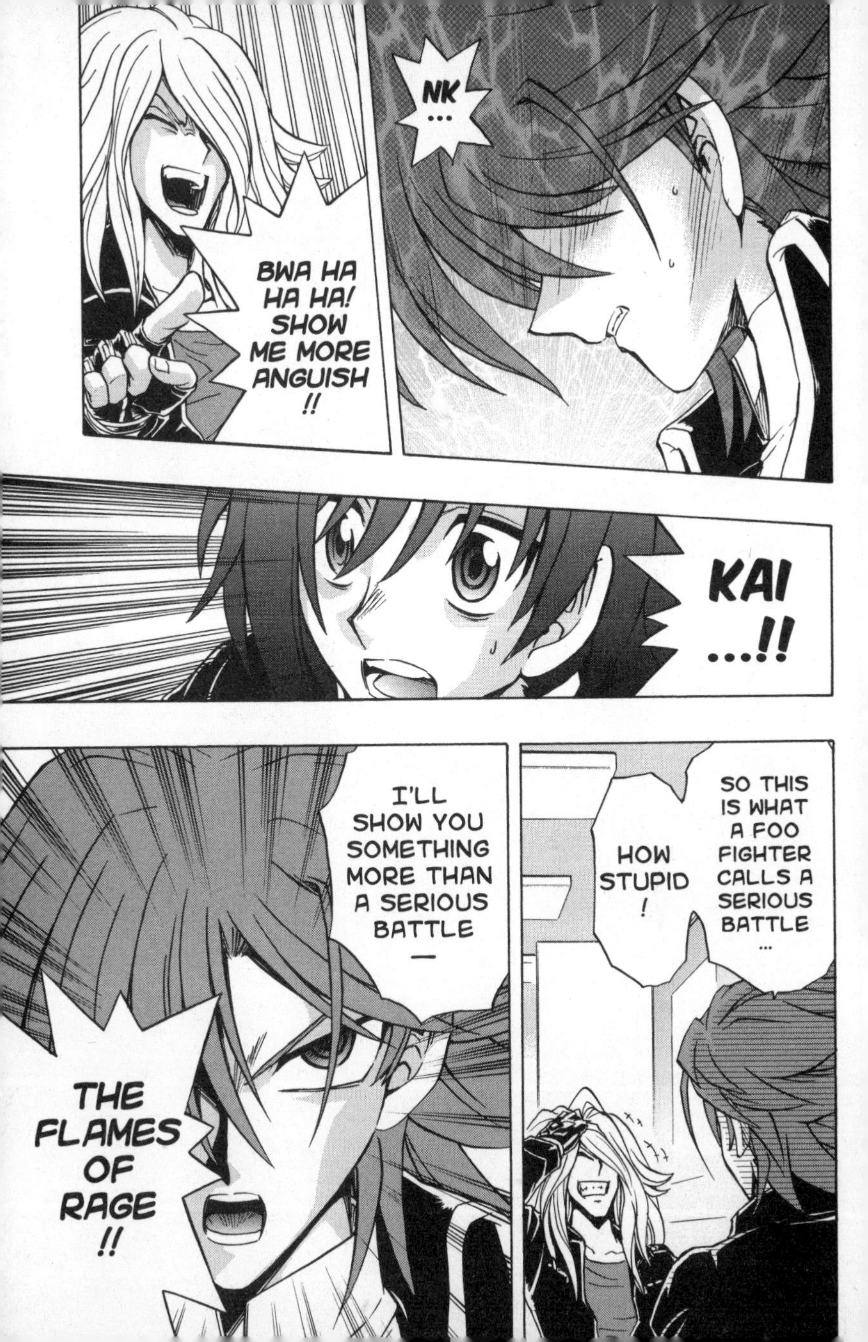
NK...
BWA HA HA HA! SHOW ME MORE ANGUISH!!
KAI...!!
SO THIS IS WHAT A FOO FIGHTER CALLS A SERIOUS BATTLE...
HOW STUPID!
I'LL SHOW YOU SOMETHING MORE THAN A SERIOUS BATTLE—
THE FLAMES OF RAGE!!

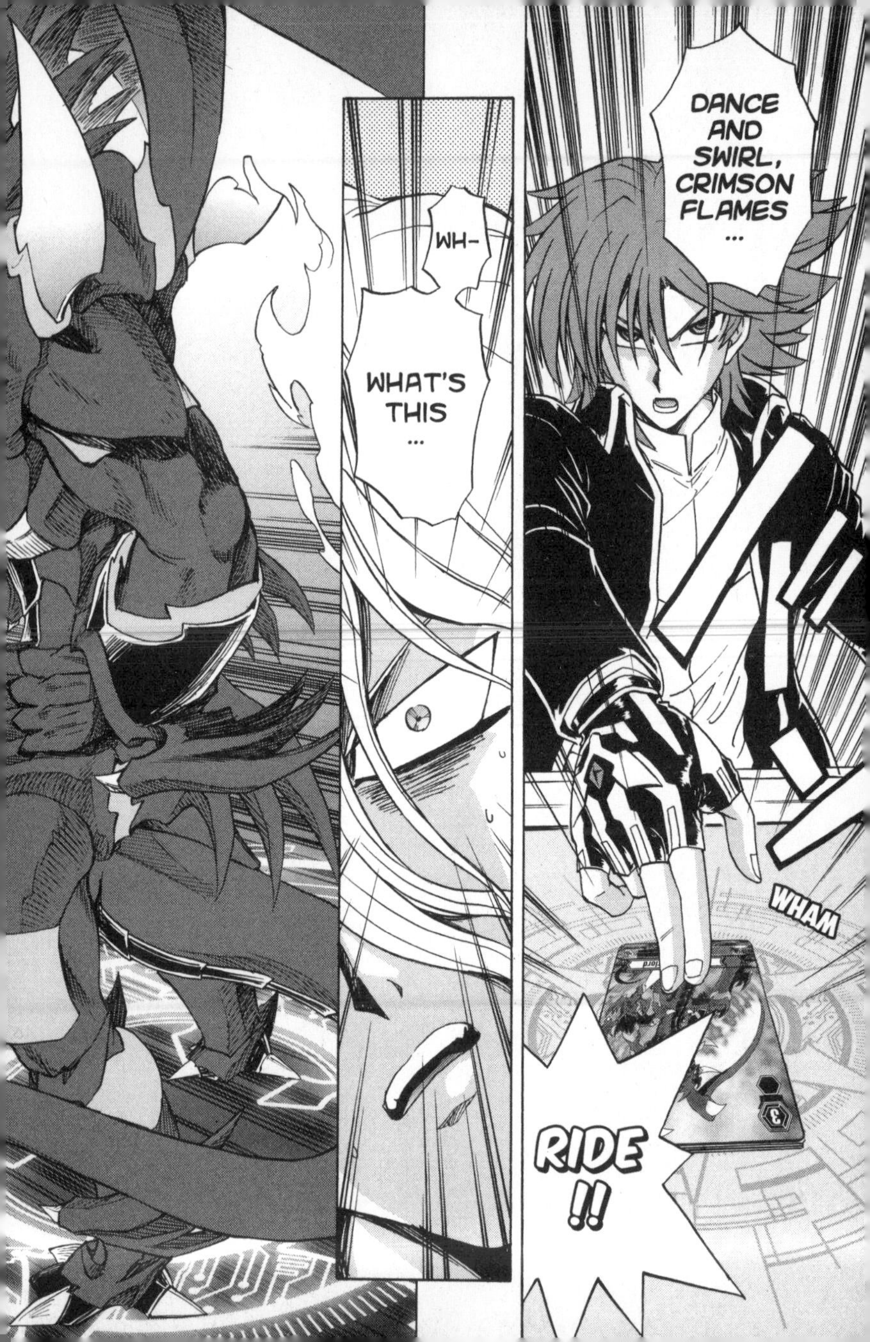
DANCE AND SWIRL, CRIMSON FLAMES ...
WHAM
RIDE !!
WH-
WHAT'S THIS ...

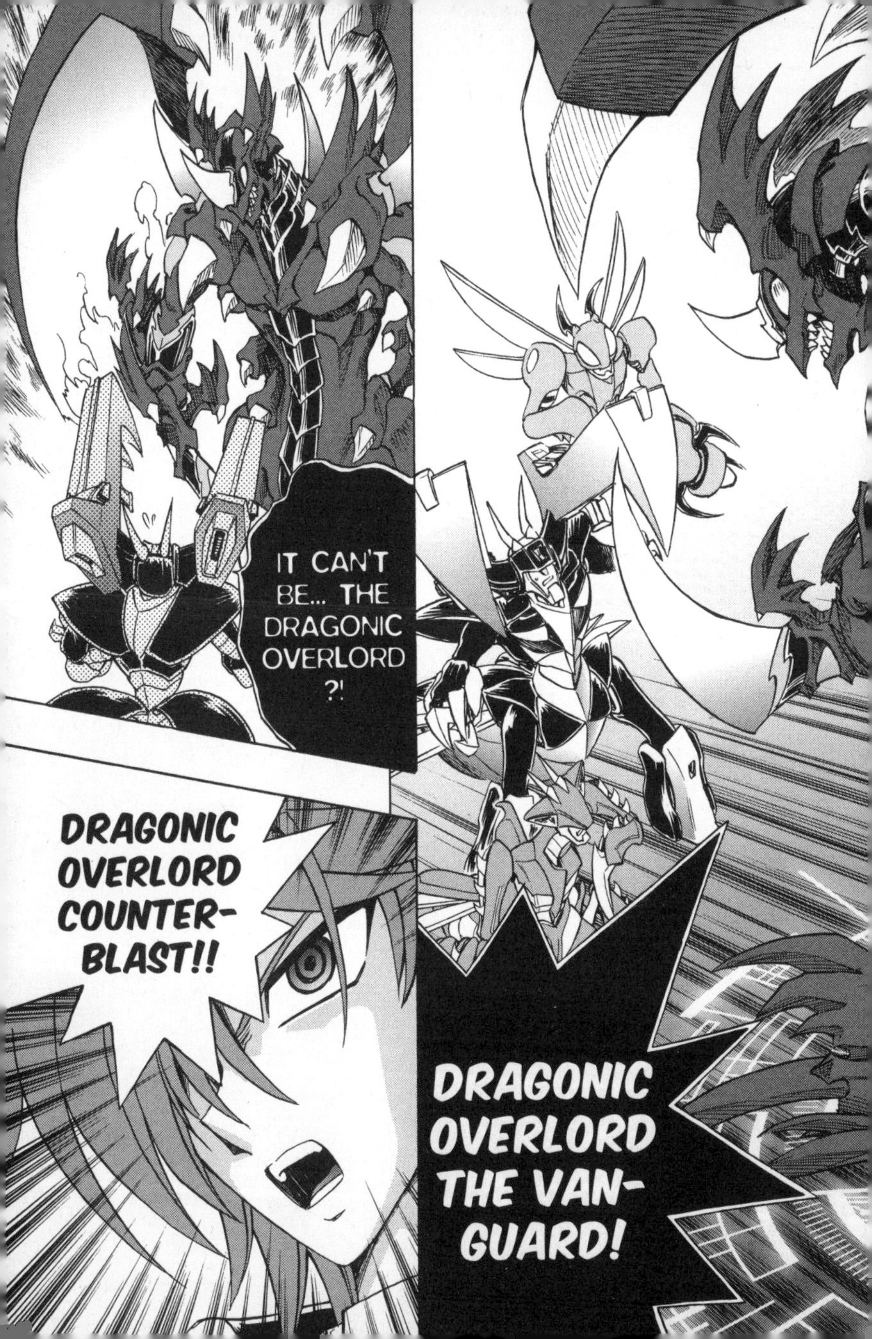
DRAGONIC OVERLORD THE VAN-GUARD!
IT CAN'T BE... THE DRAGONIC OVERLORD ?!
DRAGONIC OVERLORD COUNTER-BLAST!!

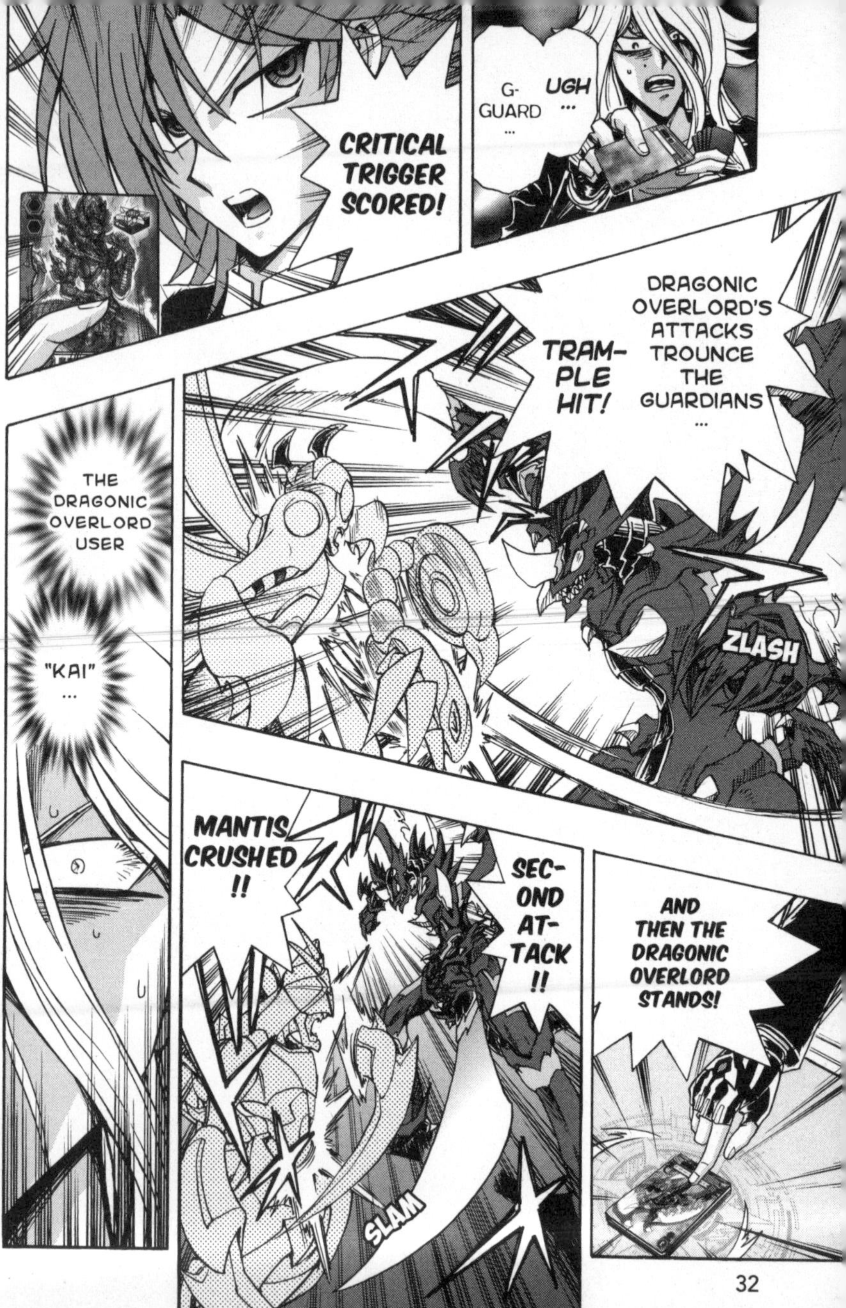
UGH ...
G-GUARD ...
CRITICAL TRIGGER SCORED!
DRAGONIC OVERLORD'S ATTACKS TROUNCE THE GUARDIANS ...
TRAMPLE HIT!
ZLASH
AND THEN THE DRAGONIC OVERLORD STANDS!
SECOND ATTACK!!
MANTIS CRUSHED!!
SLAM
THE DRAGONIC OVERLORD USER
"KAI" ...

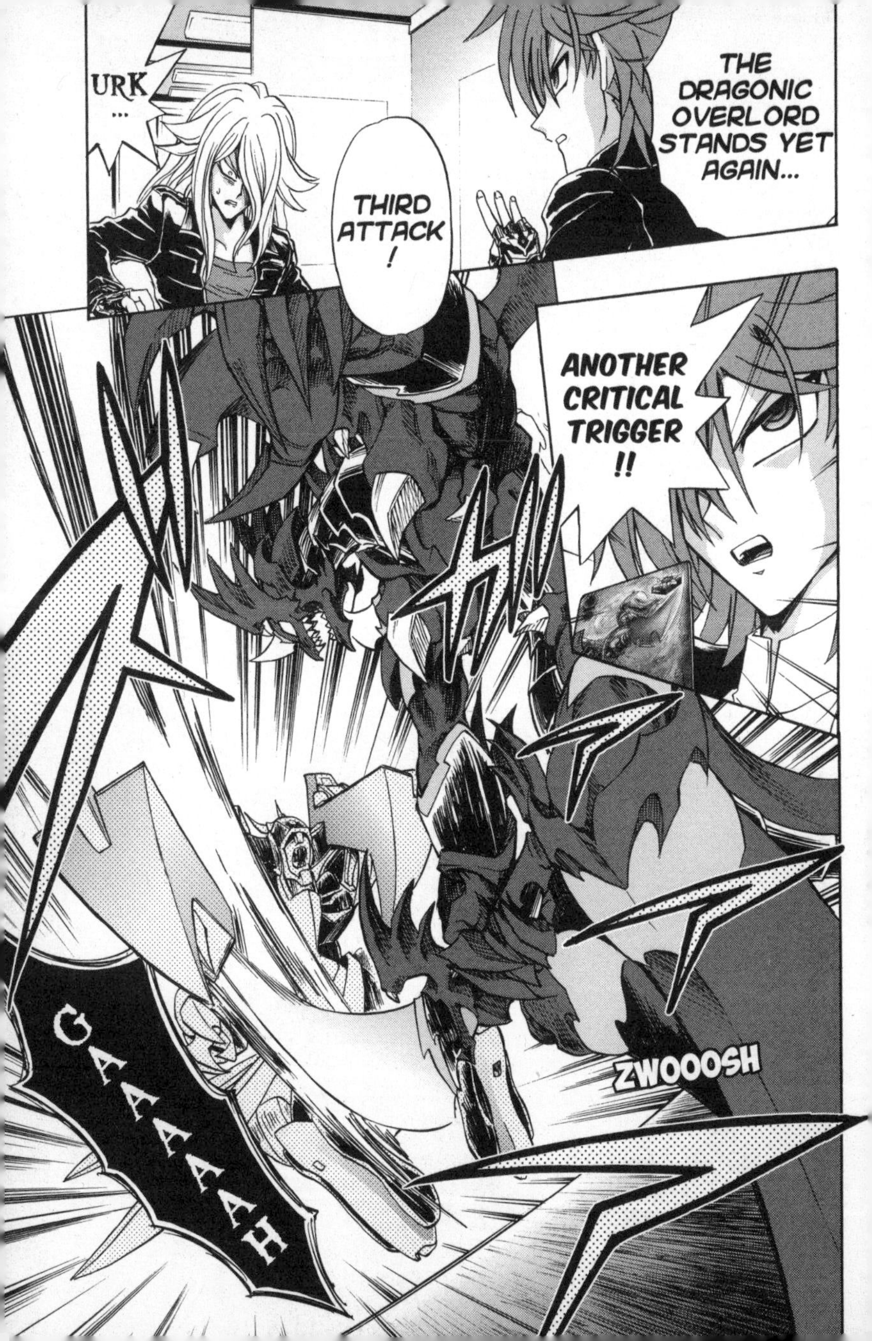
THE DRAGONIC OVERLORD STANDS YET AGAIN...
THIRD ATTACK!
URK...
ANOTHER CRITICAL TRIGGER!!
ZWOOOSH
GAAAAAH

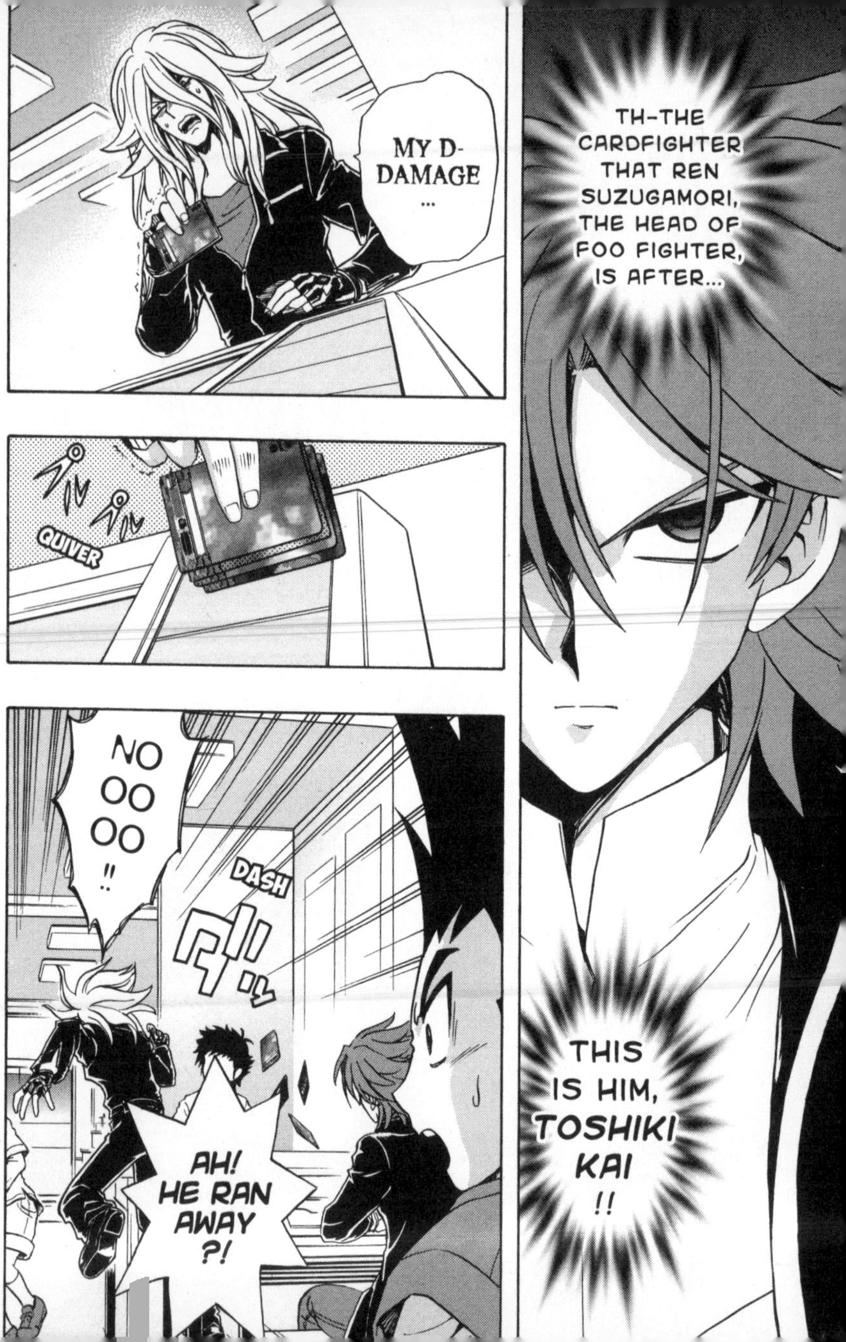
TH-THE CARDFIGHTER THAT REN SUZUGAMORI, THE HEAD OF FOO FIGHTER, IS AFTER...
THIS IS HIM, TOSHIKI KAI!!
MY D-DAMAGE ...
QUIVER
NOOOOOO!!
DASH
AH! HE RAN AWAY?!

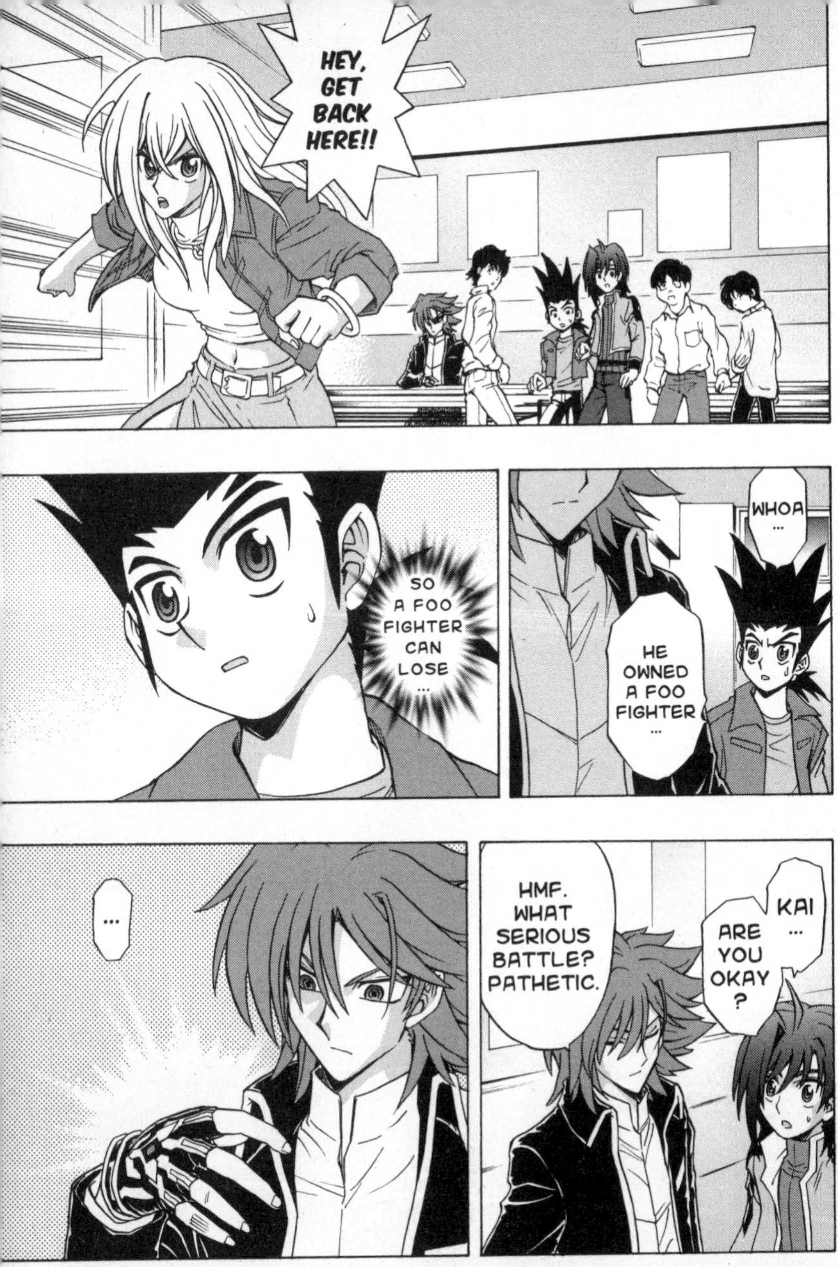
HEY, GET BACK HERE!!
WHOA ...
HE OWNED A FOO FIGHTER ...
SO A FOO FIGHTER CAN LOSE ...
KAI ...
ARE YOU OKAY?
HMF. WHAT SERIOUS BATTLE? PATHETIC.
...

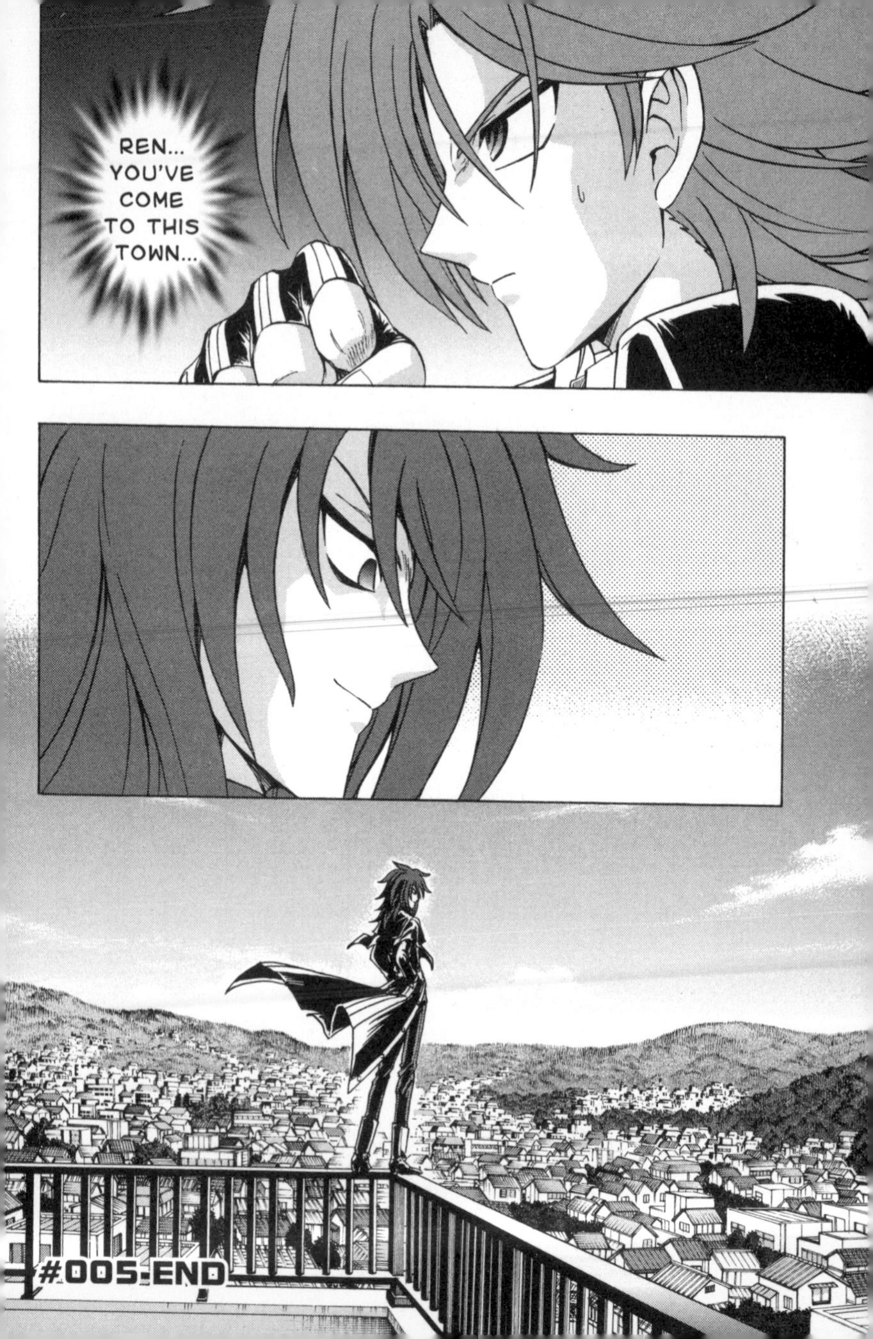
REN... YOU'VE COME TO THIS TOWN...
#005 END

BONUS! CARDFIGHT!! Vanguard NEVER-BEFORE-SEEN IMAGE BOARDS — CHARACTERS

The initial concept sketches introduced in volume 1 were a huge hit, so we're continuing the bonuses in this volume! Check out details that are slightly different from the final manga and anime versions! All illustrations and notes come from Akira Itou himself!

Main Characters Height Comparison Reference

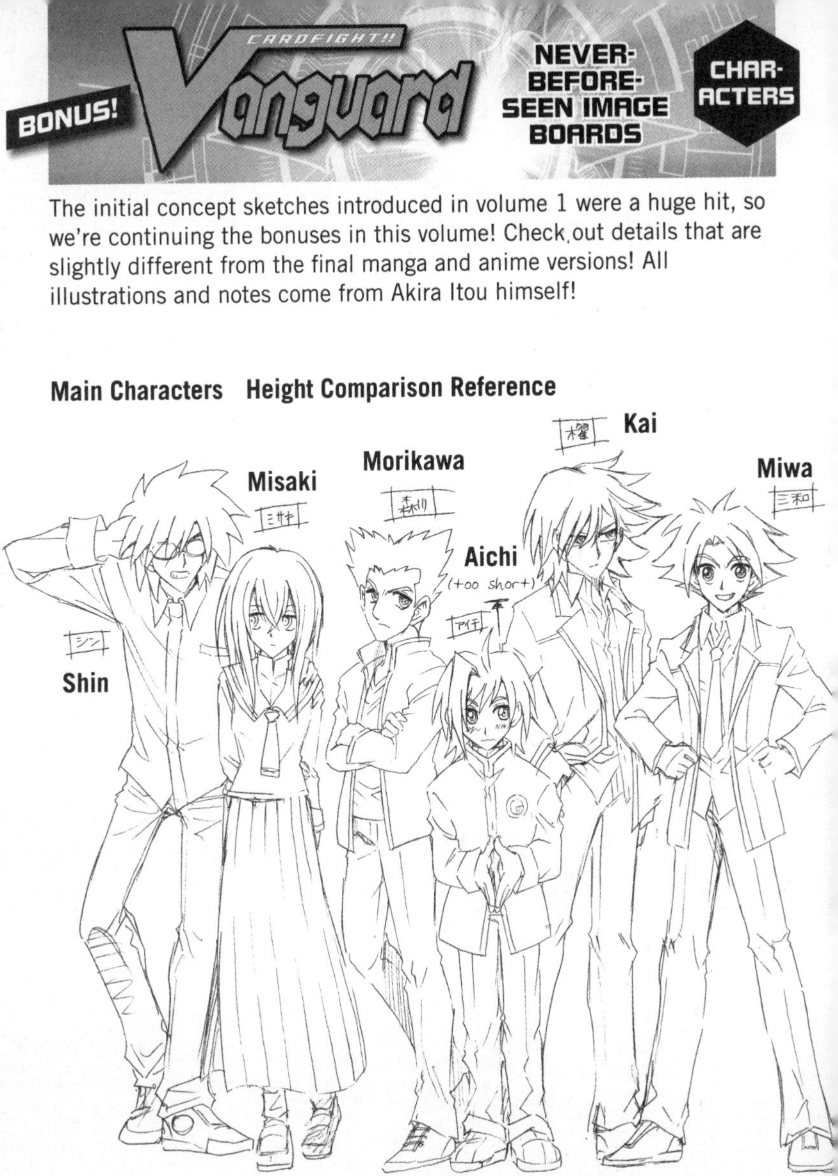
Shin
Misaki
Morikawa
Aichi
(too short)
Kai
Miwa

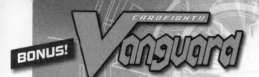

Toshiki Kai and Aichi Sendou in the Past

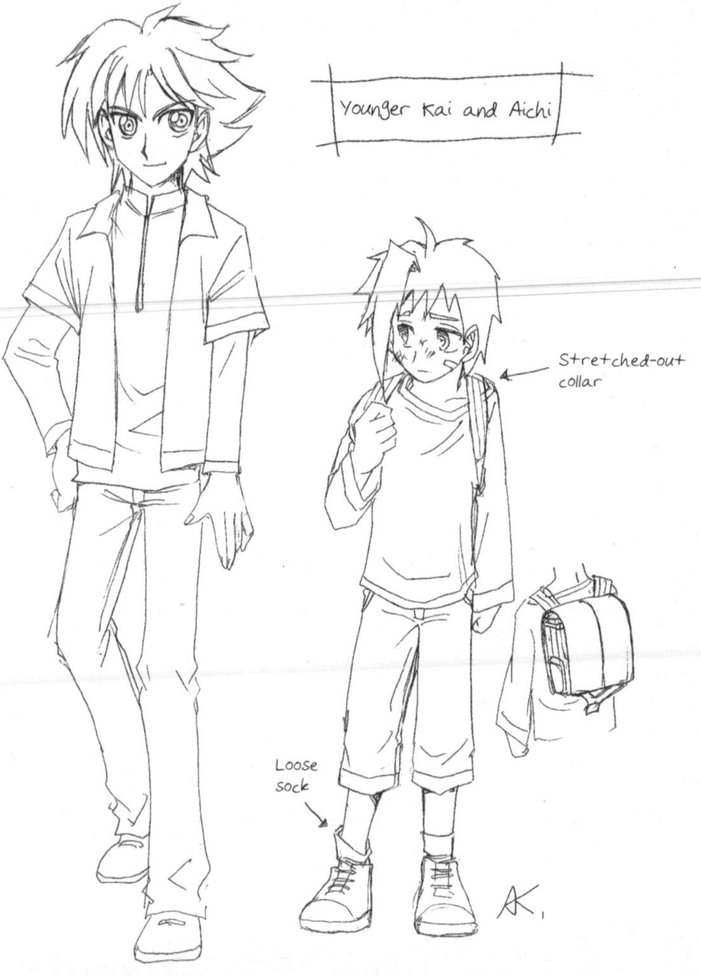
Younger Kai and Aichi
Stretched-out collar
Loose sock

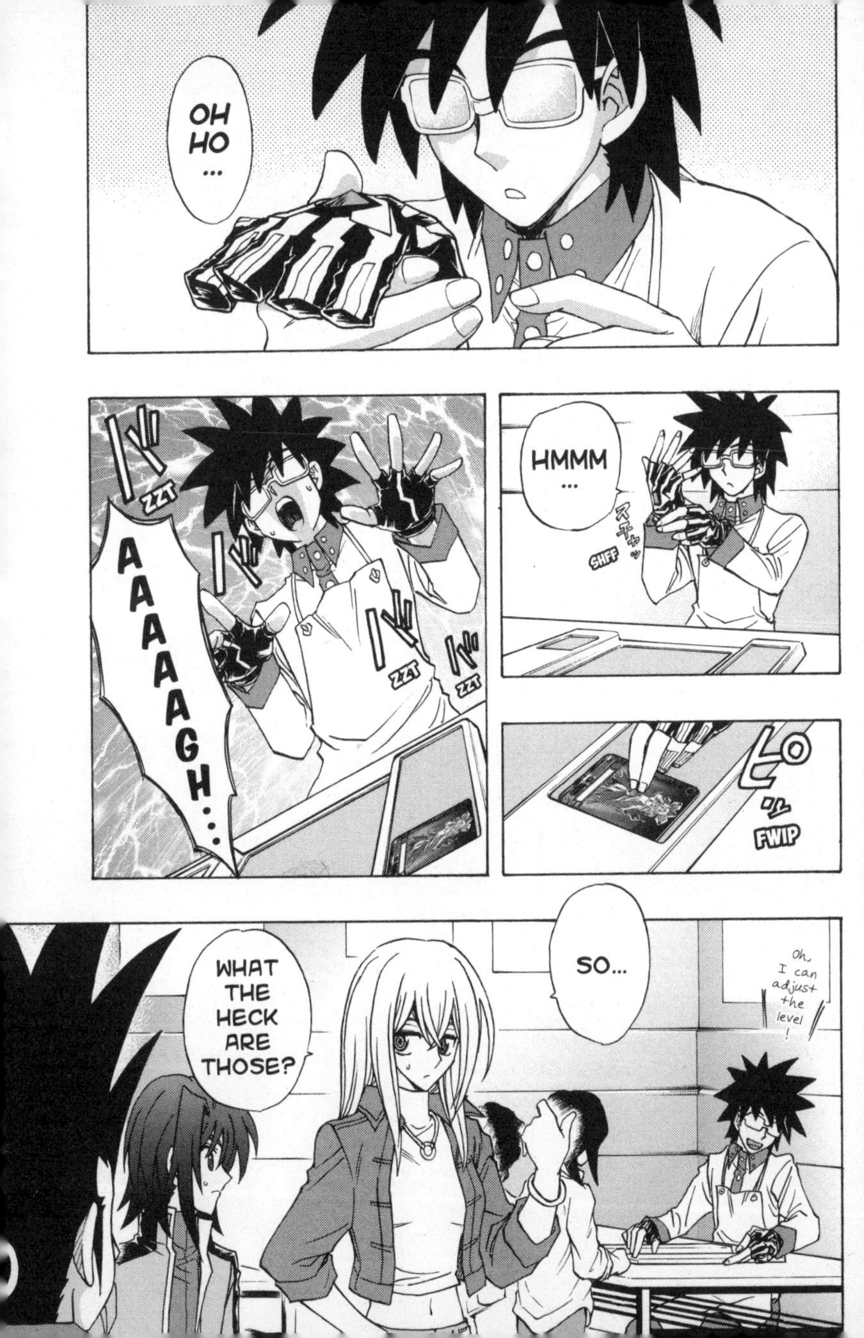
OH HO ...
HMMM ...
SHFF
FWIP
ZZT
AAAAAGH...
ZZT
ZZT
Oh, I can adjust the level!
SO...
WHAT THE HECK ARE THOSE?

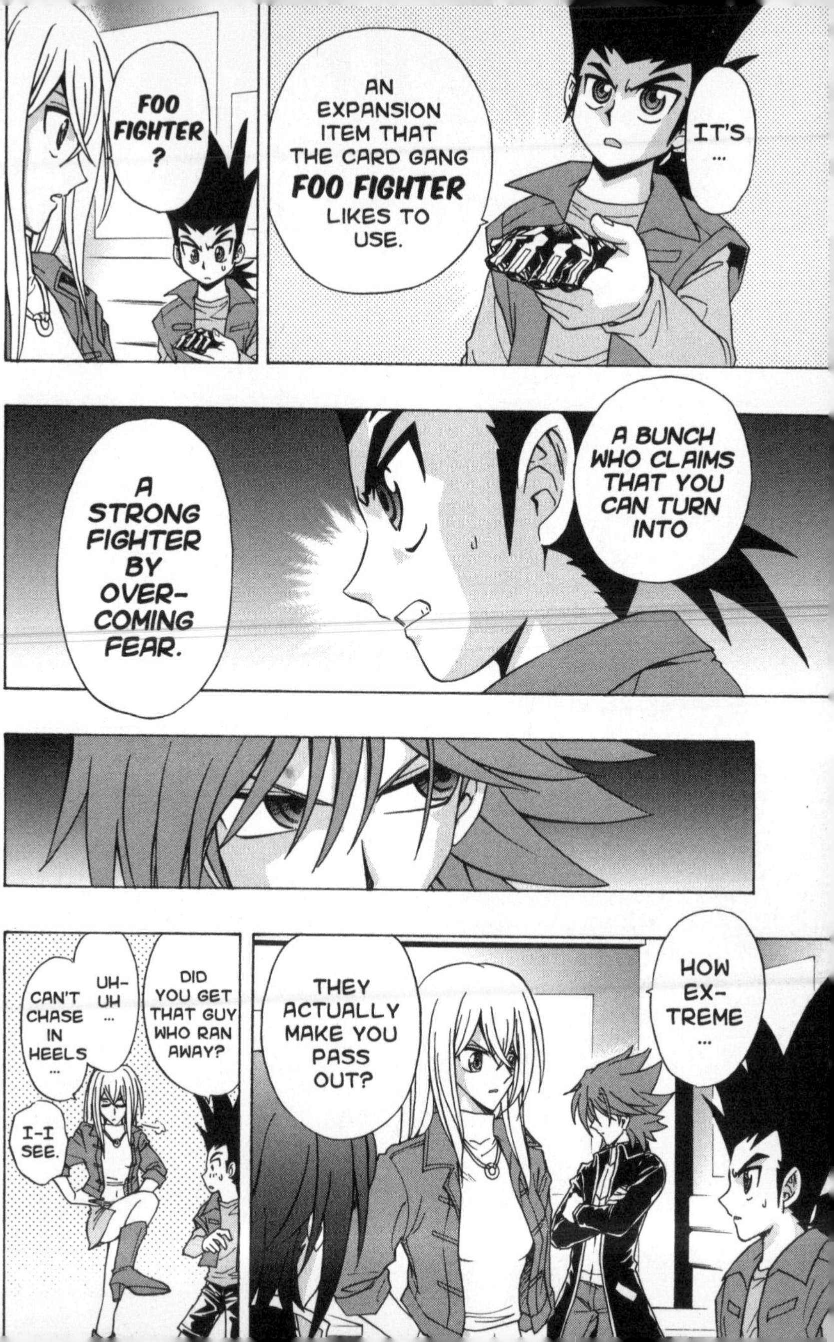
IT'S ...
AN EXPANSION ITEM THAT THE CARD GANG **FOO FIGHTER** LIKES TO USE.
FOO FIGHTER ?
A BUNCH WHO CLAIMS THAT YOU CAN TURN INTO
A STRONG FIGHTER BY OVER-COMING FEAR.
HOW EX-TREME ...
THEY ACTUALLY MAKE YOU PASS OUT?
DID YOU GET THAT GUY WHO RAN AWAY?
UH-UH ...
CAN'T CHASE IN HEELS ...
I-I SEE.

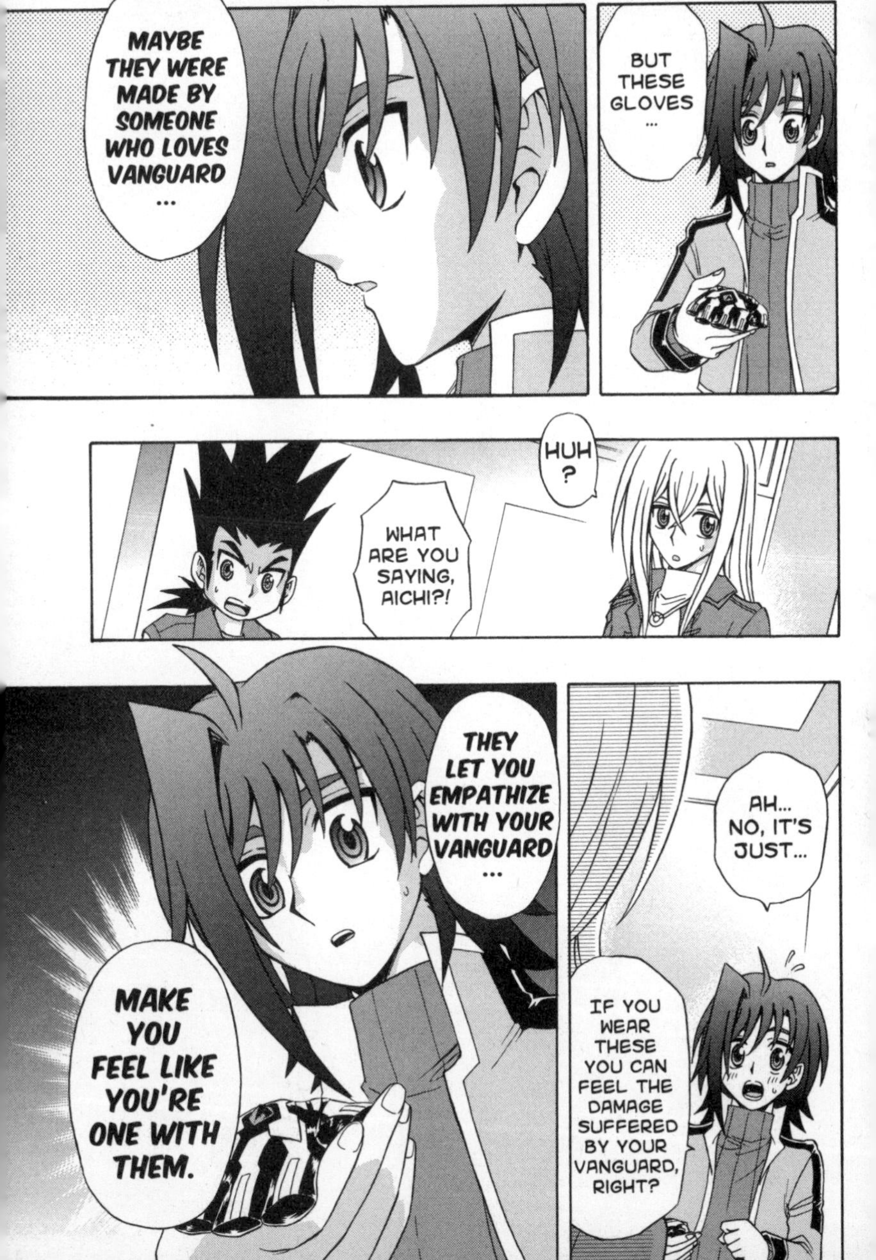
BUT THESE GLOVES ...
MAYBE THEY WERE MADE BY SOMEONE WHO LOVES VANGUARD ...
HUH?
WHAT ARE YOU SAYING, AICHI?!
AH... NO, IT'S JUST...
IF YOU WEAR THESE YOU CAN FEEL THE DAMAGE SUFFERED BY YOUR VANGUARD, RIGHT?
THEY LET YOU EMPATHIZE WITH YOUR VANGUARD ...
MAKE YOU FEEL LIKE YOU'RE ONE WITH THEM.

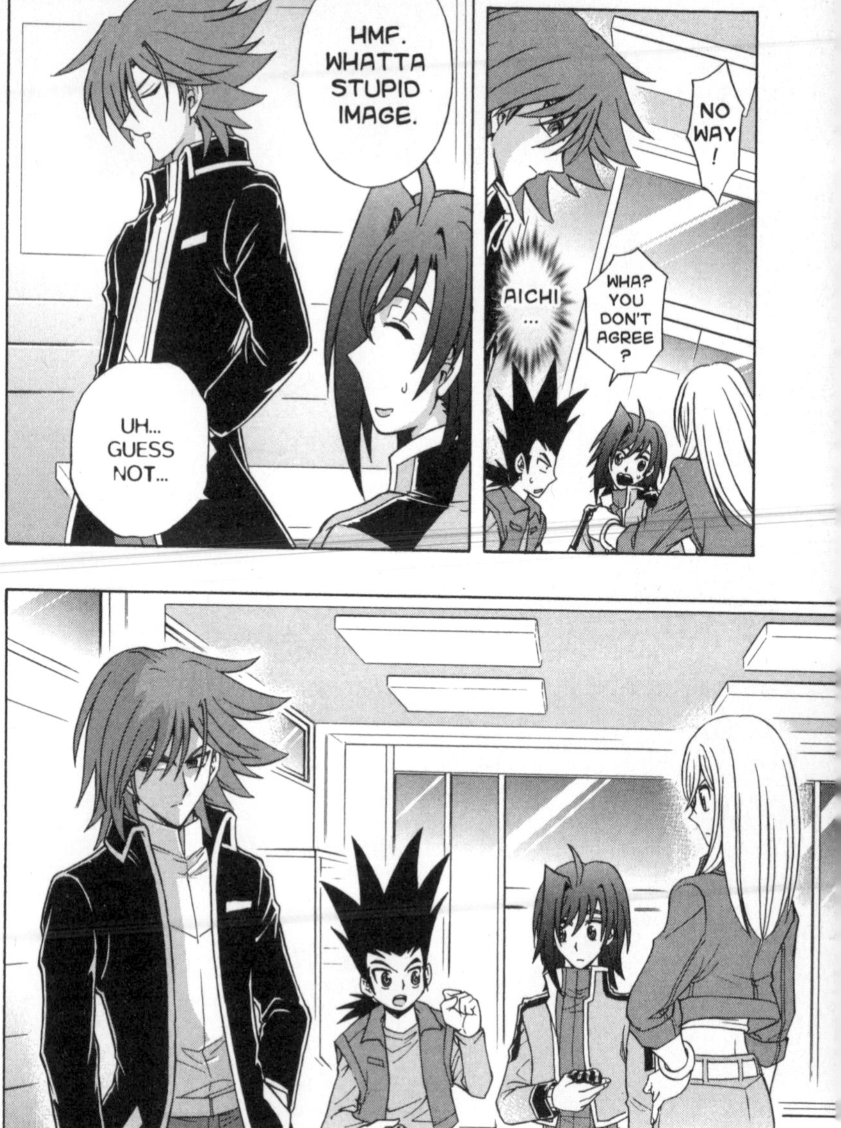
NO WAY!
WHA? YOU DON'T AGREE?
AICHI...
HMF. WHATTA STUPID IMAGE.
UH... GUESS NOT...

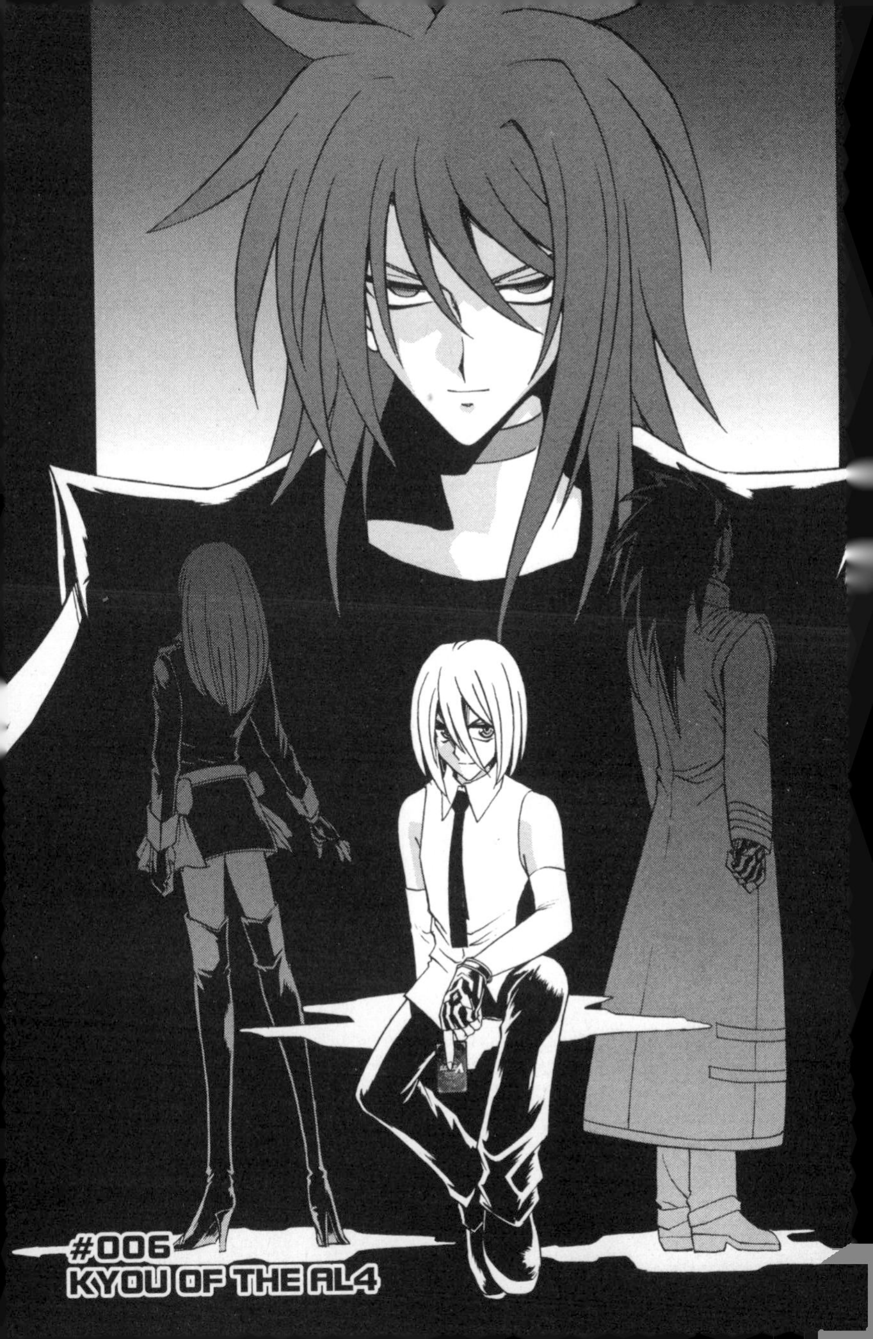
#006
KYOU OF THE AL4

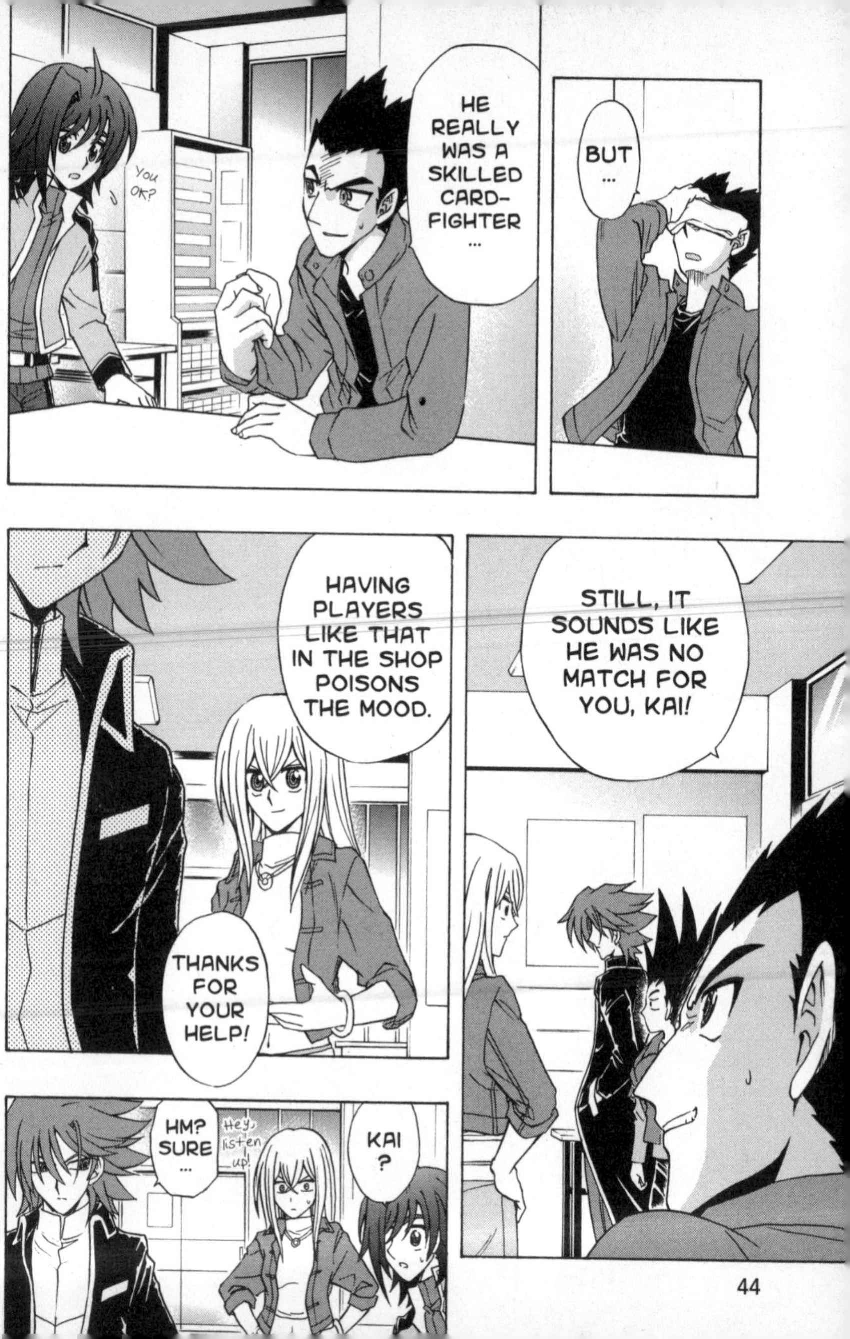
BUT ...
HE REALLY WAS A SKILLED CARD-FIGHTER ...
You OK?
STILL, IT SOUNDS LIKE HE WAS NO MATCH FOR YOU, KAI!
HAVING PLAYERS LIKE THAT IN THE SHOP POISONS THE MOOD.
THANKS FOR YOUR HELP!
KAI ?
Hey, listen up!
HM? SURE ...

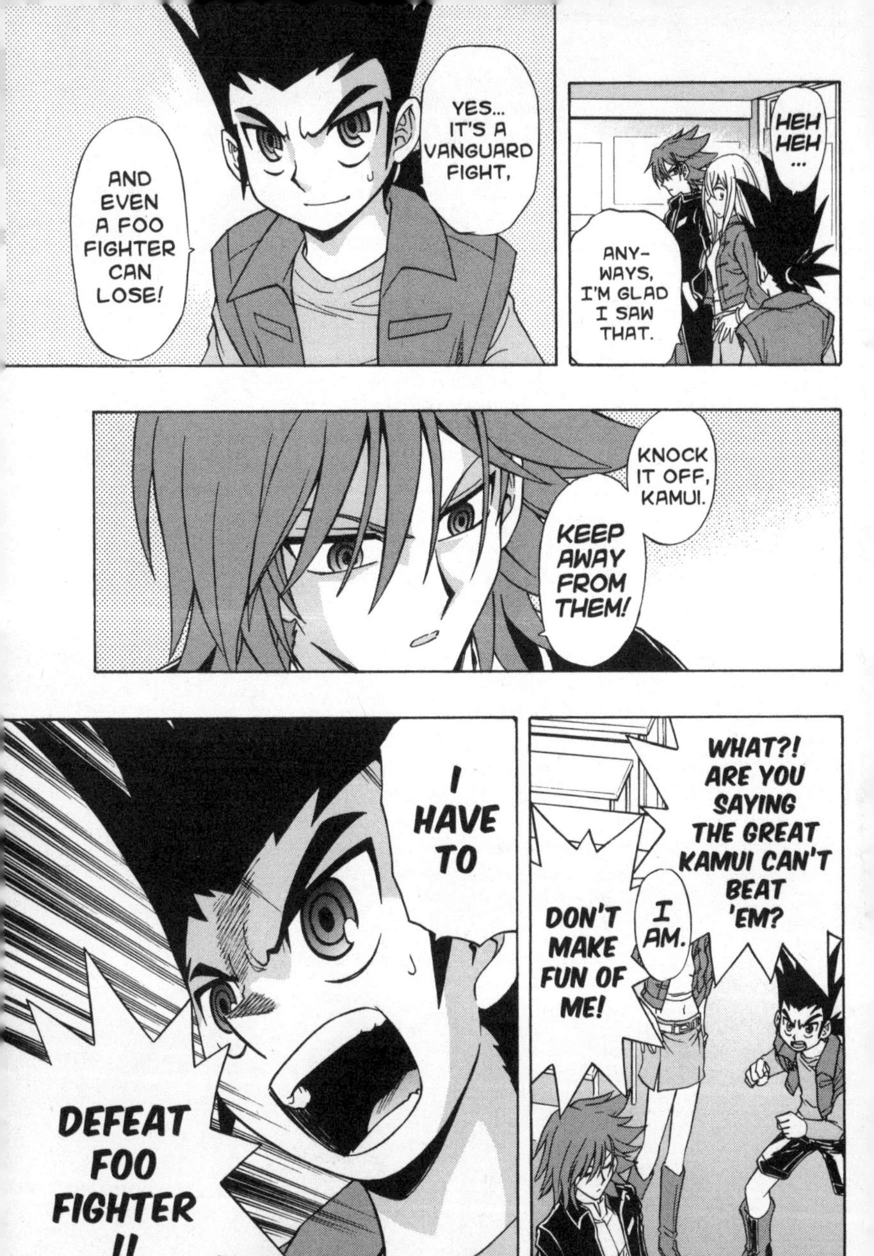
HEH HEH ...
ANY-WAYS, I'M GLAD I SAW THAT.
YES... IT'S A VANGUARD FIGHT,
AND EVEN A FOO FIGHTER CAN LOSE!
KNOCK IT OFF, KAMUI.
KEEP AWAY FROM THEM!
WHAT?! ARE YOU SAYING THE GREAT KAMUI CAN'T BEAT 'EM?
I AM.
DON'T MAKE FUN OF ME!
I HAVE TO
DEFEAT FOO FIGHTER !!

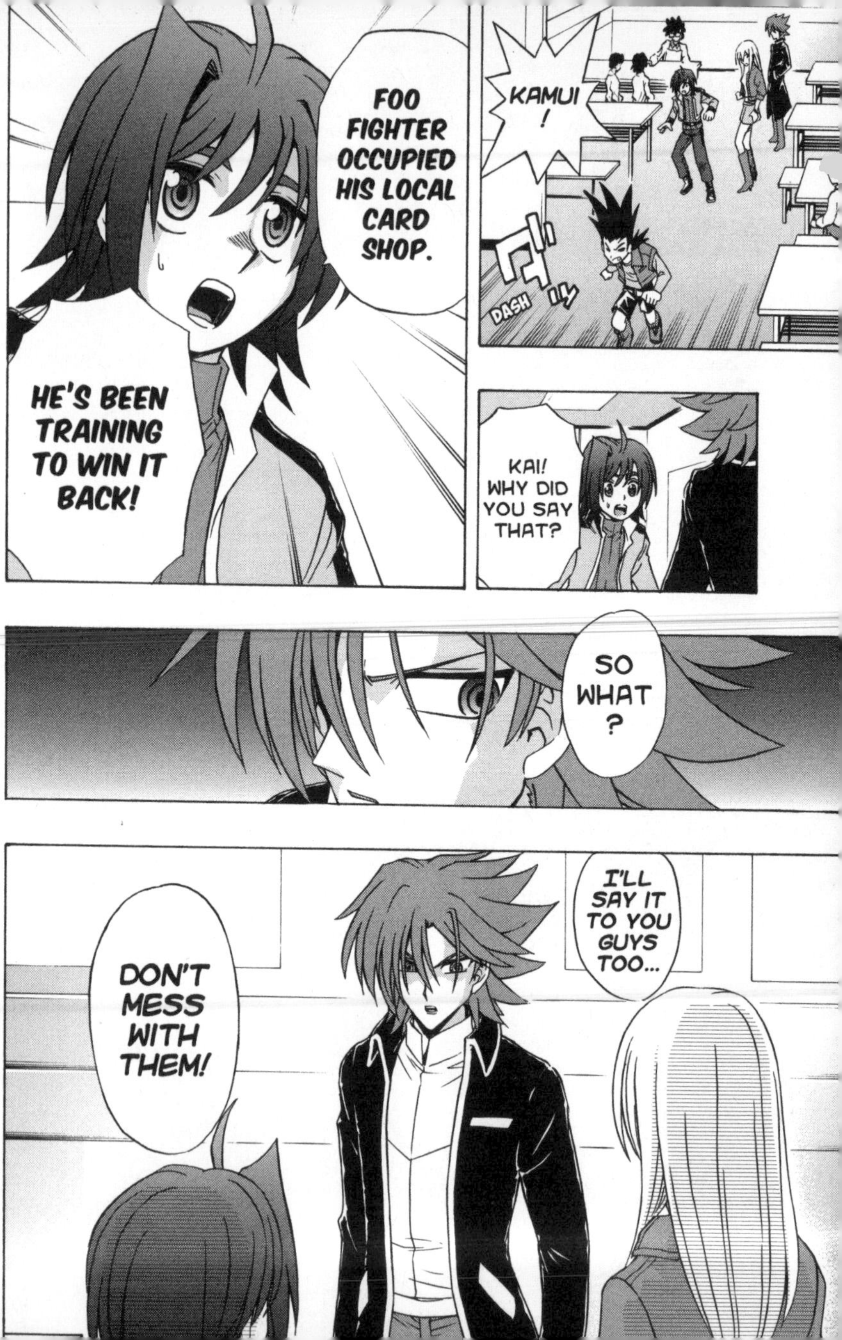
KAMUI!
DASH
KAI! WHY DID YOU SAY THAT?
FOO FIGHTER OCCUPIED HIS LOCAL CARD SHOP.
HE'S BEEN TRAINING TO WIN IT BACK!
SO WHAT?
I'LL SAY IT TO YOU GUYS TOO...
DON'T MESS WITH THEM!

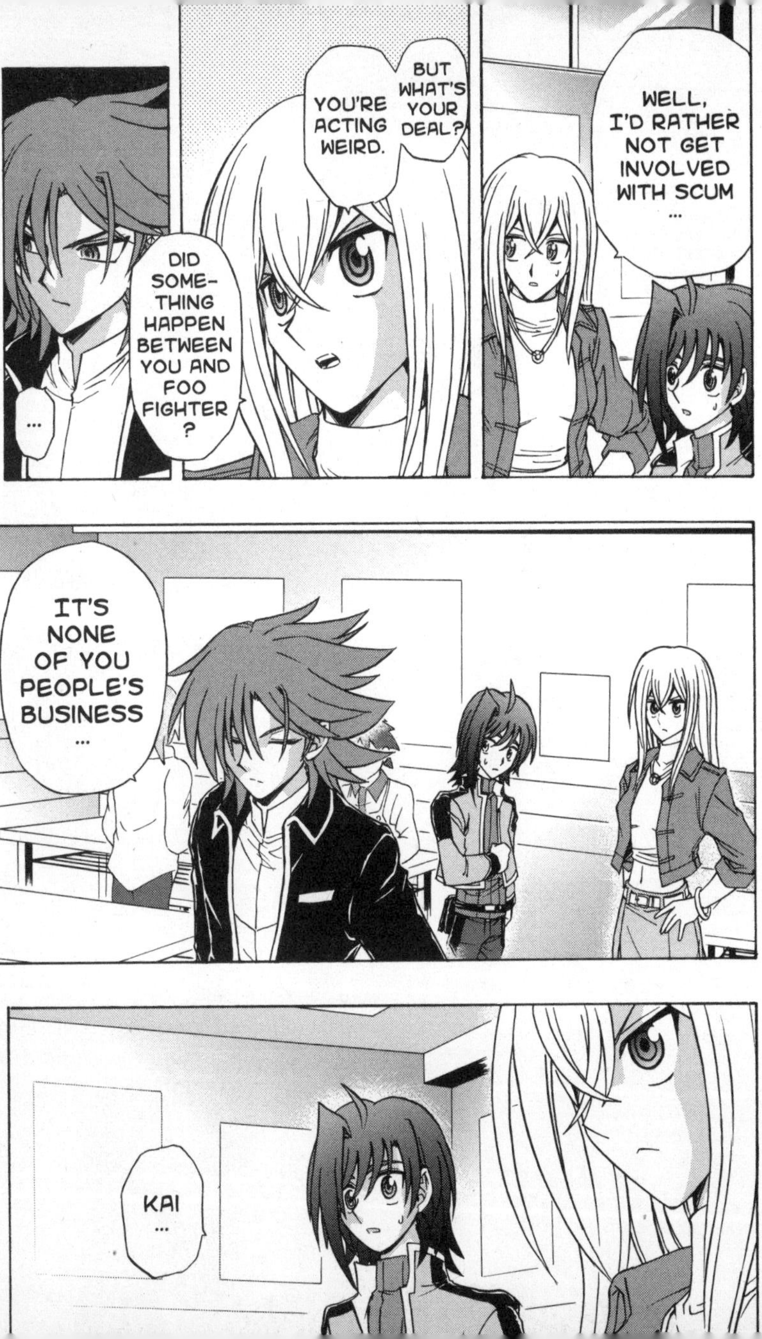
WELL, I'D RATHER NOT GET INVOLVED WITH SCUM ...
BUT WHAT'S YOUR DEAL?
YOU'RE ACTING WEIRD.
DID SOME-THING HAPPEN BETWEEN YOU AND FOO FIGHTER?
...
IT'S NONE OF YOU PEOPLE'S BUSINESS ...
KAI ...

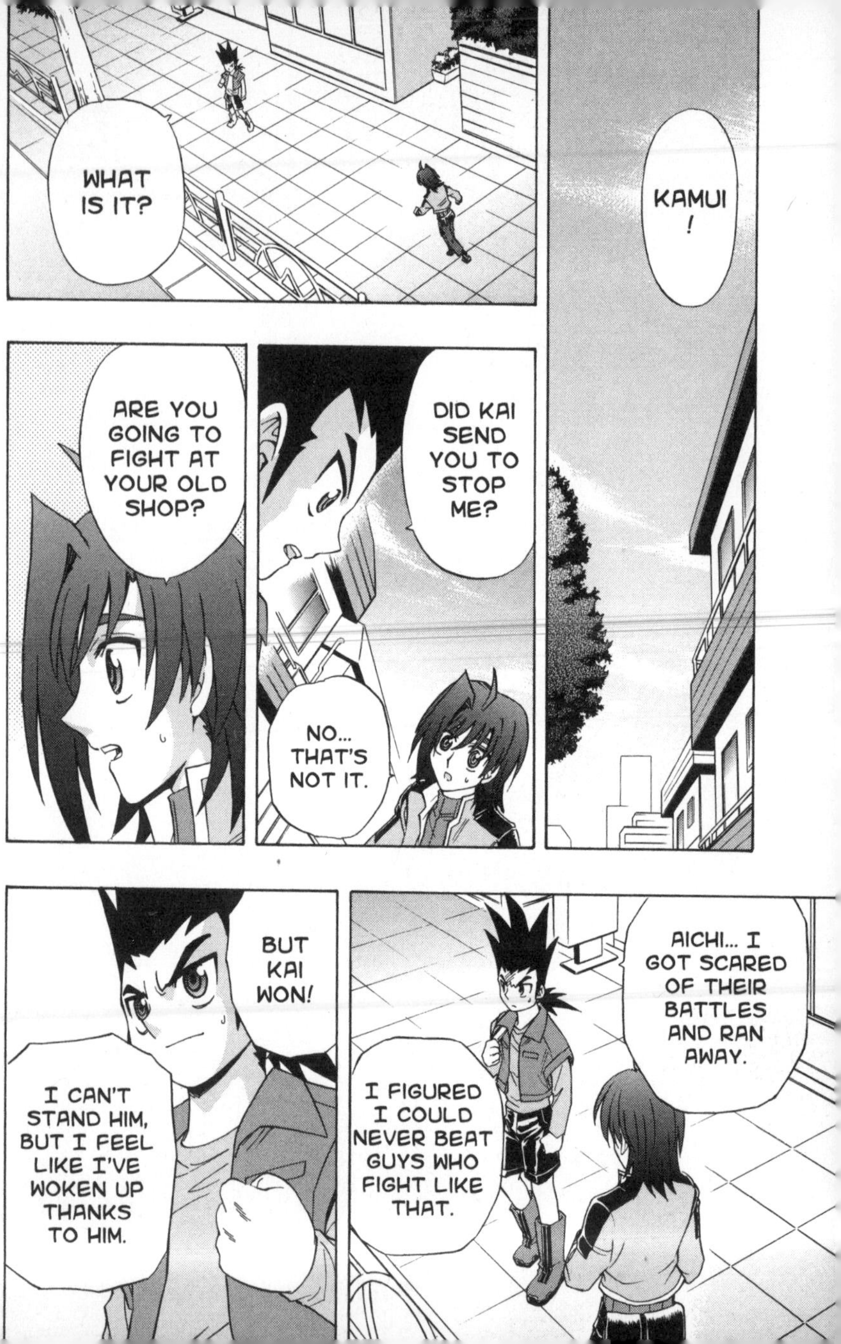
KAMUI!
WHAT IS IT?
DID KAI SEND YOU TO STOP ME?
NO... THAT'S NOT IT.
ARE YOU GOING TO FIGHT AT YOUR OLD SHOP?
AICHI... I GOT SCARED OF THEIR BATTLES AND RAN AWAY.
I FIGURED I COULD NEVER BEAT GUYS WHO FIGHT LIKE THAT.
BUT KAI WON!
I CAN'T STAND HIM, BUT I FEEL LIKE I'VE WOKEN UP THANKS TO HIM.

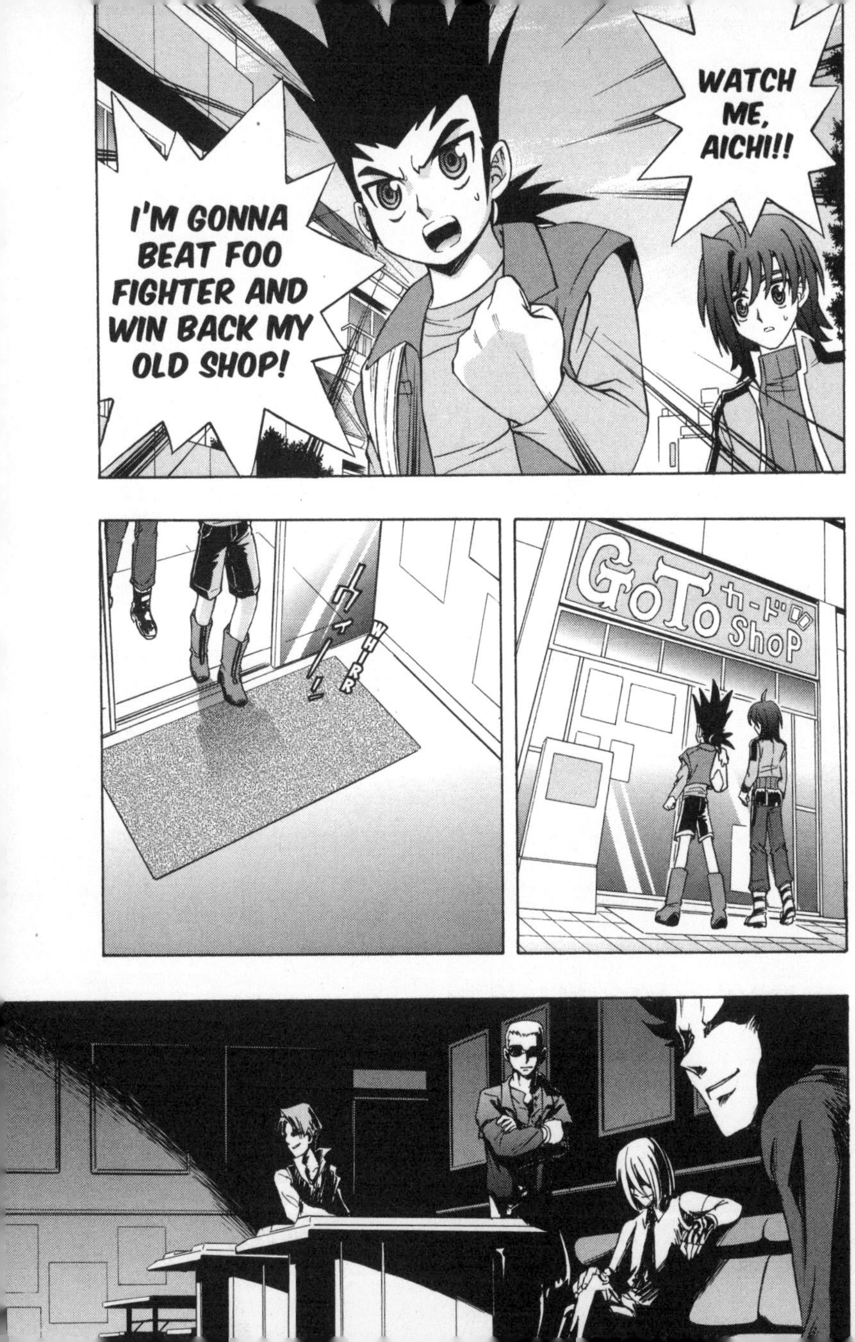
WATCH ME, AICHI!!
I'M GONNA BEAT FOO FIGHTER AND WIN BACK MY OLD SHOP!
GoTo
カード
ShoP
WHIRR

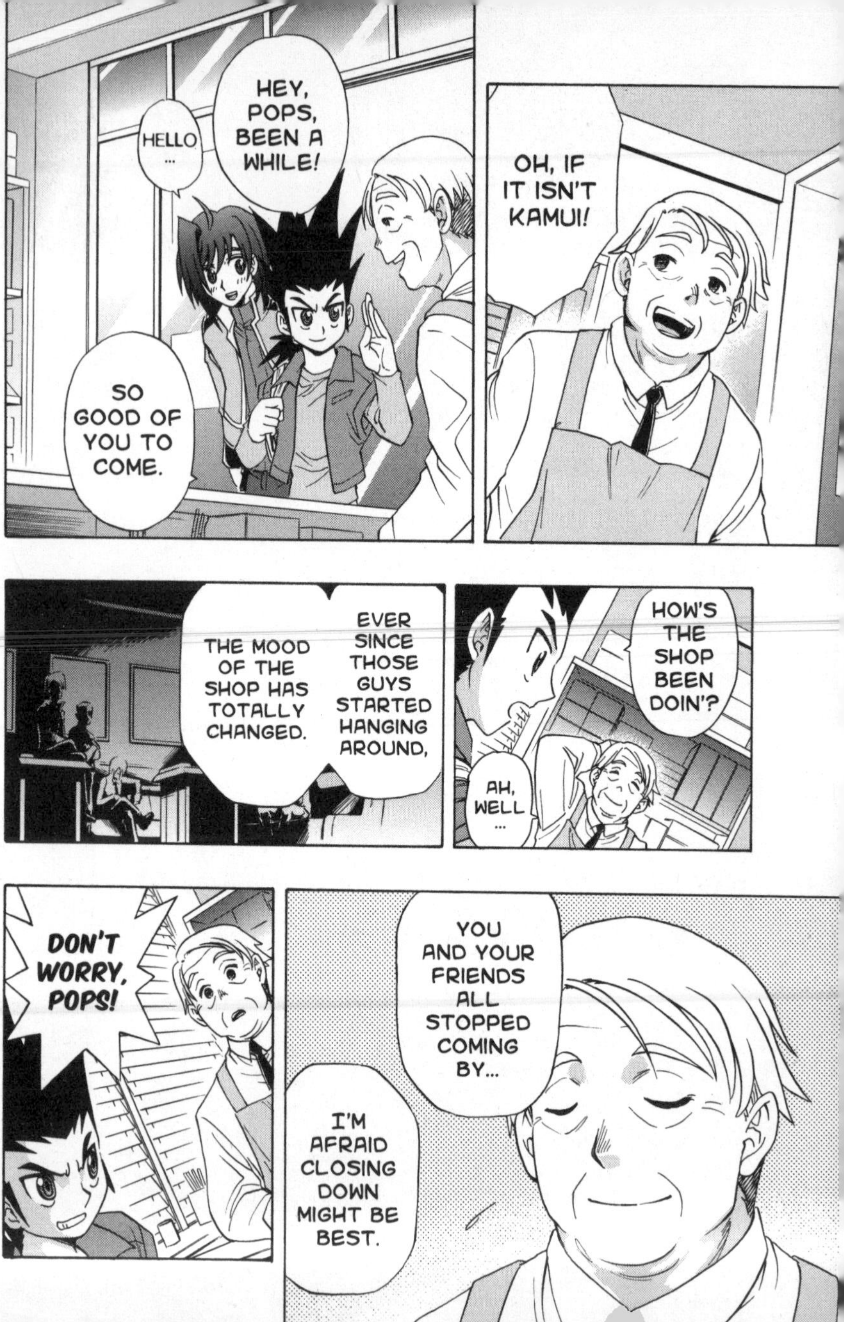
OH, IF IT ISN'T KAMUI!
HEY, POPS, BEEN A WHILE!
HELLO ...
SO GOOD OF YOU TO COME.
HOW'S THE SHOP BEEN DOIN'?
AH, WELL ...
EVER SINCE THOSE GUYS STARTED HANGING AROUND,
THE MOOD OF THE SHOP HAS TOTALLY CHANGED.
YOU AND YOUR FRIENDS ALL STOPPED COMING BY...
I'M AFRAID CLOSING DOWN MIGHT BE BEST.
DON'T WORRY, POPS!

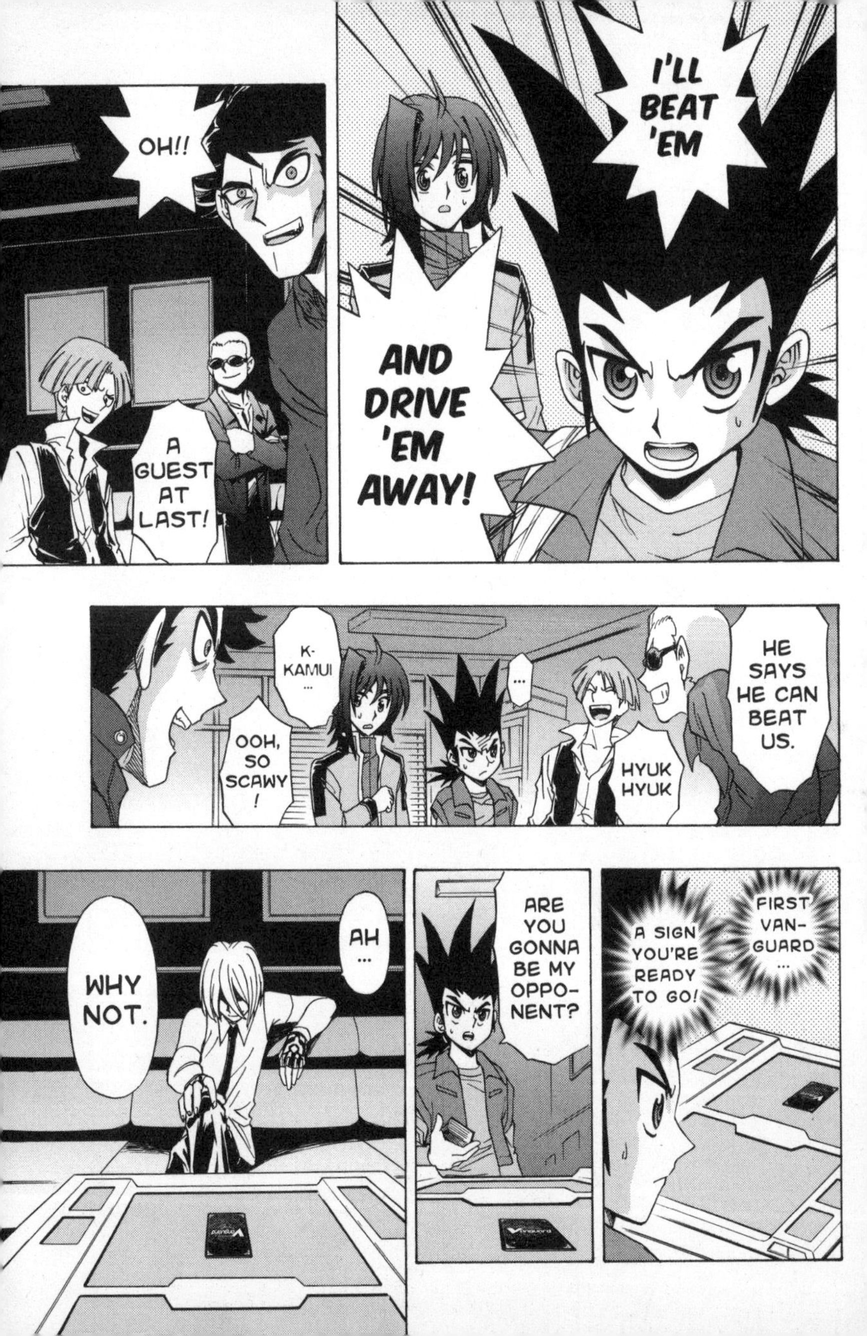
I'LL BEAT 'EM
AND DRIVE 'EM AWAY!
OH!!
A GUEST AT LAST!
HE SAYS HE CAN BEAT US.
HYUK HYUK
...
K-KAMUI ...
OOH, SO SCAWY!
FIRST VAN-GUARD ...
A SIGN YOU'RE READY TO GO!
ARE YOU GONNA BE MY OPPO-NENT?
AH ...
WHY NOT.

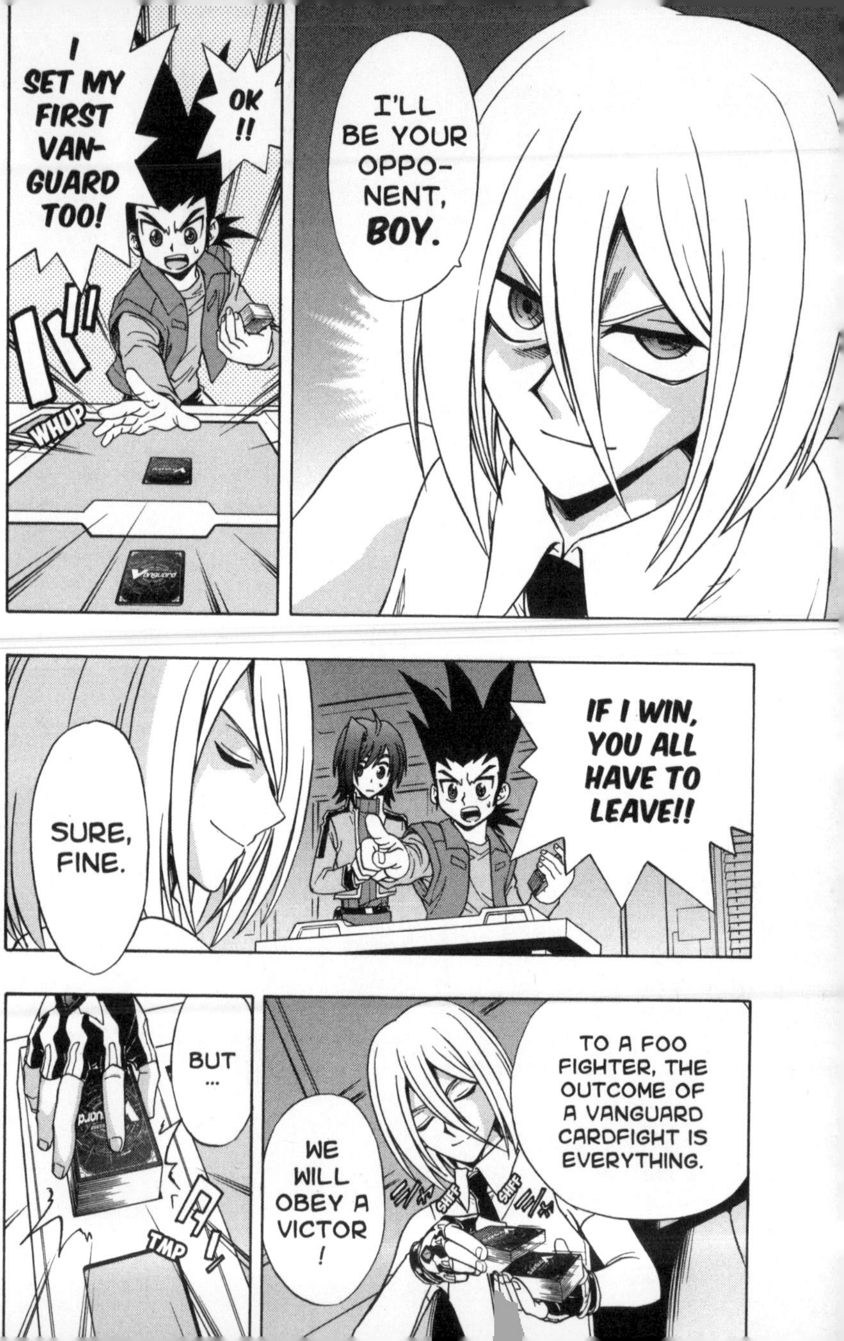

I'LL BE YOUR OPPO-NENT, BOY.
OK !!
I SET MY FIRST VAN-GUARD TOO!
WHUP
IF I WIN, YOU ALL HAVE TO LEAVE!!
SURE, FINE.
TO A FOO FIGHTER, THE OUTCOME OF A VANGUARD CARDFIGHT IS EVERYTHING.
SHFF
SHFF
WE WILL OBEY A VICTOR !
BUT ...
TMP

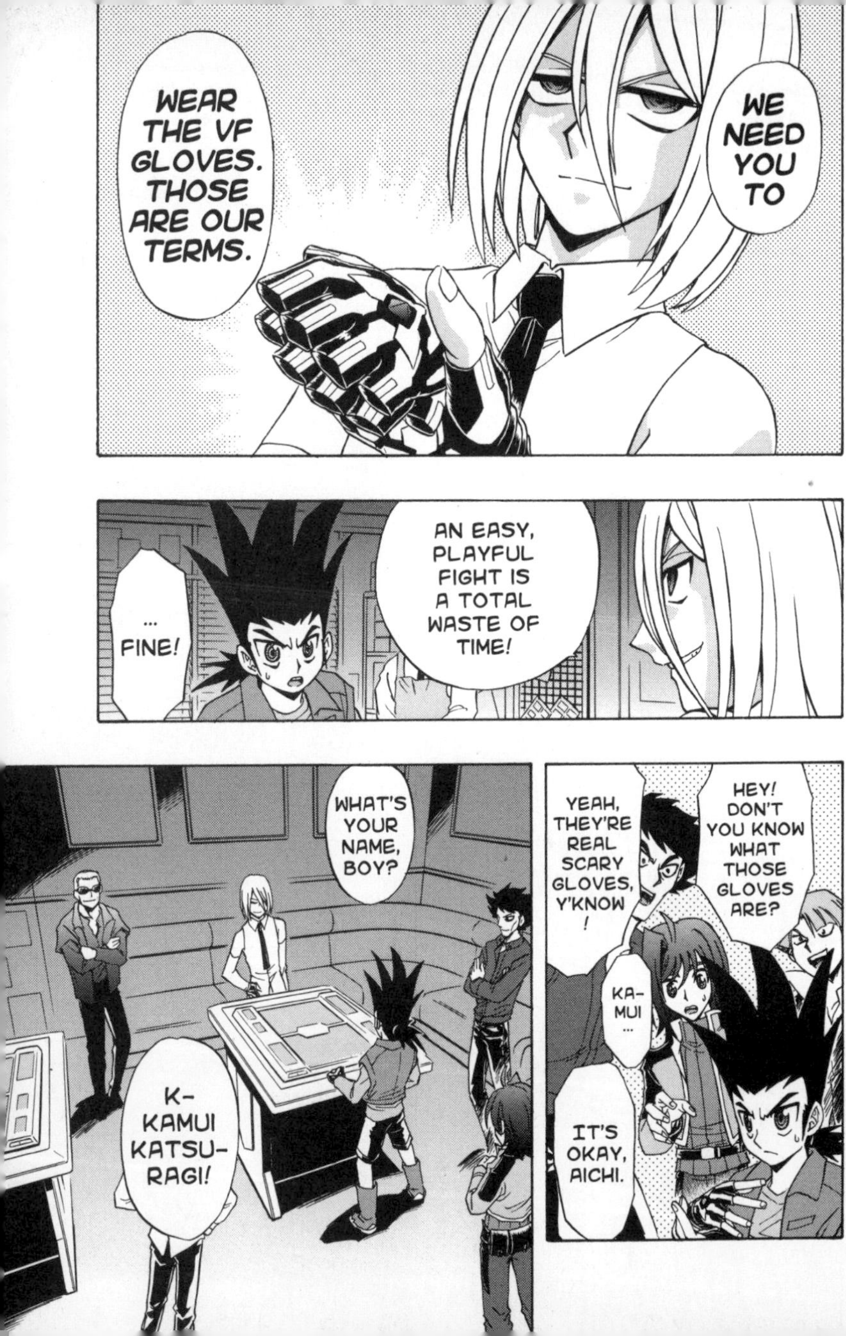
WE NEED YOU TO
WEAR THE VF GLOVES. THOSE ARE OUR TERMS.
AN EASY, PLAYFUL FIGHT IS A TOTAL WASTE OF TIME!
... FINE!
HEY! DON'T YOU KNOW WHAT THOSE GLOVES ARE?
YEAH, THEY'RE REAL SCARY GLOVES, Y'KNOW!
KA-MUI ...
IT'S OKAY, AICHI.
WHAT'S YOUR NAME, BOY?
K-KAMUI KATSURAGI!

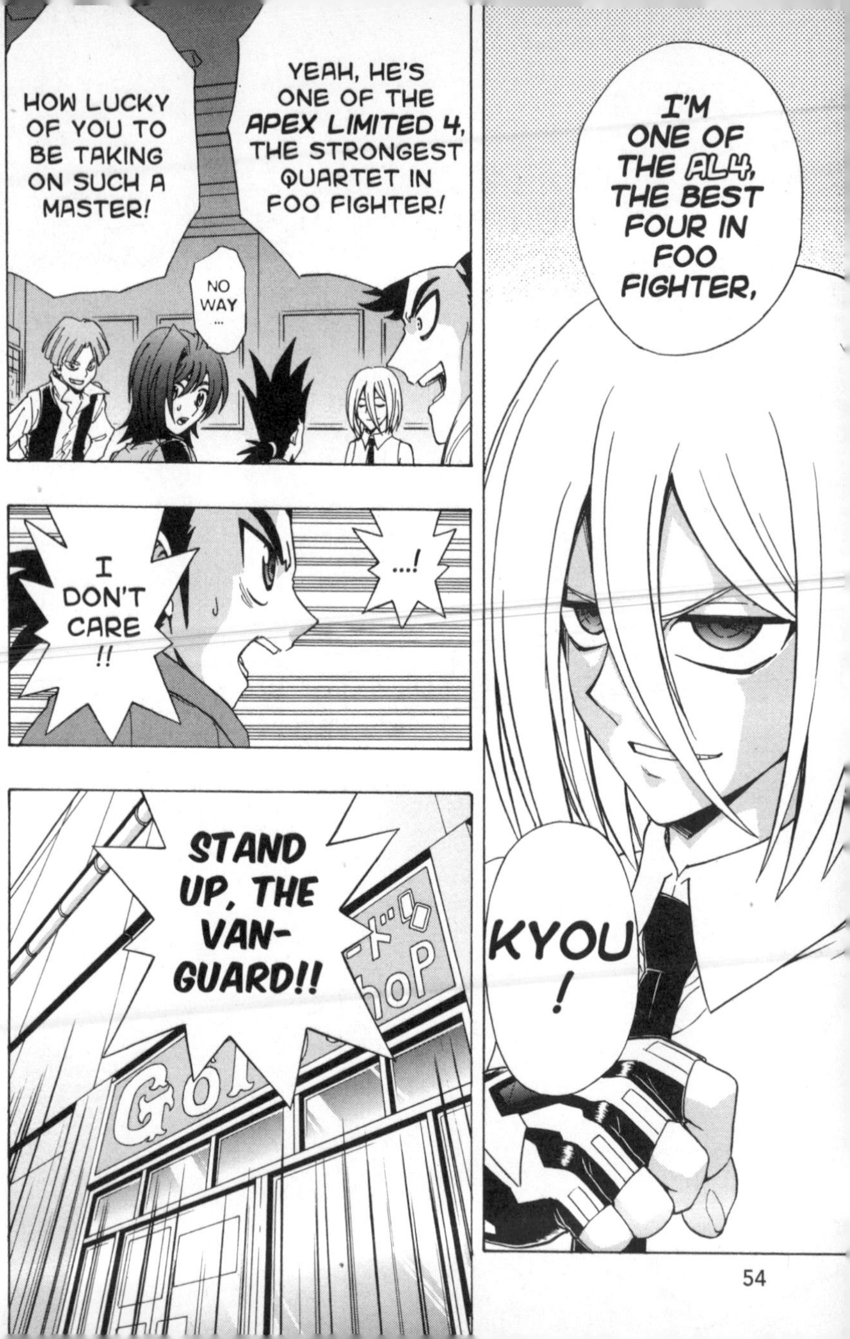
I'M ONE OF THE AL4, THE BEST FOUR IN FOO FIGHTER,
KYOU!
YEAH, HE'S ONE OF THE APEX LIMITED 4, THE STRONGEST QUARTET IN FOO FIGHTER!
HOW LUCKY OF YOU TO BE TAKING ON SUCH A MASTER!
NO WAY...
...!
I DON'T CARE!!
STAND UP, THE VAN-GUARD!!

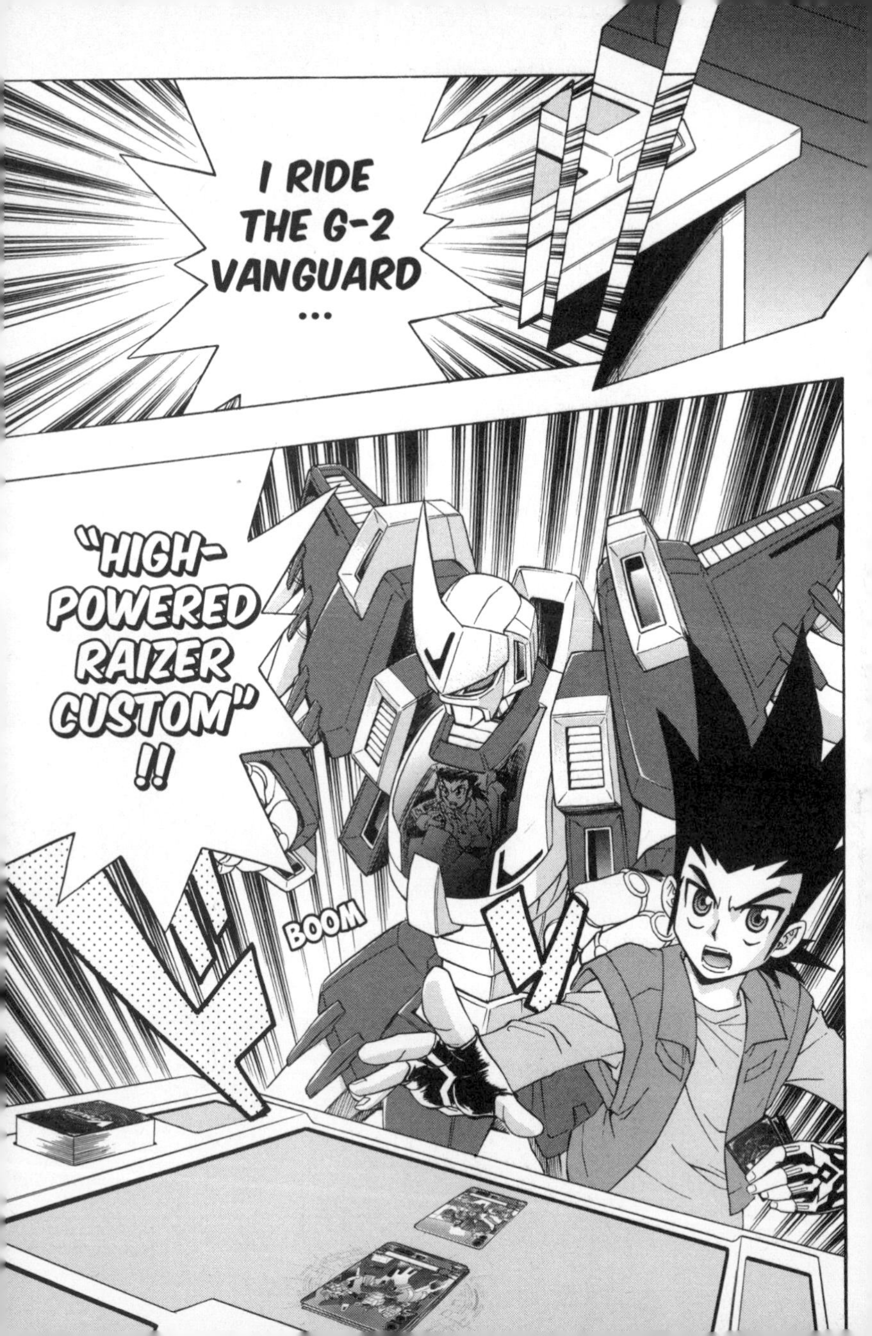
I RIDE THE G-2 VANGUARD ...
"HIGH-POWERED RAIZER CUSTOM" !!
BOOM

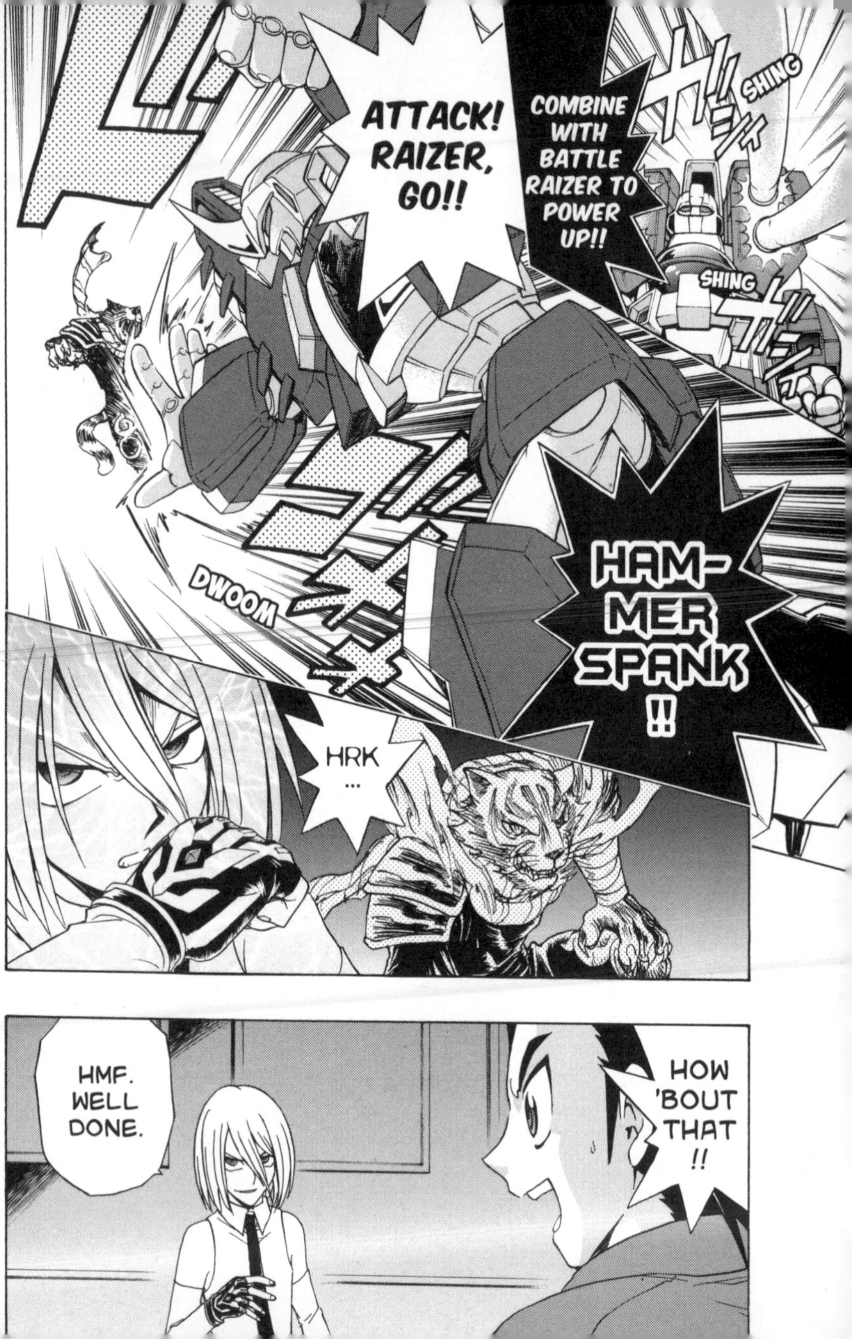
SHING
COMBINE WITH BATTLE RAIZER TO POWER UP!!
ATTACK! RAIZER, GO!!
SHING
DWOOM
HAM-MER SPANK!!
HRK...
HOW 'BOUT THAT!!
HMF. WELL DONE.

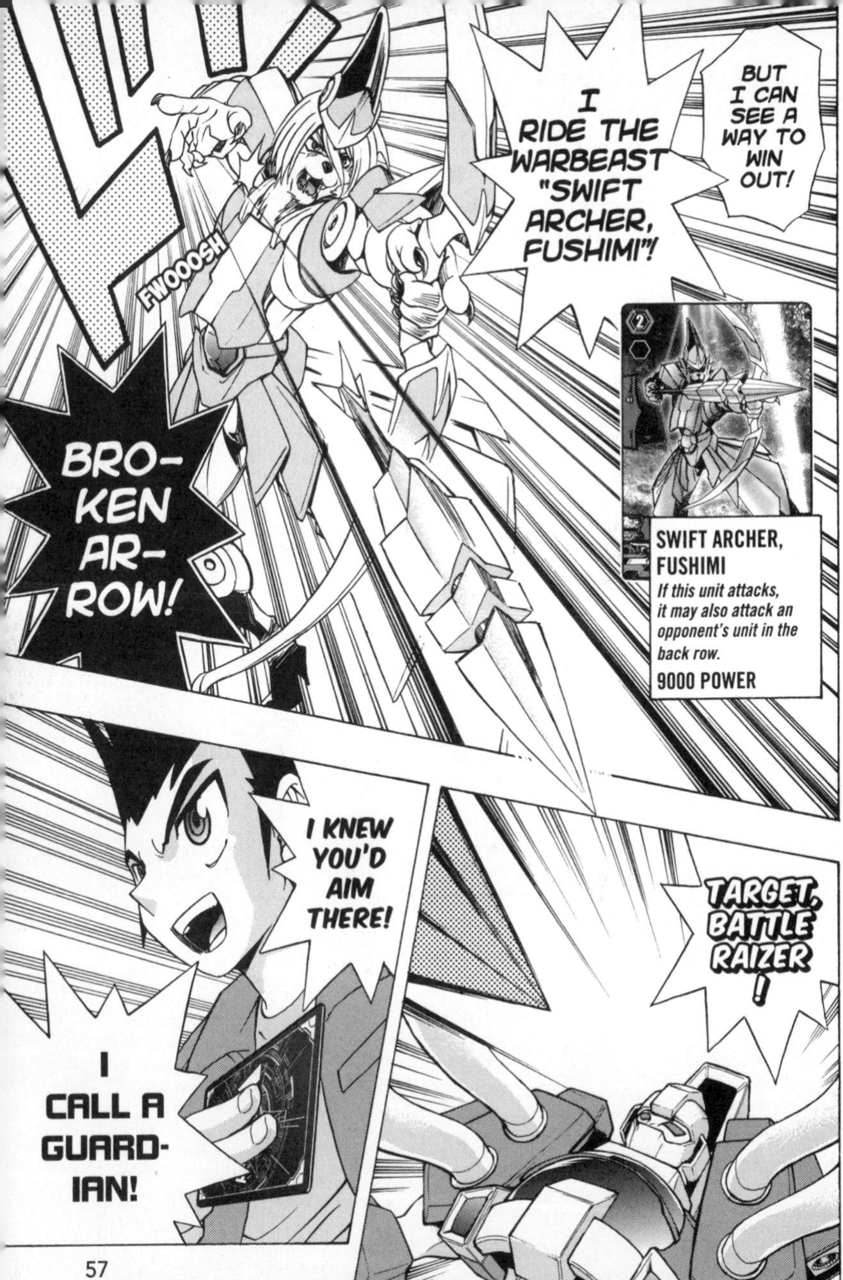
BUT I CAN SEE A WAY TO WIN OUT!
I RIDE THE WARBEAST "SWIFT ARCHER, FUSHIMI"!
2
SWIFT ARCHER, FUSHIMI
If this unit attacks, it may also attack an opponent's unit in the back row.
9000 POWER
FWOOOSH
BRO-KEN AR-ROW!
TARGET, BATTLE RAIZER!
I KNEW YOU'D AIM THERE!
I CALL A GUARD-IAN!

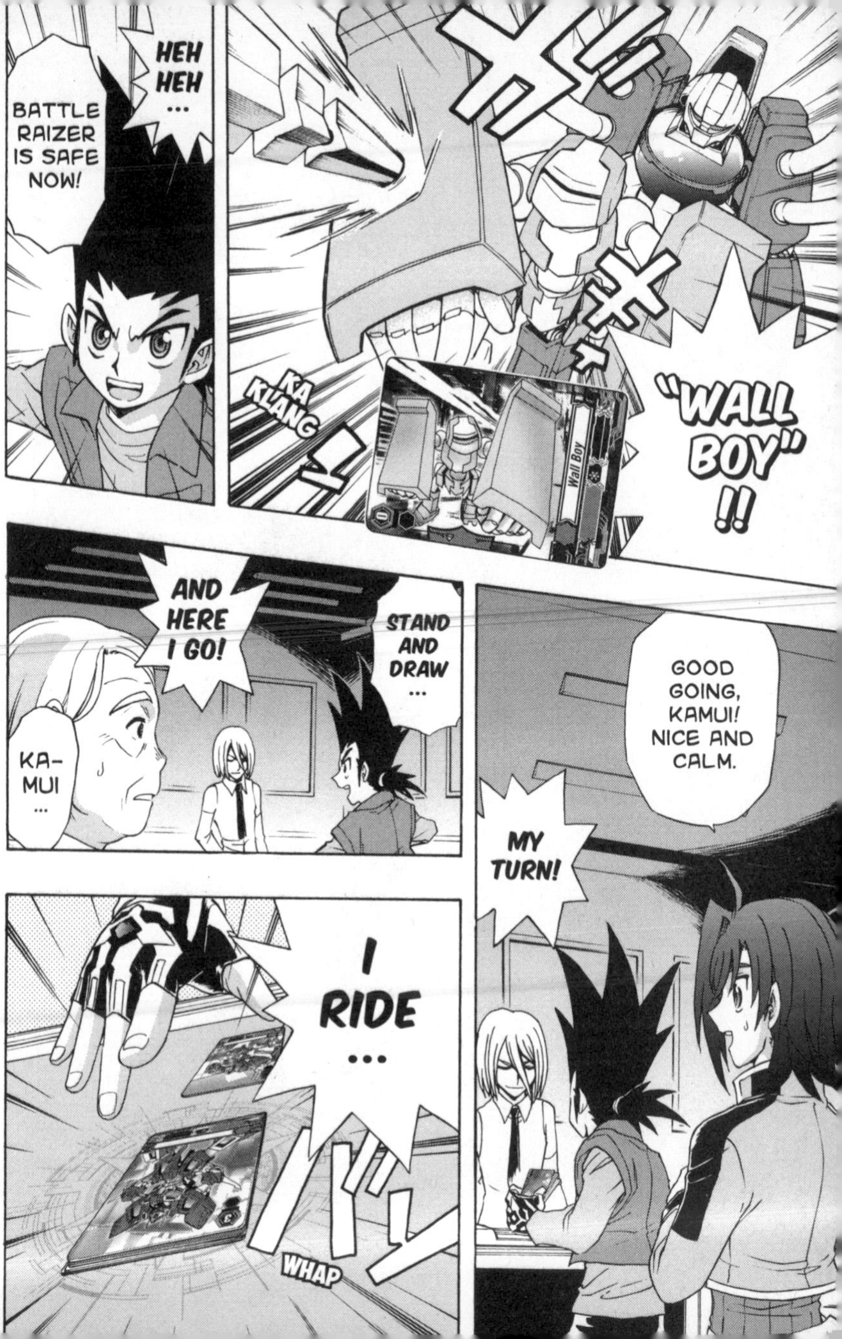
"WALL BOY" !!
Wall Boy
KA KLANG
HEH HEH ...
BATTLE RAIZER IS SAFE NOW!
GOOD GOING, KAMUI! NICE AND CALM.
MY TURN!
STAND AND DRAW ...
AND HERE I GO!
KA-MUI ...
I RIDE ...
WHAP

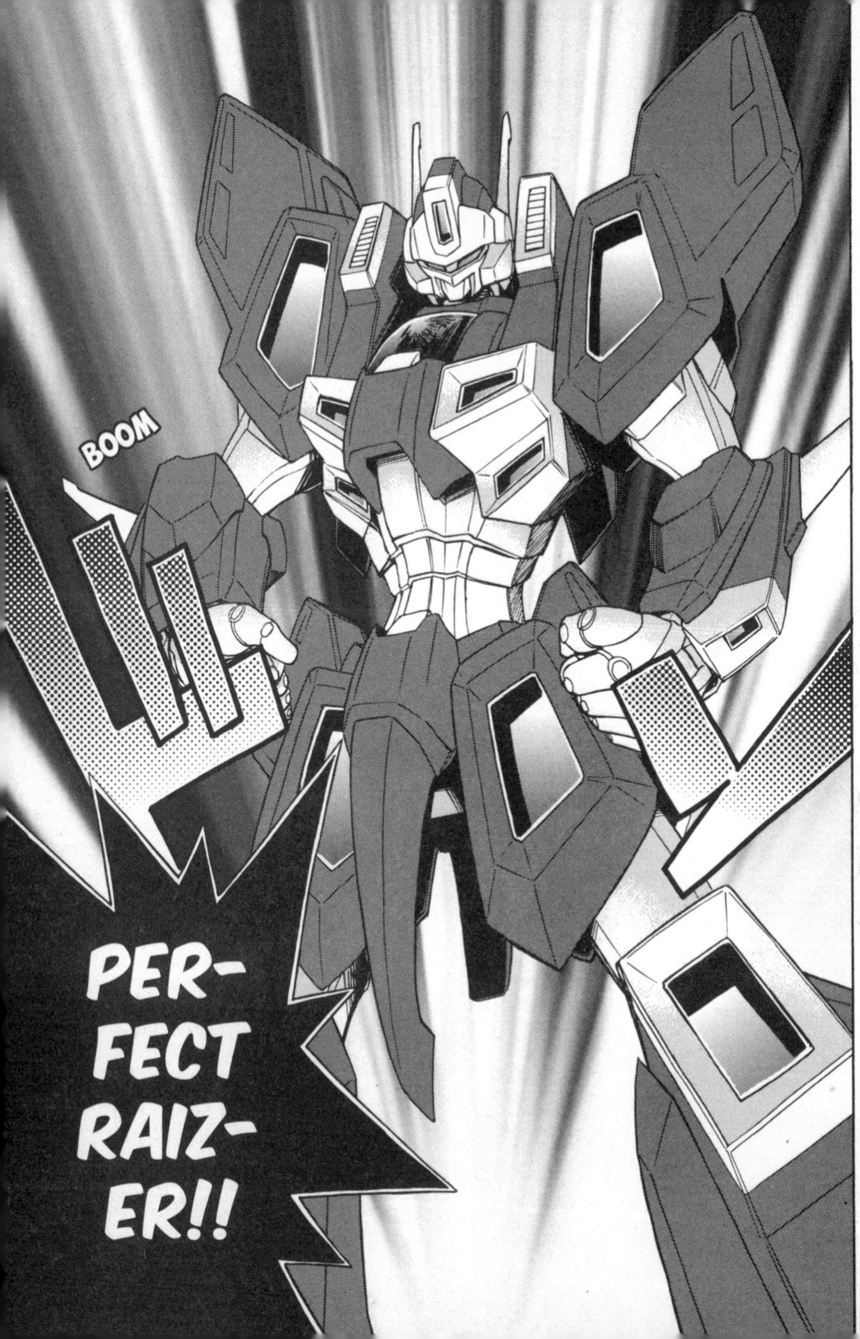
BOOM
PER-FECT RAIZ-ER!!

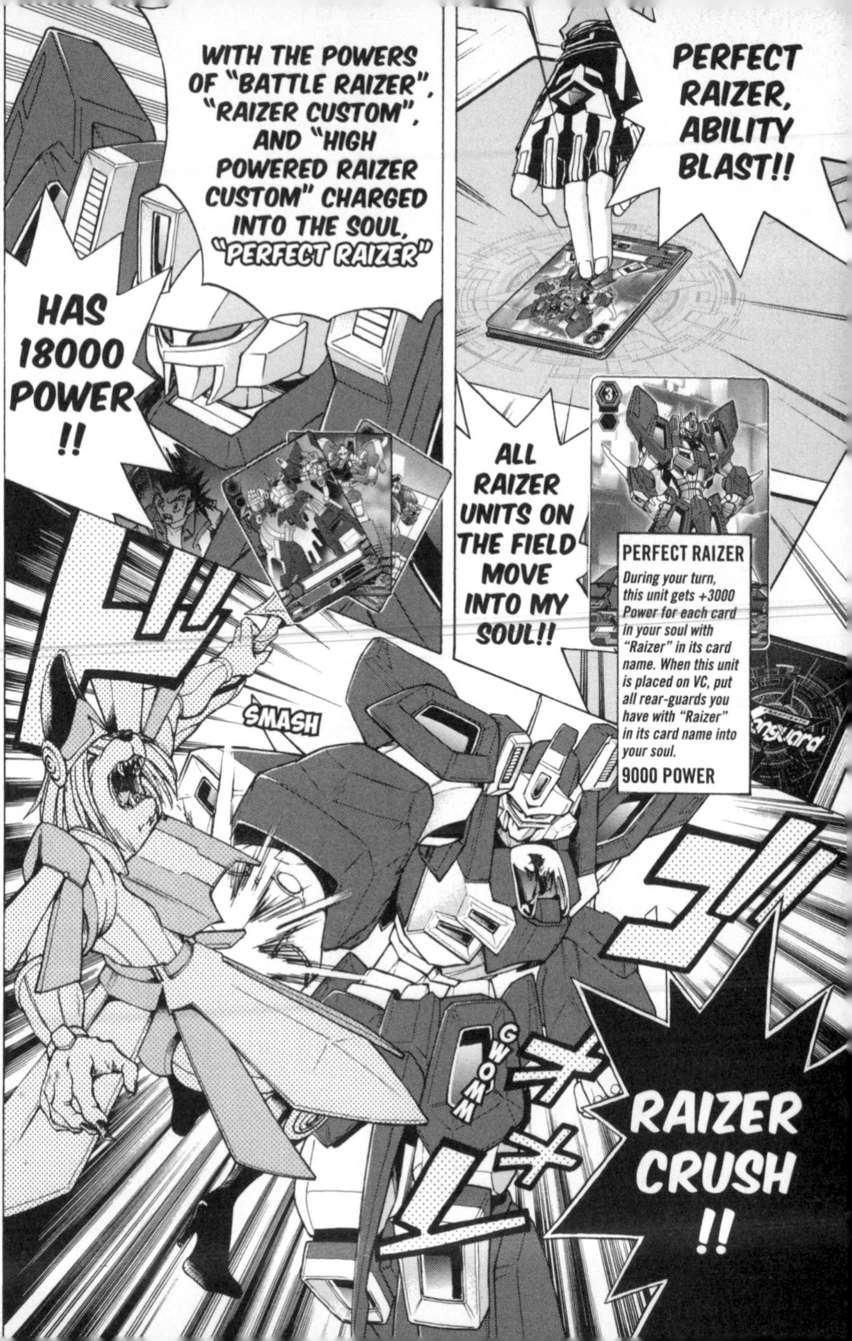
PERFECT RAIZER, ABILITY BLAST!!
ALL RAIZER UNITS ON THE FIELD MOVE INTO MY SOUL!!
PERFECT RAIZER
During your turn, this unit gets +3000 Power for each card in your soul with "Raizer" in its card name. When this unit is placed on VC, put all rear-guards you have with "Raizer" in its card name into your soul.
9000 POWER
WITH THE POWERS OF "BATTLE RAIZER", "RAIZER CUSTOM", AND "HIGH POWERED RAIZER CUSTOM" CHARGED INTO THE SOUL, "PERFECT RAIZER"
HAS 18000 POWER!!
SMASH
GWOMM
RAIZER CRUSH!!

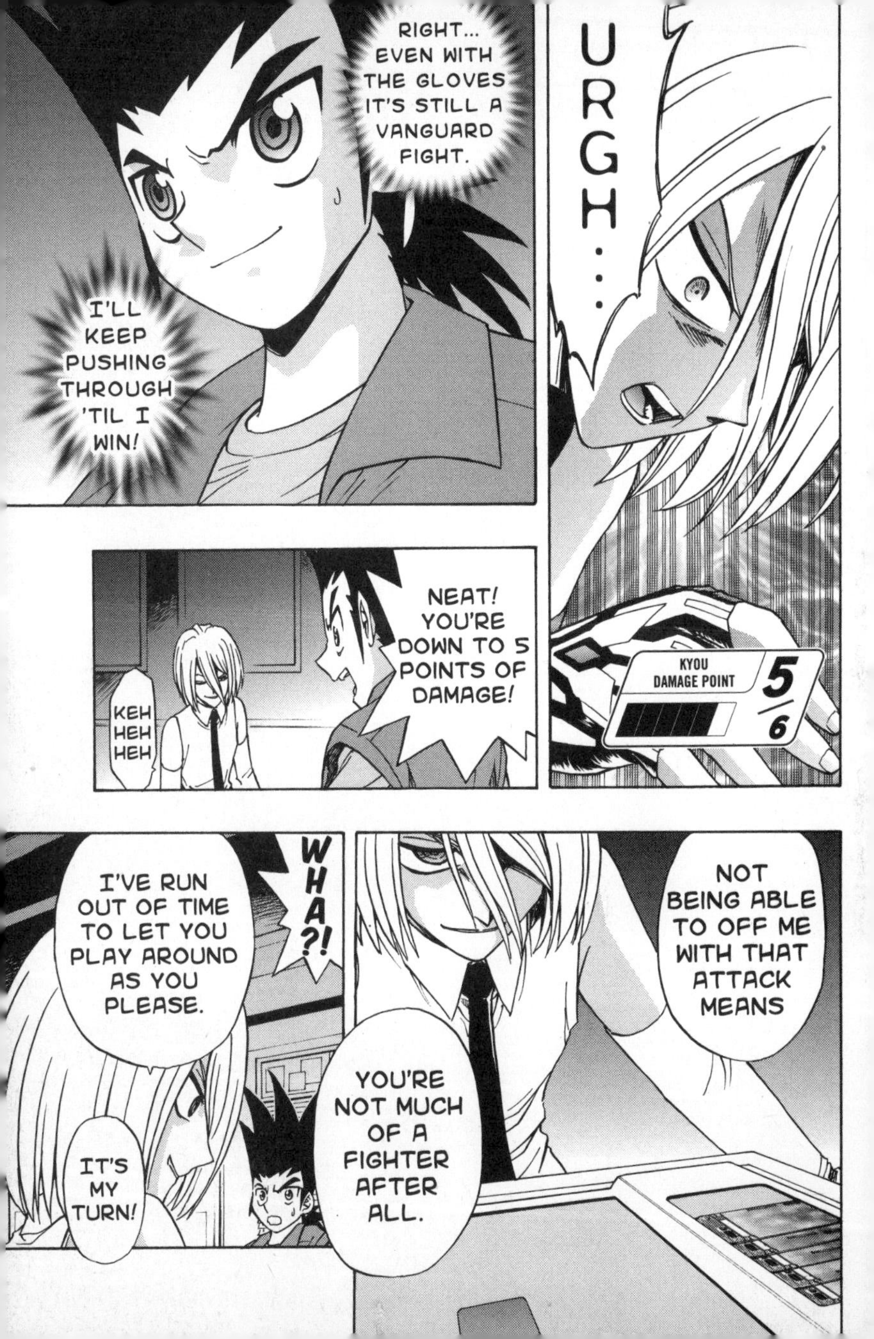
URGH...
KYOU
DAMAGE POINT
5/6
RIGHT... EVEN WITH THE GLOVES IT'S STILL A VANGUARD FIGHT.
I'LL KEEP PUSHING THROUGH 'TIL I WIN!
NEAT! YOU'RE DOWN TO 5 POINTS OF DAMAGE!
KEH HEH HEH
NOT BEING ABLE TO OFF ME WITH THAT ATTACK MEANS
YOU'RE NOT MUCH OF A FIGHTER AFTER ALL.
WHA?!
I'VE RUN OUT OF TIME TO LET YOU PLAY AROUND AS YOU PLEASE.
IT'S MY TURN!

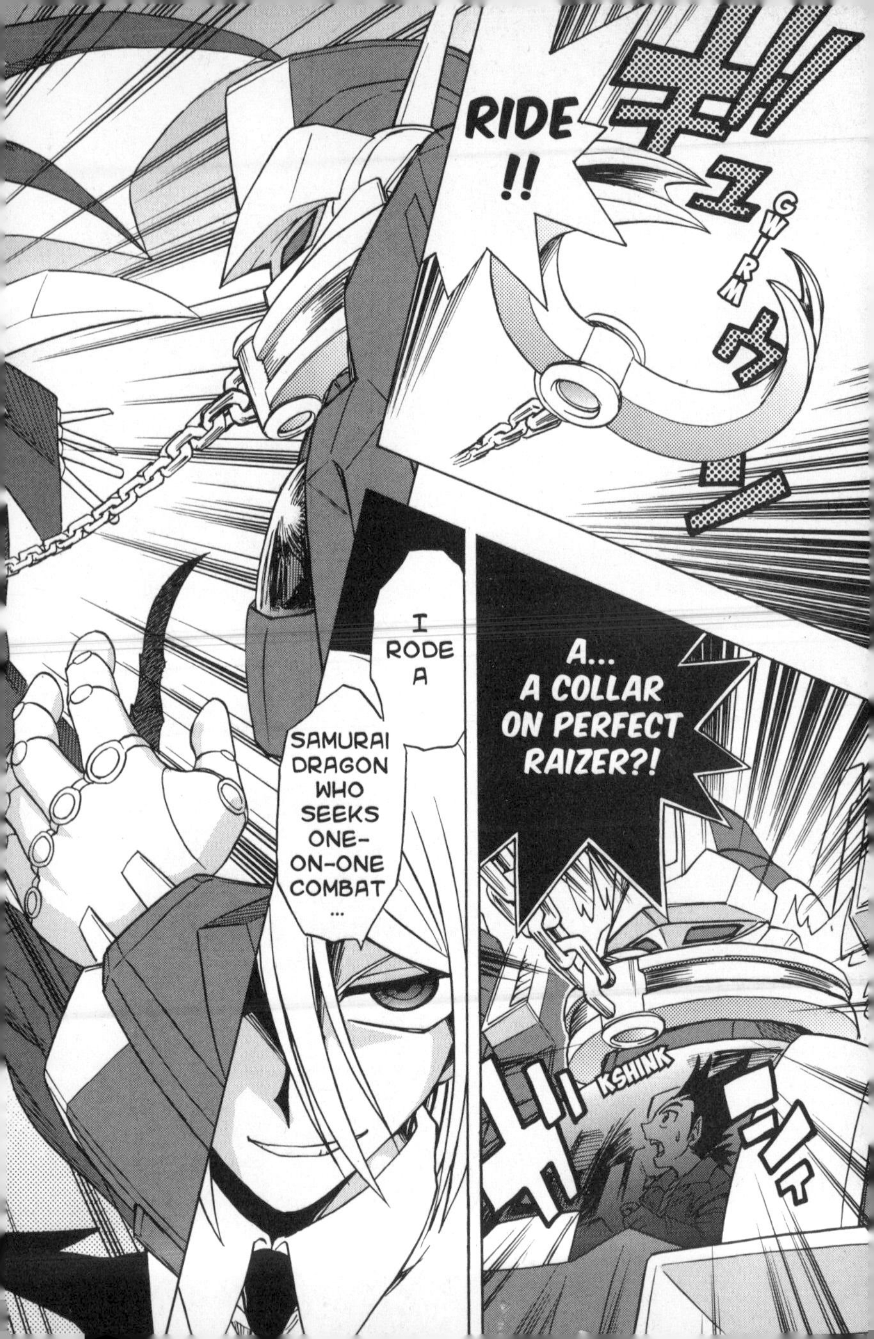
RIDE !!
GWIRM
A... A COLLAR ON PERFECT RAIZER?!
KSHINK
I RODE A
SAMURAI DRAGON WHO SEEKS ONE-ON-ONE COMBAT ...

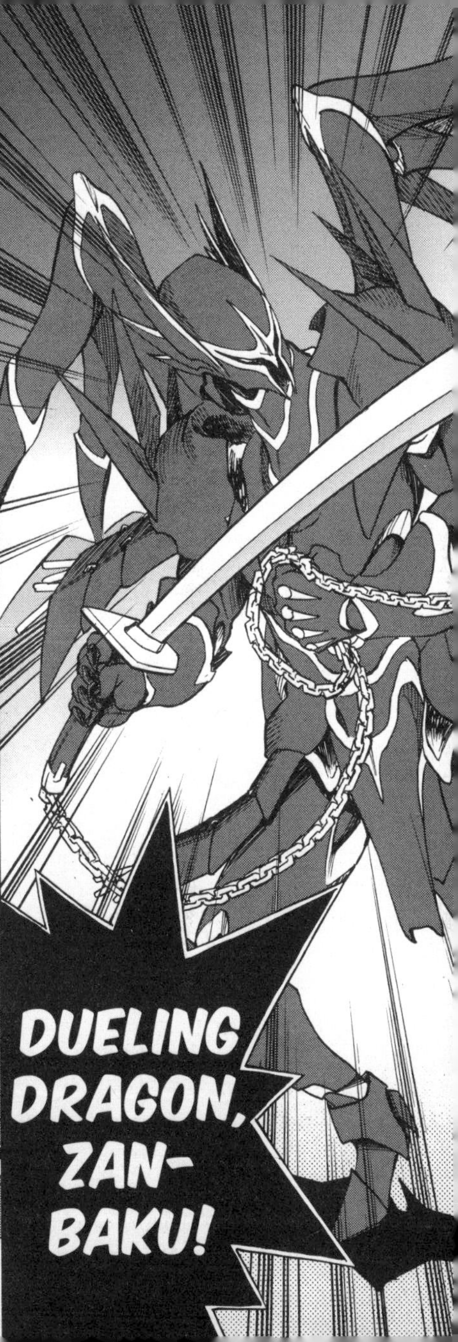
DUELING DRAGON, ZAN-BAKU!

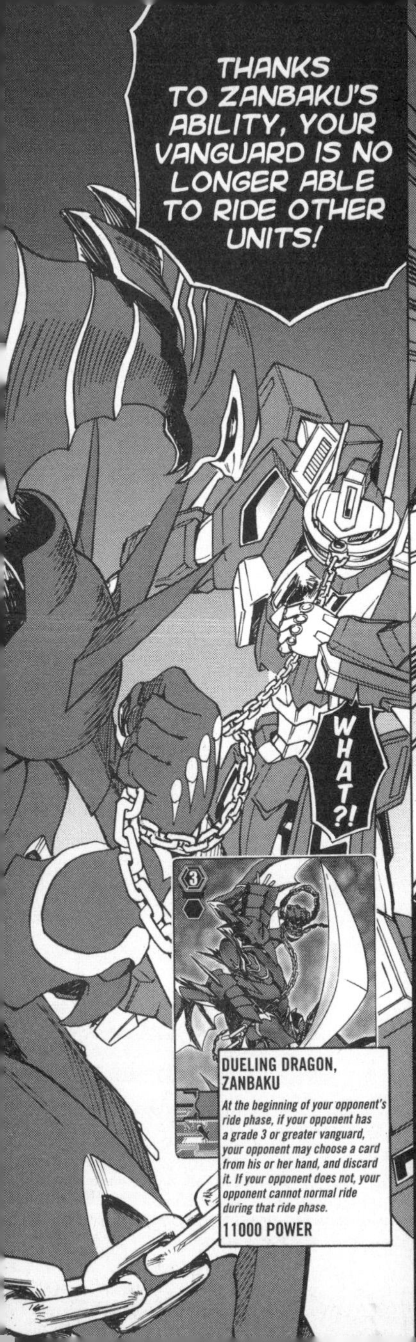
THANKS TO ZANBAKU'S ABILITY, YOUR VANGUARD IS NO LONGER ABLE TO RIDE OTHER UNITS!
WHAT?!
3
DUELING DRAGON, ZANBAKU
At the beginning of your opponent's ride phase, if your opponent has a grade 3 or greater vanguard, your opponent may choose a card from his or her hand, and discard it. If your opponent does not, your opponent cannot normal ride during that ride phase.
11000 POWER

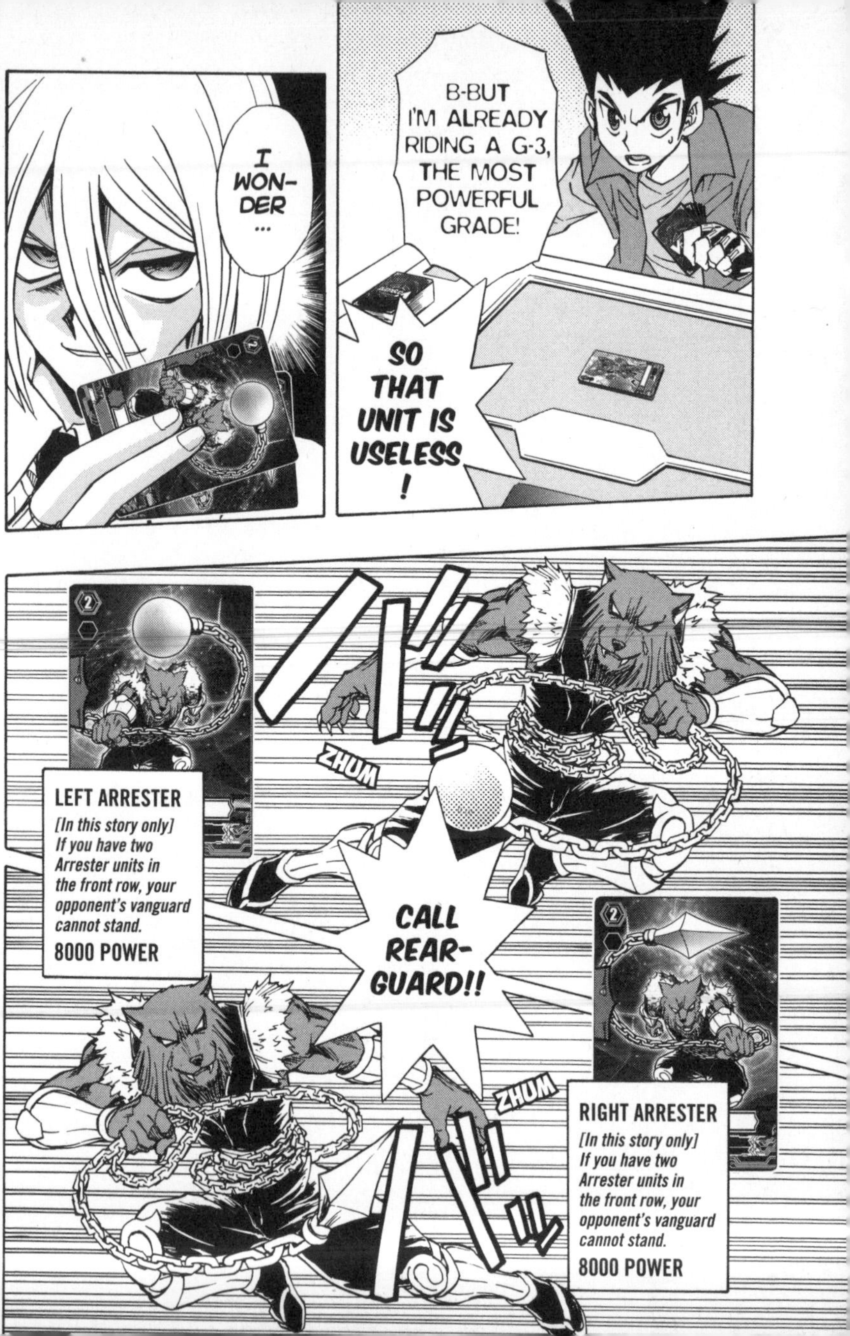
B-BUT I'M ALREADY RIDING A G-3, THE MOST POWERFUL GRADE!
SO THAT UNIT IS USELESS!
I WONDER...
ZHUM
LEFT ARRESTER
[In this story only]
If you have two Arrester units in the front row, your opponent's vanguard cannot stand.
8000 POWER
CALL REAR-GUARD!!
ZHUM
RIGHT ARRESTER
[In this story only]
If you have two Arrester units in the front row, your opponent's vanguard cannot stand.
8000 POWER

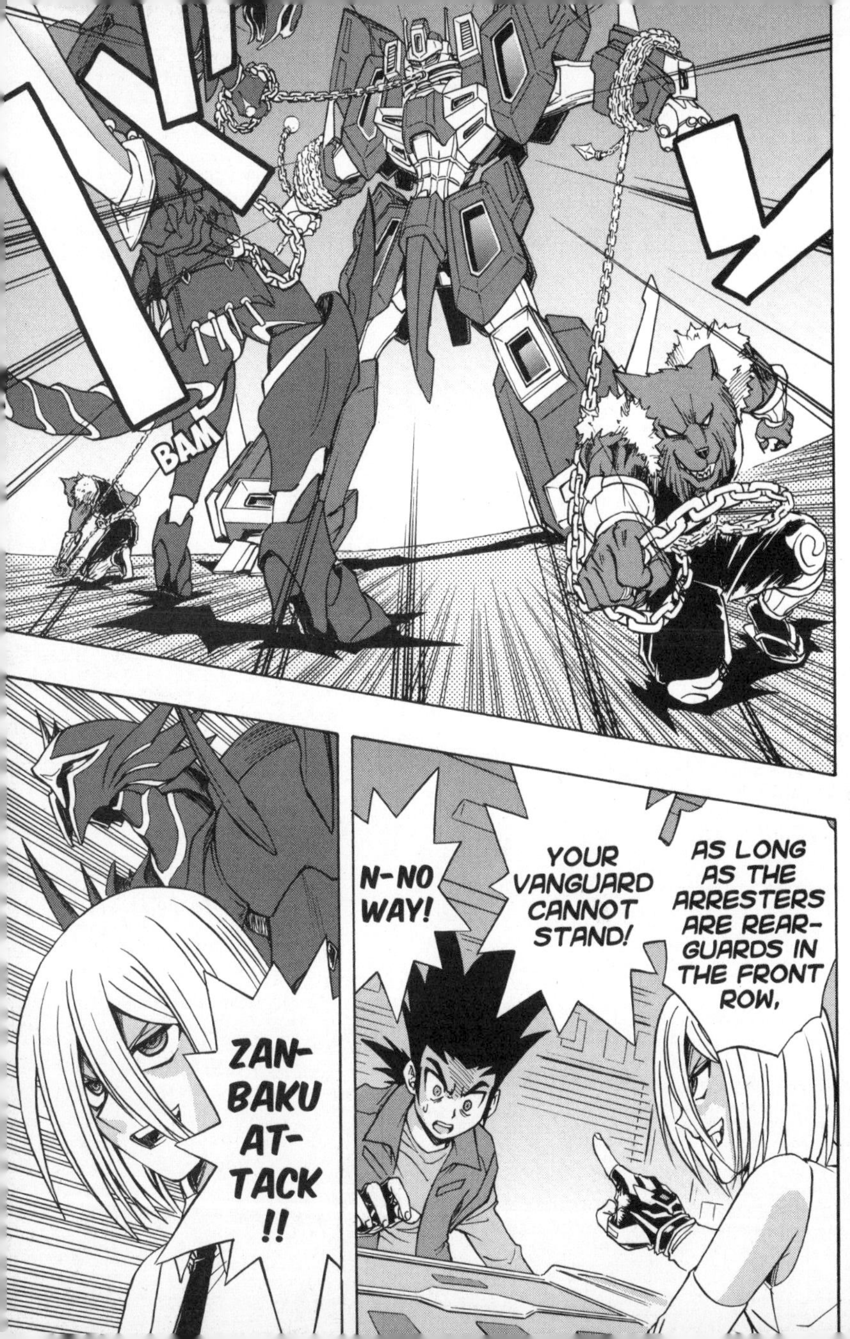
BAM
AS LONG AS THE ARRESTERS ARE REAR-GUARDS IN THE FRONT ROW,
YOUR VANGUARD CANNOT STAND!
N-NO WAY!
ZAN-BAKU AT-TACK!!

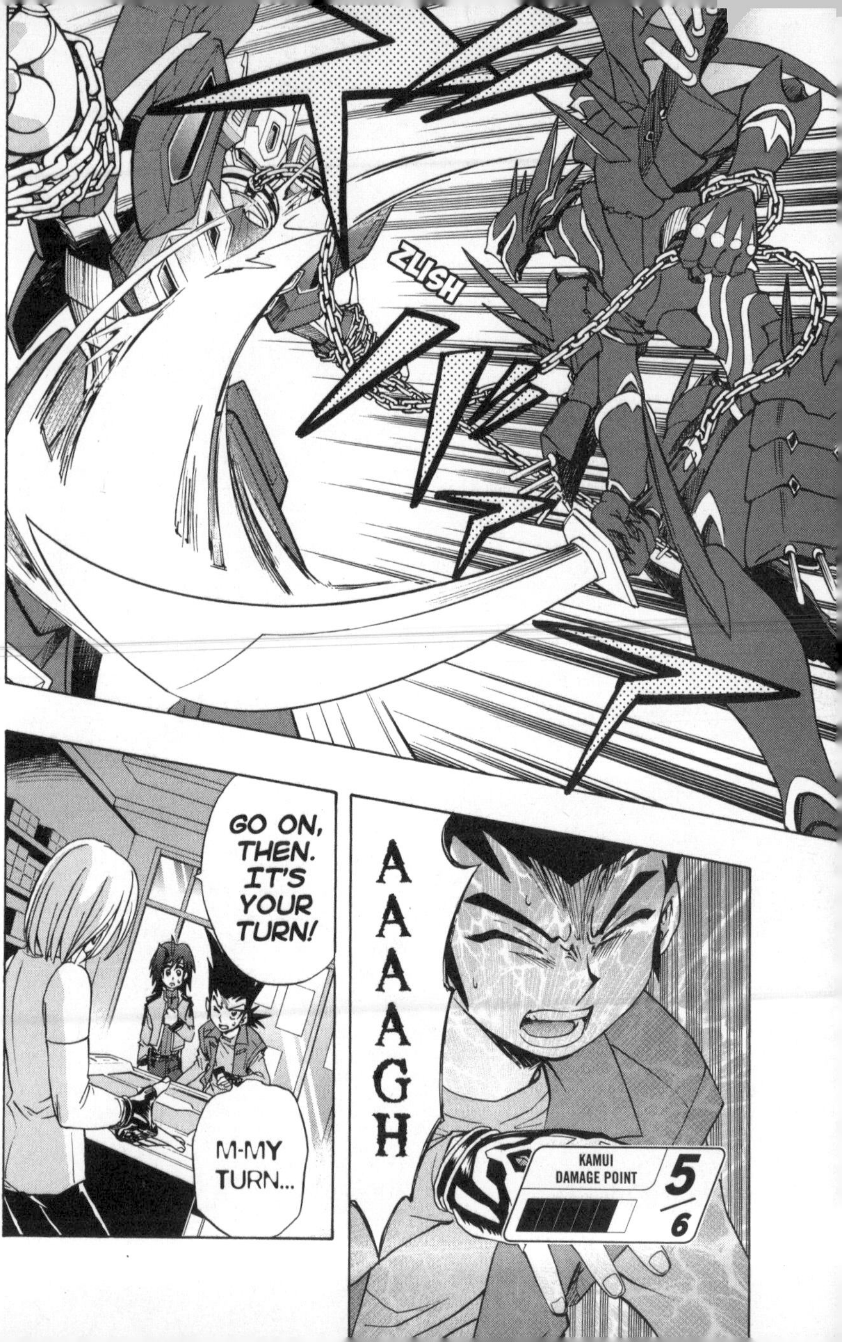
ZLISH
AAAAGH
KAMUI
DAMAGE POINT
5/6
GO ON, THEN. IT'S YOUR TURN!
M-MY TURN...

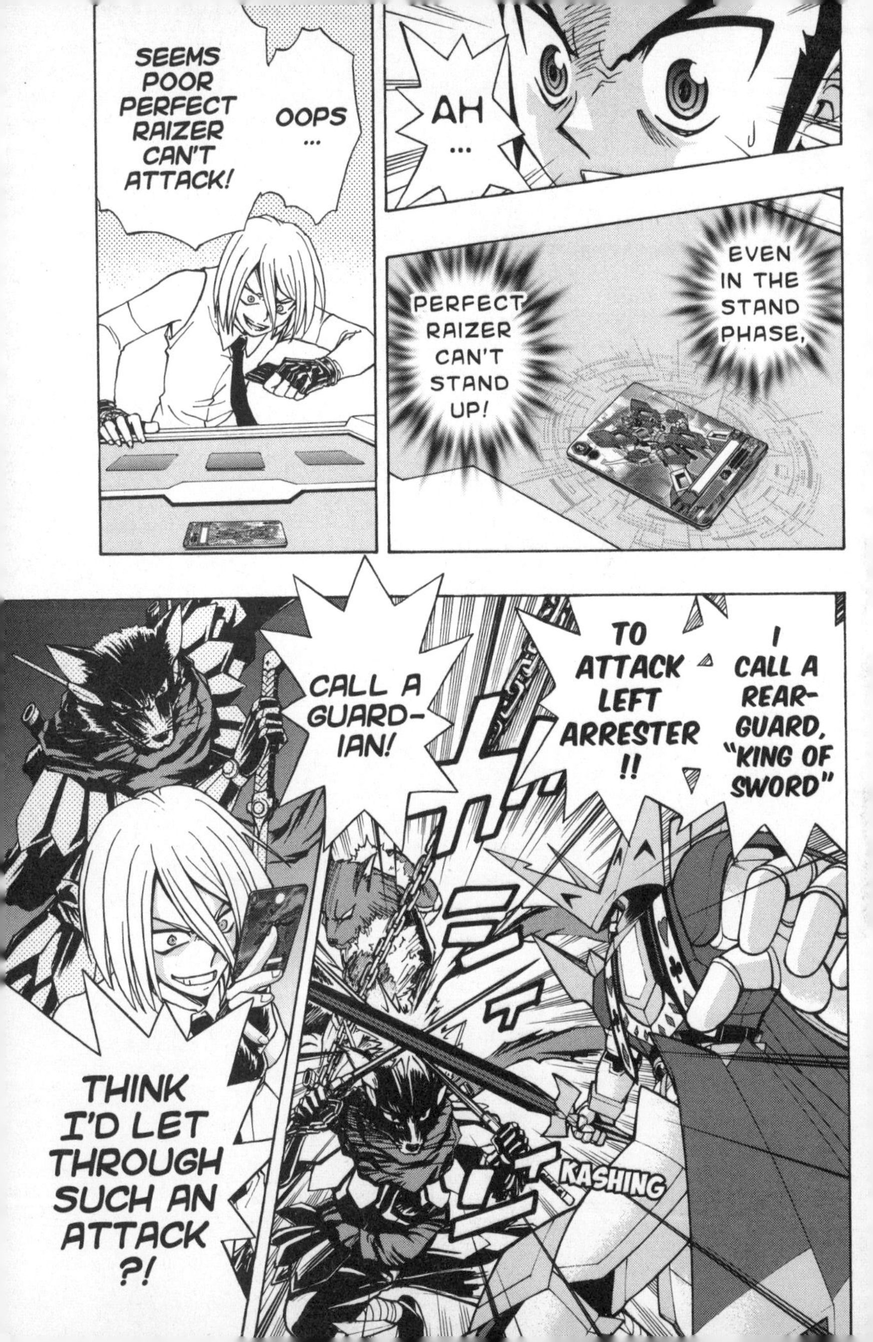
AH ...
EVEN IN THE STAND PHASE,
PERFECT RAIZER CAN'T STAND UP!
OOPS ...
SEEMS POOR PERFECT RAIZER CAN'T ATTACK!
I CALL A REAR-GUARD, "KING OF SWORD"
TO ATTACK LEFT ARRESTER !!
CALL A GUARD-IAN!
KASHING
THINK I'D LET THROUGH SUCH AN ATTACK ?!

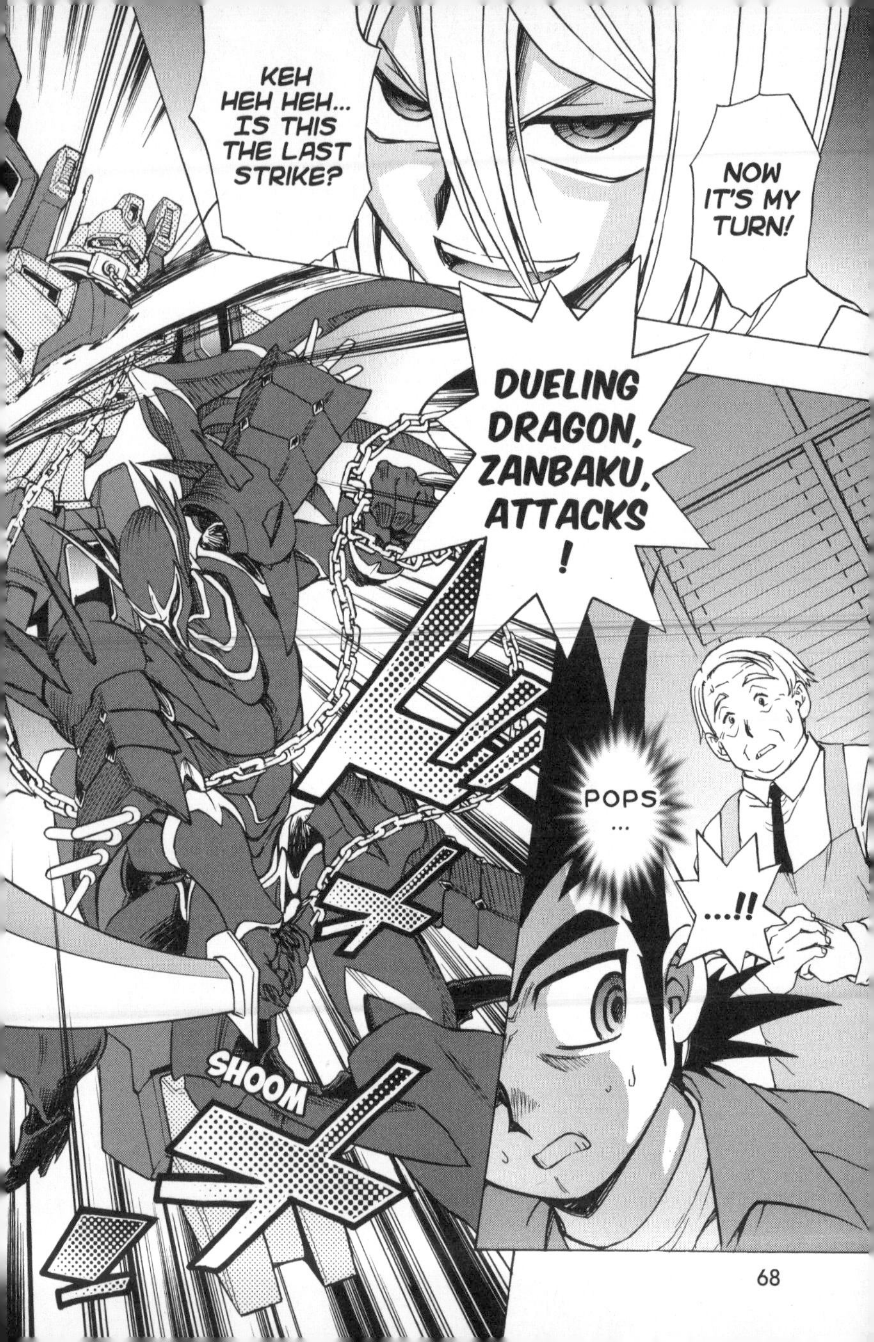
KEH HEH HEH... IS THIS THE LAST STRIKE?
NOW IT'S MY TURN!
DUELING DRAGON, ZANBAKU, ATTACKS!
SHOOM
...!!
POPS...

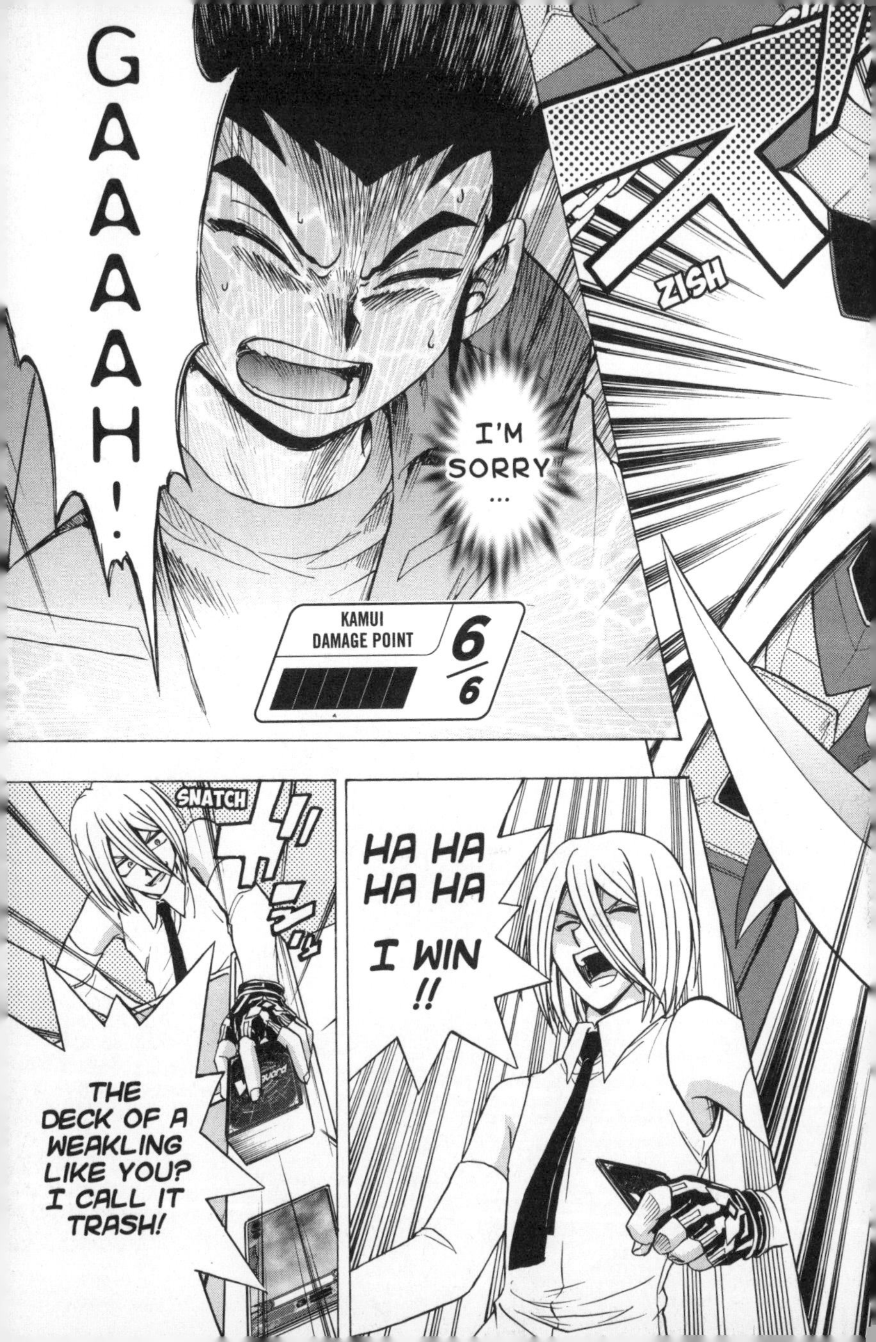
ZISH
I'M SORRY ...
GAAAAH!
KAMUI DAMAGE POINT 6/6
HA HA HA HA
I WIN !!
SNATCH
THE DECK OF A WEAKLING LIKE YOU? I CALL IT TRASH!

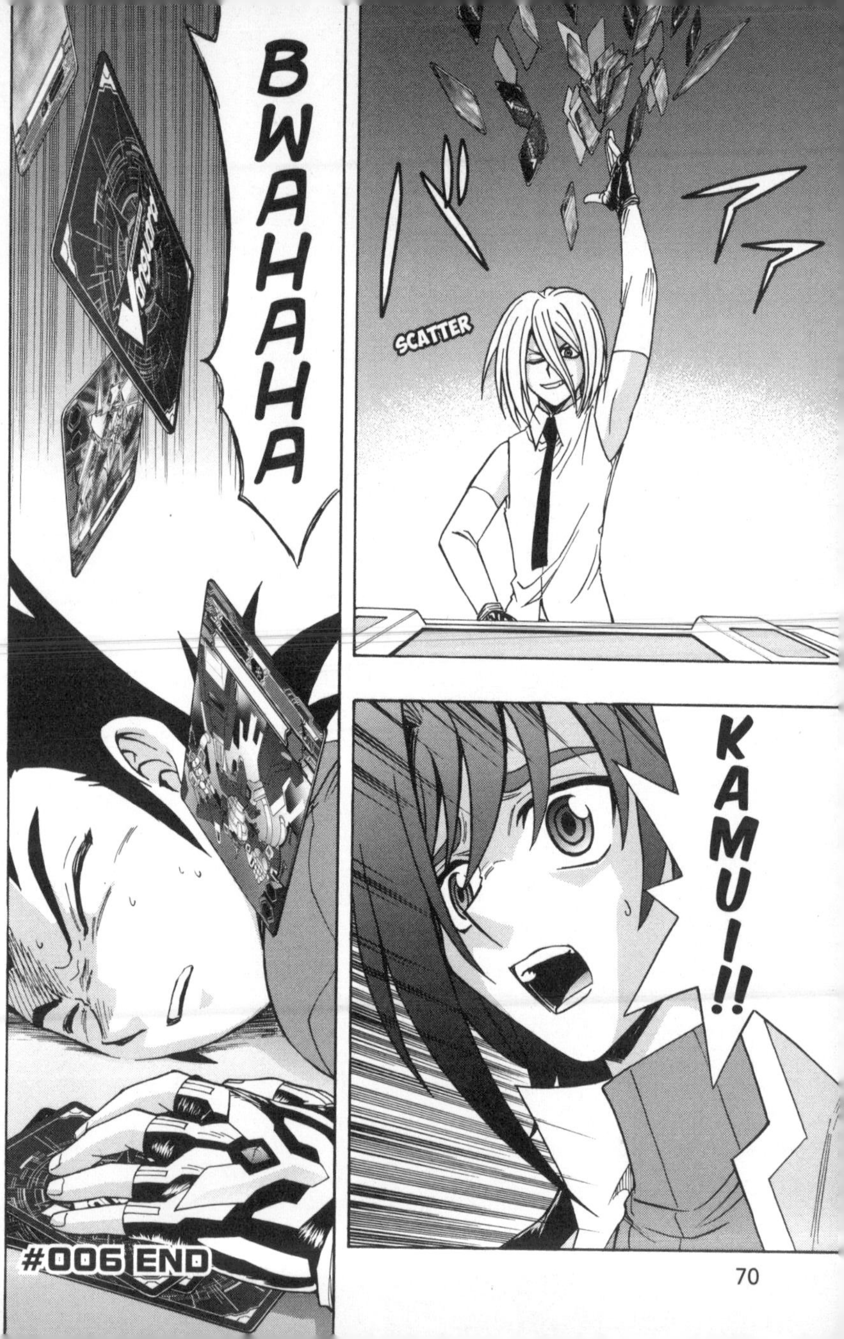
SCATTER
KAMUI!!
BWAHAHAHA
#006 END

BONUS! CARDFIGHT!! Vanguard NEVER-BEFORE-SEEN IMAGE BOARDS: CHARACTERS

Here we'll reveal Aichi's little sister Emi Sendou, who hasn't appeared yet in the comics but is a central character in the anime. We're also showing school uniform sketches! Perhaps you'll also see why Misaki dresses as she does?

Emi Sendou

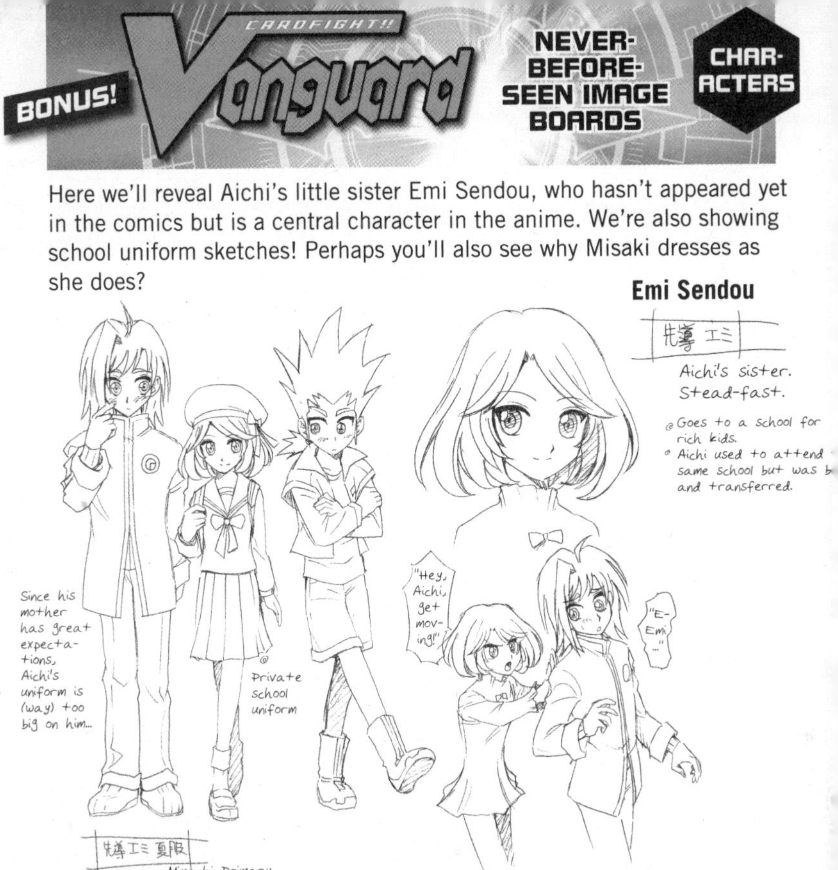
先導 エミ
Aichi's sister. Stead-fast.
Goes to a school for rich kids.
Aichi used to attend same school but was
and transferred.
Since his mother has great expectations, Aichi's uniform is (way) too big on him...
Private school uniform
"Hey, Aichi, get moving!"
"E-Emi..."

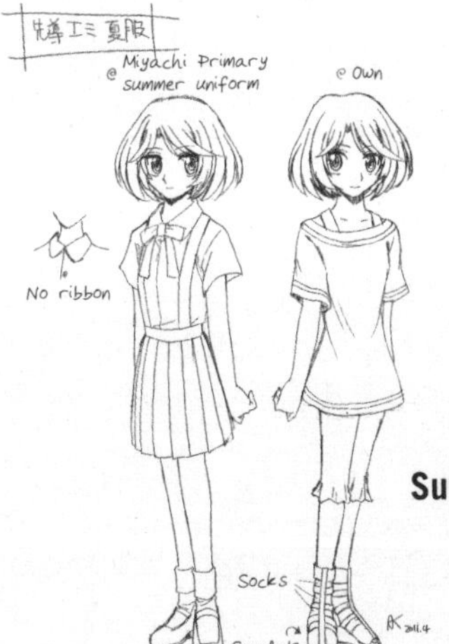
先導エミ夏服
Miyachi Primary summer uniform
Own
No ribbon
Socks
Sandals
AK 2011.4

Summer Clothes: Emi Sendou

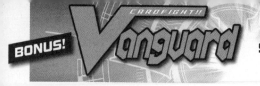

BONUS! CARDFIGHT!! Vanguard NEVER-BEFORE-SEEN IMAGE BOARDS CHAR-ACTERS

Mr. Mark Whiting

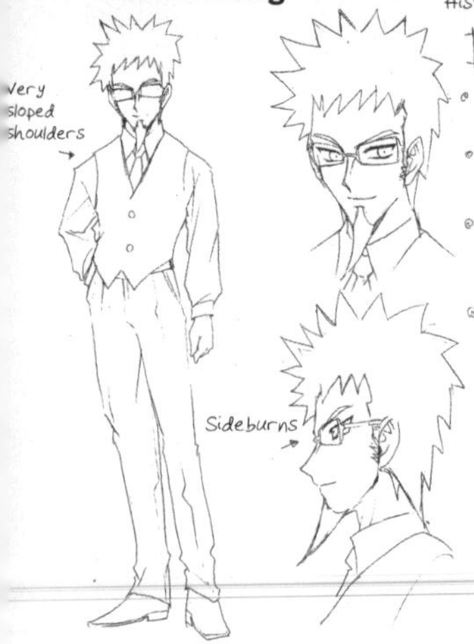

History Teacher
マーク・ホワイティング
Very sloped shoulders
A very enthusiastic Japanese history teacher!
Grew a beard out of admiration for feudal generals
Uses an armored warrior deck during Vanguard cardfights.
Classmates with Shin Nitta
Sideburns

Morikawa's Buddies

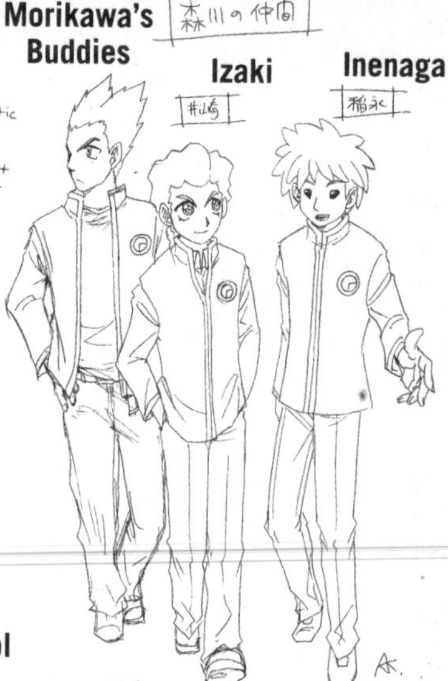

森川の仲間
Izaki
井崎
Inenaga
稲永

Girls' Uniform for Aichi's Middle School

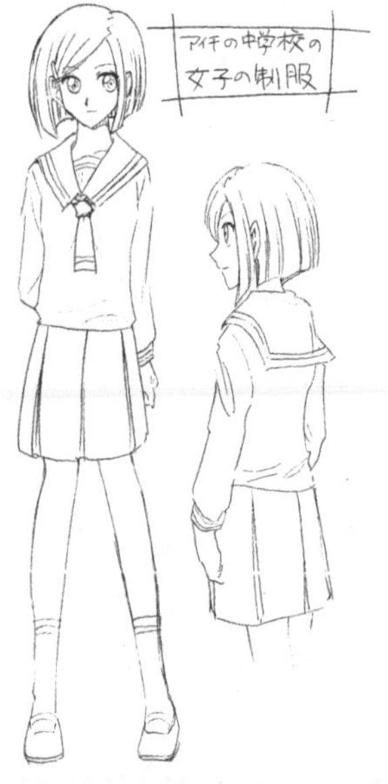

アイチの中学校の女子の制服

Uniform for Misaki's High School

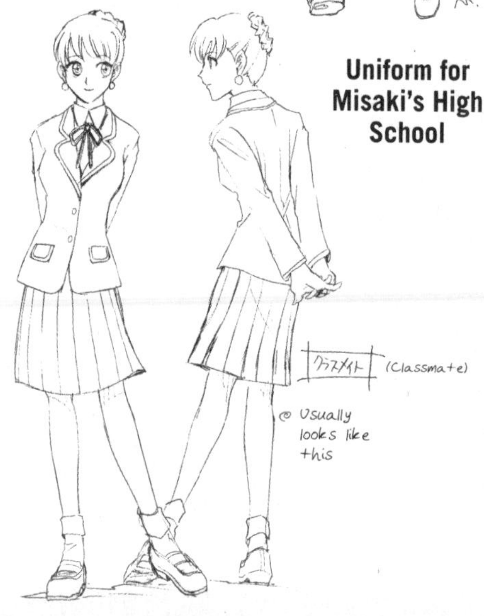

クラスメイト (Classmate)
Usually looks like this

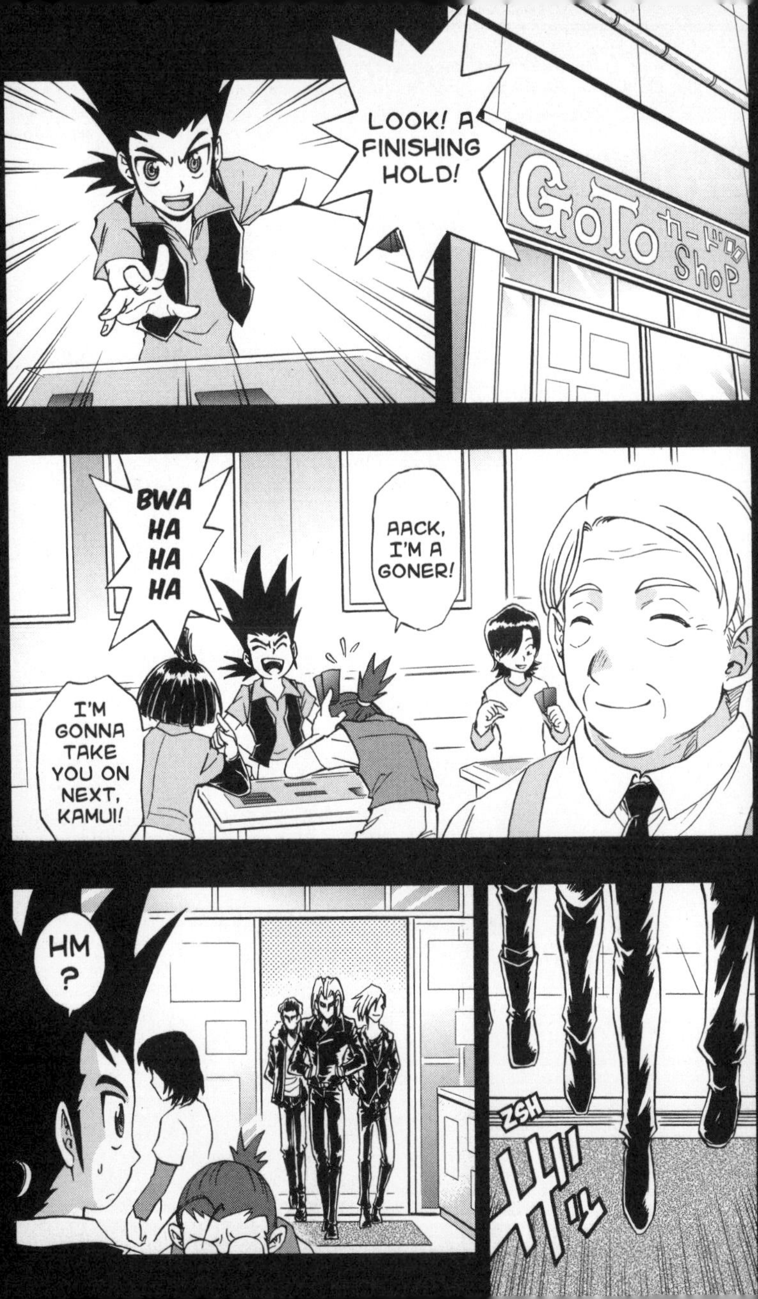
GoTo
ShoP
LOOK! A FINISHING HOLD!
AACK, I'M A GONER!
BWA HA HA HA
I'M GONNA TAKE YOU ON NEXT, KAMUI!
ZSH
ザッ
HM?

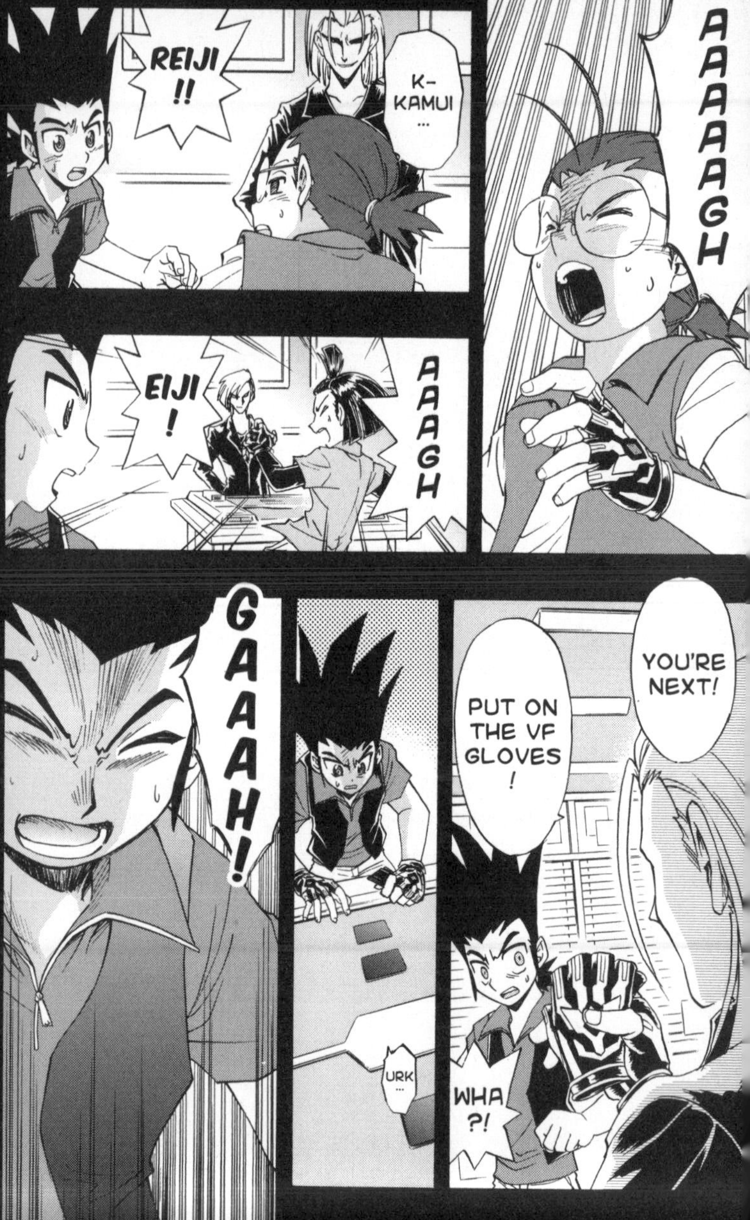
AAAAAAAGH
K-KAMUI ...
REIJI !!
AAAAGH
EIJI !
YOU'RE NEXT!
PUT ON THE VF GLOVES !
WHA ?!
URK ...
GAAAAH!

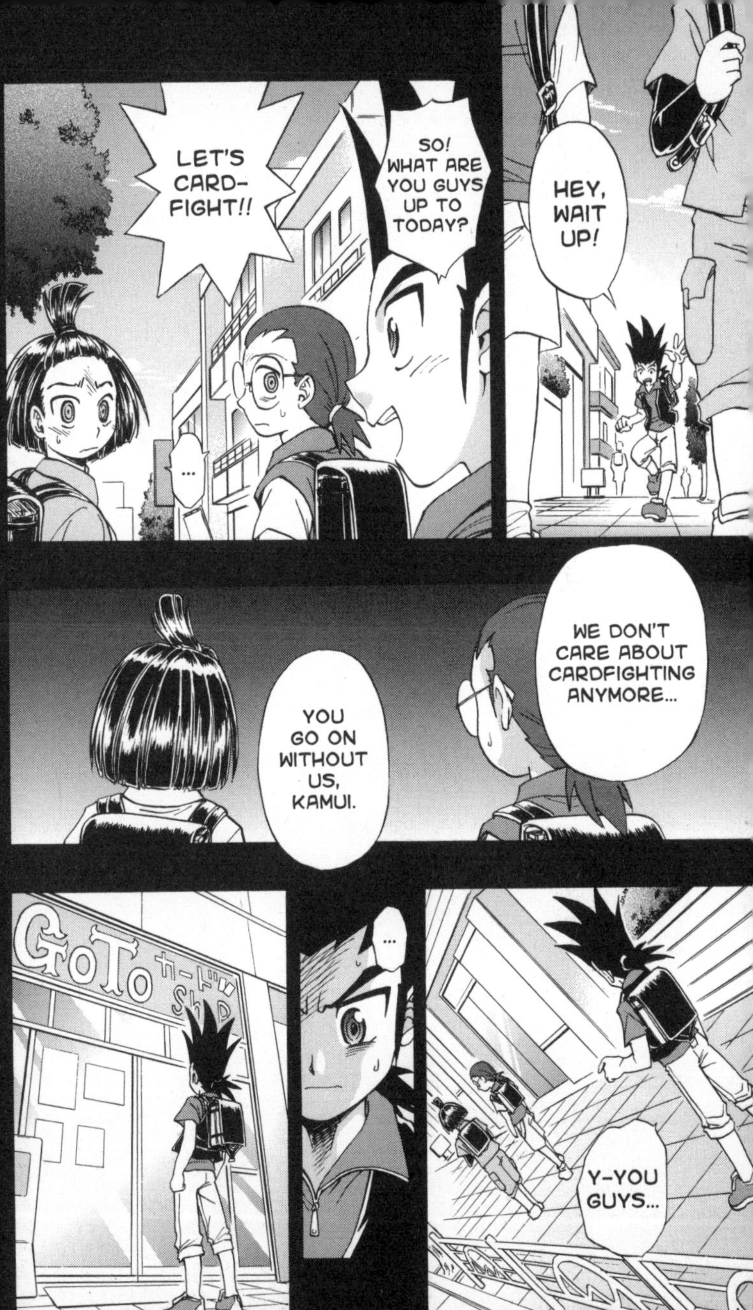
HEY, WAIT UP!
SO! WHAT ARE YOU GUYS UP TO TODAY?
LET'S CARD-FIGHT!!
...
WE DON'T CARE ABOUT CARDFIGHTING ANYMORE...
YOU GO ON WITHOUT US, KAMUI.
Y-YOU GUYS...
...
GoTo

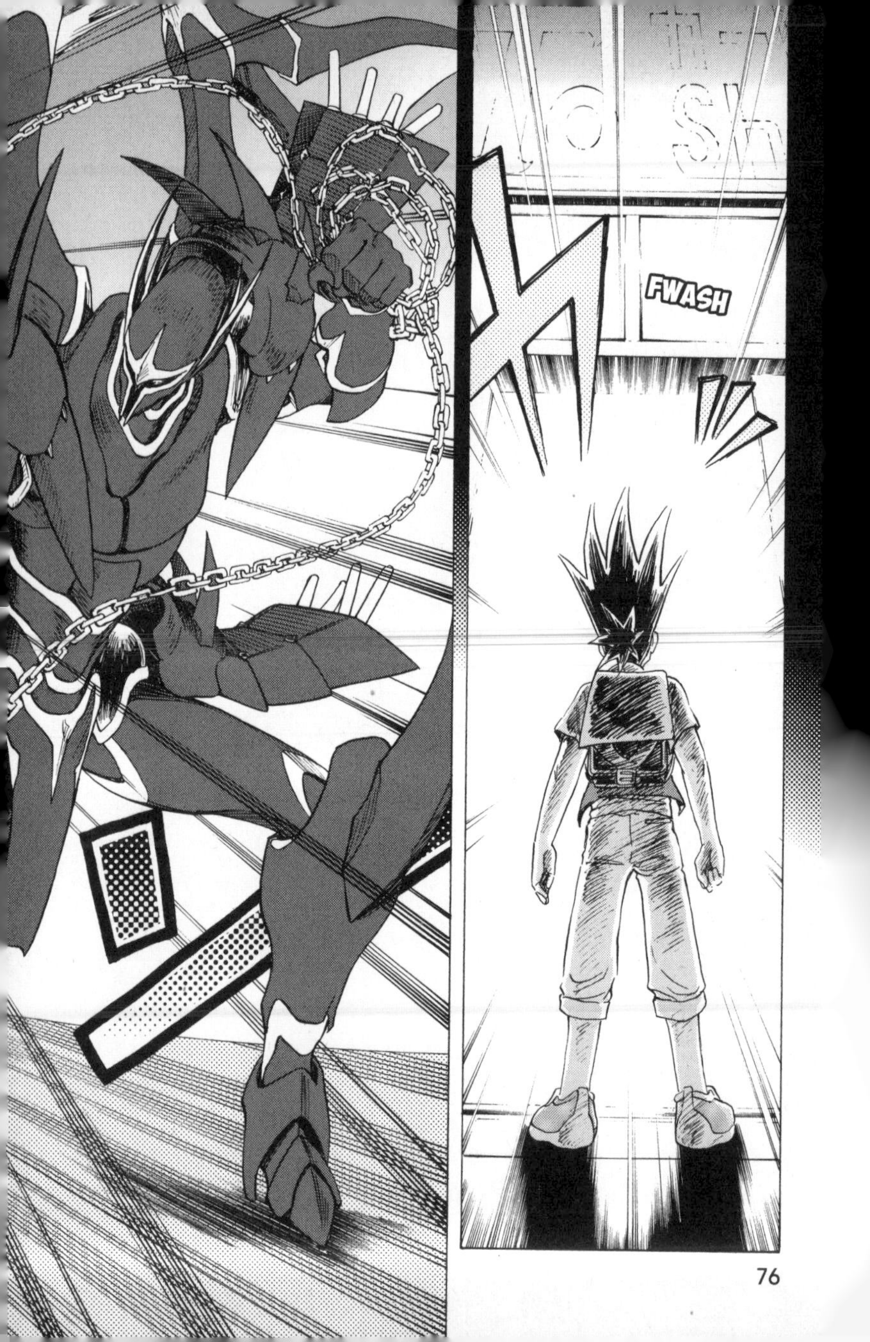
FWASH

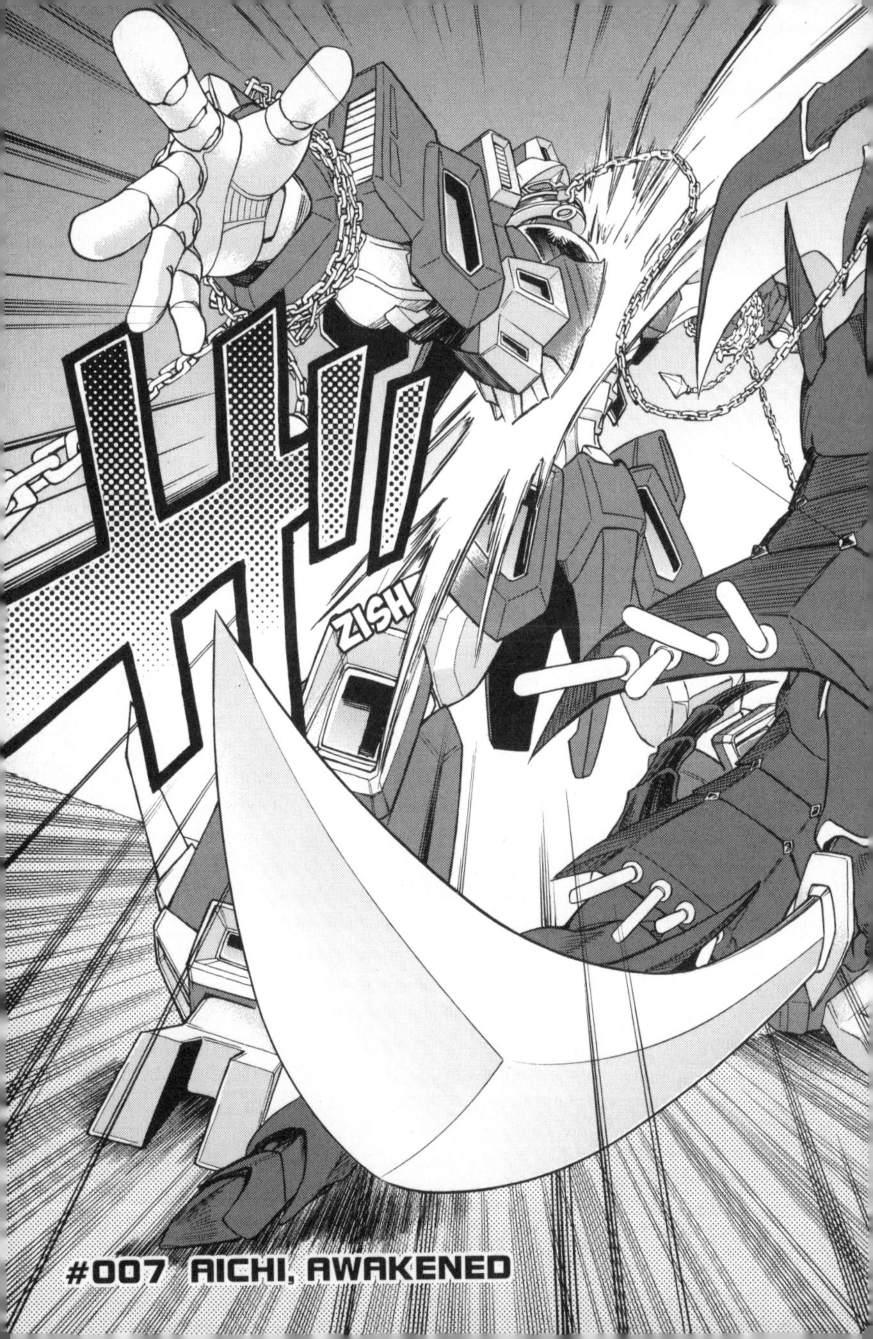
ZISH

#007 AICHI, AWAKENED

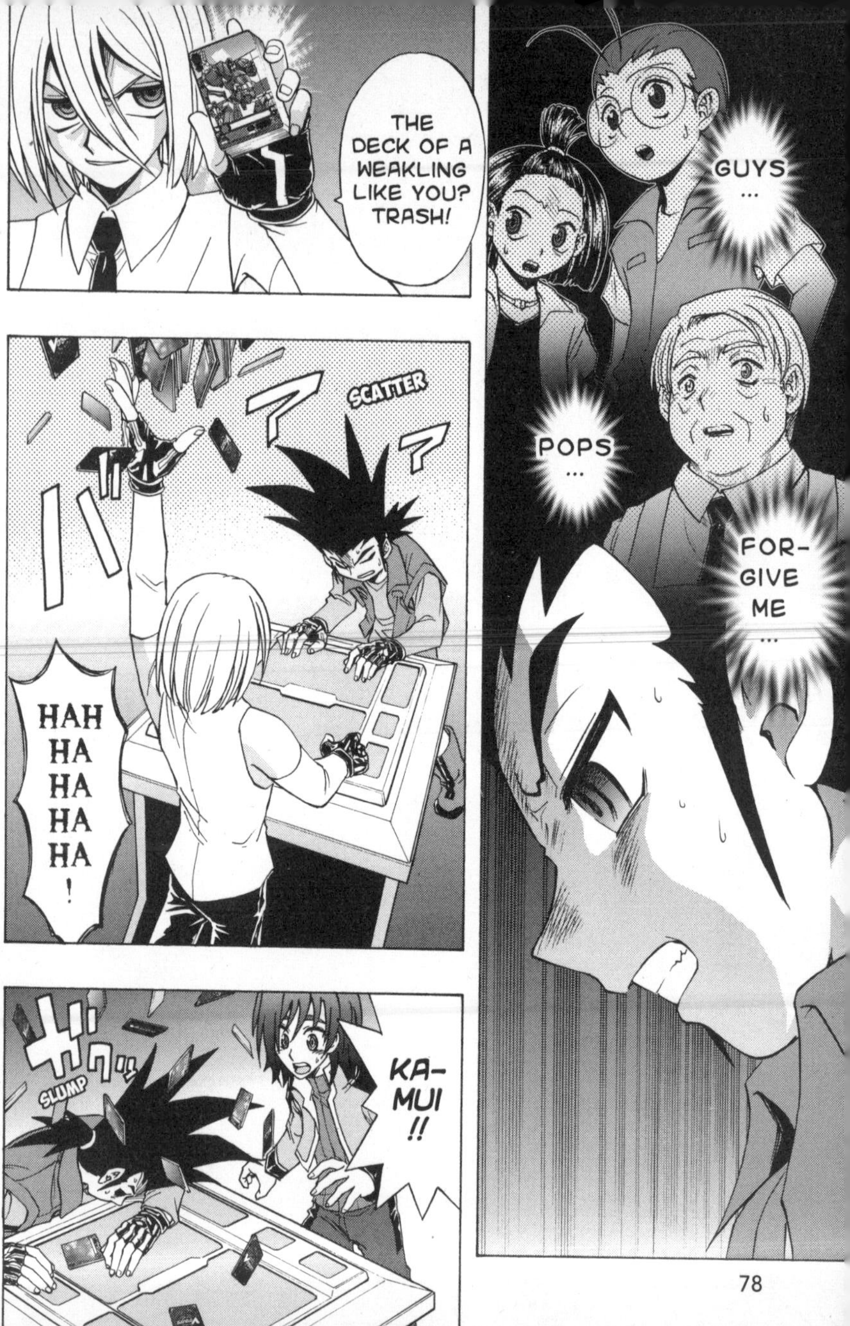
GUYS ...
POPS ...
FOR-GIVE ME ...
THE DECK OF A WEAKLING LIKE YOU? TRASH!
SCATTER
HAH HA HA HA HA !
KA-MUI !!
SLUMP

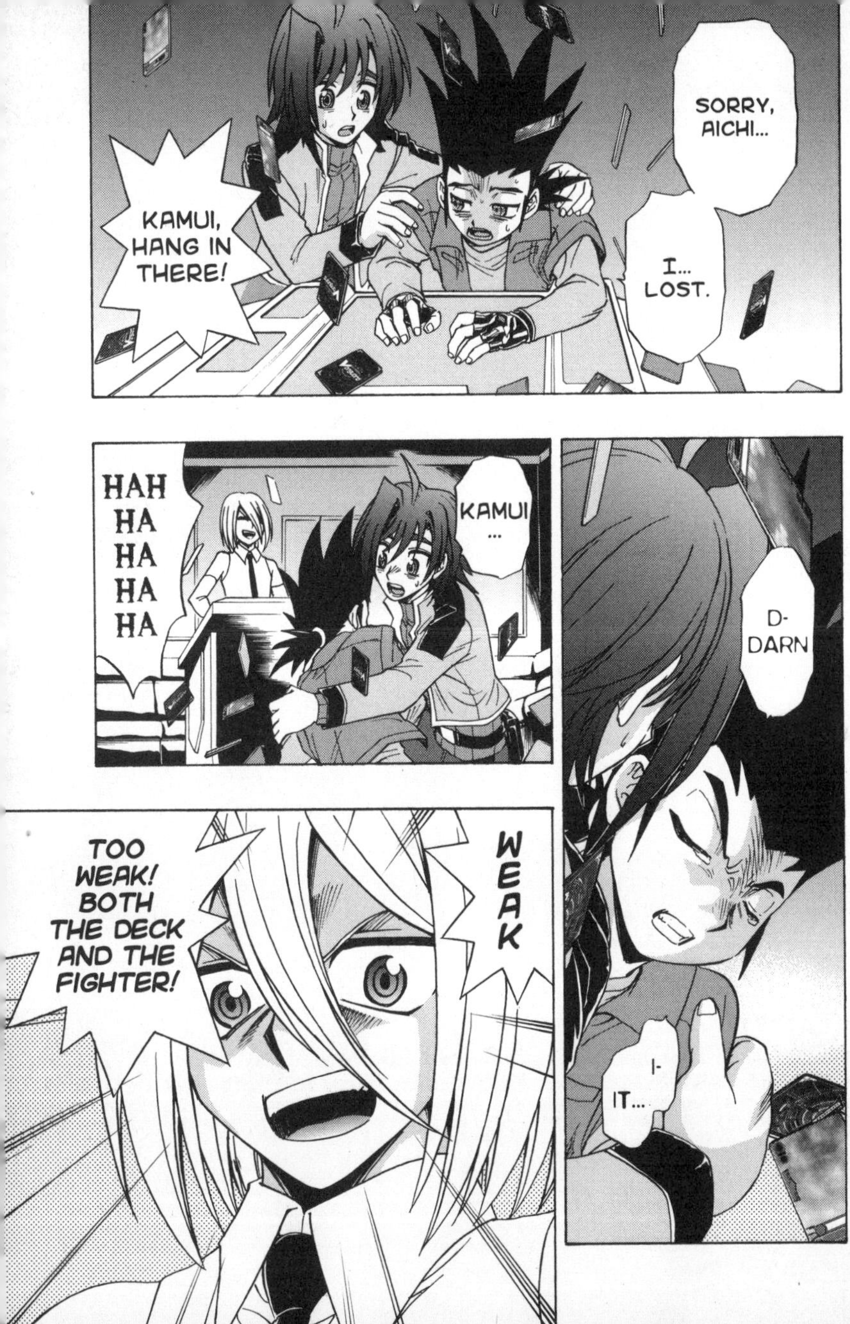
SORRY, AICHI...
I... LOST.
KAMUI, HANG IN THERE!
D-DARN
I-IT...
KAMUI...
HAH HA HA HA HA
WEAK
TOO WEAK! BOTH THE DECK AND THE FIGHTER!

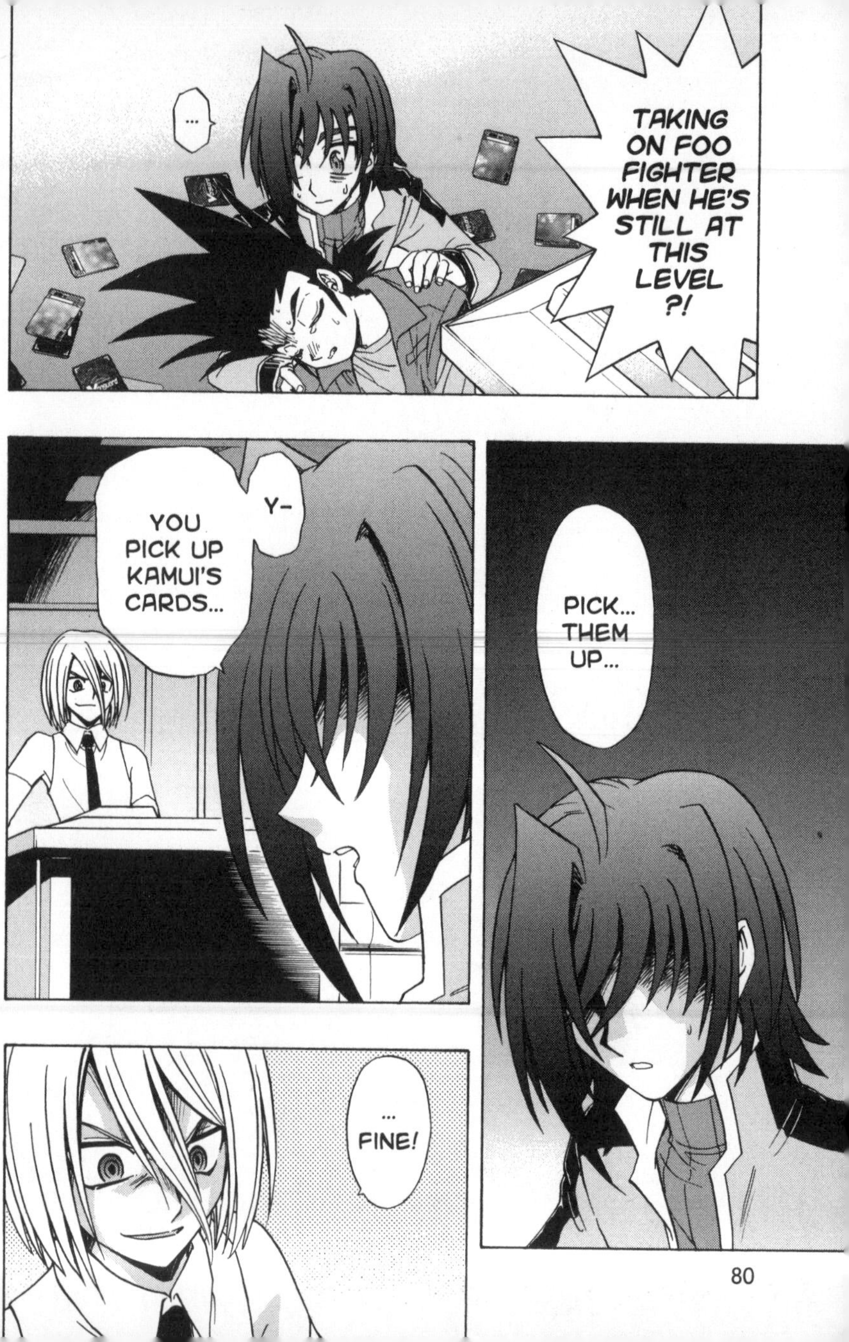

TAKING ON FOO FIGHTER WHEN HE'S STILL AT THIS LEVEL ?!
...
PICK... THEM UP...
Y-
YOU PICK UP KAMUI'S CARDS...
... FINE!

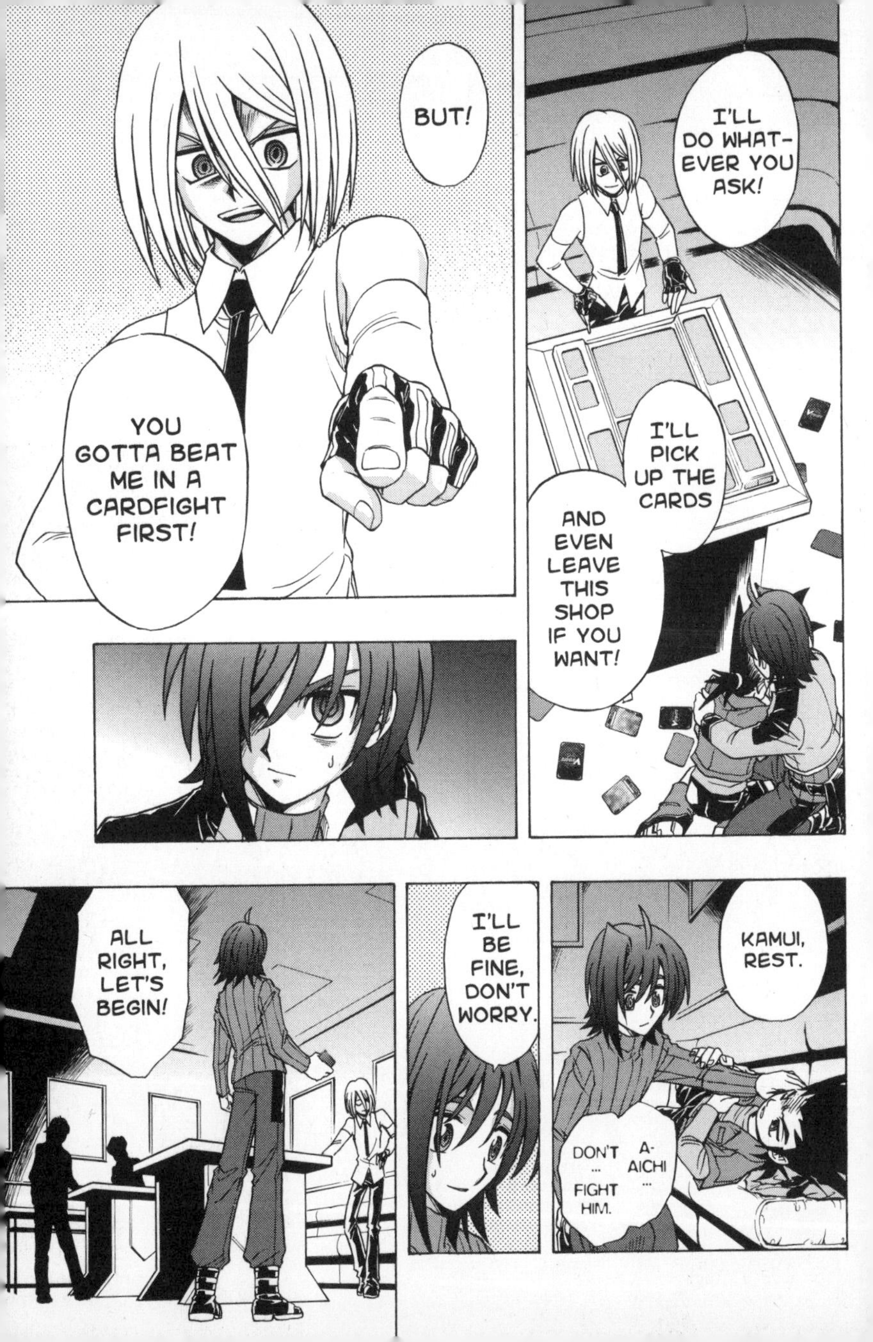
I'LL DO WHAT-EVER YOU ASK!
I'LL PICK UP THE CARDS
AND EVEN LEAVE THIS SHOP IF YOU WANT!
BUT!
YOU GOTTA BEAT ME IN A CARDFIGHT FIRST!
KAMUI, REST.
A-AICHI ...
DON'T ... FIGHT HIM.
I'LL BE FINE, DON'T WORRY.
ALL RIGHT, LET'S BEGIN!

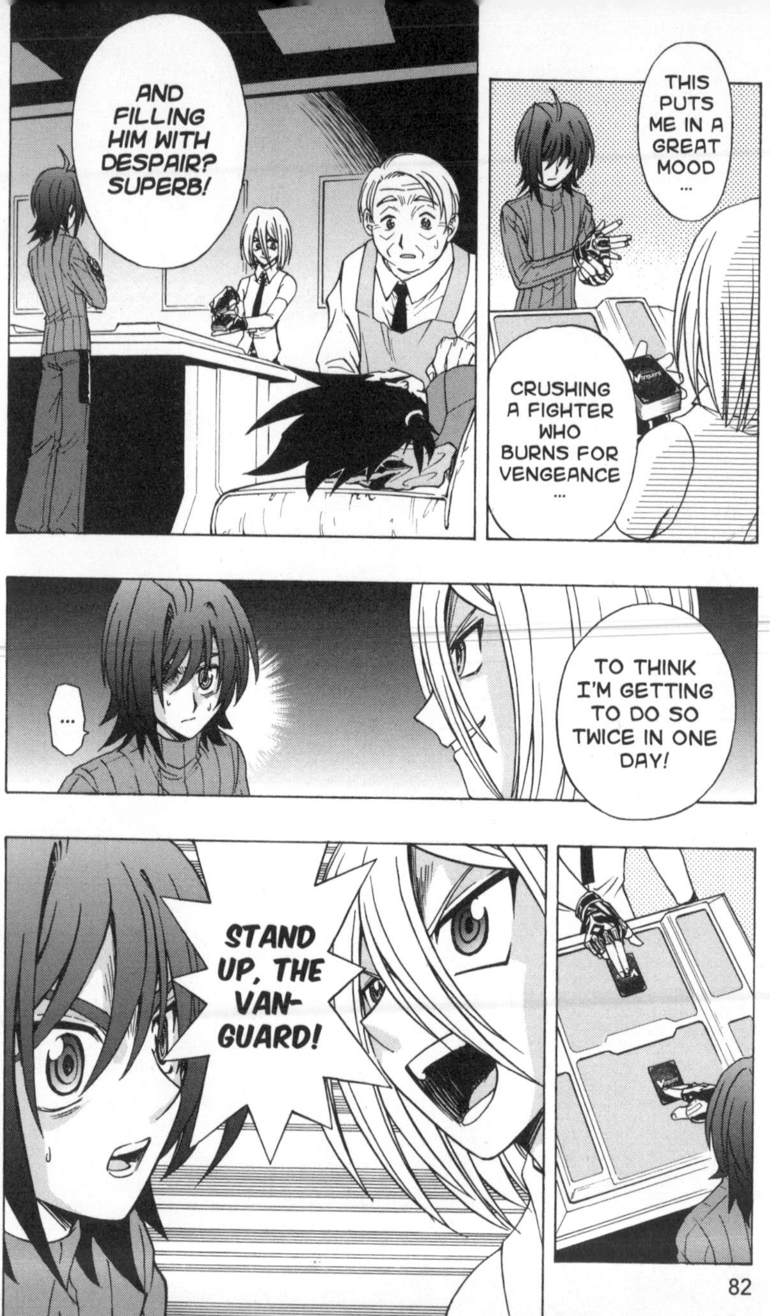
THIS PUTS ME IN A GREAT MOOD ...
CRUSHING A FIGHTER WHO BURNS FOR VENGEANCE ...
AND FILLING HIM WITH DESPAIR? SUPERB!
TO THINK I'M GETTING TO DO SO TWICE IN ONE DAY!
...
STAND UP, THE VAN-GUARD!

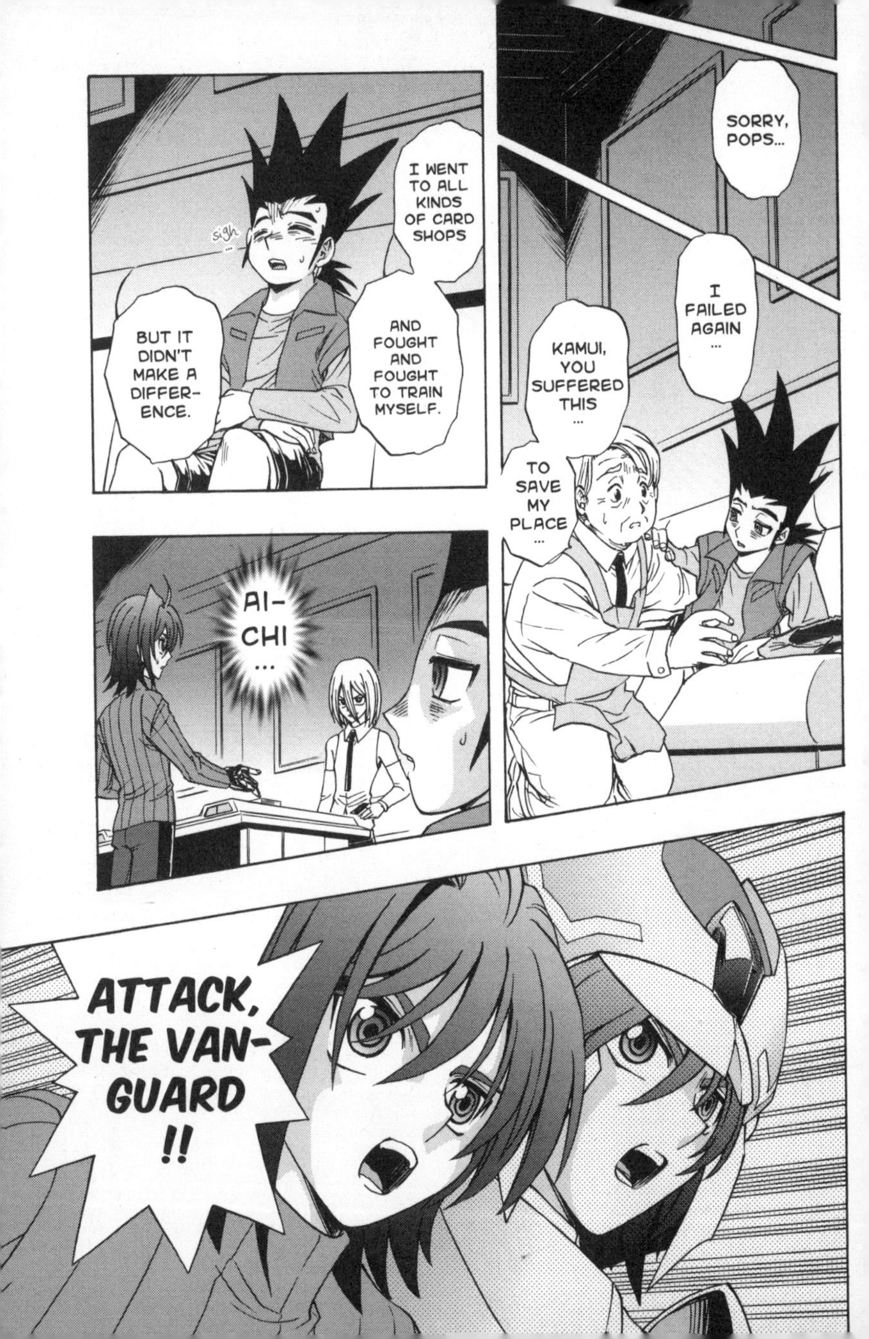
SORRY, POPS...
I FAILED AGAIN ...
KAMUI, YOU SUFFERED THIS ...
TO SAVE MY PLACE ...
sigh ...
I WENT TO ALL KINDS OF CARD SHOPS
AND FOUGHT AND FOUGHT TO TRAIN MYSELF.
BUT IT DIDN'T MAKE A DIFFER-ENCE.
AI-CHI ...
ATTACK, THE VAN-GUARD !!

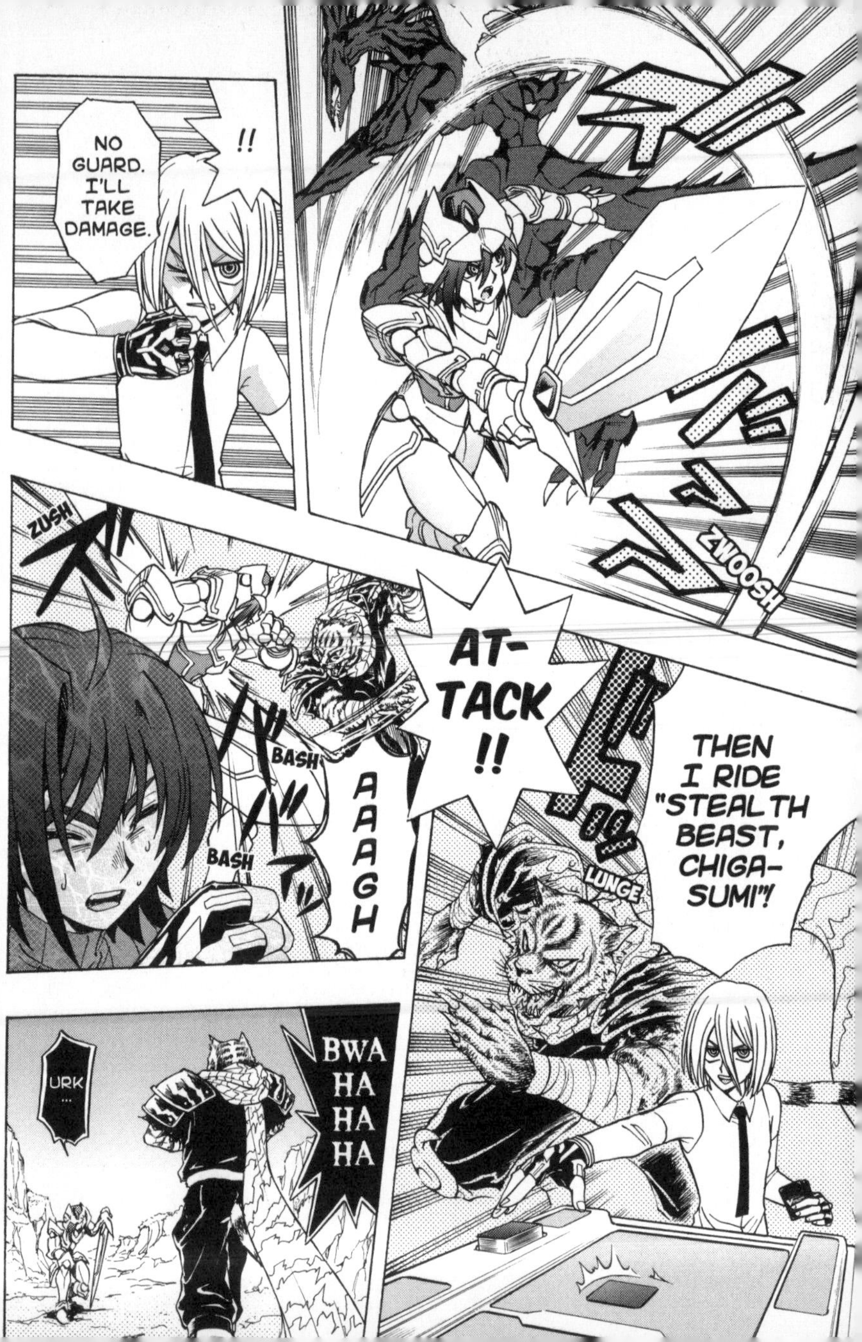
ZWOOSH
NO GUARD. I'LL TAKE DAMAGE.
!!
AT-TACK!!
THEN I RIDE "STEALTH BEAST, CHIGA-SUMI"!
LUNGE
ZUSH
BASH
BASH
AAAAGH
BWA HA HA HA
URK...

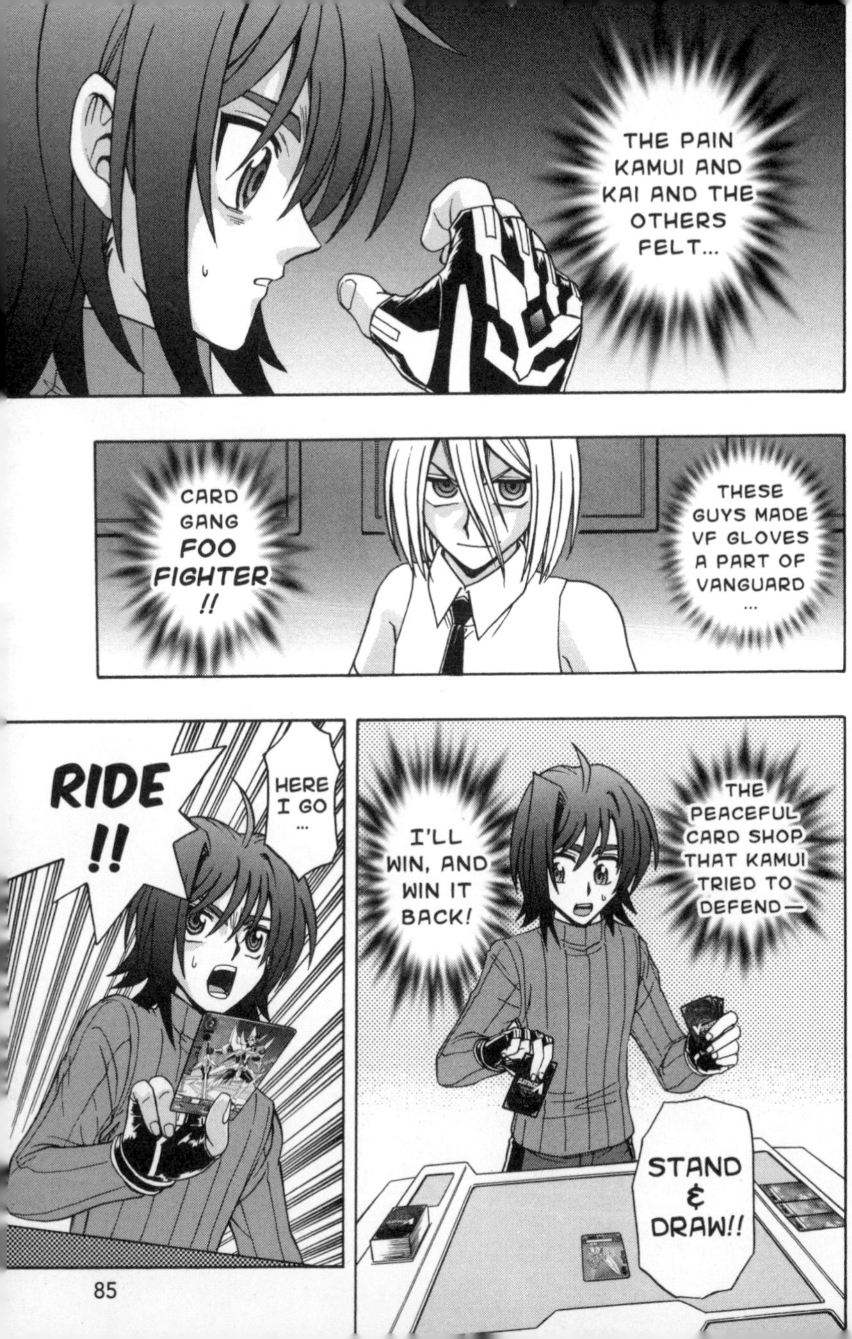
THE PAIN KAMUI AND KAI AND THE OTHERS FELT...
THESE GUYS MADE VF GLOVES A PART OF VANGUARD ...
CARD GANG **FOO FIGHTER** !!
THE PEACEFUL CARD SHOP THAT KAMUI TRIED TO DEFEND—
I'LL WIN, AND WIN IT BACK!
STAND & DRAW!!
HERE I GO ...
RIDE !!

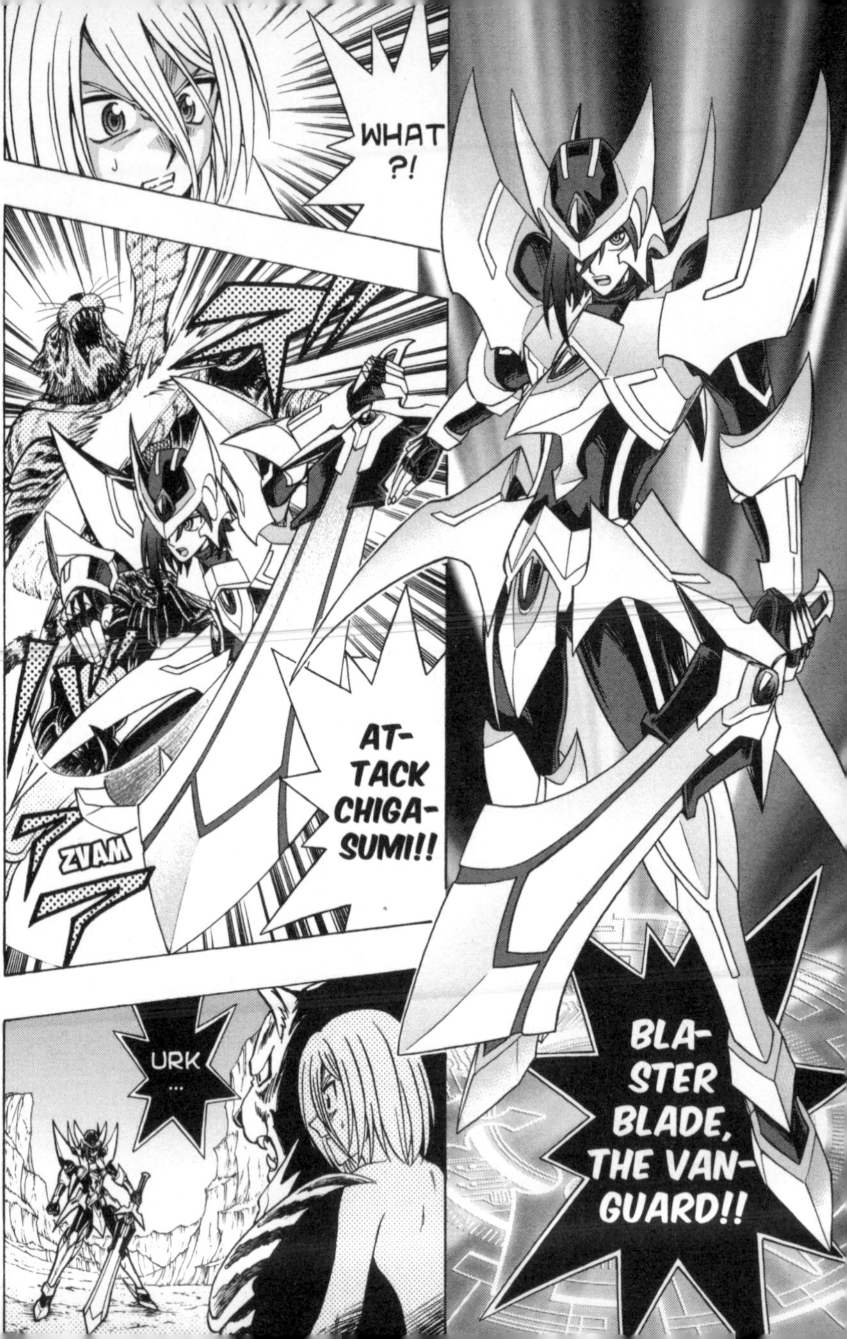
BLASTER BLADE, THE VANGUARD!!
WHAT ?!
ATTACK CHIGASUMI!!
ZVAM
URK ...

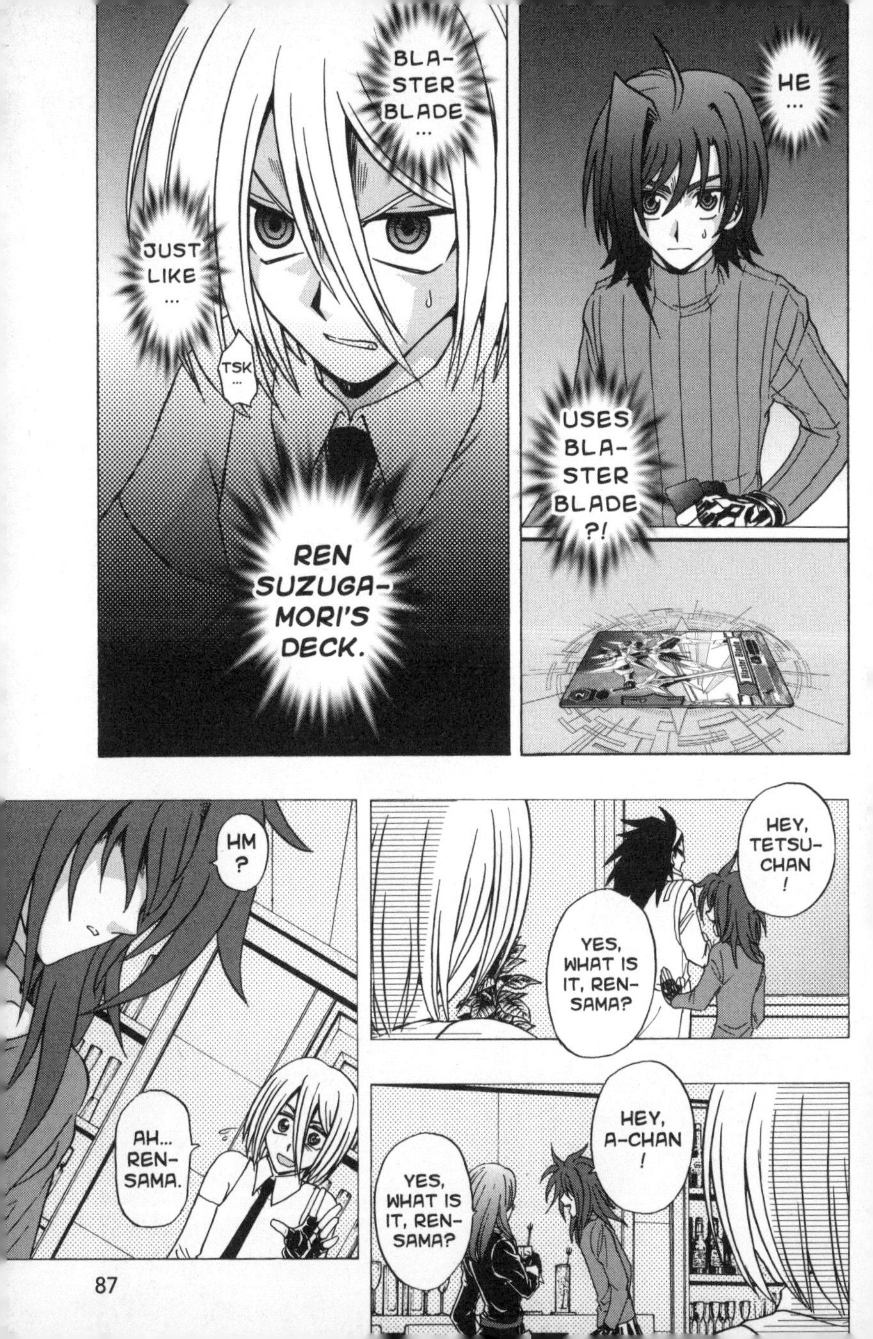
HE...
USES BLASTER BLADE?!
BLASTER BLADE...
JUST LIKE...
TSK...
REN SUZUGAMORI'S DECK.
HEY, TETSU-CHAN!
YES, WHAT IS IT, REN-SAMA?
HEY, A-CHAN!
YES, WHAT IS IT, REN-SAMA?
HM?
AH... REN-SAMA.

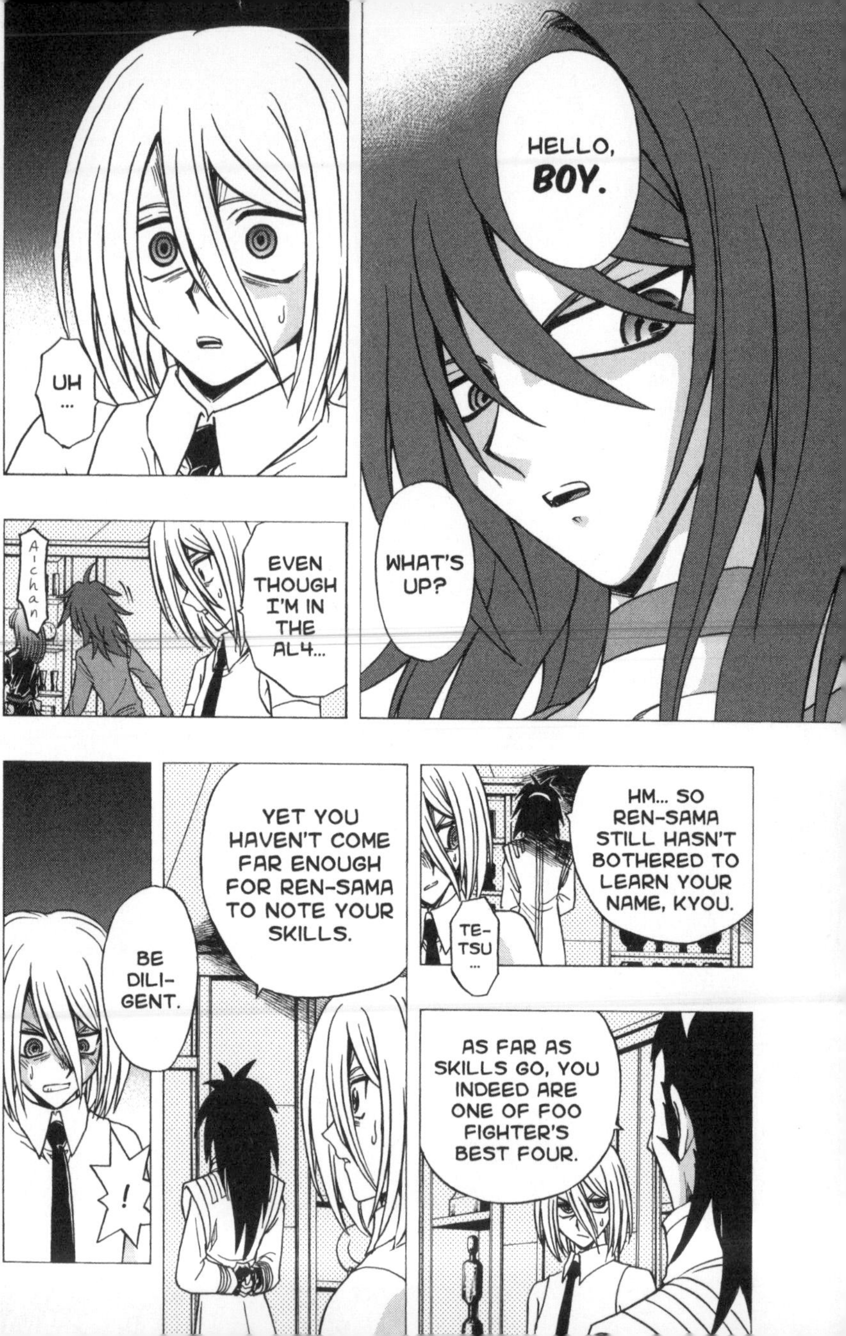
HELLO, BOY.
WHAT'S UP?
UH ...
Aichan
EVEN THOUGH I'M IN THE AL4...
HM... SO REN-SAMA STILL HASN'T BOTHERED TO LEARN YOUR NAME, KYOU.
TE-TSU ...
AS FAR AS SKILLS GO, YOU INDEED ARE ONE OF FOO FIGHTER'S BEST FOUR.
YET YOU HAVEN'T COME FAR ENOUGH FOR REN-SAMA TO NOTE YOUR SKILLS.
BE DILI-GENT.
!

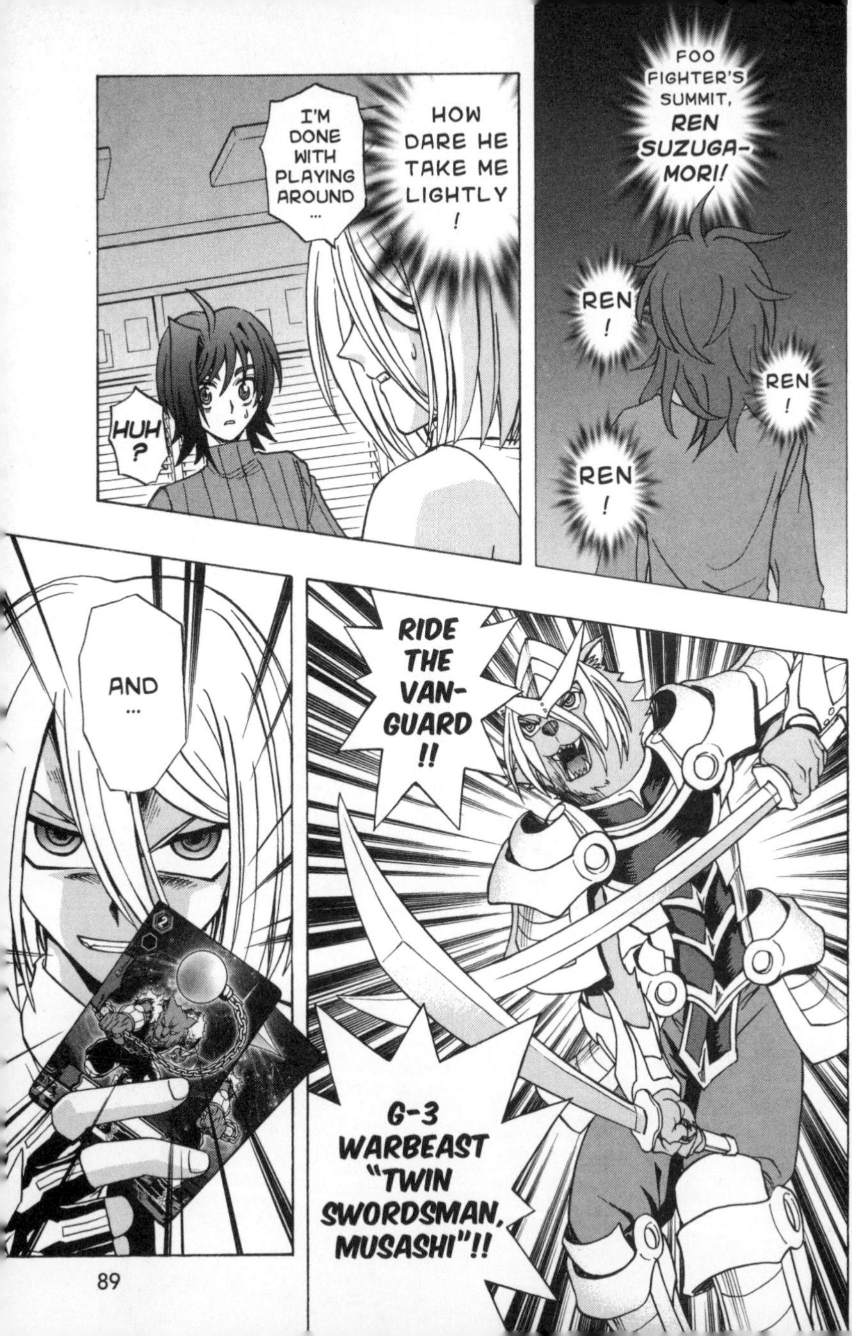
FOO FIGHTER'S SUMMIT, REN SUZUGA-MORI!
REN!
REN!
REN!
HOW DARE HE TAKE ME LIGHTLY!
I'M DONE WITH PLAYING AROUND...
HUH?
RIDE THE VAN-GUARD!!
G-3 WARBEAST "TWIN SWORDSMAN, MUSASHI"!!
AND...

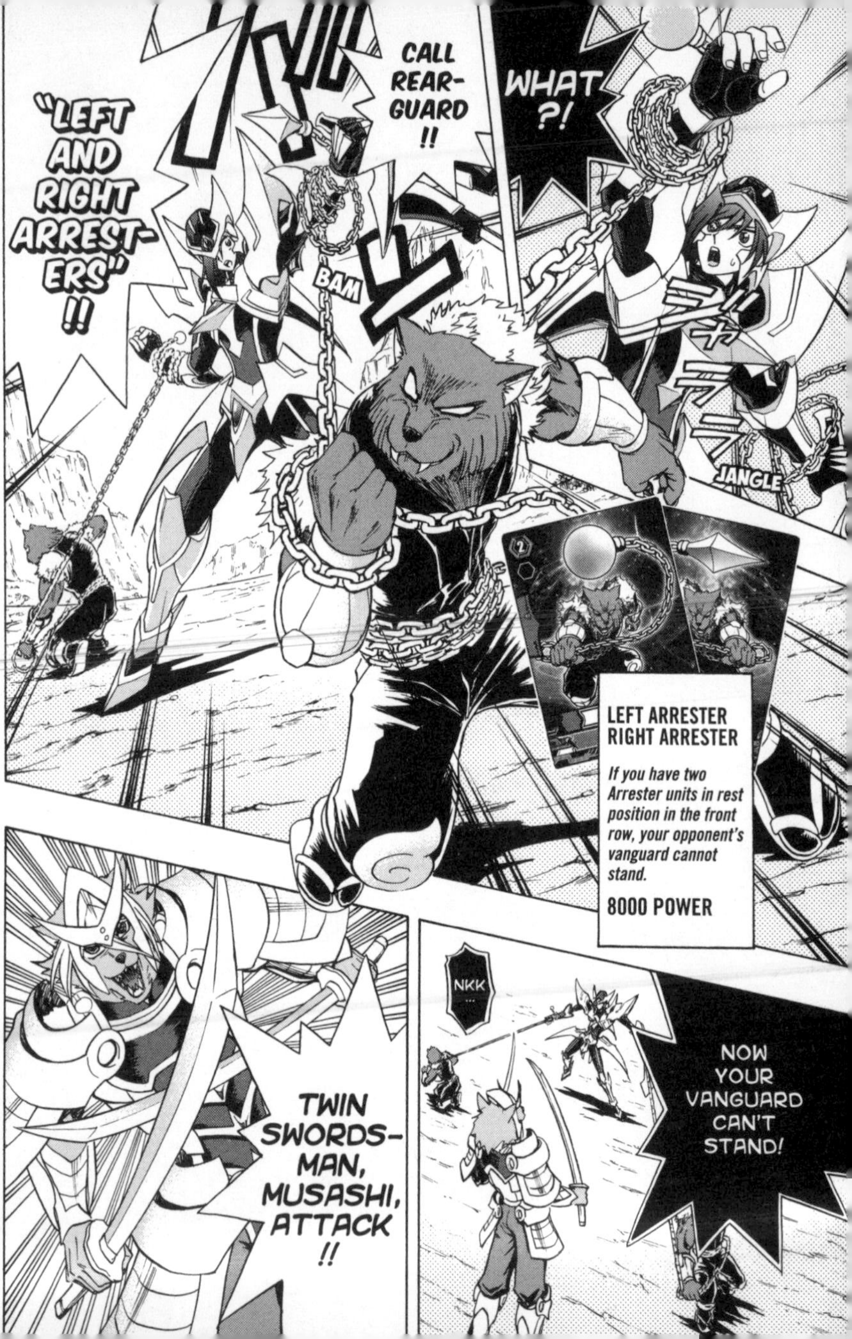
WHAT?!
CALL REAR-GUARD!!
"LEFT AND RIGHT ARRESTERS"!!
BAM
JANGLE
LEFT ARRESTER
RIGHT ARRESTER
If you have two Arrester units in rest position in the front row, your opponent's vanguard cannot stand.
8000 POWER
NKK...
NOW YOUR VANGUARD CAN'T STAND!
TWIN SWORDSMAN, MUSASHI, ATTACK!!

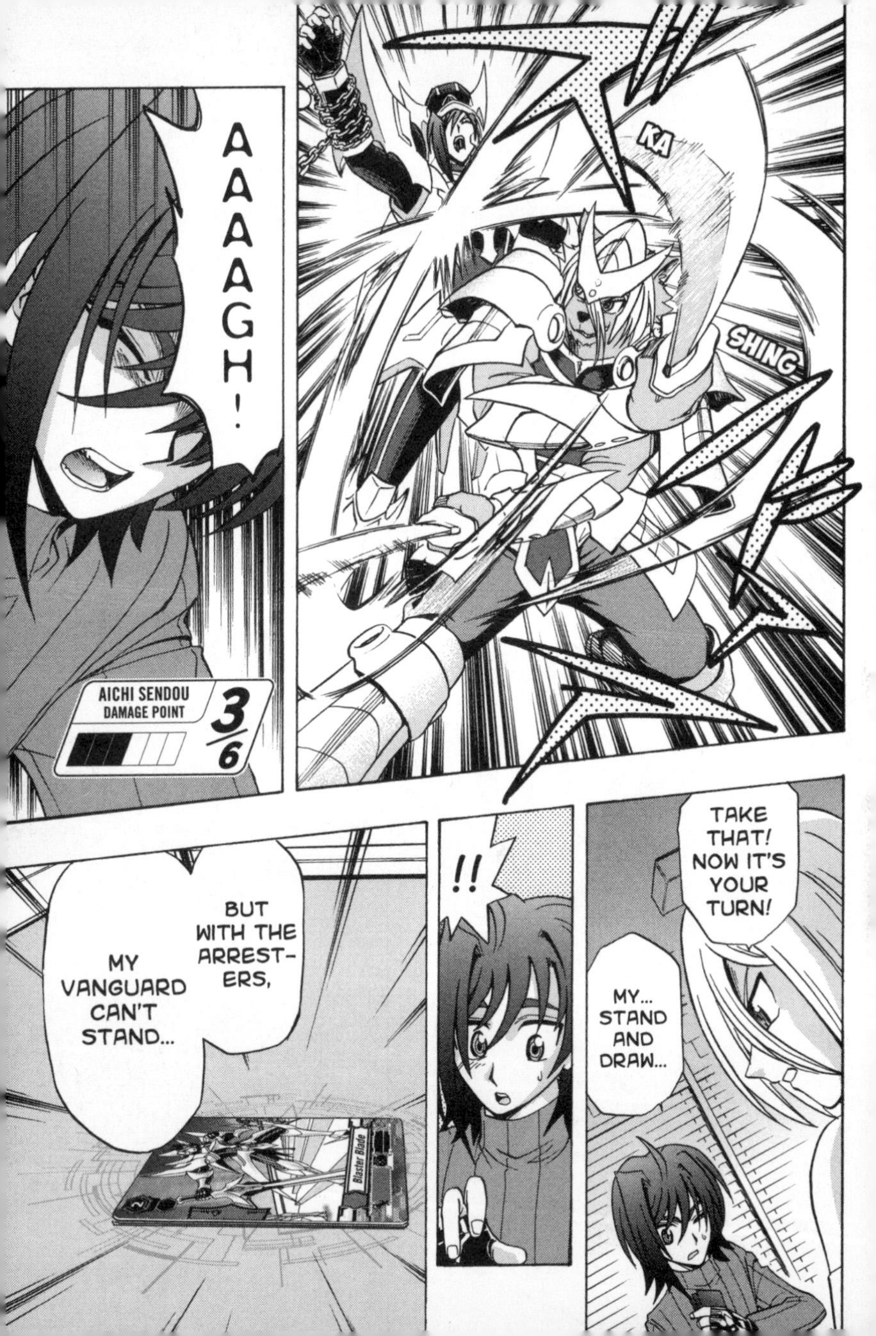
KA
SHING
AAAAAGH!
AICHI SENDOU DAMAGE POINT 3/6
TAKE THAT! NOW IT'S YOUR TURN!
MY... STAND AND DRAW...
!!
BUT WITH THE ARREST-ERS,
MY VANGUARD CAN'T STAND...
Blaster Blade

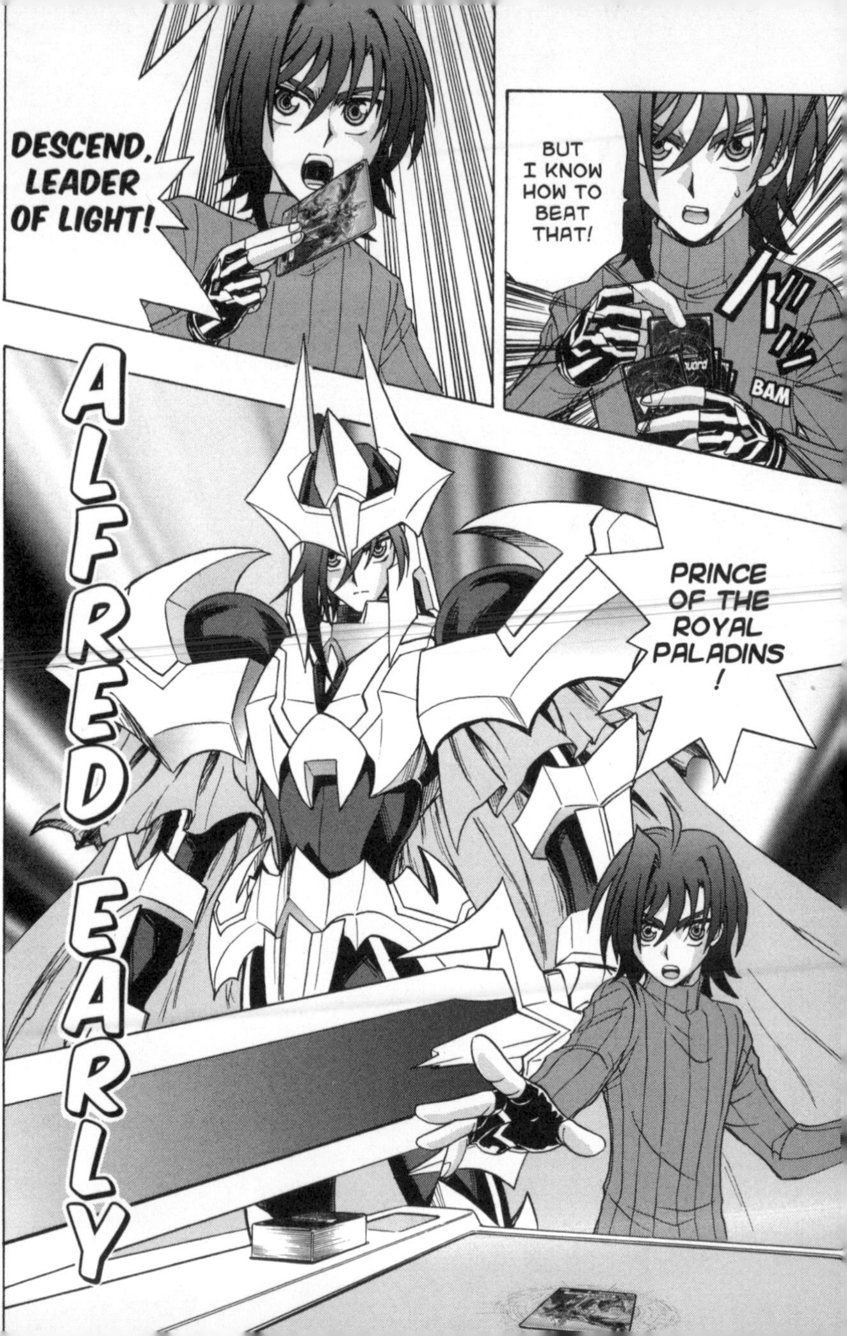
BUT I KNOW HOW TO BEAT THAT!
BAM
DESCEND, LEADER OF LIGHT!
PRINCE OF THE ROYAL PALADINS!
ALFRED EARLY

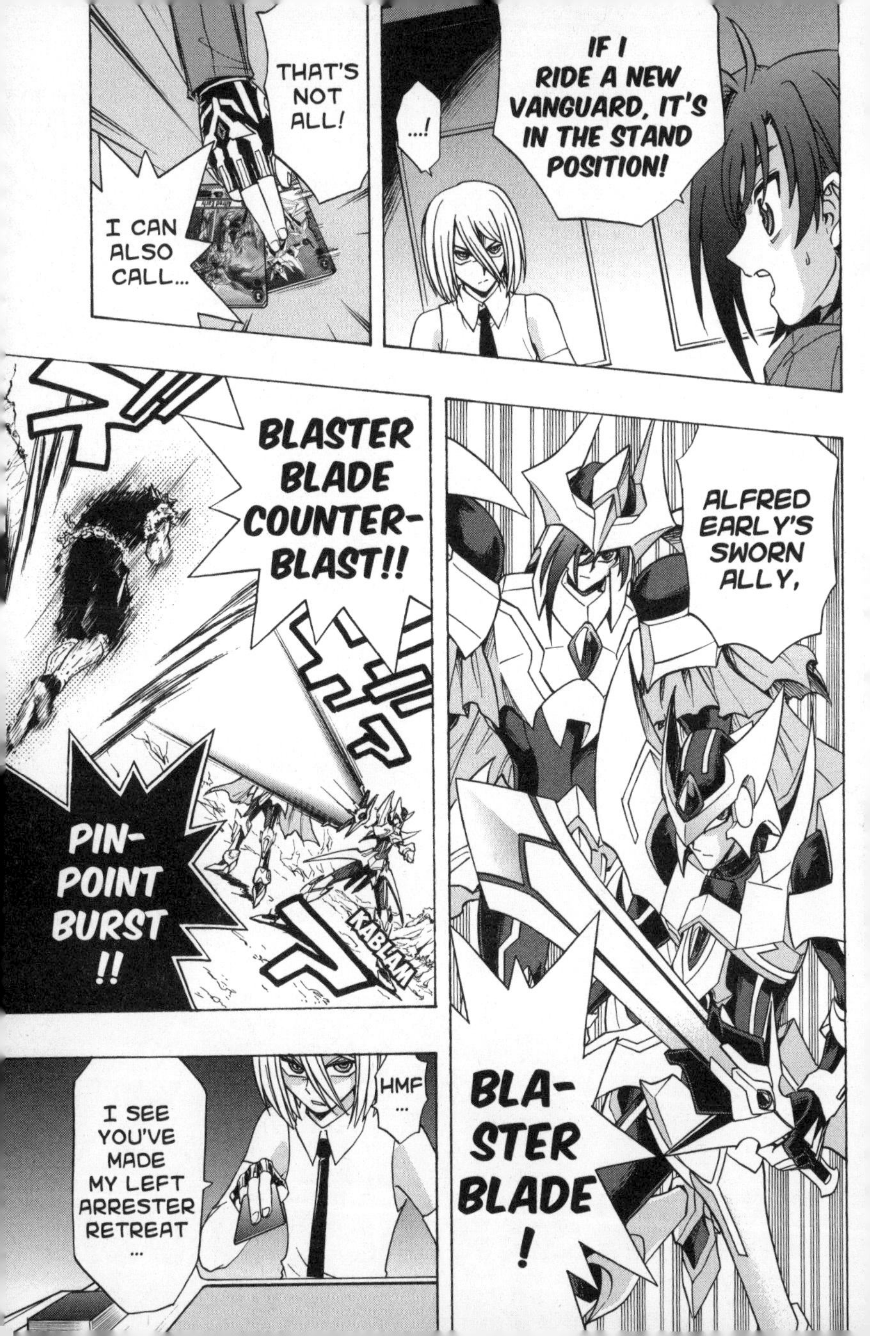
IF I RIDE A NEW VANGUARD, IT'S IN THE STAND POSITION!
...!
THAT'S NOT ALL!
I CAN ALSO CALL...
ALFRED EARLY'S SWORN ALLY,
BLA-STER BLADE!
BLASTER BLADE COUNTER-BLAST!!
PIN-POINT BURST!!
KABLAM
HMF...
I SEE YOU'VE MADE MY LEFT ARRESTER RETREAT...

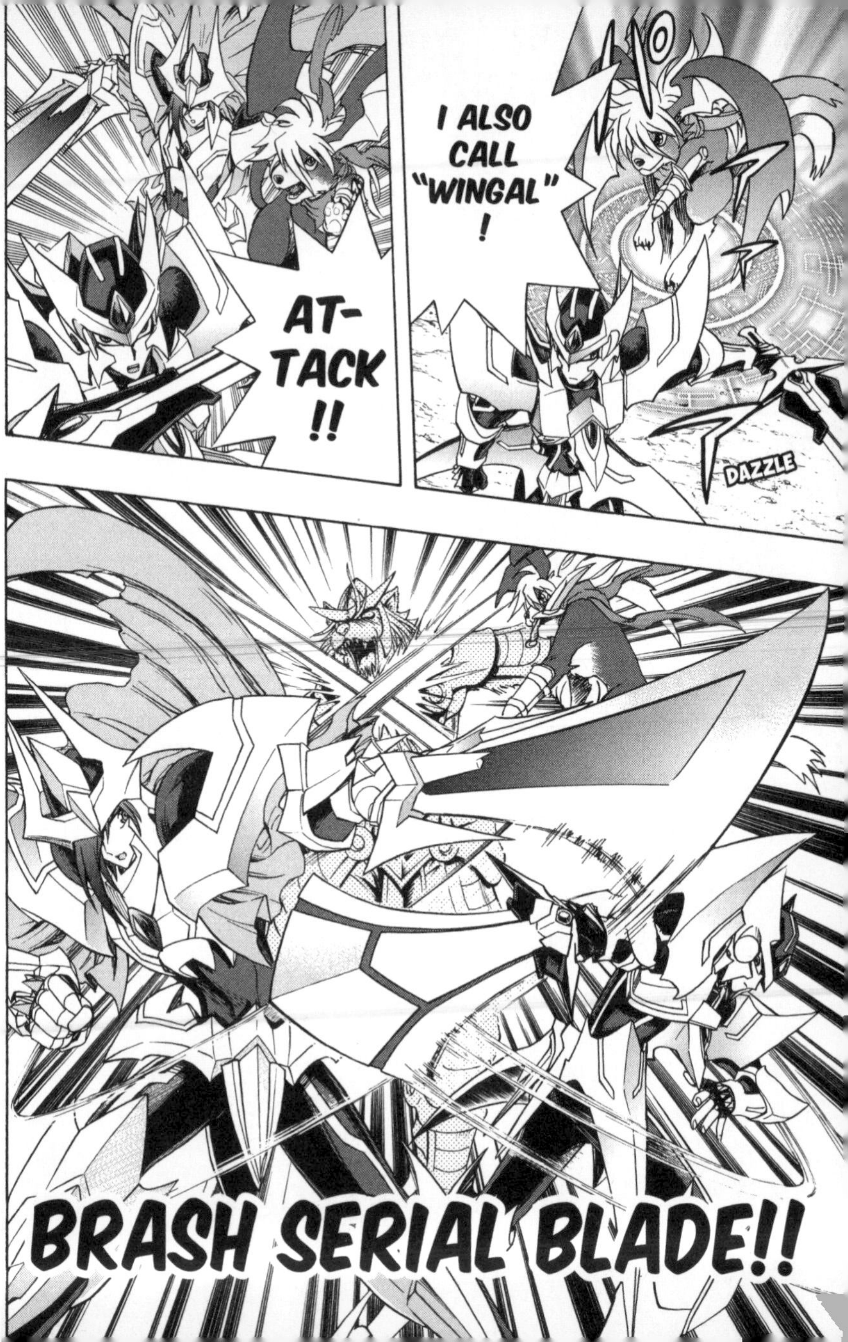
I ALSO CALL "WINGAL"!
DAZZLE
AT-TACK!!
BRASH SERIAL BLADE!!

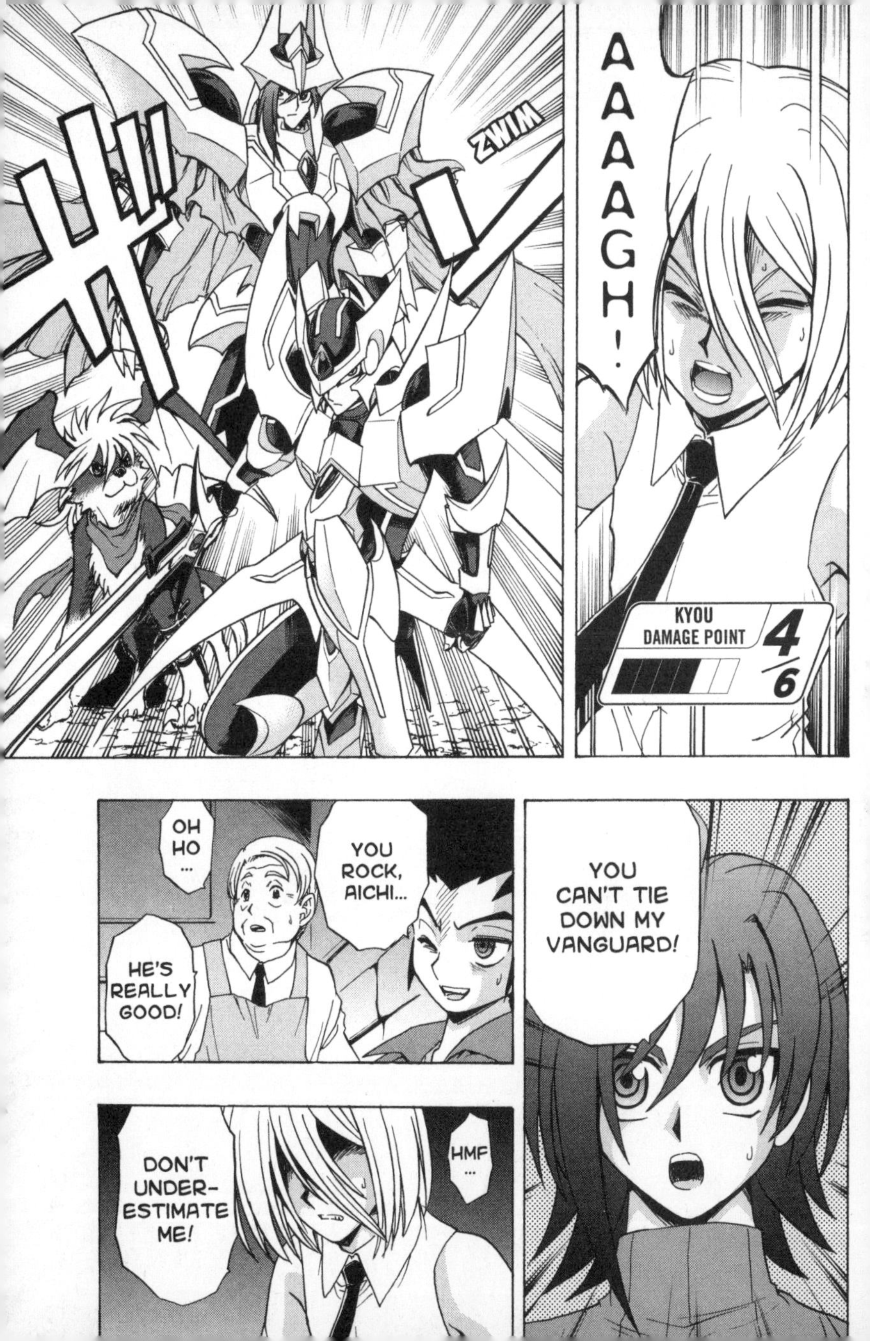
AAAAAGH!
KYOU DAMAGE POINT 4/6
ZWIM
YOU CAN'T TIE DOWN MY VANGUARD!
YOU ROCK, AICHI...
OH HO ...
HE'S REALLY GOOD!
HMF ...
DON'T UNDER-ESTIMATE ME!

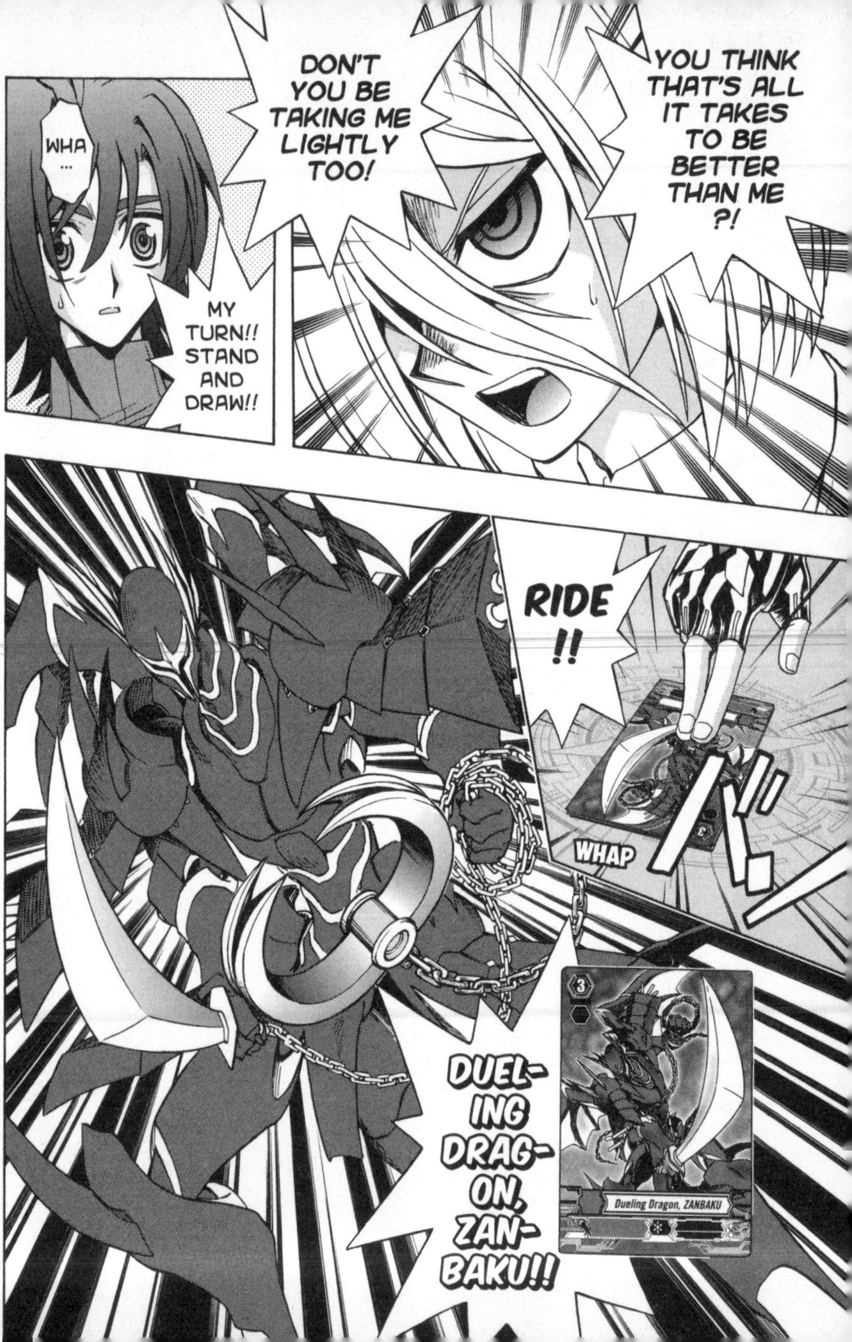
YOU THINK THAT'S ALL IT TAKES TO BE BETTER THAN ME?!
DON'T YOU BE TAKING ME LIGHTLY TOO!
WHA...
MY TURN!! STAND AND DRAW!!
RIDE!!
WHAP
Dueling Dragon, ZANBAKU
DUEL-ING DRAG-ON, ZAN-BAKU!!

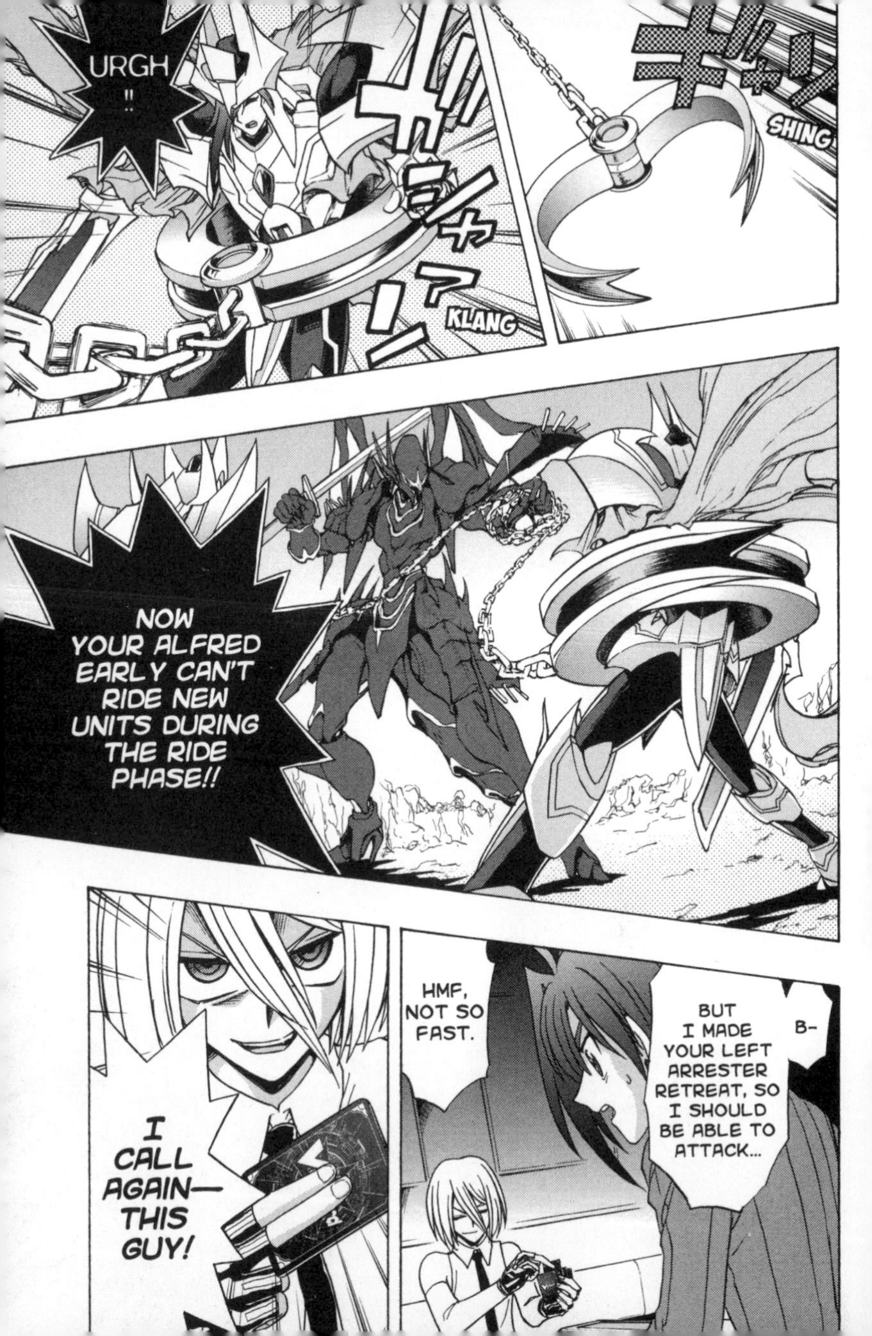
SHING
URGH!!
KLANG
NOW YOUR ALFRED EARLY CAN'T RIDE NEW UNITS DURING THE RIDE PHASE!!
B-
BUT I MADE YOUR LEFT ARRESTER RETREAT, SO I SHOULD BE ABLE TO ATTACK...
HMF, NOT SO FAST.
I CALL AGAIN—THIS GUY!

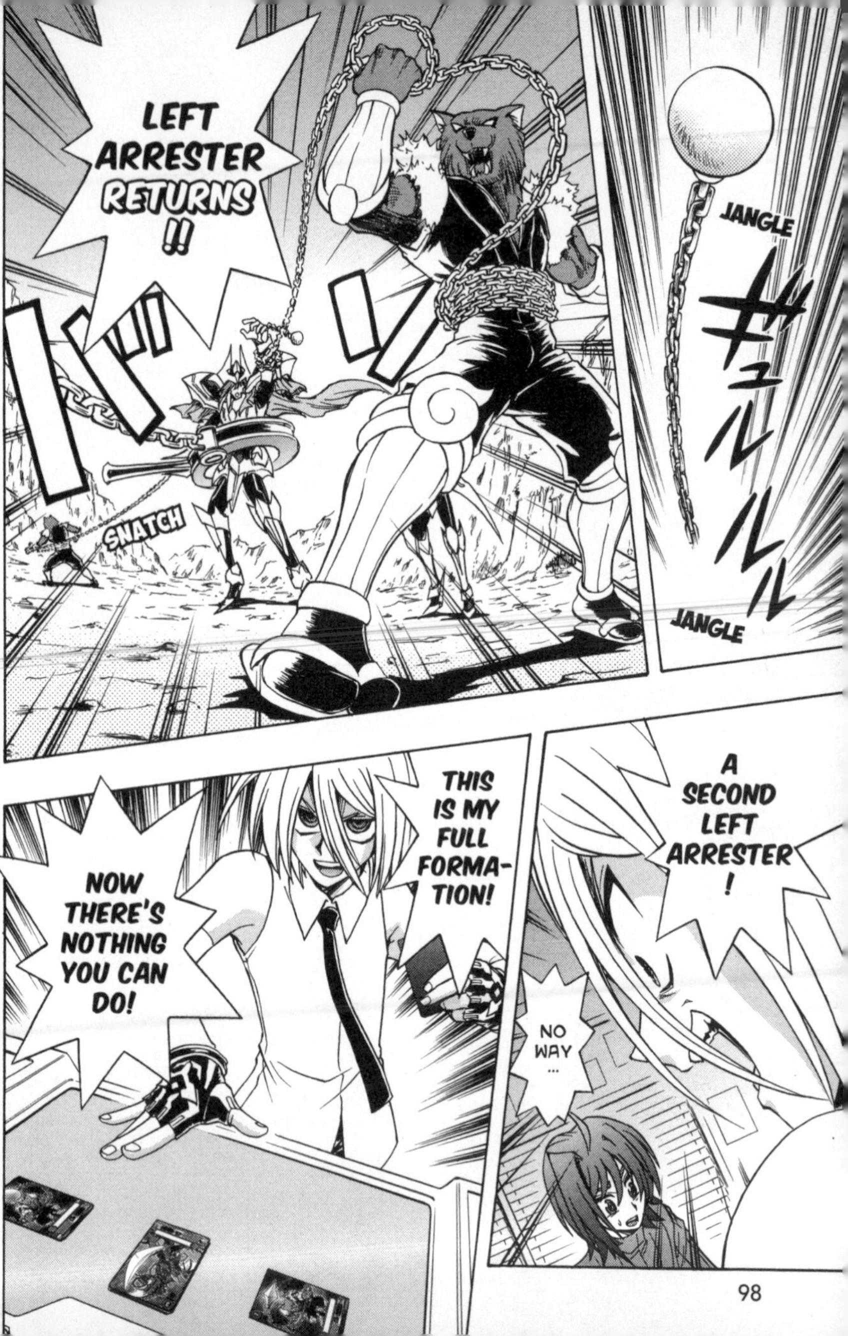
JANGLE
ギュルルル
JANGLE
LEFT ARRESTER RETURNS !!
SNATCH
A SECOND LEFT ARRESTER !
NO WAY ...
THIS IS MY FULL FORMATION!
NOW THERE'S NOTHING YOU CAN DO!

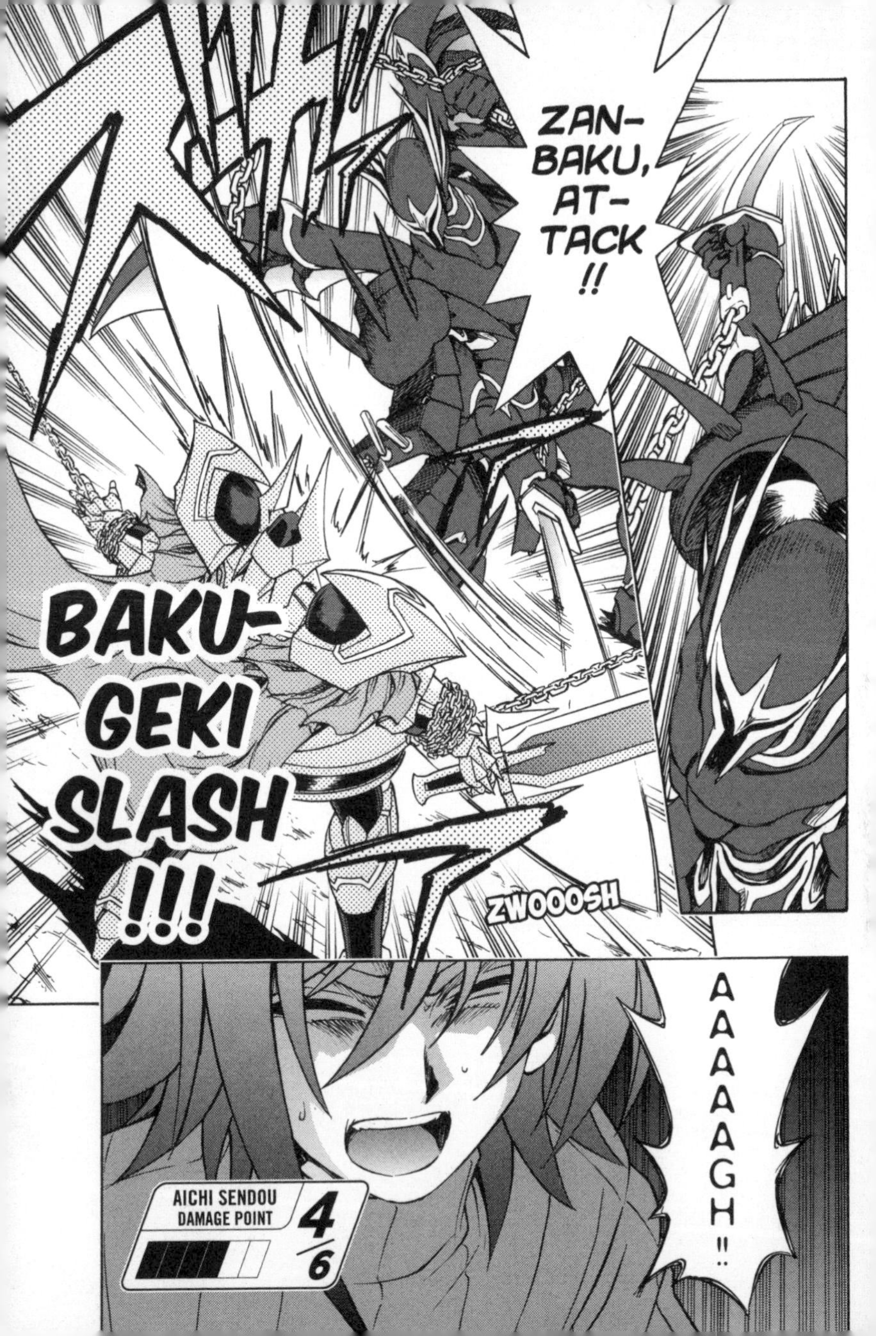
ZAN-BAKU, AT-TACK!!
BAKU-GEKI SLASH!!!
ZWOOOSH
AAAAAAGH!!
AICHI SENDOU
DAMAGE POINT
4/6

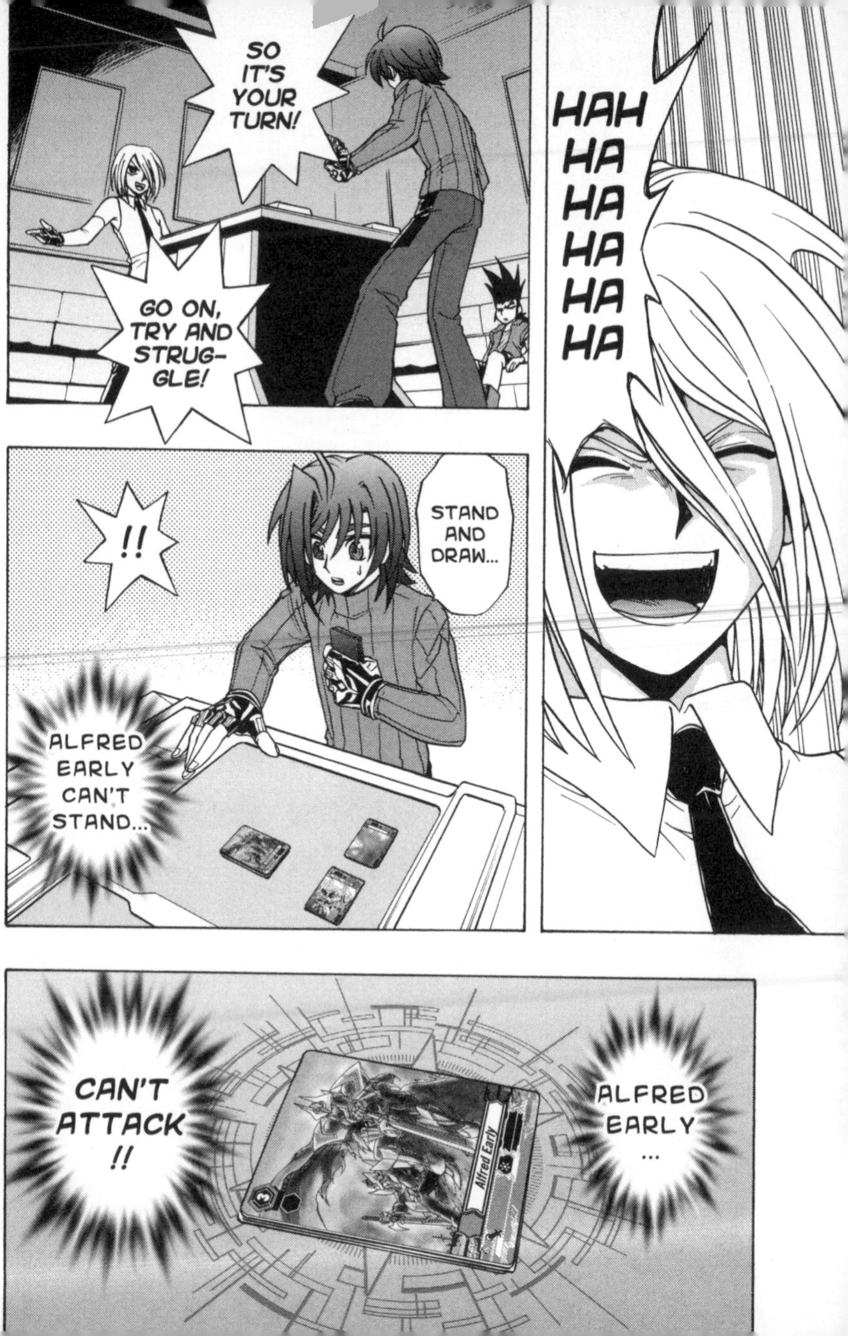
HAH HA HA HA HA HA
SO IT'S YOUR TURN!
GO ON, TRY AND STRUG-GLE!
STAND AND DRAW...
!!
ALFRED EARLY CAN'T STAND...
ALFRED EARLY ...
Alfred Early
CAN'T ATTACK !!

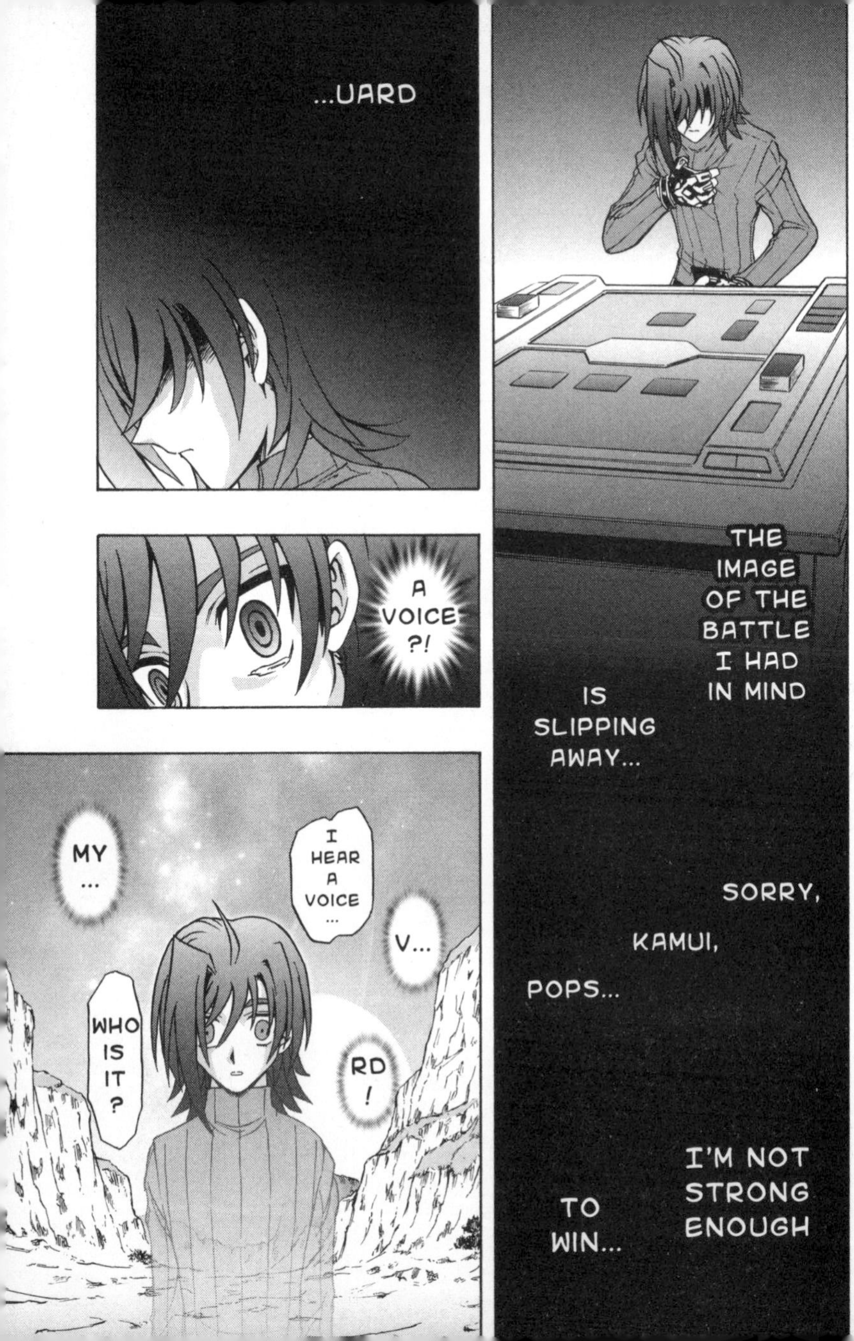
THE IMAGE OF THE BATTLE I HAD IN MIND
IS SLIPPING AWAY...
SORRY,
KAMUI,
POPS...
I'M NOT STRONG ENOUGH
TO WIN...
...UARD
A VOICE?!
I HEAR A VOICE...
MY...
V...
RD!
WHO IS IT?

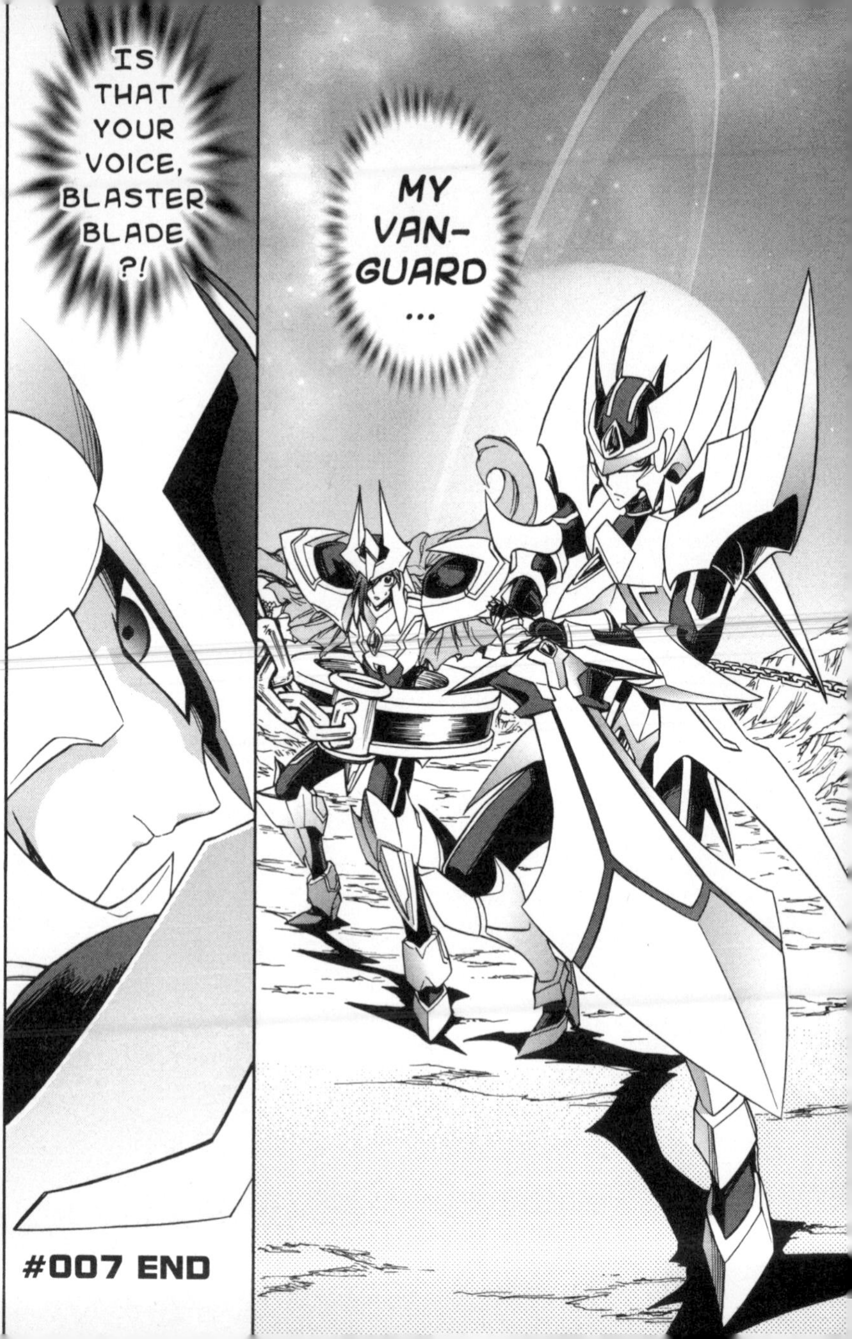
MY VAN-GUARD ...
IS THAT YOUR VOICE, BLASTER BLADE ?!
#007 END

BONUS! CARDFIGHT!! Vanguard

NEVER-BEFORE-SEEN IMAGE BOARDS

CHARACTERS

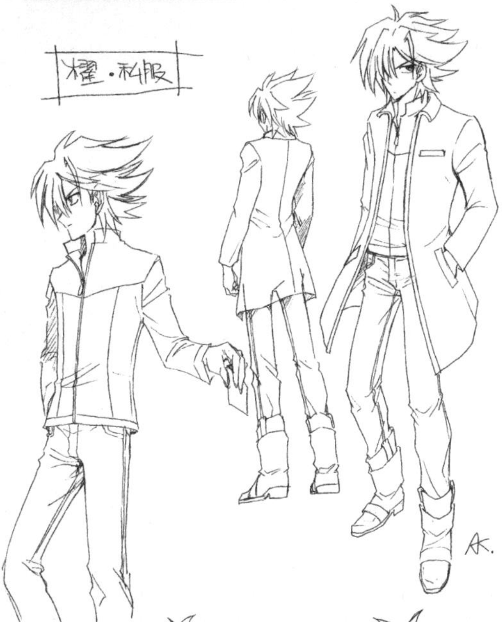
櫂・私服
AK.

Kai: Casual Clothes

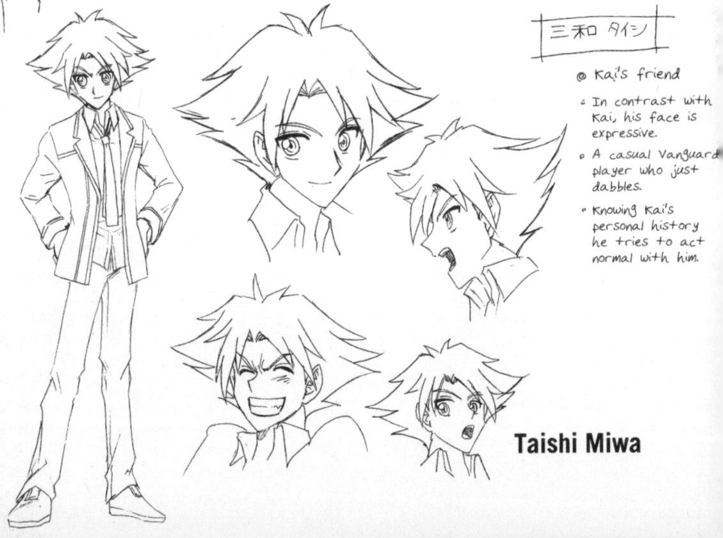
三和 タイシ
◎ Kai's friend
◦ In contrast with Kai, his face is expressive.
◦ A casual Vanguard player who just dabbles.
◦ Knowing Kai's personal history he tries to act normal with him.

Taishi Miwa

BONUS! CARDFIGHT!! Vanguard NEVER-BEFORE-SEEN IMAGE BOARDS: CHARACTERS

Miwa and Nitta: Casual Summer Clothes

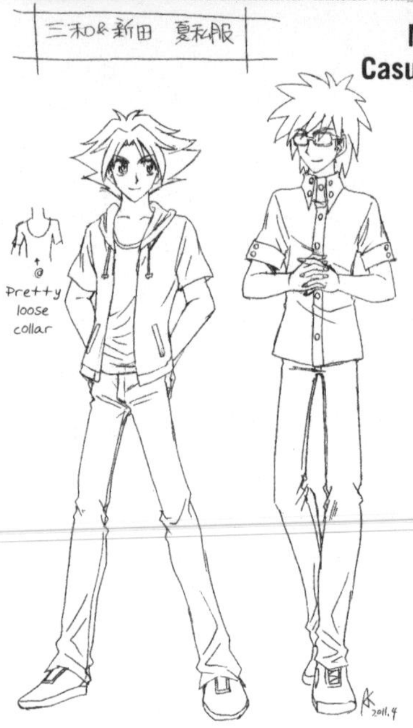
三和&新田 夏私服
Pretty loose collar
2011.4

Shin Nitta

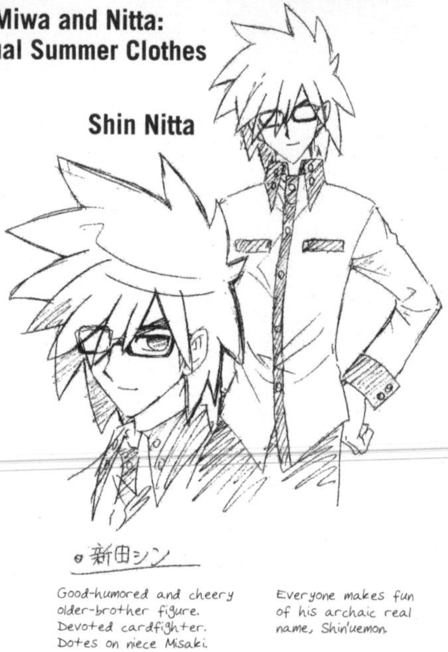
新田シン
Good-humored and cheery older-brother figure. Devoted cardfighter. Dotes on niece Misaki.
Everyone makes fun of his archaic real name, Shin'uemon.

Katsumi Morikawa

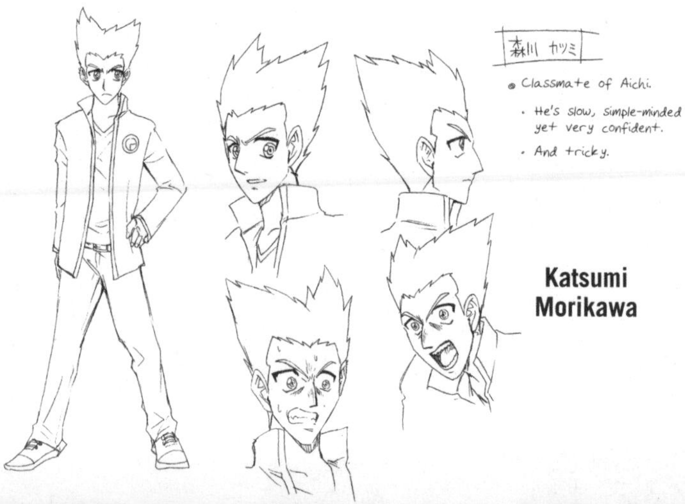
森川 カツミ
Classmate of Aichi.
He's slow, simple-minded yet very confident.
And tricky.

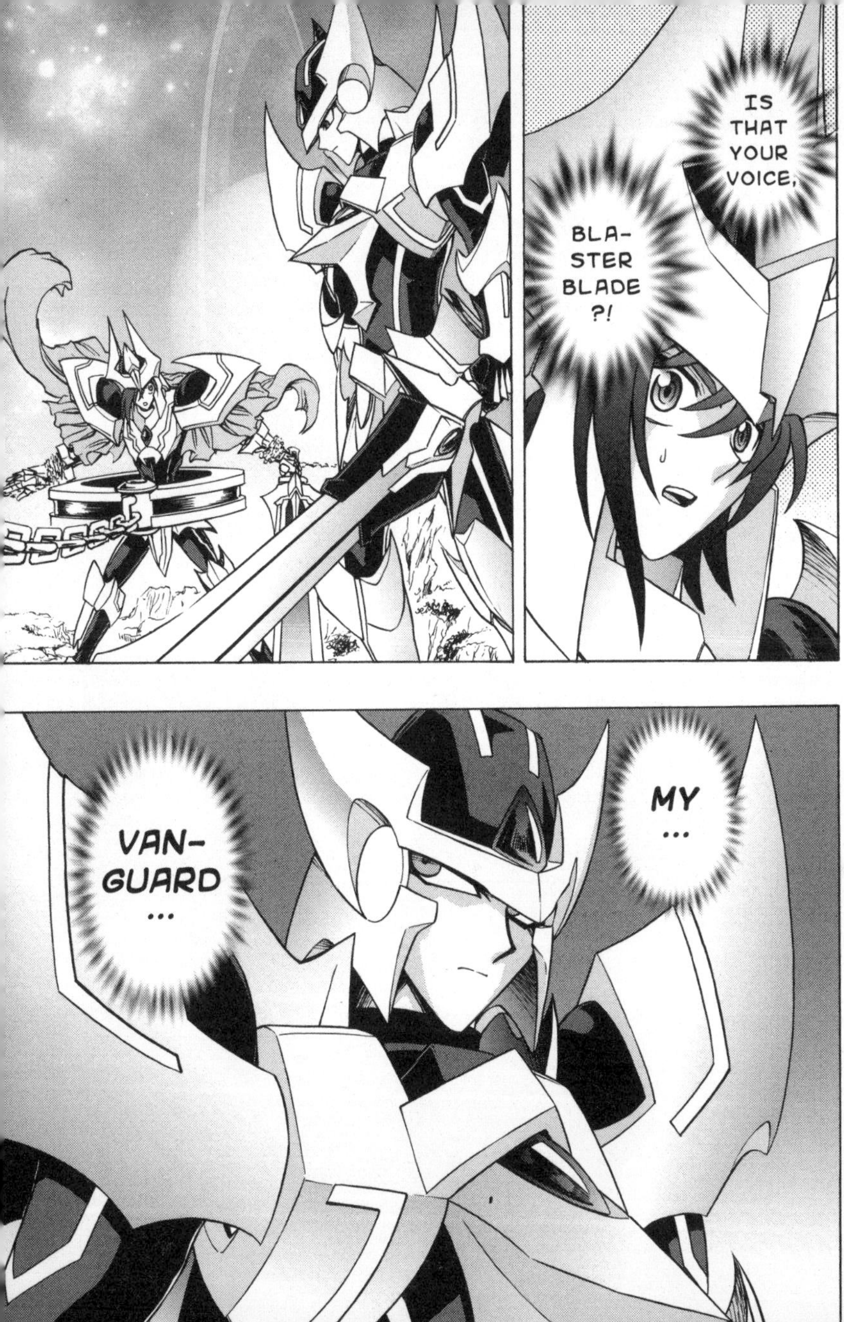
IS THAT YOUR VOICE,
BLA-STER BLADE ?!
MY ...
VAN-GUARD ...

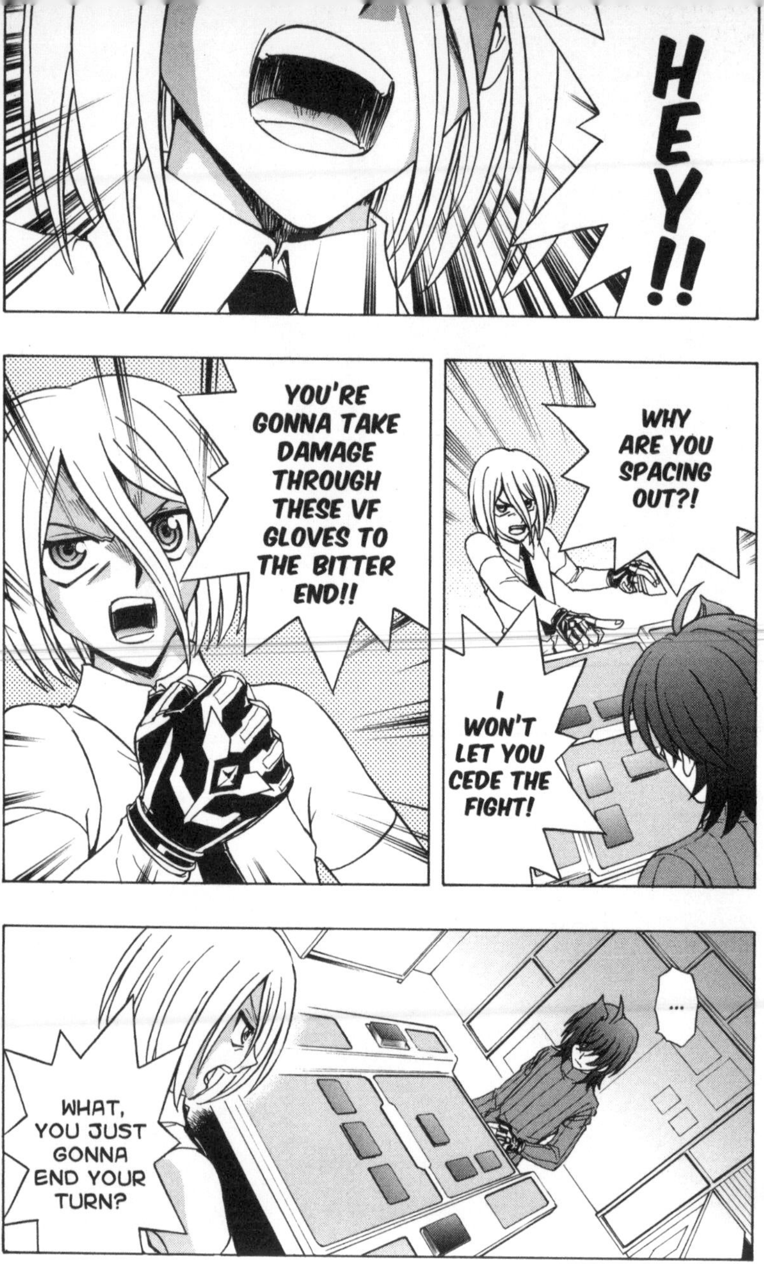
HEY!!
WHY ARE YOU SPACING OUT?!
I WON'T LET YOU CEDE THE FIGHT!
YOU'RE GONNA TAKE DAMAGE THROUGH THESE VF GLOVES TO THE BITTER END!!
...
WHAT, YOU JUST GONNA END YOUR TURN?

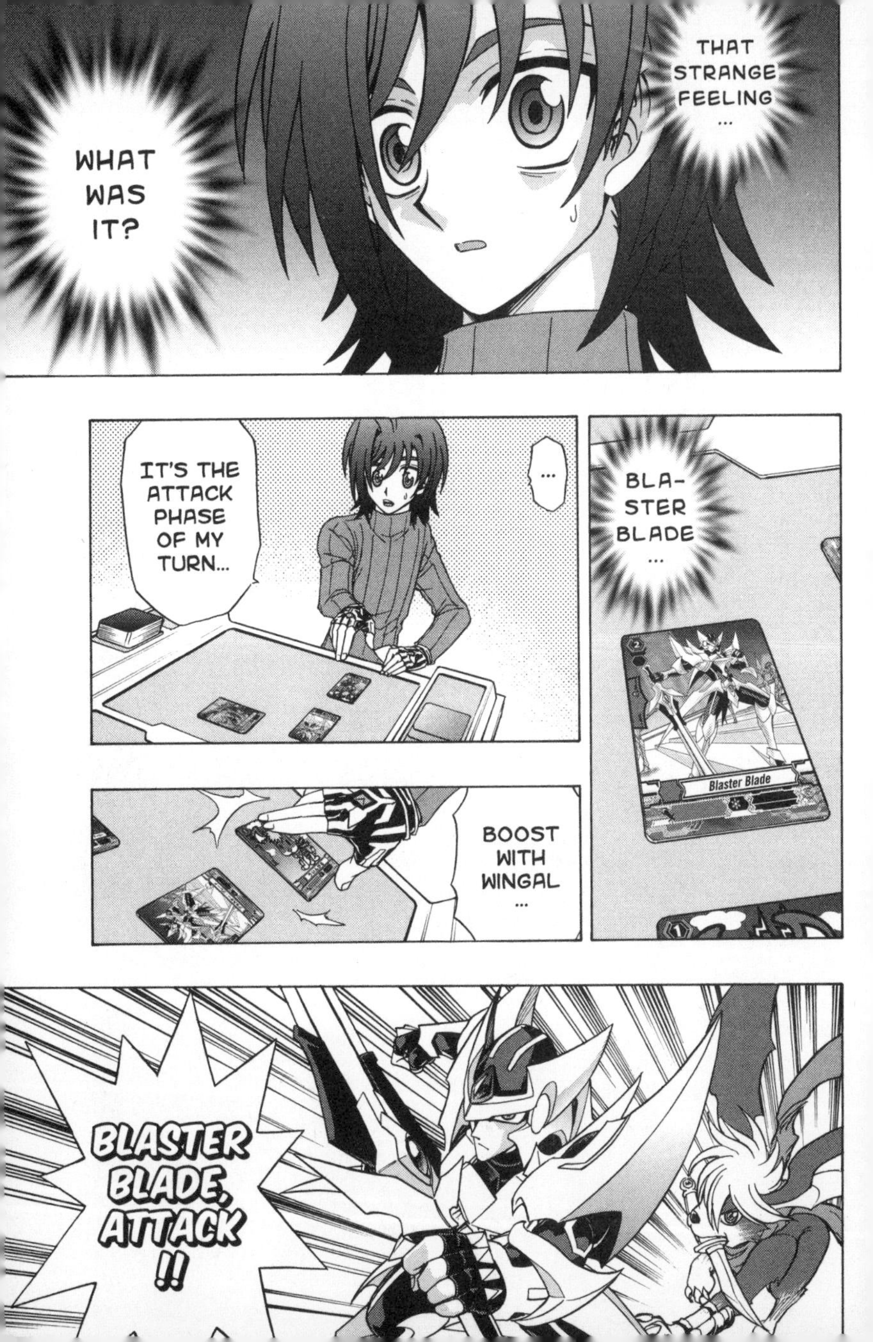
THAT STRANGE FEELING ...
WHAT WAS IT?
BLA- STER BLADE ...
Blaster Blade
...
IT'S THE ATTACK PHASE OF MY TURN...
BOOST WITH WINGAL ...
BLASTER BLADE, ATTACK !!

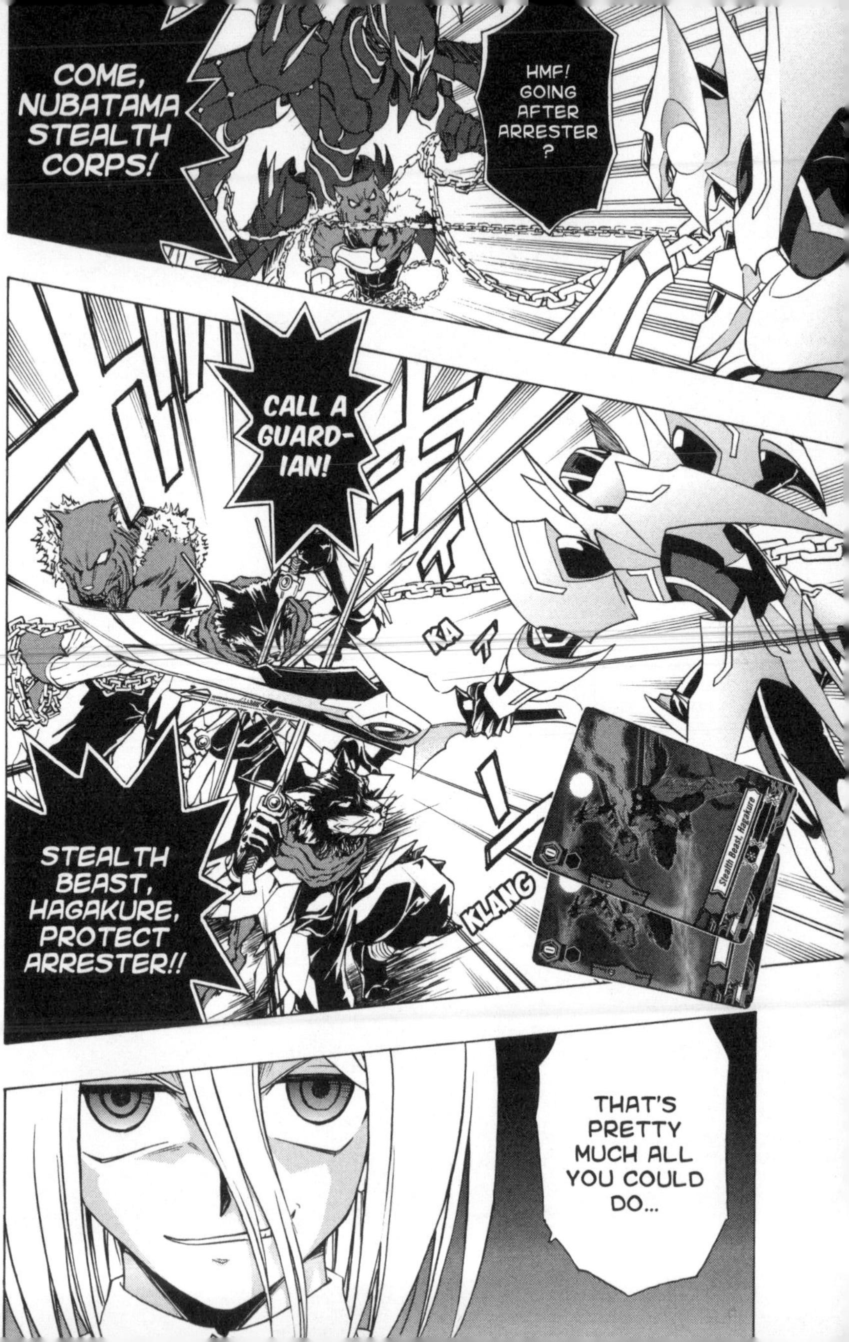
HMF! GOING AFTER ARRESTER?
COME, NUBATAMA STEALTH CORPS!
CALL A GUARDIAN!
KA
KLANG
Stealth Beast, Hagakure
STEALTH BEAST, HAGAKURE, PROTECT ARRESTER!!
THAT'S PRETTY MUCH ALL YOU COULD DO...

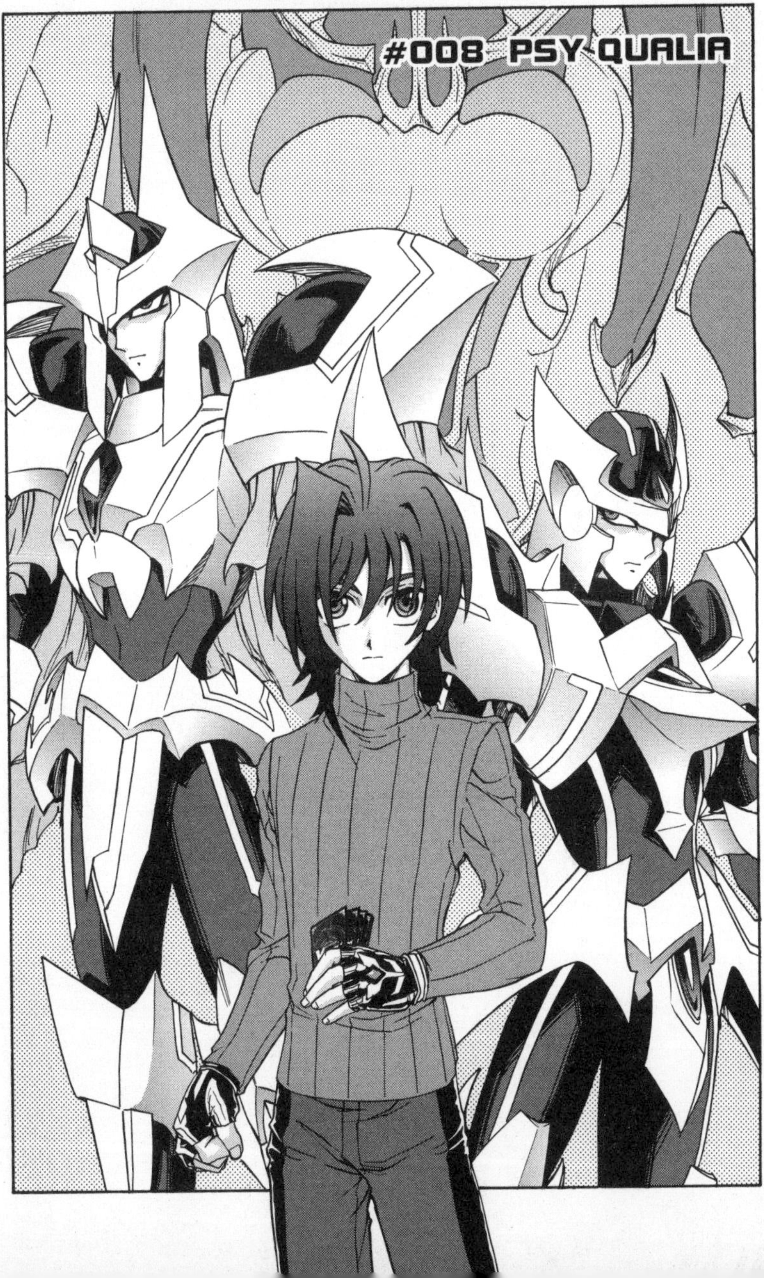
#008 PSY QUALIA

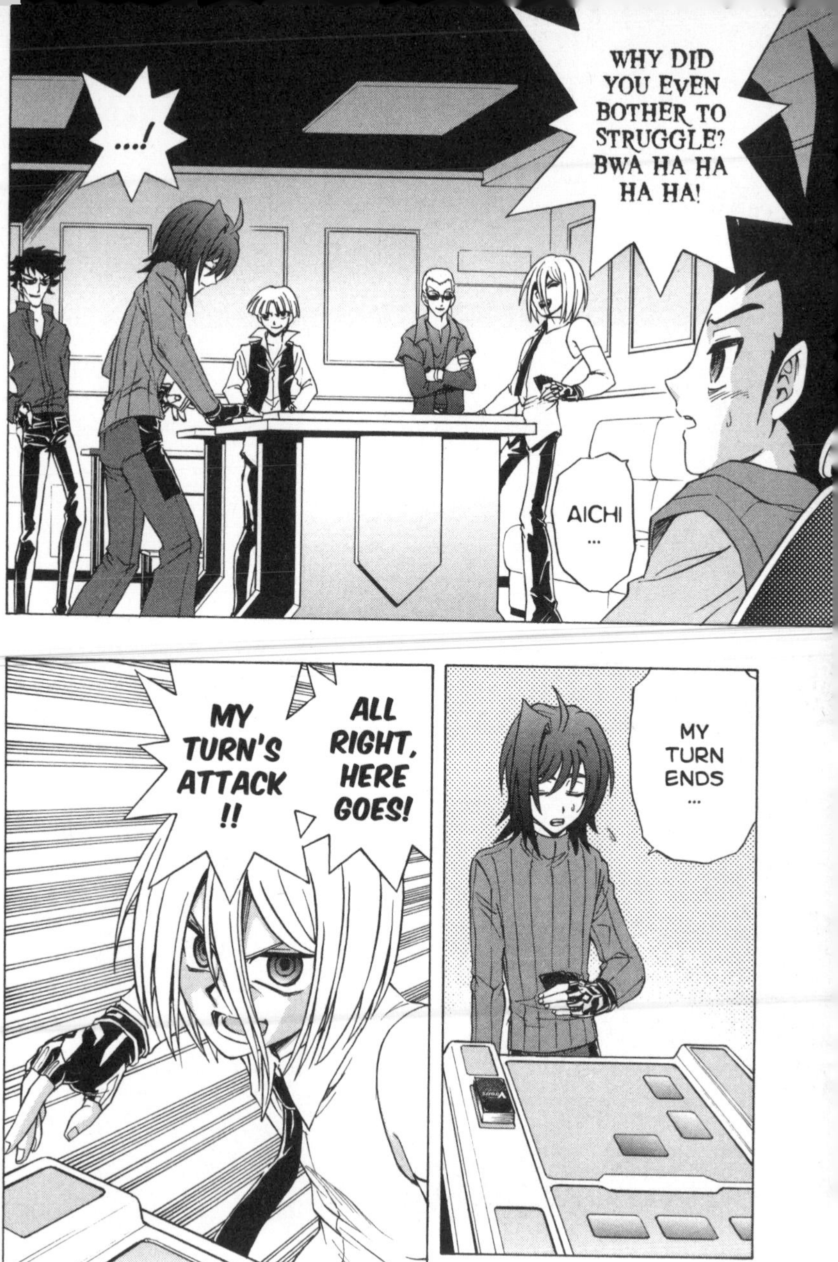
WHY DID YOU EVEN BOTHER TO STRUGGLE? BWA HA HA HA HA!
...!
AICHI ...
MY TURN ENDS ...
ALL RIGHT, HERE GOES!
MY TURN'S ATTACK !!

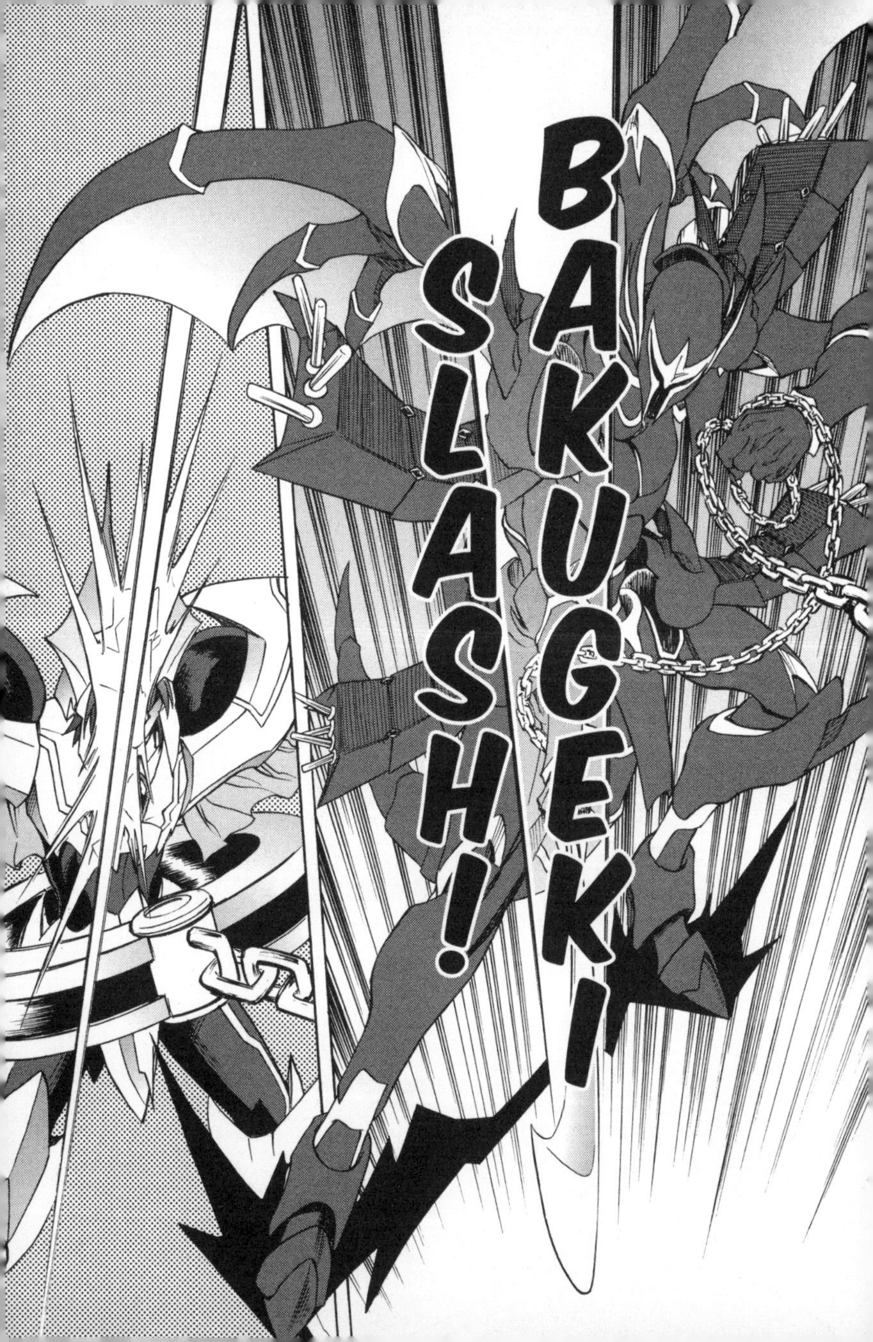
BAKUGEKI
SLASH!

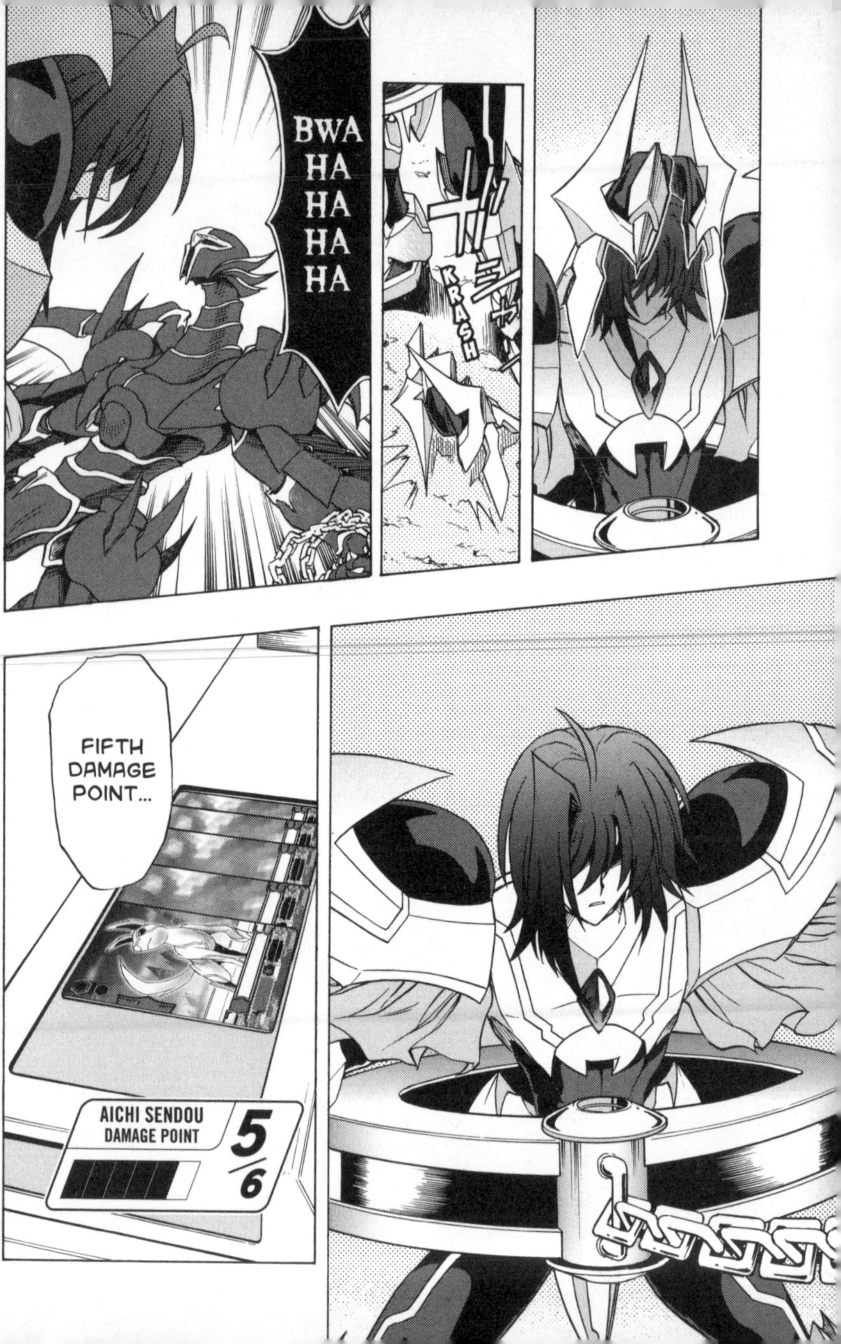
KRASH
BWA HA HA HA HA
FIFTH DAMAGE POINT...
AICHI SENDOU DAMAGE POINT
5/6

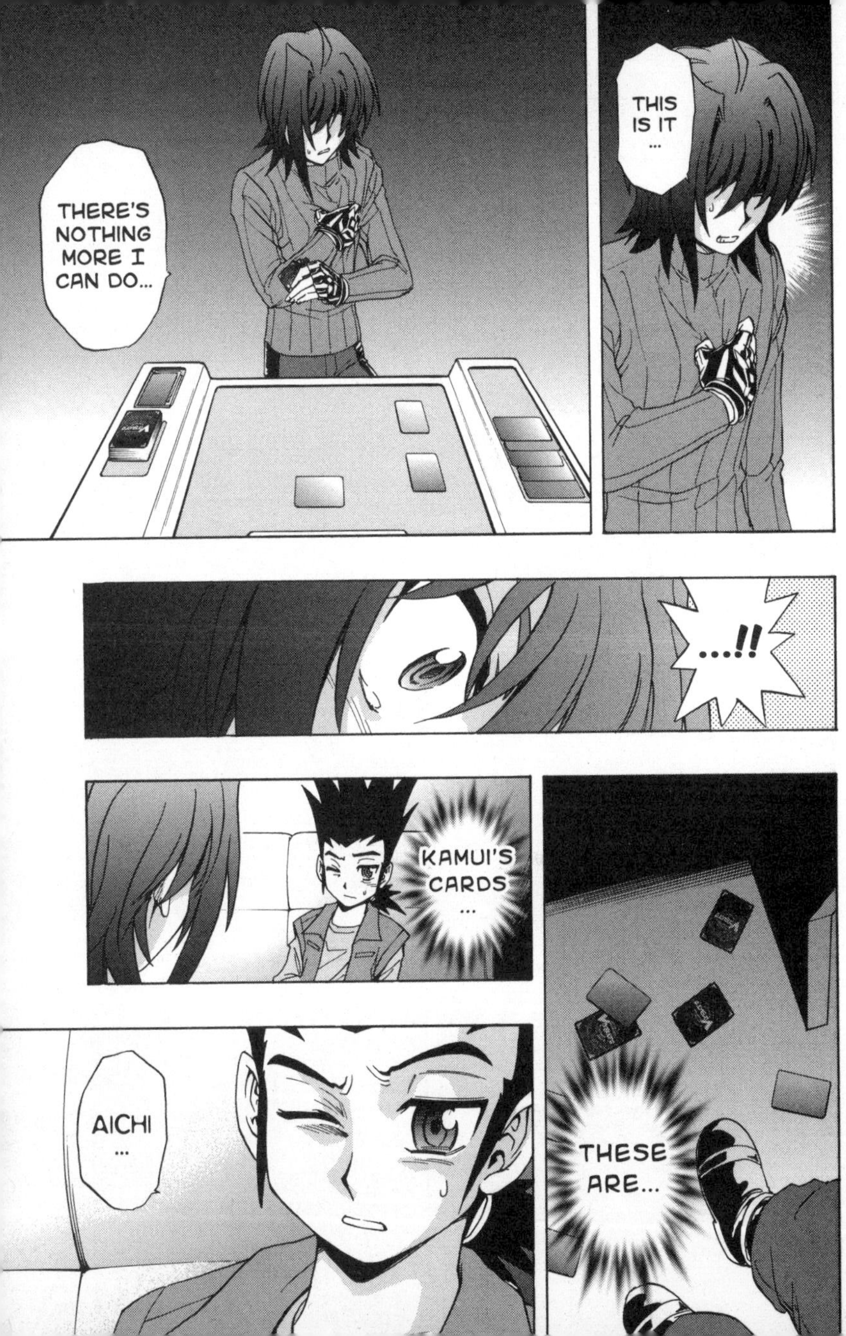
THIS IS IT ...
THERE'S NOTHING MORE I CAN DO...
...!!
THESE ARE...
KAMUI'S CARDS ...
AICHI ...

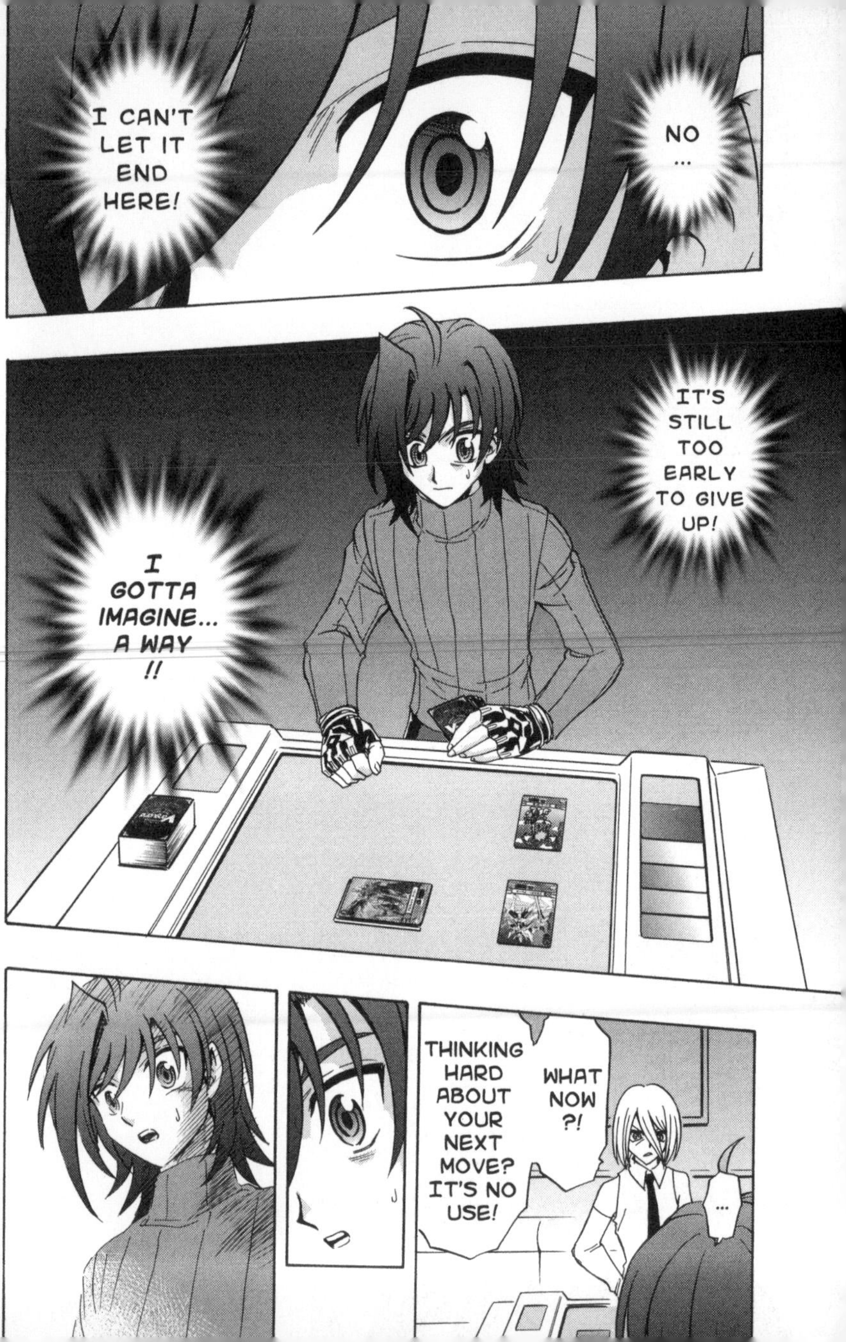
NO ...
I CAN'T LET IT END HERE!
IT'S STILL TOO EARLY TO GIVE UP!
I GOTTA IMAGINE... A WAY !!
WHAT NOW ?!
...
THINKING HARD ABOUT YOUR NEXT MOVE? IT'S NO USE!

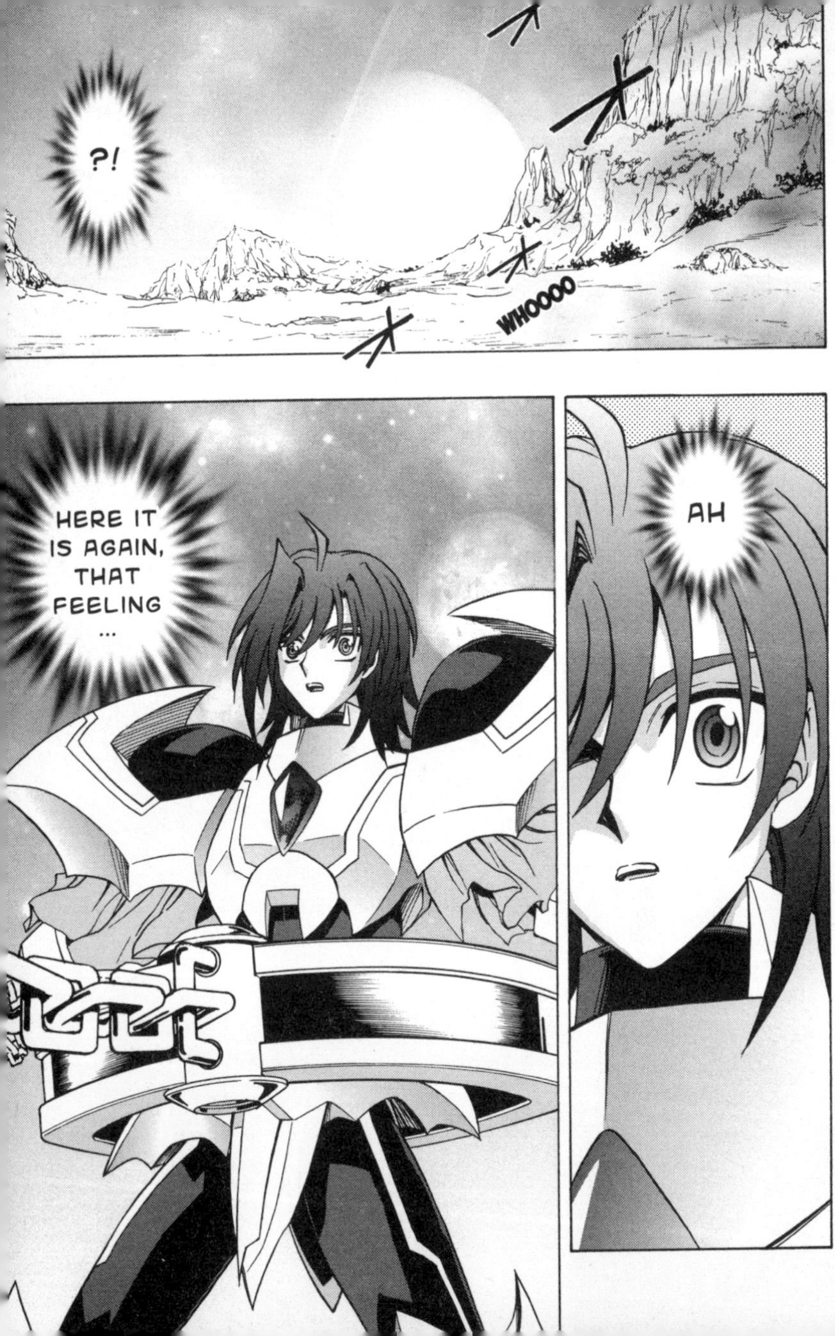
?!
WHOOOO
AH
HERE IT IS AGAIN, THAT FEELING ...

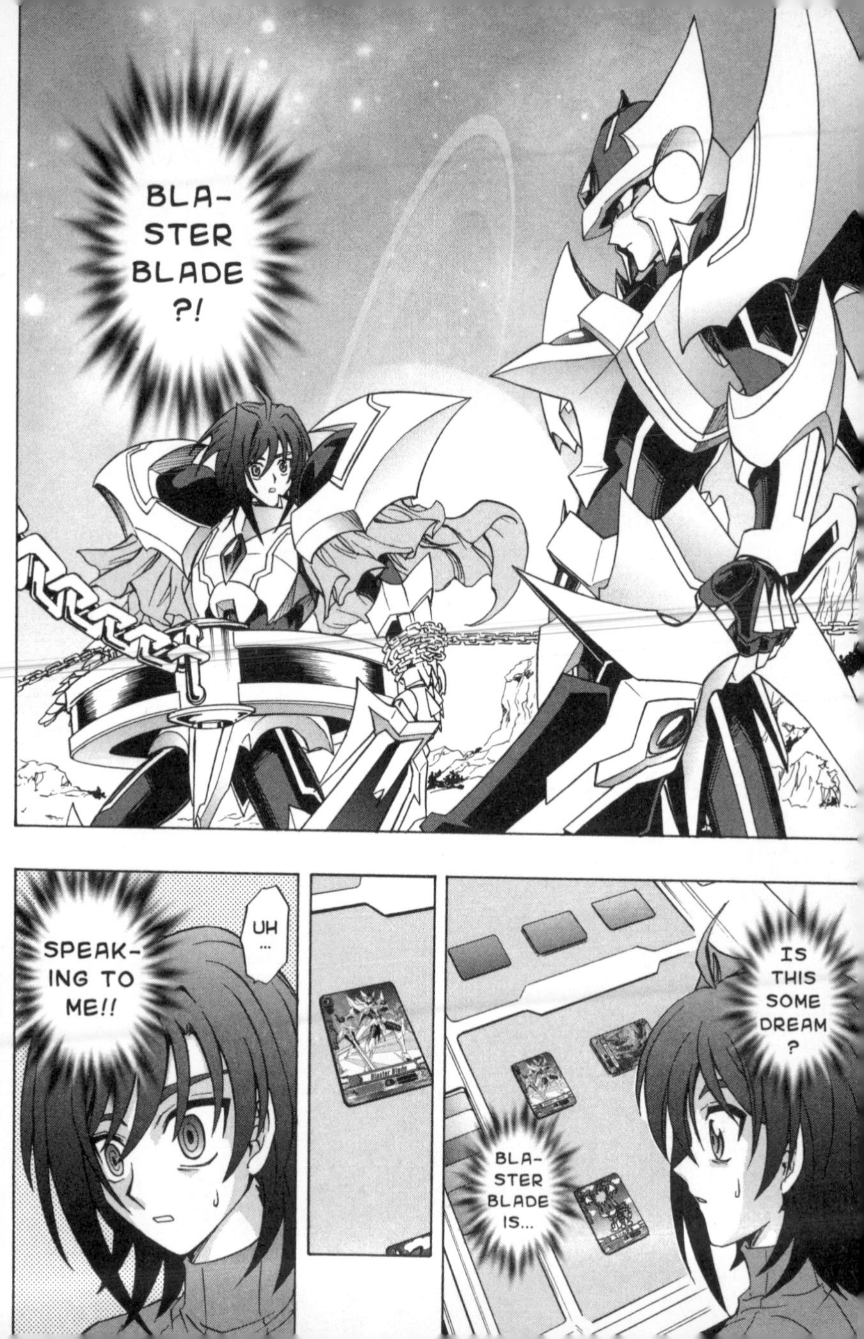
BLA-
STER
BLADE
?!
IS THIS SOME DREAM?
BLA-
STER
BLADE
IS...
UH...
SPEAK-
ING TO
ME!!

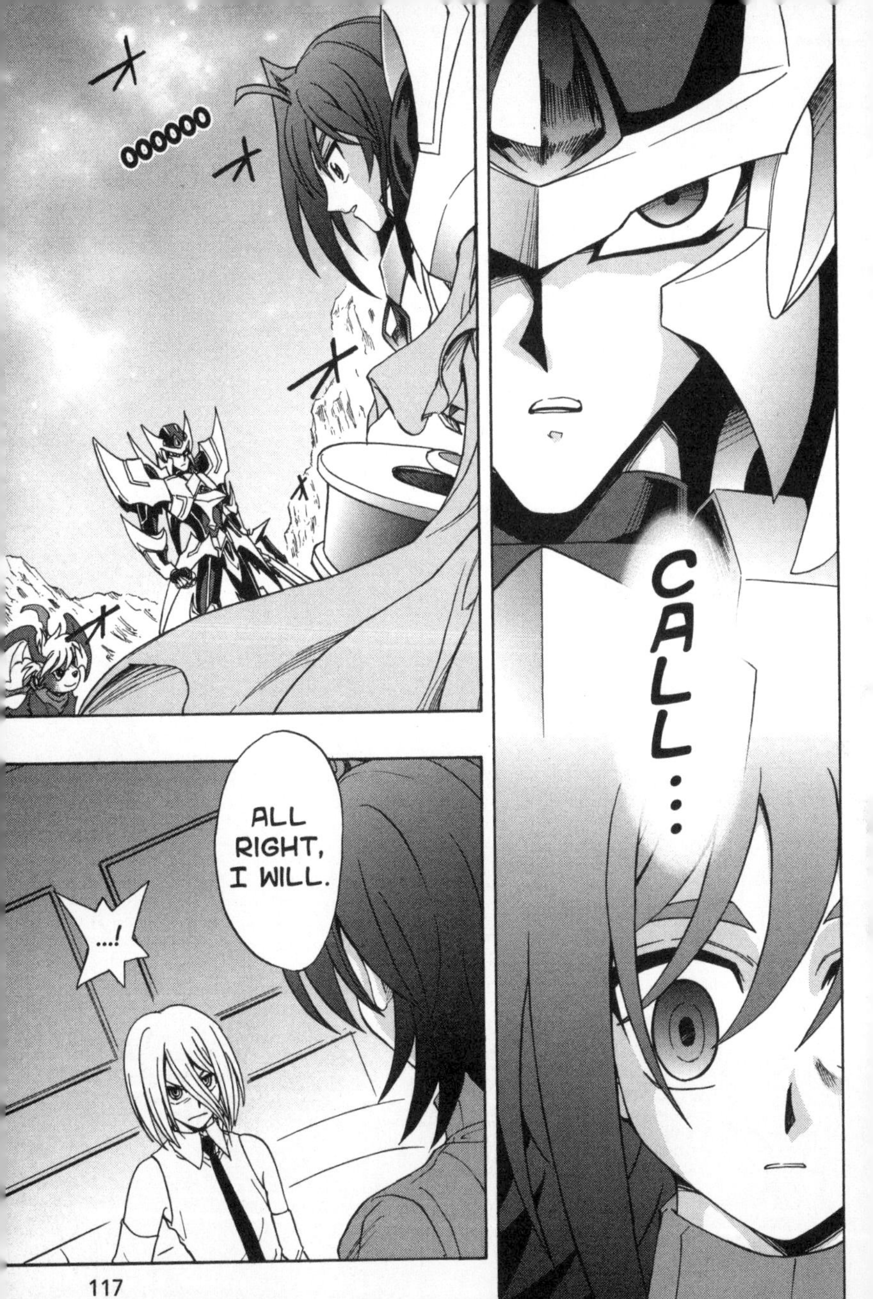
CALL...
OOOOOO
ALL RIGHT, I WILL.
...!

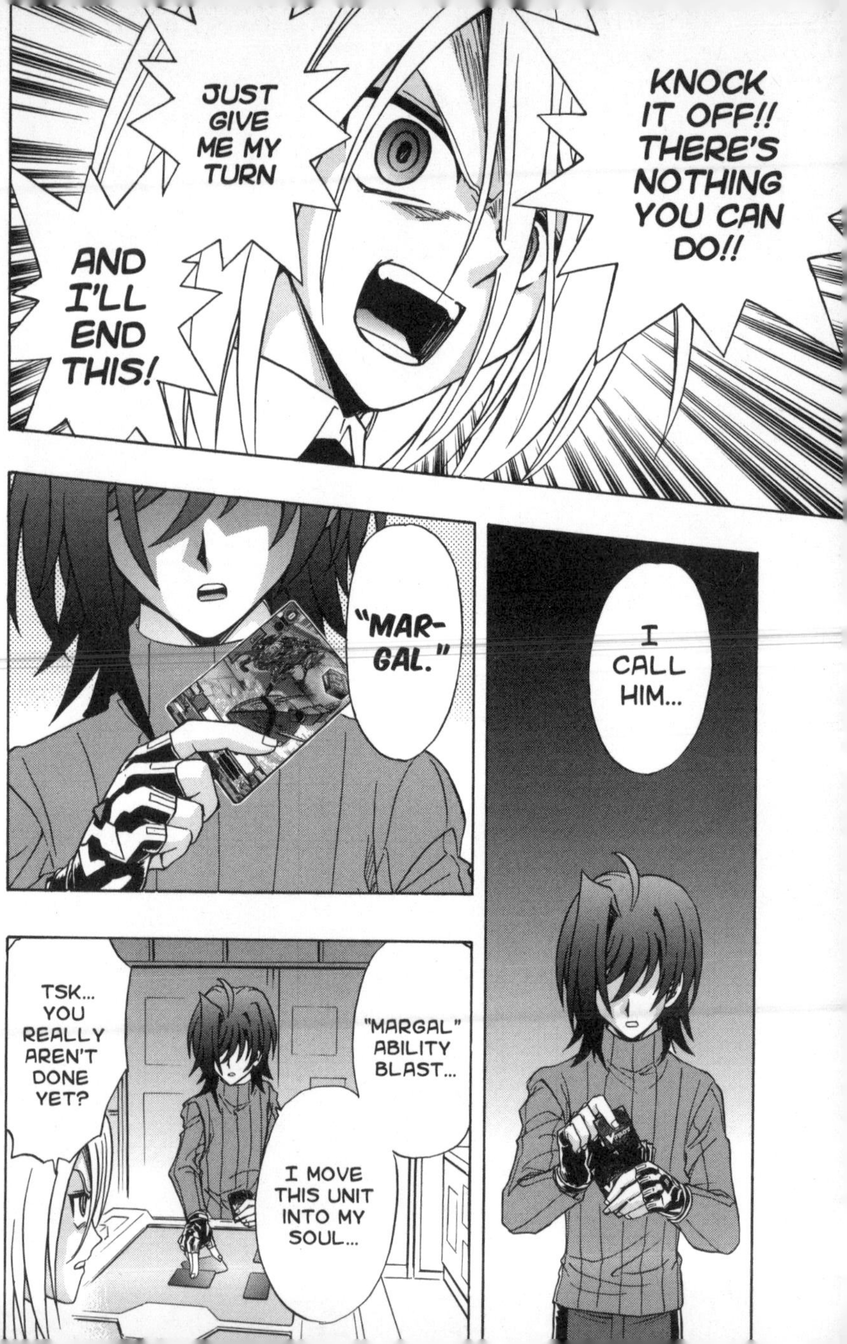
KNOCK IT OFF!! THERE'S NOTHING YOU CAN DO!!
JUST GIVE ME MY TURN
AND I'LL END THIS!
I CALL HIM...
“MAR-GAL.”
"MARGAL" ABILITY BLAST...
I MOVE THIS UNIT INTO MY SOUL...
TSK... YOU REALLY AREN'T DONE YET?

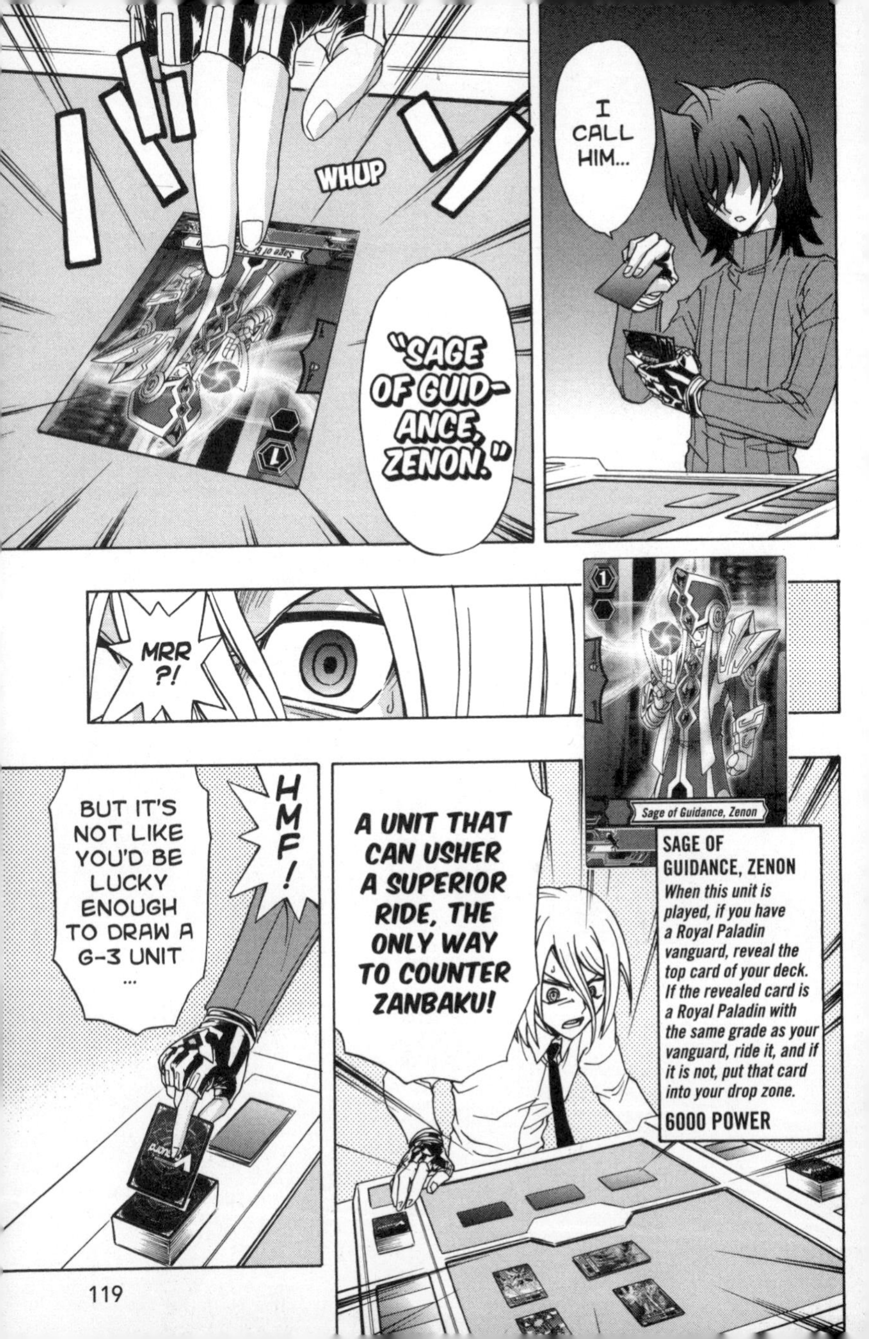

I CALL HIM...
WHUP
"SAGE OF GUIDANCE, ZENON."
Sage of Guidance, Zenon
MRR ?!
A UNIT THAT CAN USHER A SUPERIOR RIDE, THE ONLY WAY TO COUNTER ZANBAKU!
SAGE OF GUIDANCE, ZENON
When this unit is played, if you have a Royal Paladin vanguard, reveal the top card of your deck. If the revealed card is a Royal Paladin with the same grade as your vanguard, ride it, and if it is not, put that card into your drop zone.
6000 POWER
HMF!
BUT IT'S NOT LIKE YOU'D BE LUCKY ENOUGH TO DRAW A G-3 UNIT ...

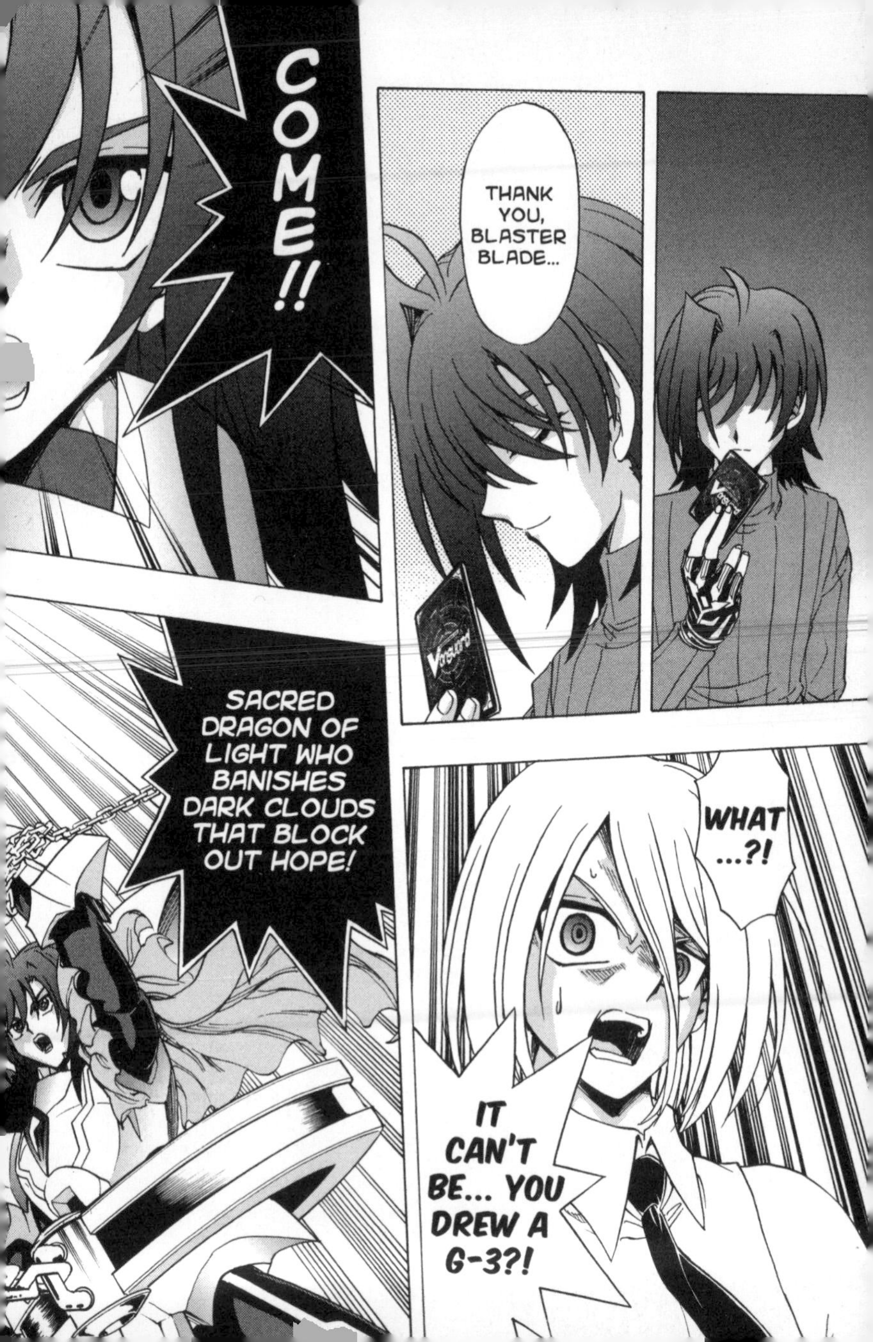
THANK YOU, BLASTER BLADE...
COME!!
WHAT ...?!
IT CAN'T BE... YOU DREW A G-3?!
SACRED DRAGON OF LIGHT WHO BANISHES DARK CLOUDS THAT BLOCK OUT HOPE!

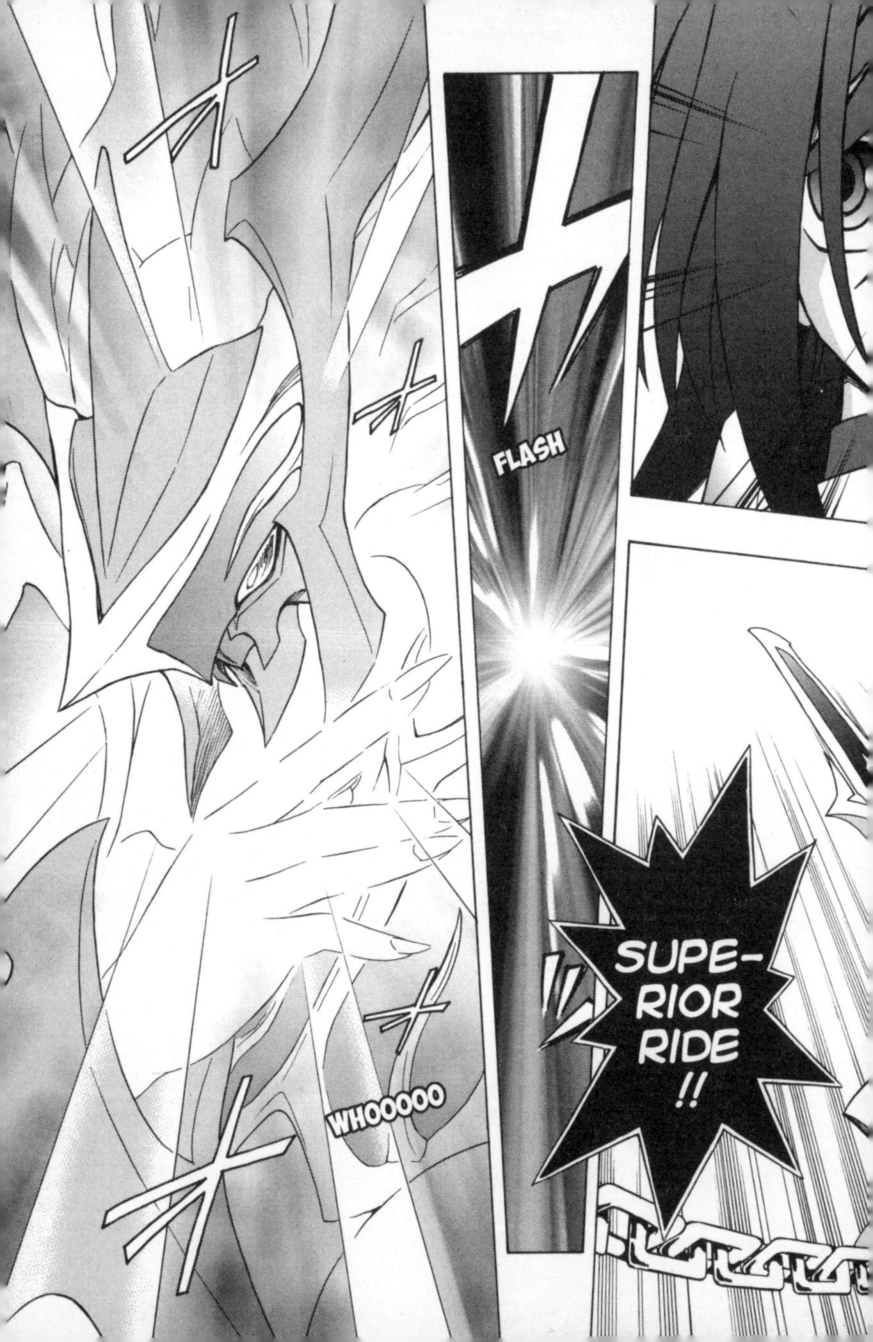
SUPE-RIOR RIDE !!
FLASH
WHOOOOO

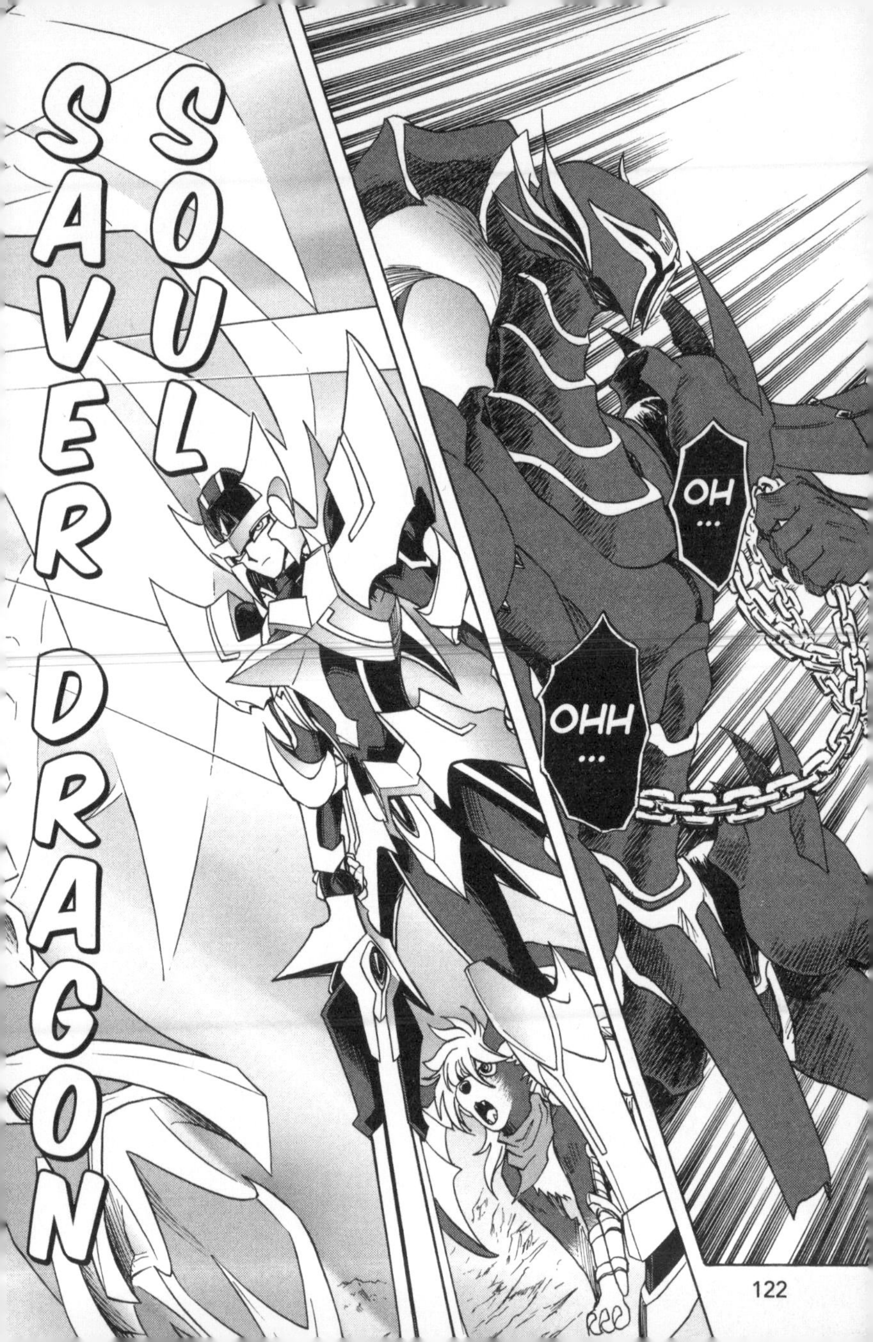
SOUL
SAVER DRAGON
OH ...
OHH ...

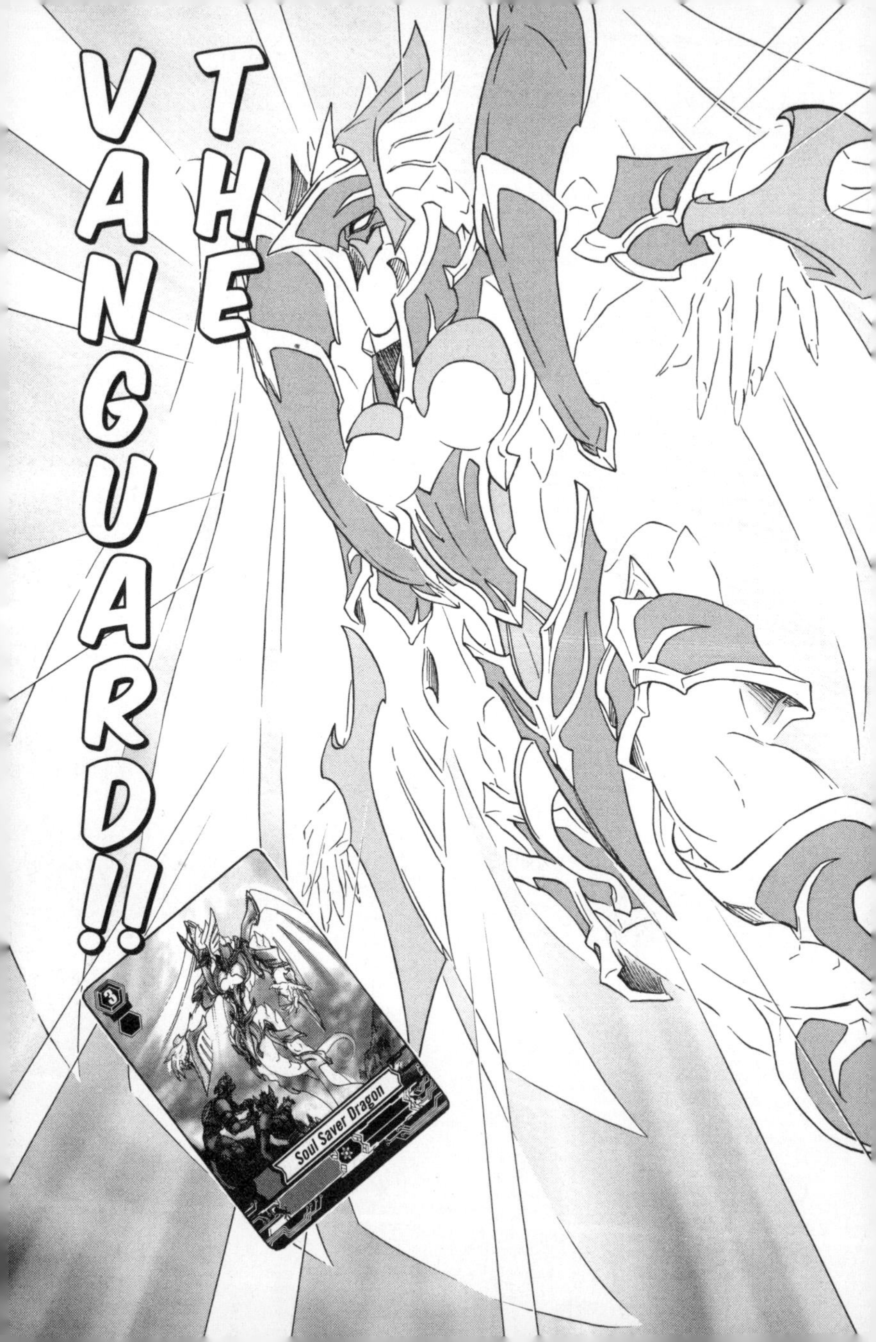
THE VANGUARD!!
Soul Saver Dragon

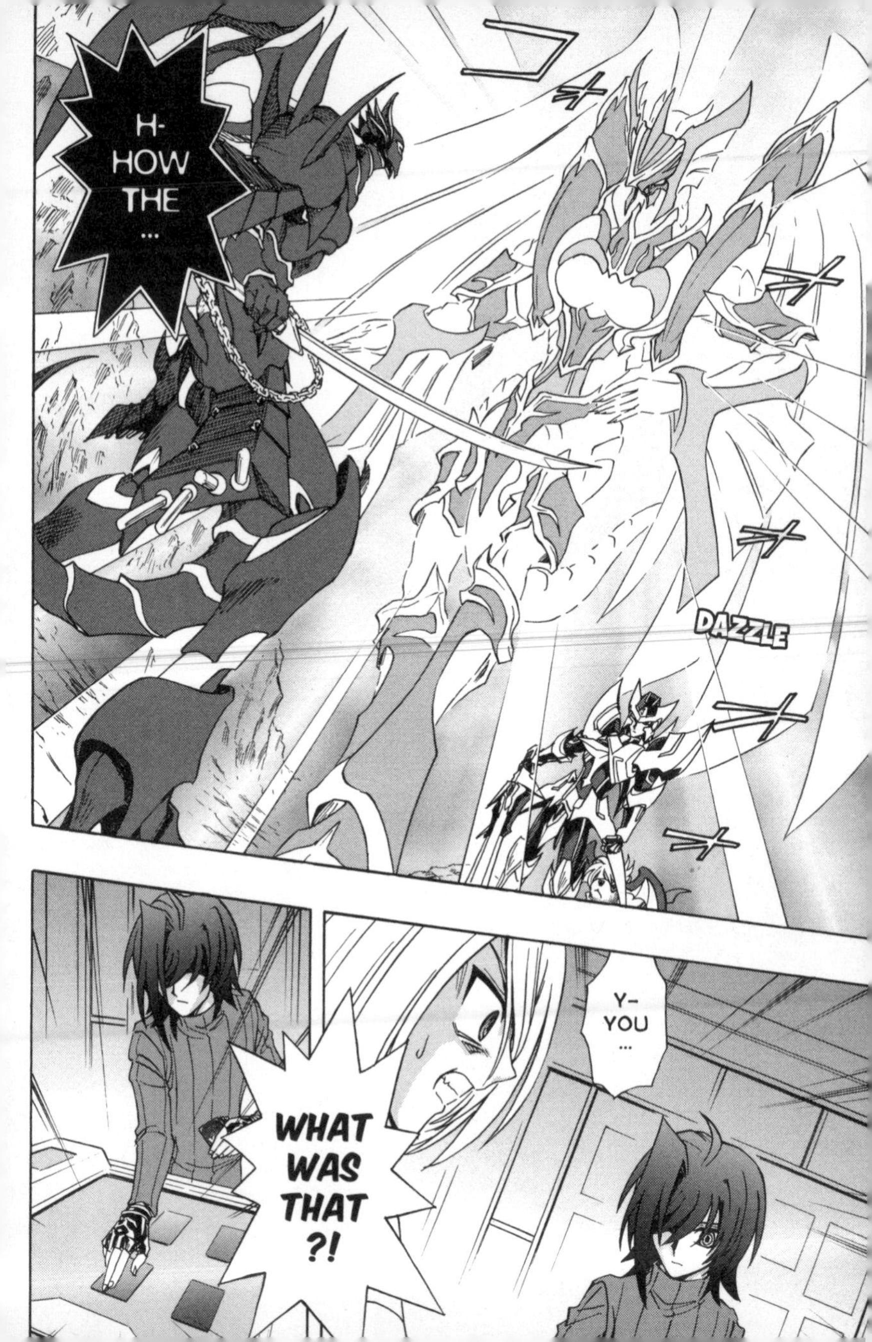
H-HOW THE ...
DAZZLE
Y-YOU ...
WHAT WAS THAT?!

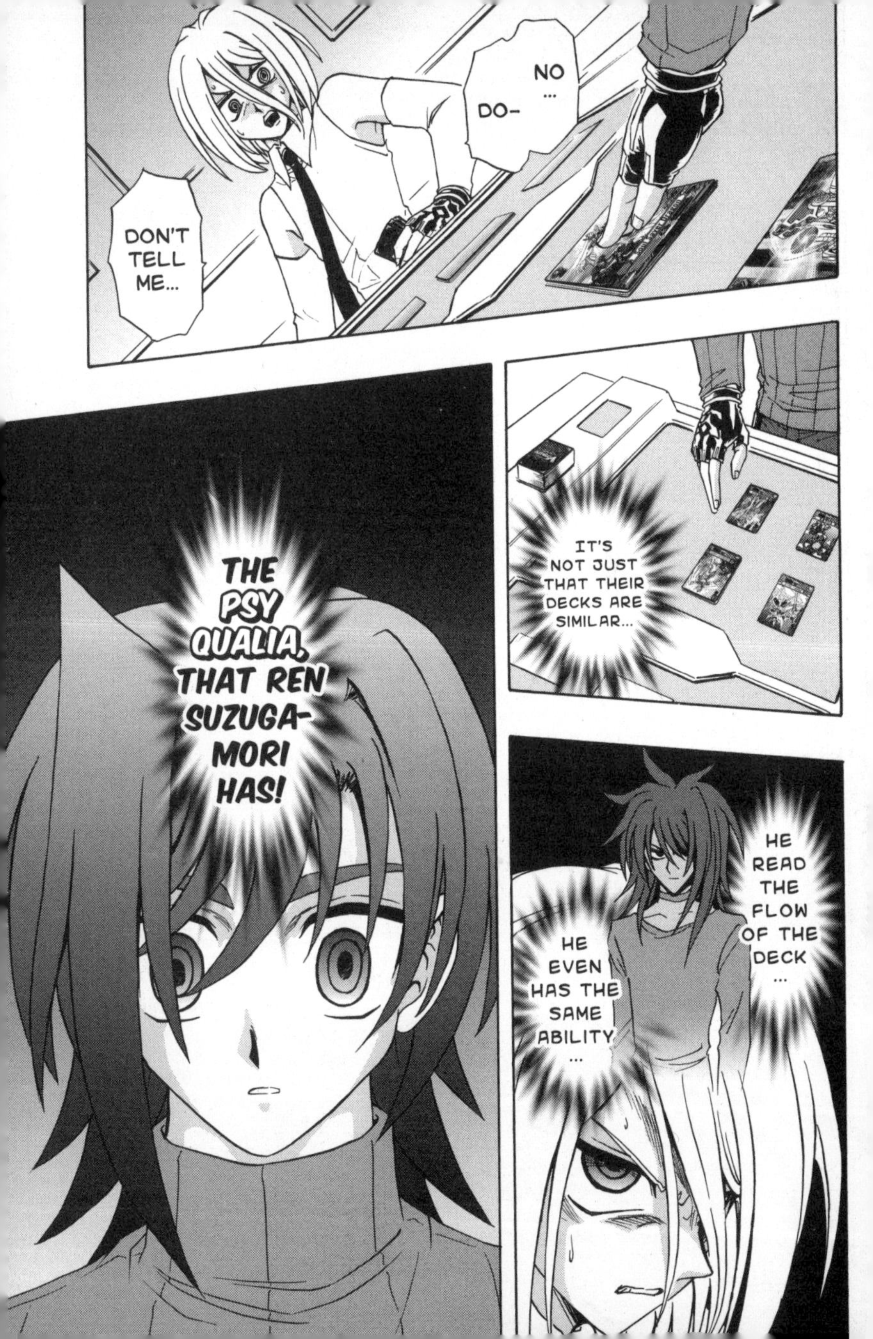
NO ...
DO-
DON'T TELL ME...
IT'S NOT JUST THAT THEIR DECKS ARE SIMILAR...
HE READ THE FLOW OF THE DECK ...
HE EVEN HAS THE SAME ABILITY ...
THE PSY QUALIA, THAT REN SUZUGA-MORI HAS!

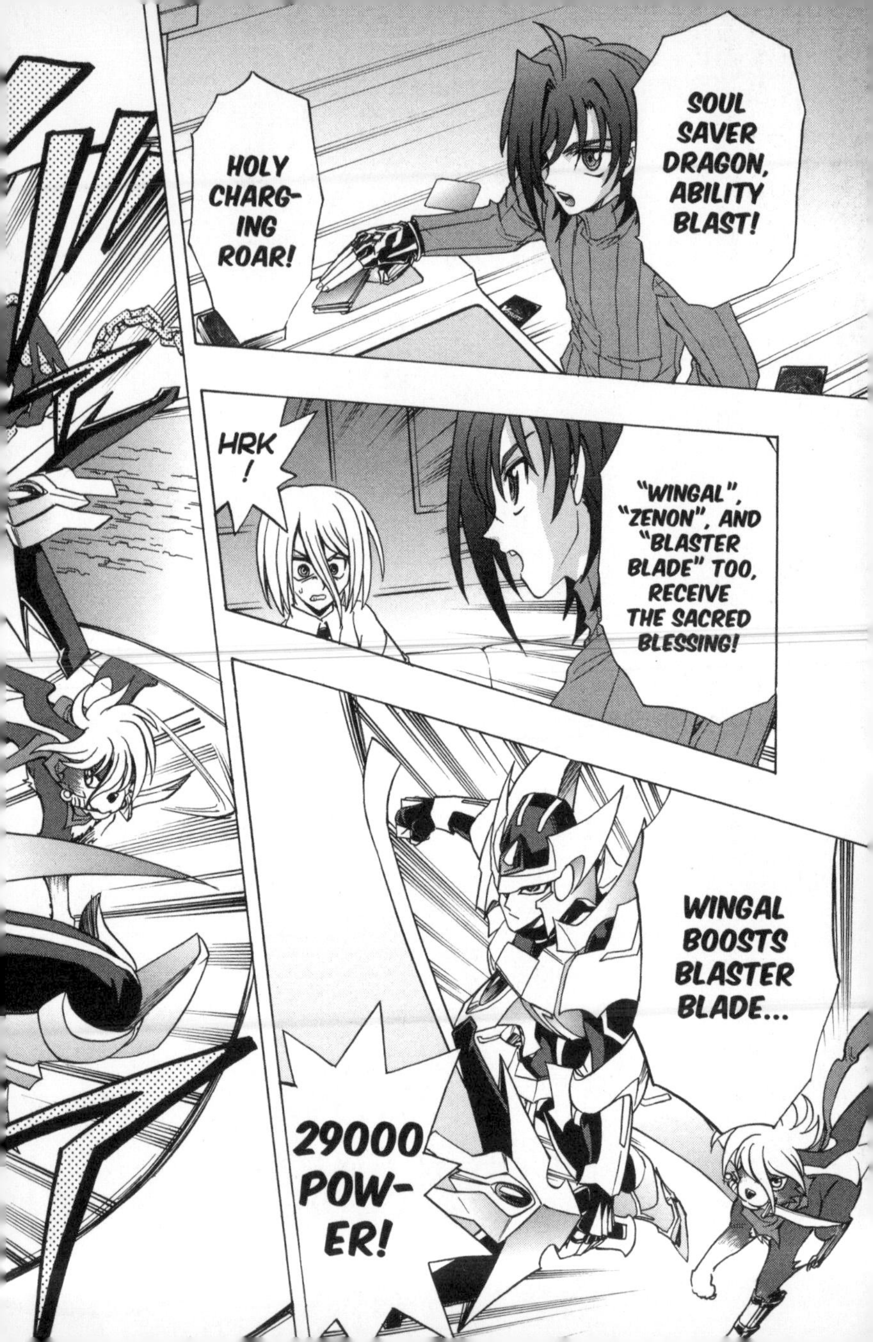
SOUL SAVER DRAGON, ABILITY BLAST!
HOLY CHARG-ING ROAR!
"WINGAL", "ZENON", AND "BLASTER BLADE" TOO, RECEIVE THE SACRED BLESSING!
HRK!
WINGAL BOOSTS BLASTER BLADE...
29000 POW-ER!

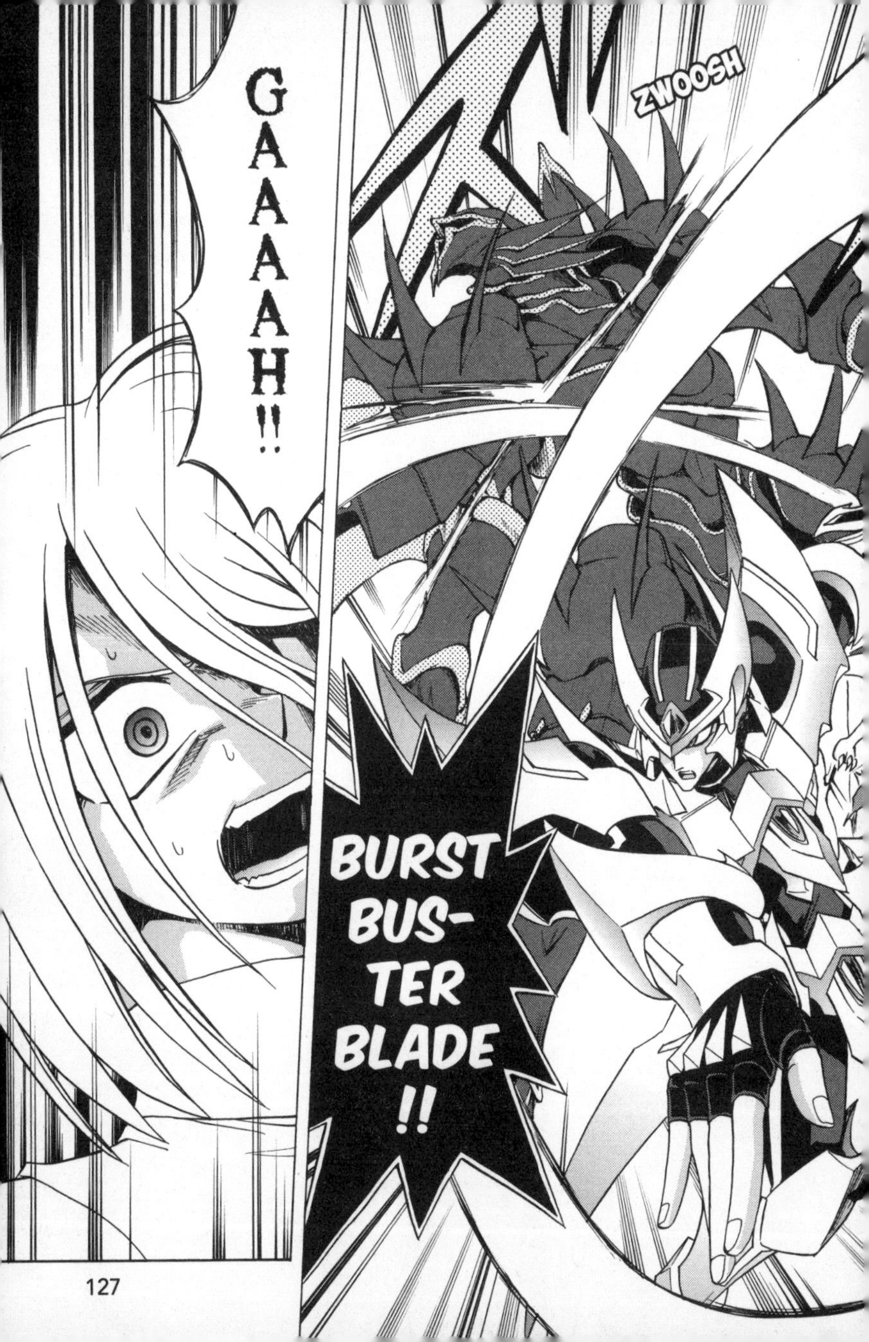
ZWOOSH
BURST BUS-TER BLADE!!
GAAAAH!!

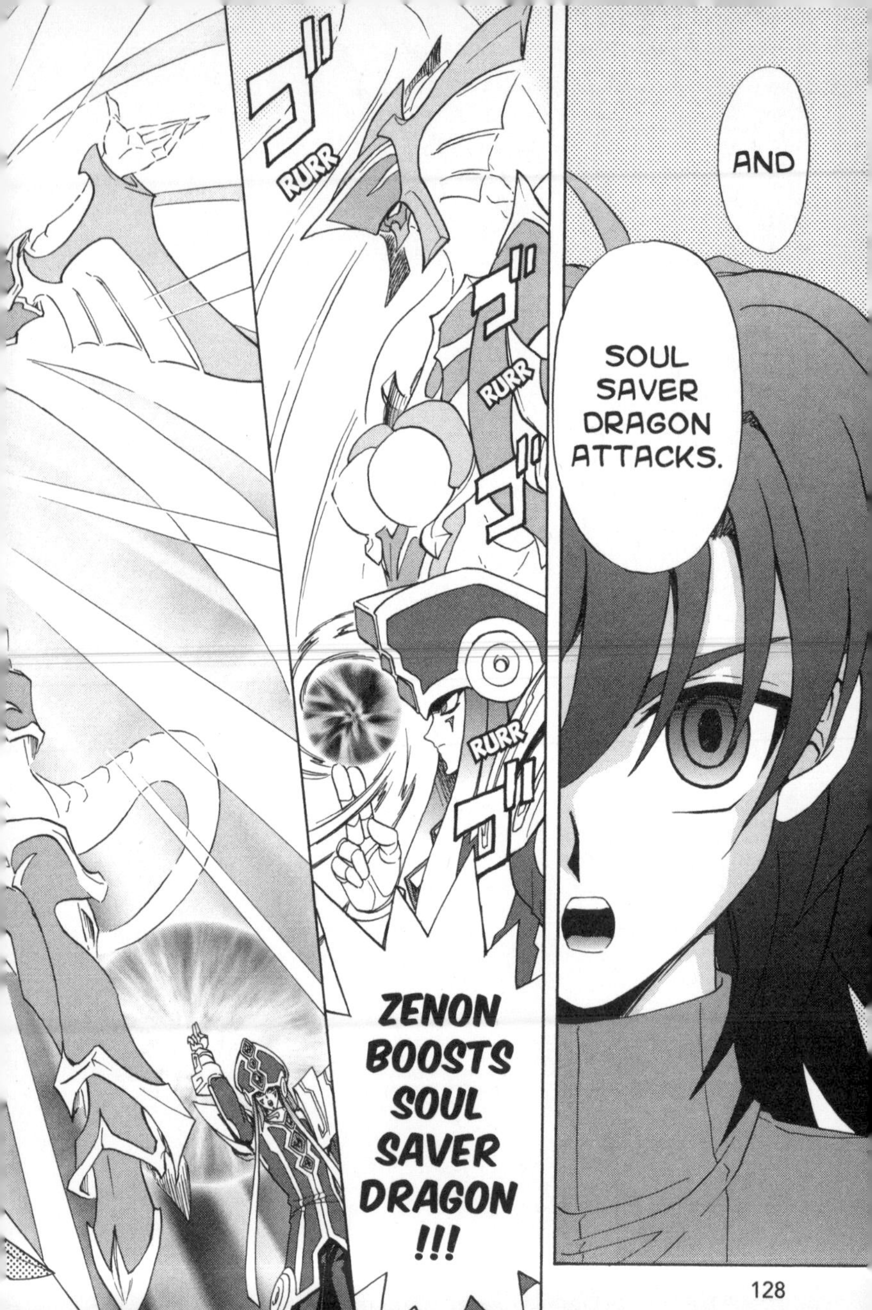
AND
SOUL SAVER DRAGON ATTACKS.
ゴ
RURR
ゴ
RURR
ゴ
RURR
ゴ
ZENON BOOSTS SOUL SAVER DRAGON !!!

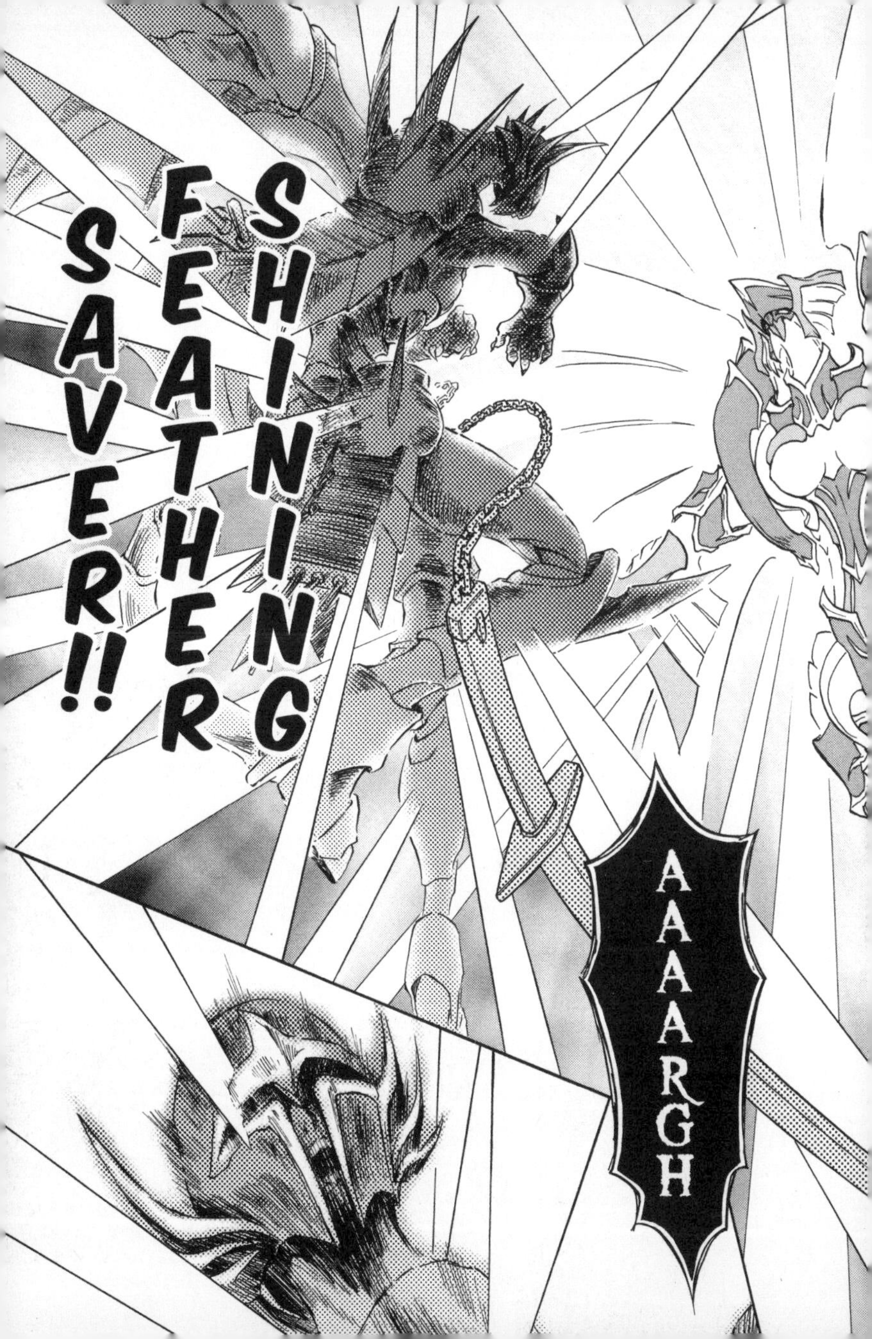
SHINING FEATHER SAVER!!
AAAARGH

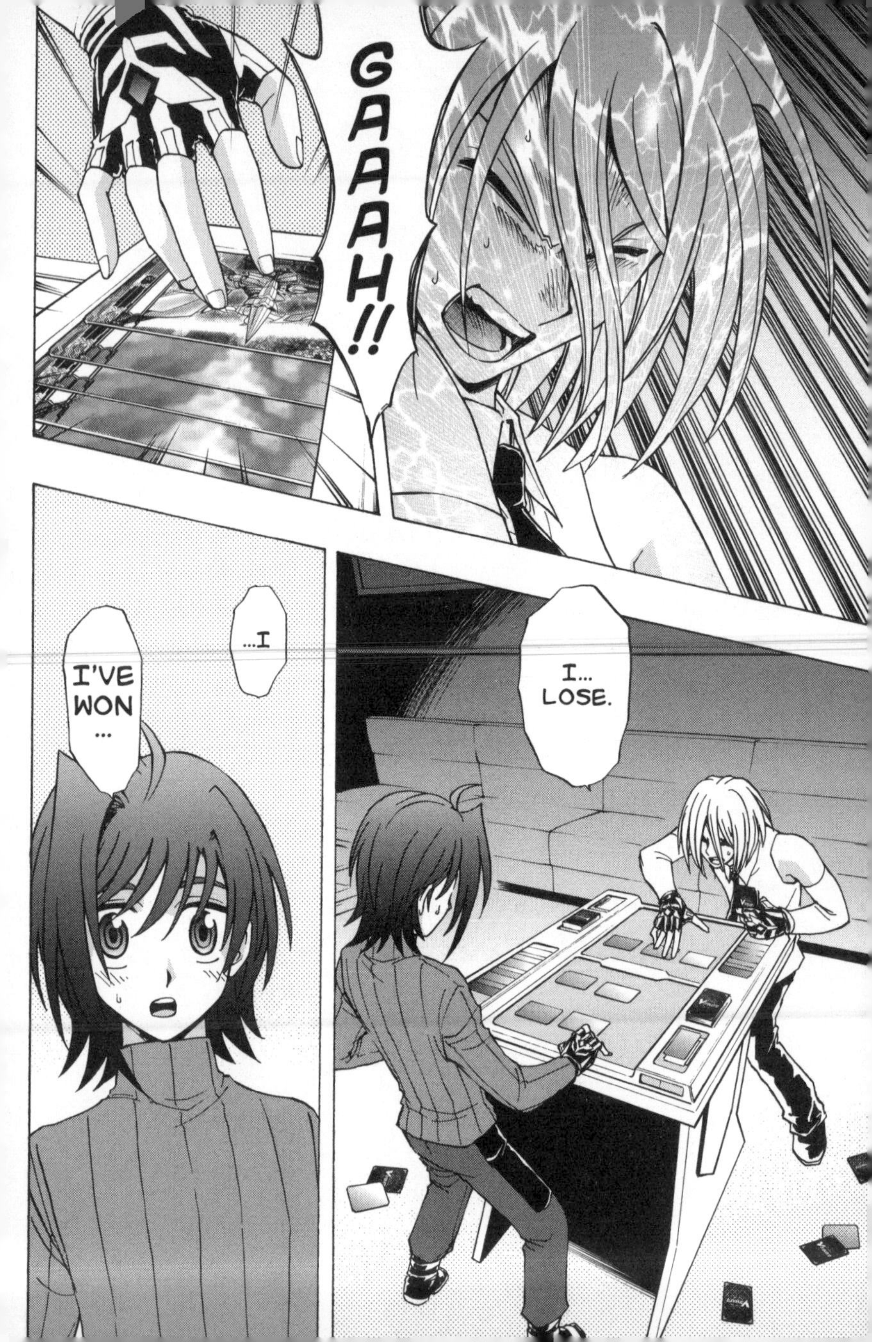
GAAAAH!!
I... LOSE.
...I
I'VE WON ...

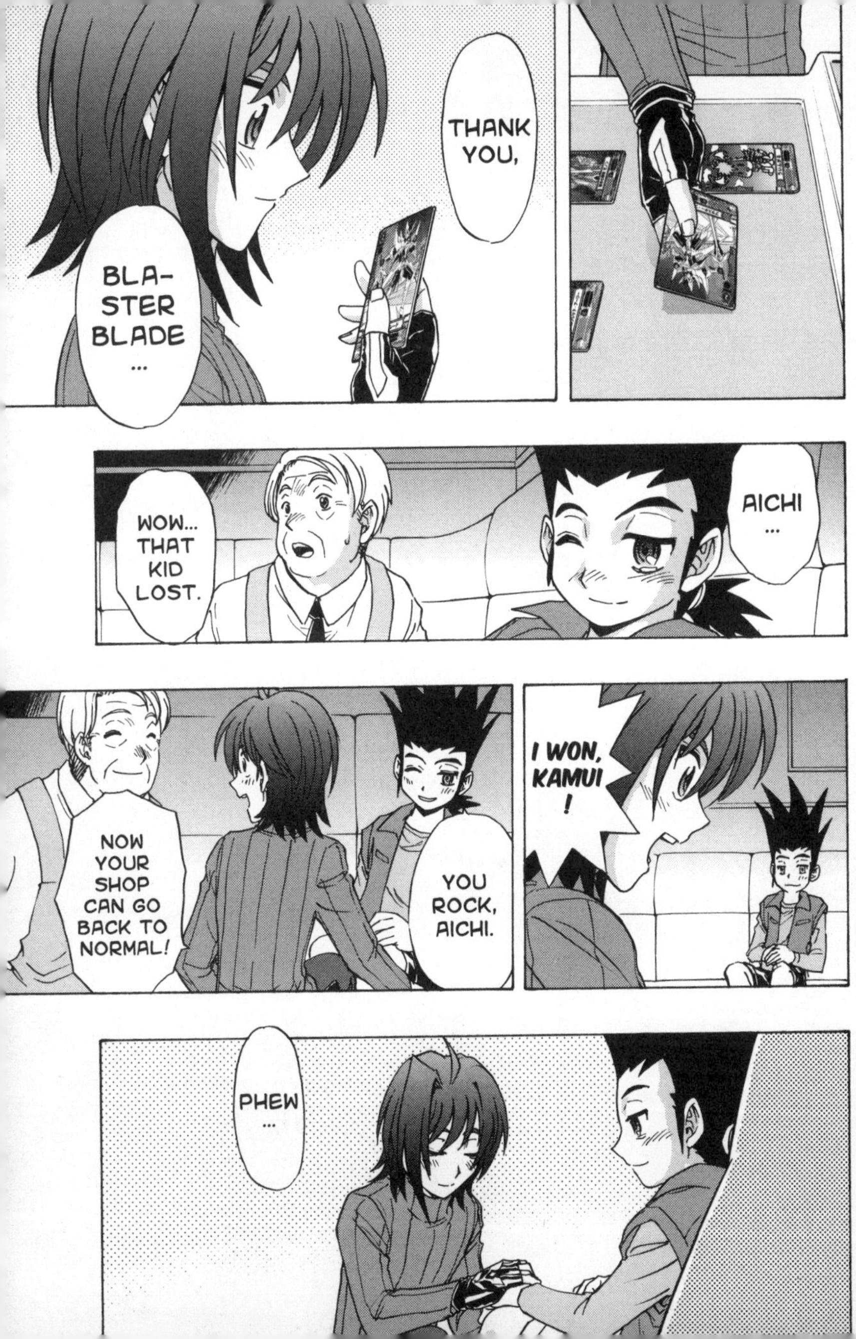
THANK YOU,
BLA-STER BLADE ...
AICHI ...
WOW... THAT KID LOST.
I WON, KAMUI!
YOU ROCK, AICHI.
NOW YOUR SHOP CAN GO BACK TO NORMAL!
PHEW ...

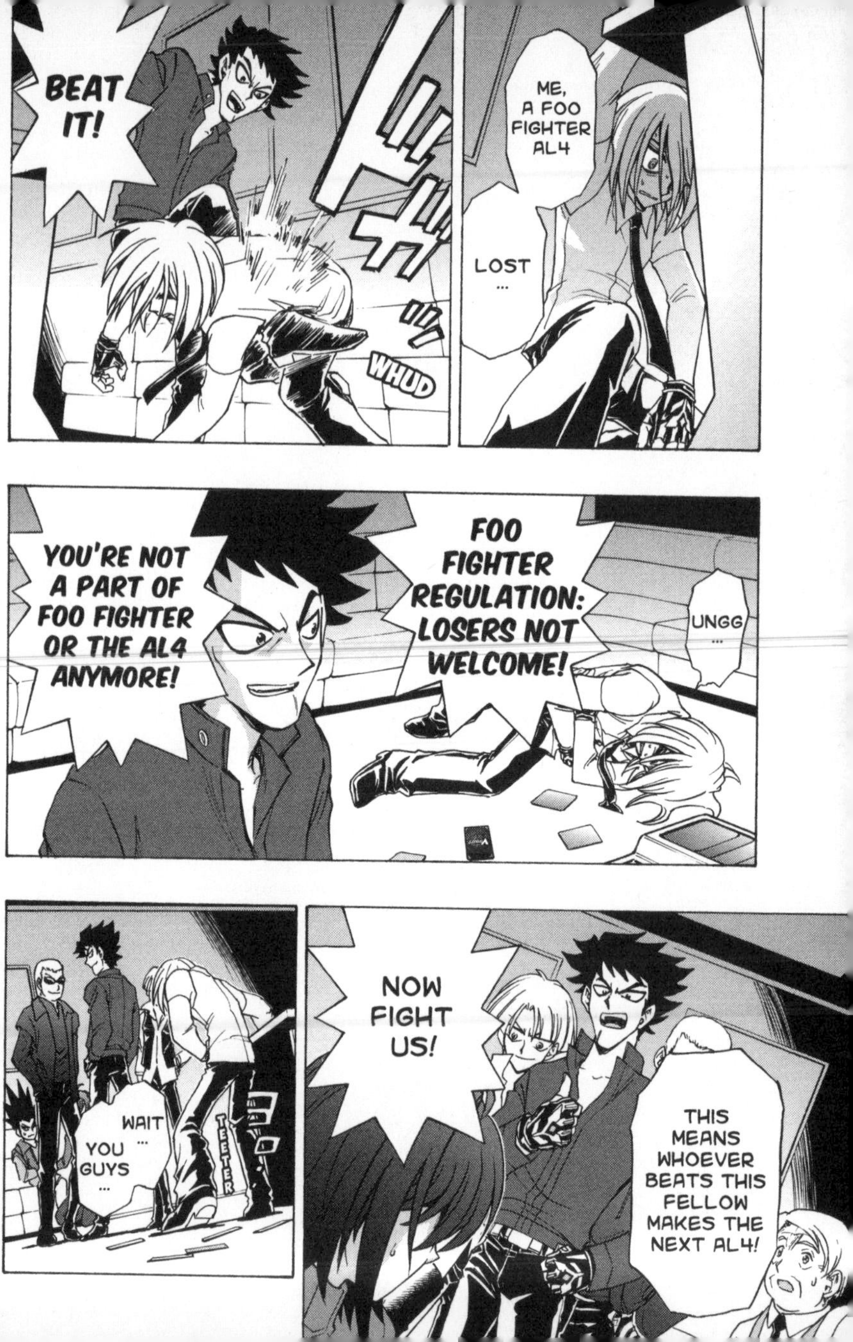
ME, A FOO FIGHTER AL4
LOST ...
BEAT IT!
WHUD
FOO FIGHTER REGULATION: LOSERS NOT WELCOME!
UNGG ...
YOU'RE NOT A PART OF FOO FIGHTER OR THE AL4 ANYMORE!
NOW FIGHT US!
THIS MEANS WHOEVER BEATS THIS FELLOW MAKES THE NEXT AL4!
WAIT ... YOU GUYS ...
TEETER

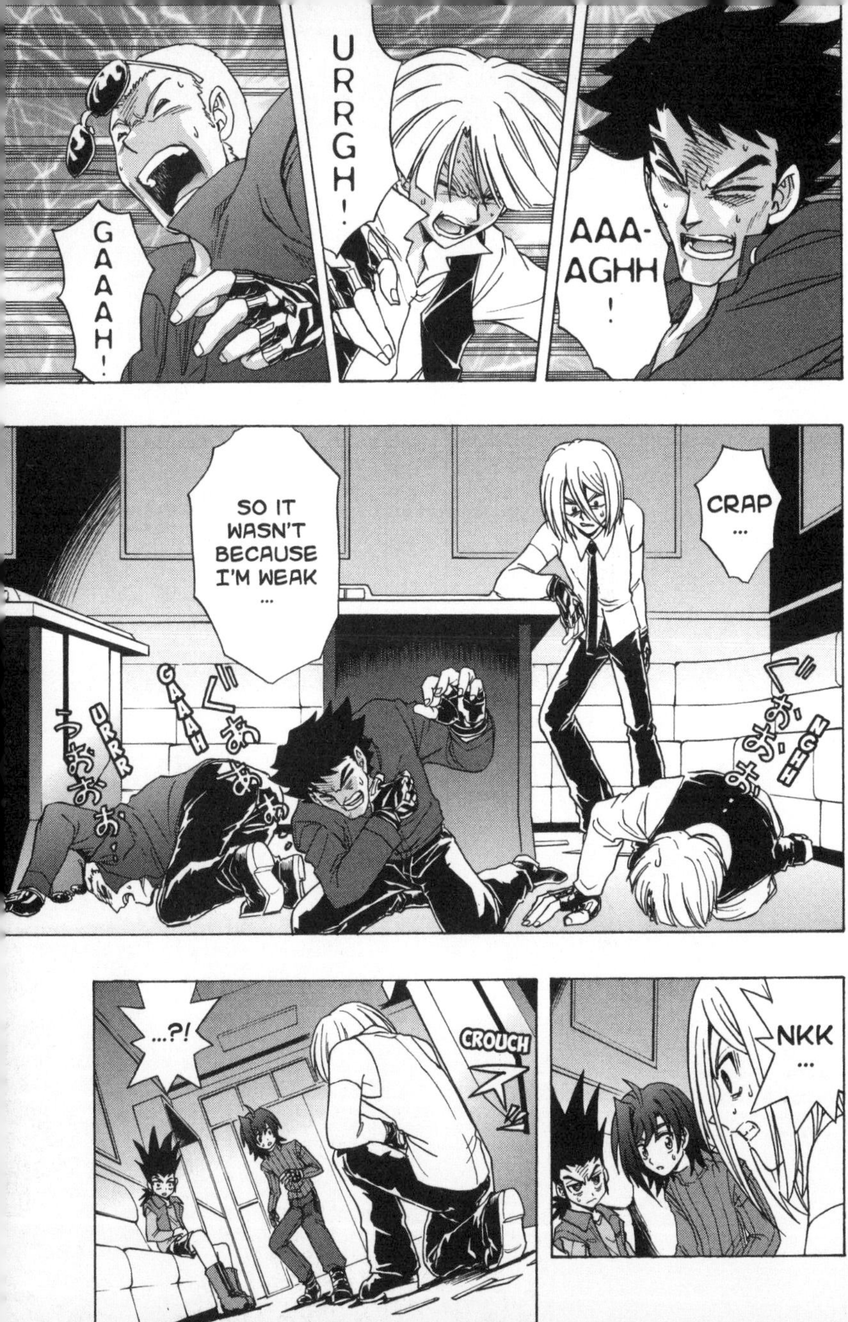

AAA-AGHH!
URRGH!
GAAAAH!
CRAP...
NGHH
SO IT WASN'T BECAUSE I'M WEAK...
GAAAH
URRR
NKK...
CROUCH
...?!

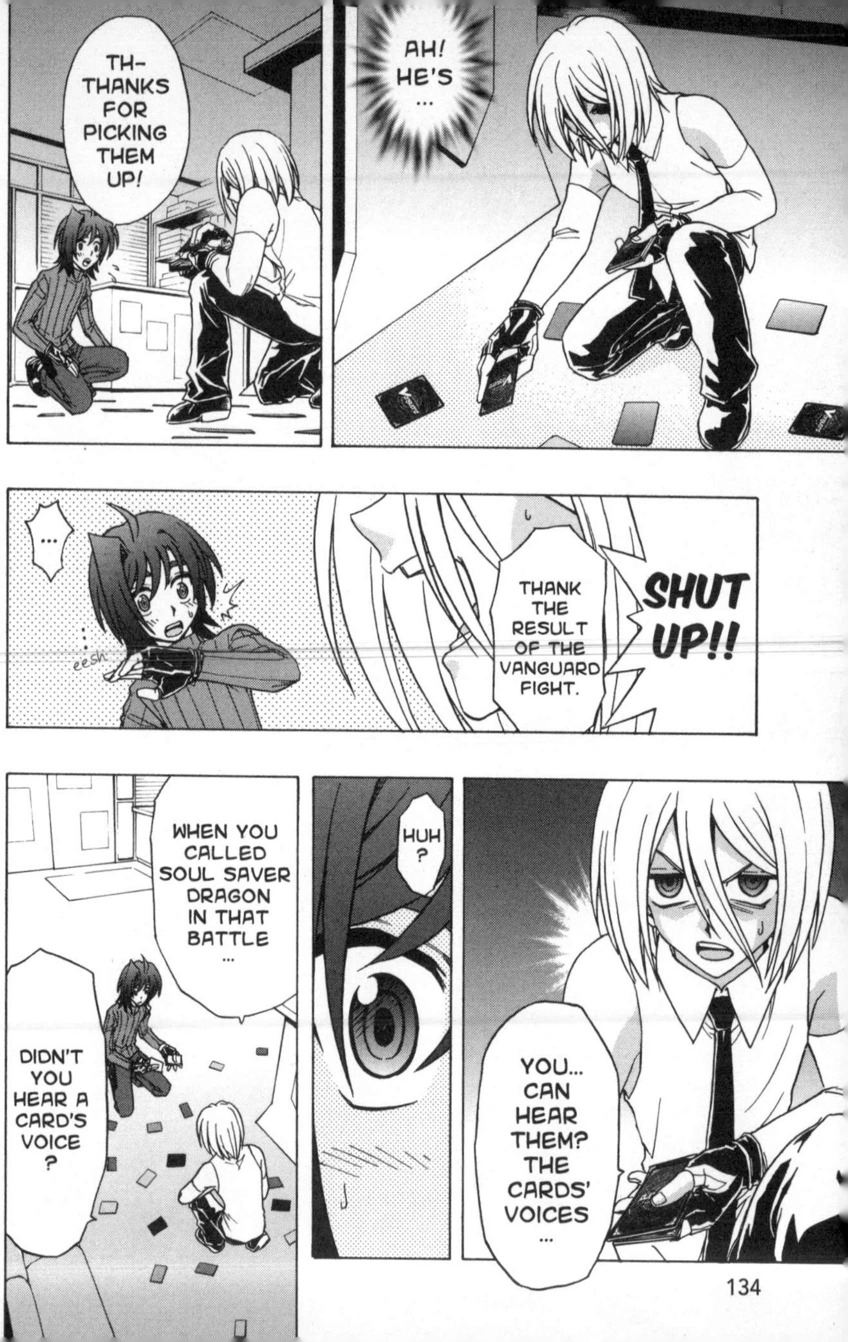
AH! HE'S ...
TH-THANKS FOR PICKING THEM UP!
SHUT UP!!
THANK THE RESULT OF THE VANGUARD FIGHT.
...
eesh
YOU... CAN HEAR THEM? THE CARDS' VOICES ...
HUH ?
WHEN YOU CALLED SOUL SAVER DRAGON IN THAT BATTLE ...
DIDN'T YOU HEAR A CARD'S VOICE ?

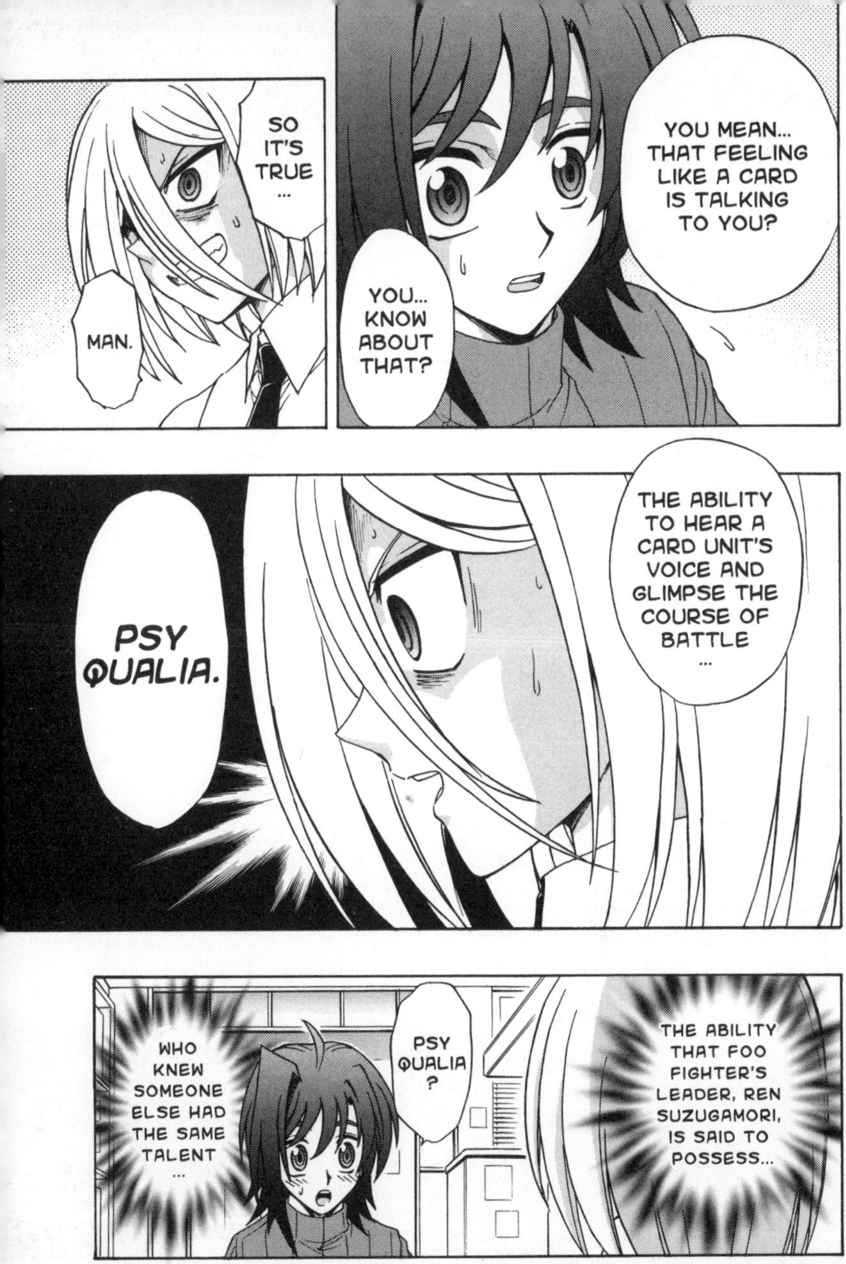
YOU MEAN... THAT FEELING LIKE A CARD IS TALKING TO YOU?
YOU... KNOW ABOUT THAT?
SO IT'S TRUE ...
MAN.
THE ABILITY TO HEAR A CARD UNIT'S VOICE AND GLIMPSE THE COURSE OF BATTLE ...
PSY QUALIA.
THE ABILITY THAT FOO FIGHTER'S LEADER, REN SUZUGAMORI, IS SAID TO POSSESS...
PSY QUALIA ?
WHO KNEW SOMEONE ELSE HAD THE SAME TALENT ...

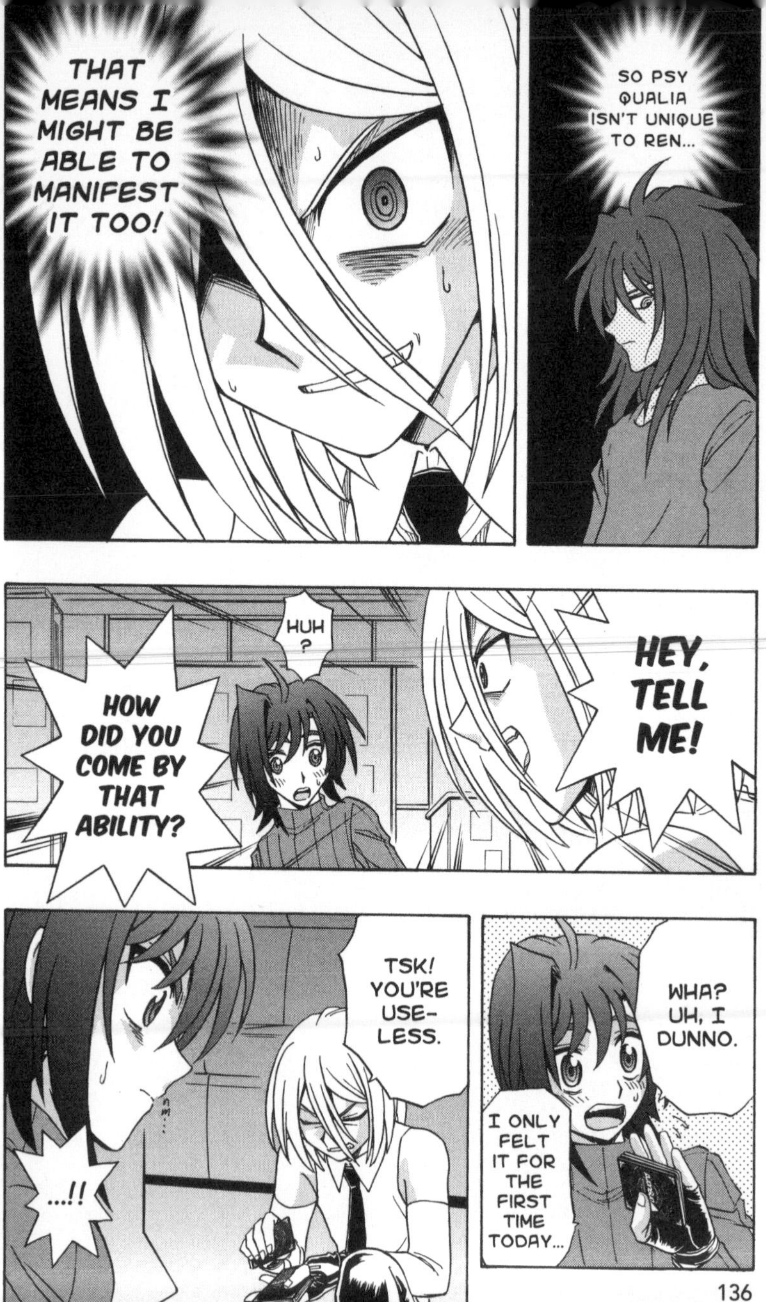
SO PSY QUALIA ISN'T UNIQUE TO REN...
THAT MEANS I MIGHT BE ABLE TO MANIFEST IT TOO!
HEY, TELL ME!
HUH?
HOW DID YOU COME BY THAT ABILITY?
WHA? UH, I DUNNO.
I ONLY FELT IT FOR THE FIRST TIME TODAY...
TSK! YOU'RE USE-LESS.
...!!

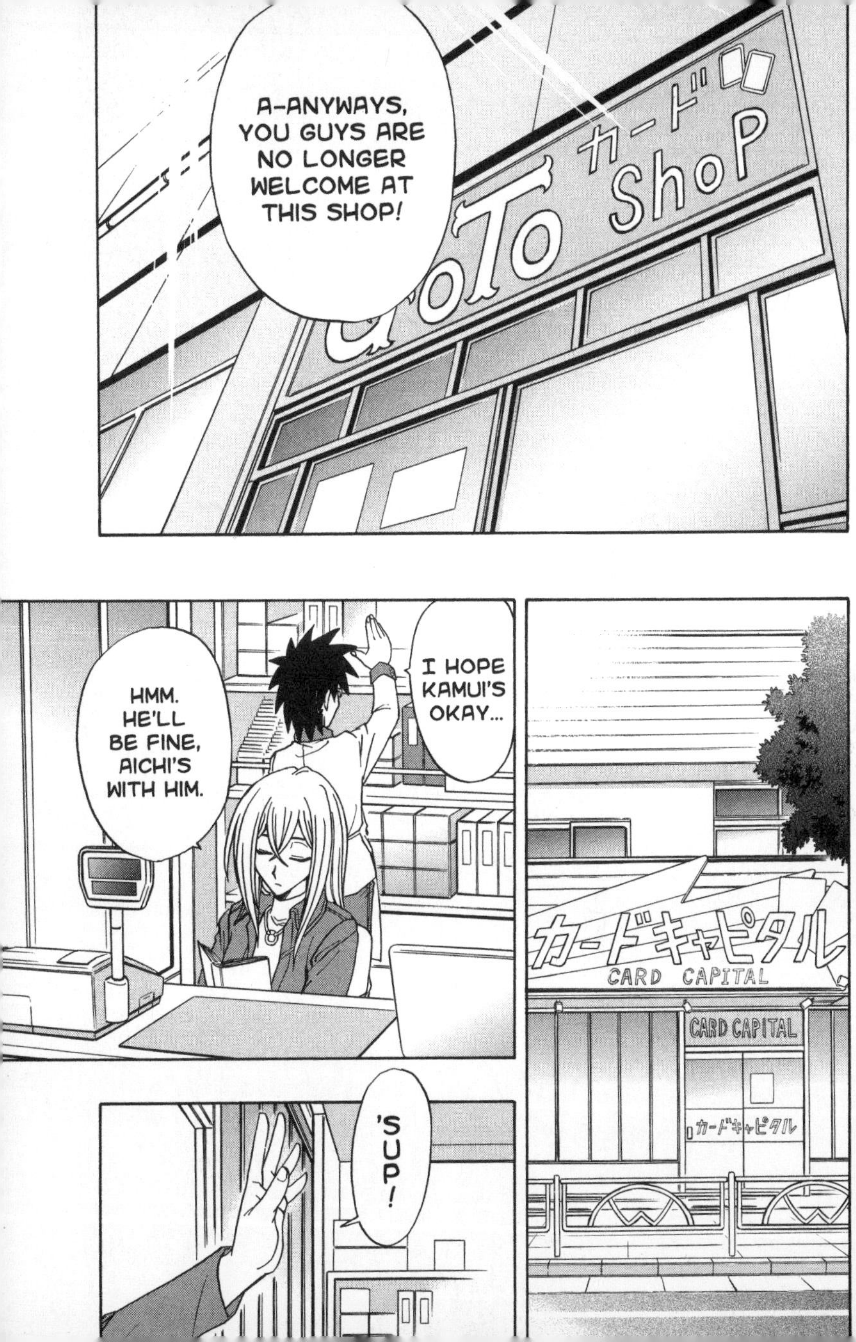
A-ANYWAYS, YOU GUYS ARE NO LONGER WELCOME AT THIS SHOP!
カード ShoP
カードキャピタル
CARD CAPITAL
CARD CAPITAL
カードキャピタル
I HOPE KAMUI'S OKAY...
HMM. HE'LL BE FINE, AICHI'S WITH HIM.
'SUP!

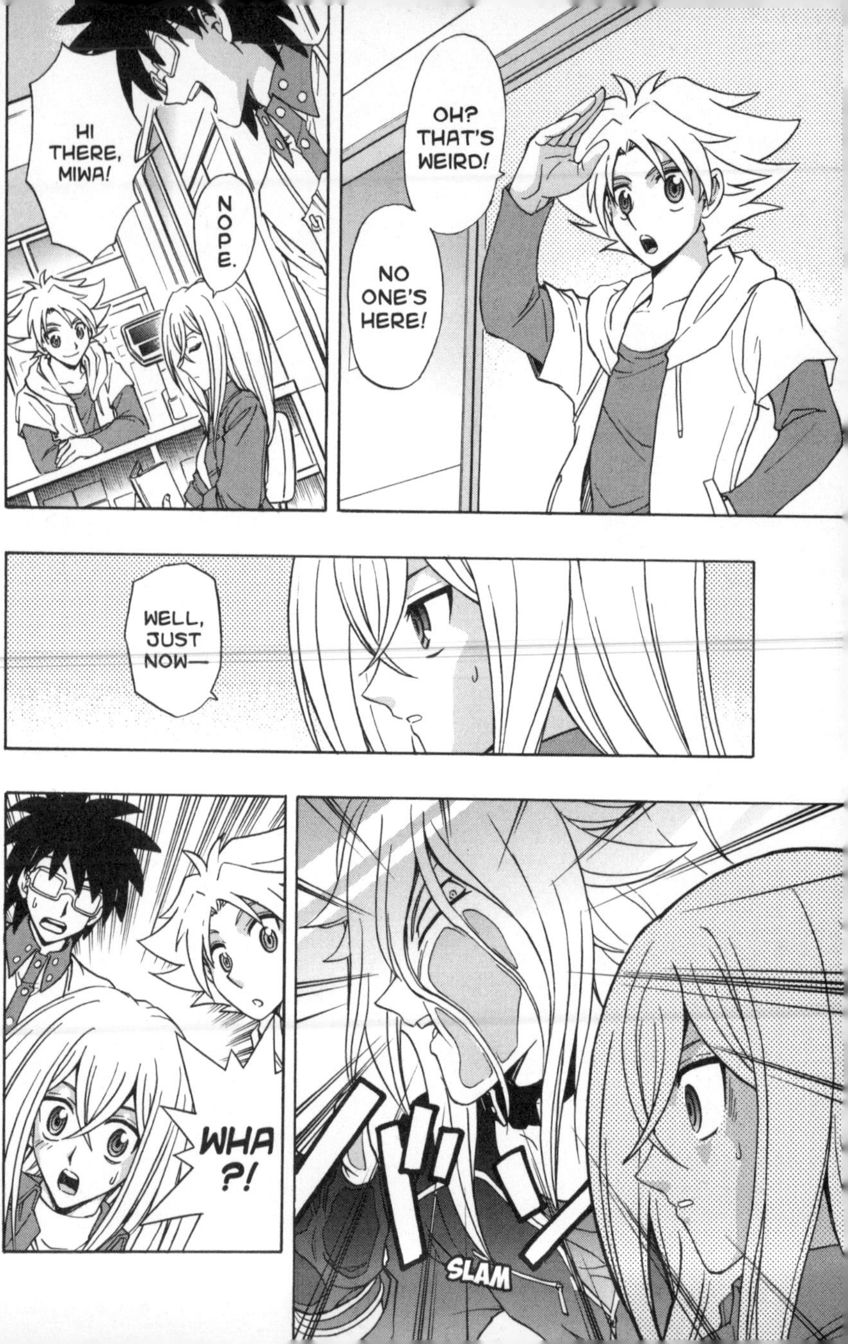
OH? THAT'S WEIRD!
NO ONE'S HERE!
HI THERE, MIWA!
NOPE.
WELL, JUST NOW—
SLAM
WHA ?!

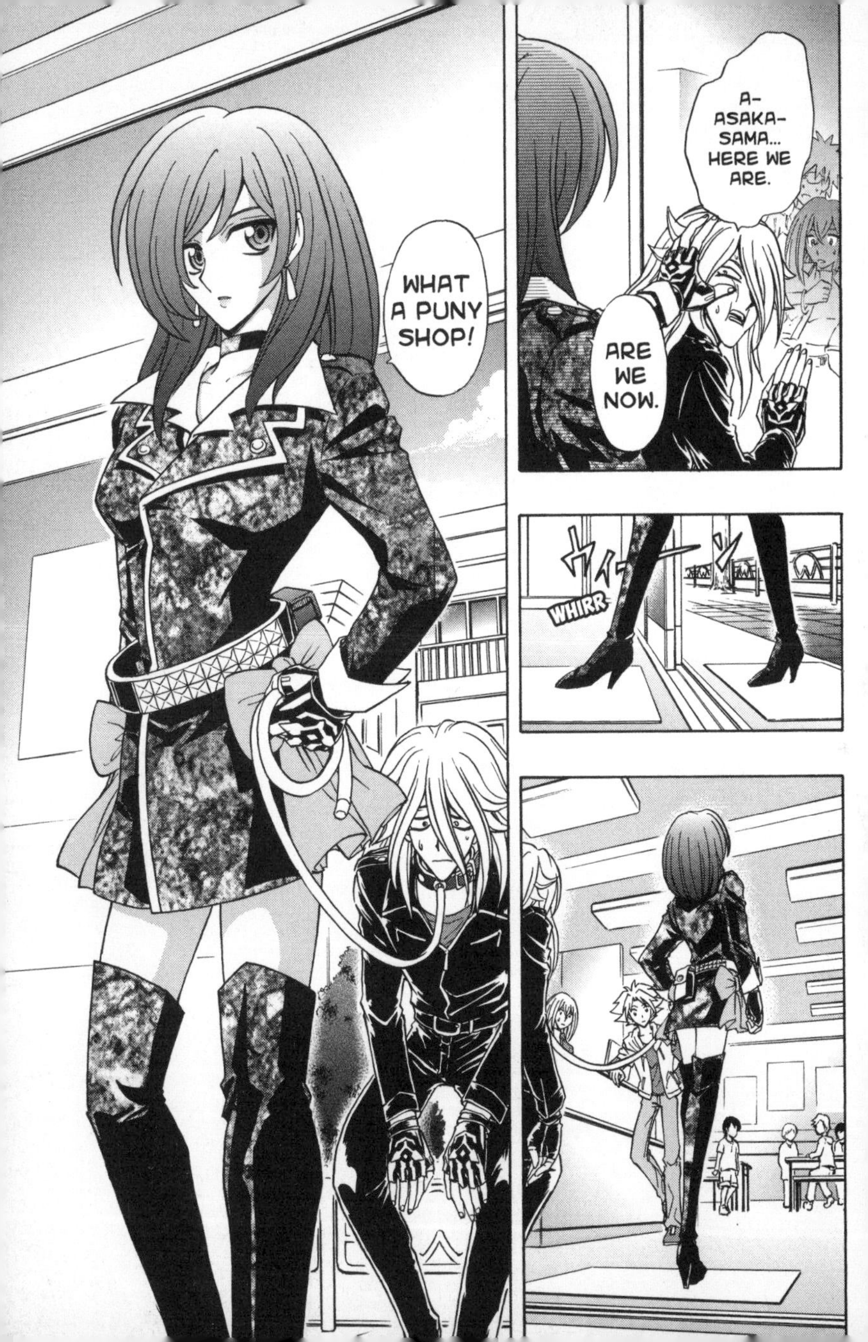
A-ASAKA-SAMA... HERE WE ARE.
ARE WE NOW.
ヴィーン
WHIRR
WHAT A PUNY SHOP!

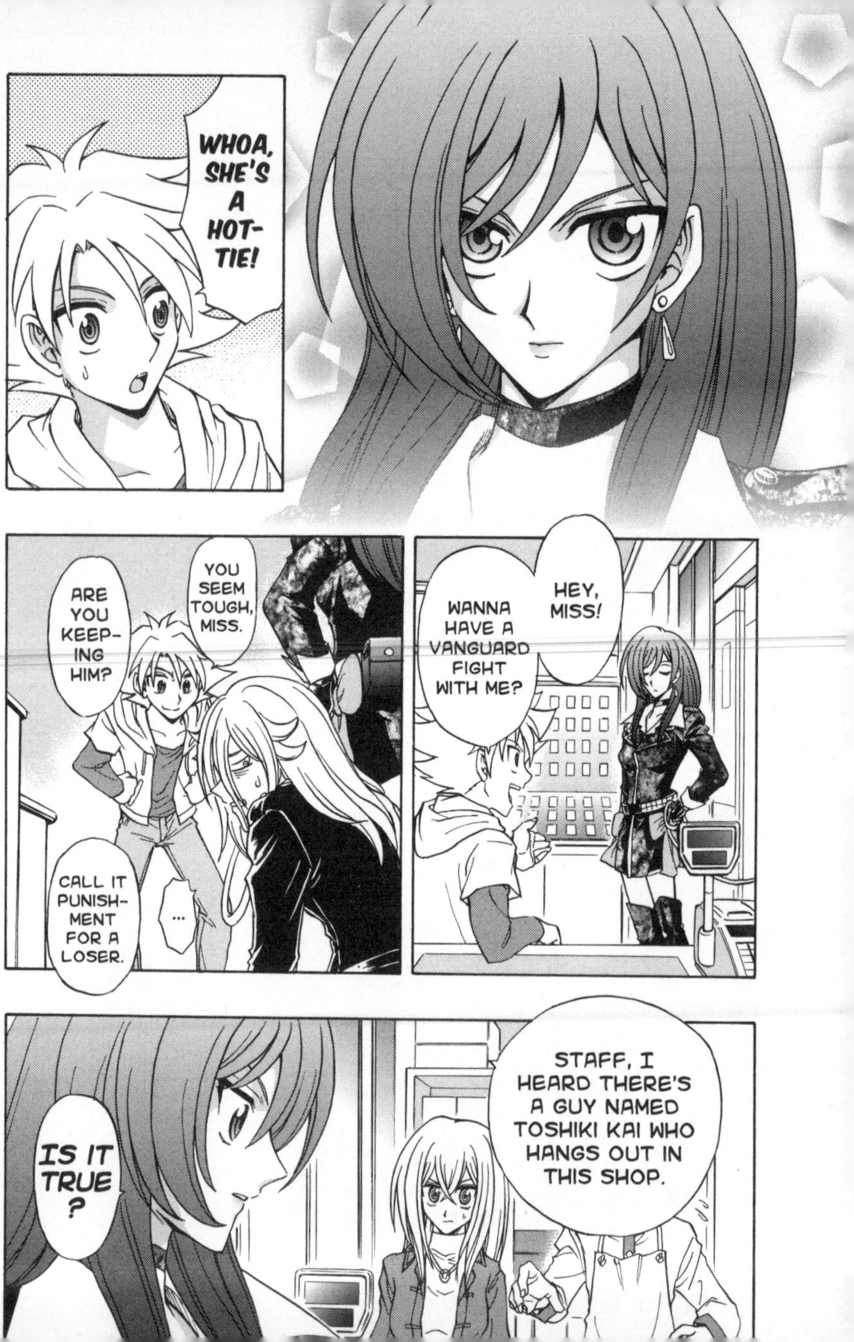
WHOA, SHE'S A HOT-TIE!
HEY, MISS!
WANNA HAVE A VANGUARD FIGHT WITH ME?
YOU SEEM TOUGH, MISS.
ARE YOU KEEP-ING HIM?
...
CALL IT PUNISH-MENT FOR A LOSER.
STAFF, I HEARD THERE'S A GUY NAMED TOSHIKI KAI WHO HANGS OUT IN THIS SHOP.
IS IT TRUE?

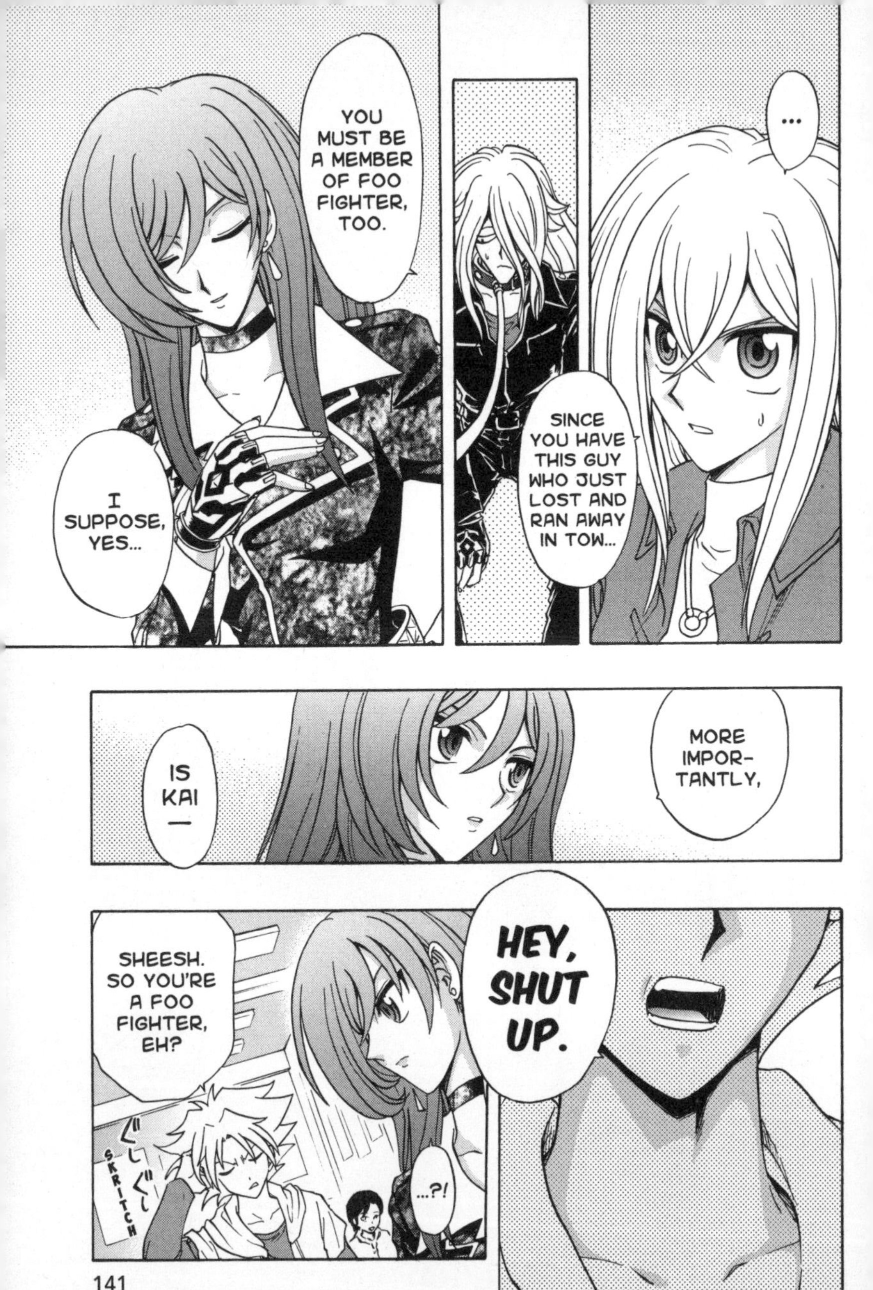
...
SINCE YOU HAVE THIS GUY WHO JUST LOST AND RAN AWAY IN TOW...
YOU MUST BE A MEMBER OF FOO FIGHTER, TOO.
I SUPPOSE, YES...
MORE IMPOR-TANTLY,
IS KAI —
HEY, SHUT UP.
SHEESH. SO YOU'RE A FOO FIGHTER, EH?
...?!
ぐしぐし
SKRITCH

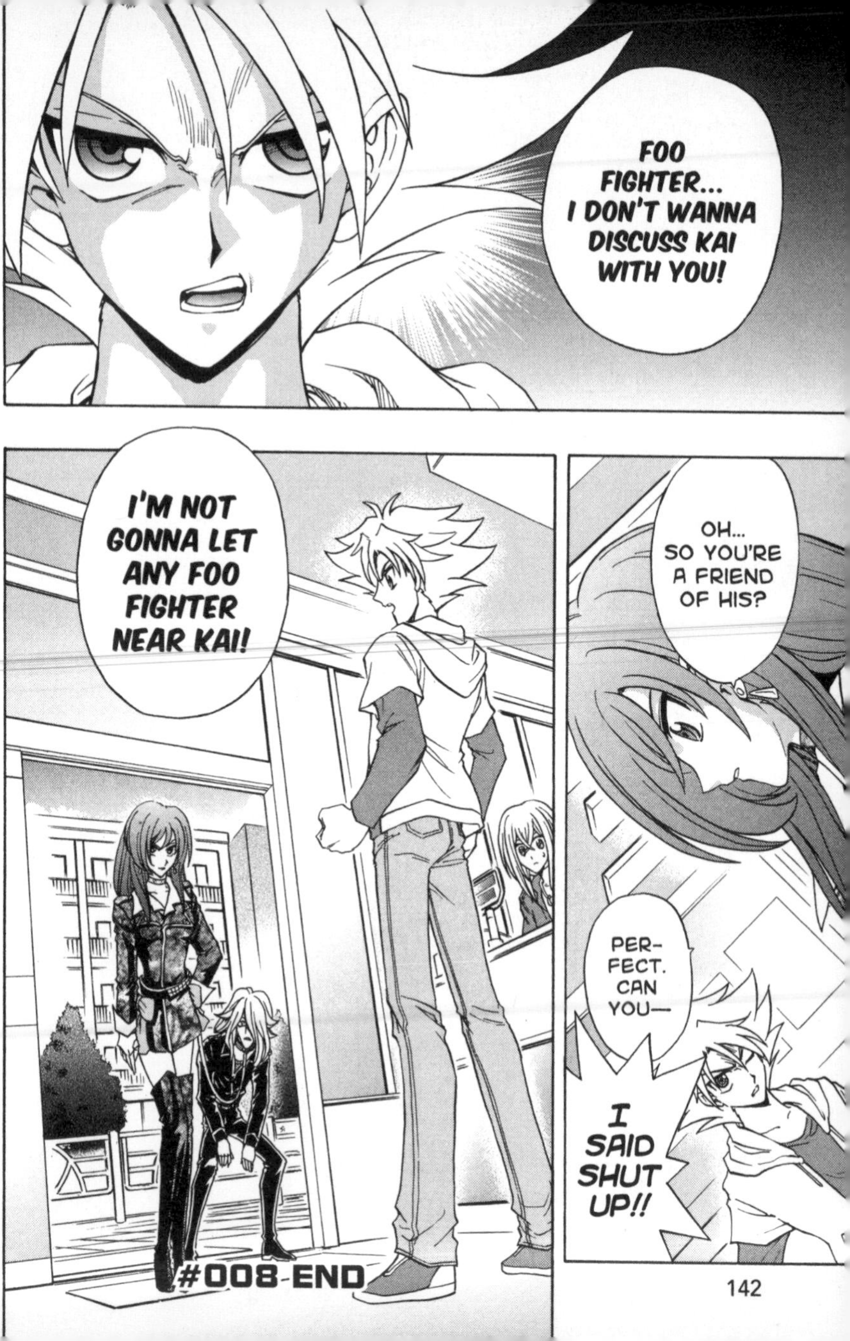
FOO FIGHTER... I DON'T WANNA DISCUSS KAI WITH YOU!
OH... SO YOU'RE A FRIEND OF HIS?
PER-FECT. CAN YOU—
I SAID SHUT UP!!
I'M NOT GONNA LET ANY FOO FIGHTER NEAR KAI!
#008-END

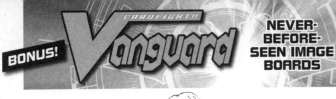

BONUS! CARDFIGHT!! Vanguard NEVER-BEFORE-SEEN IMAGE BOARDS CHARACTERS

Misaki: Casual Clothes

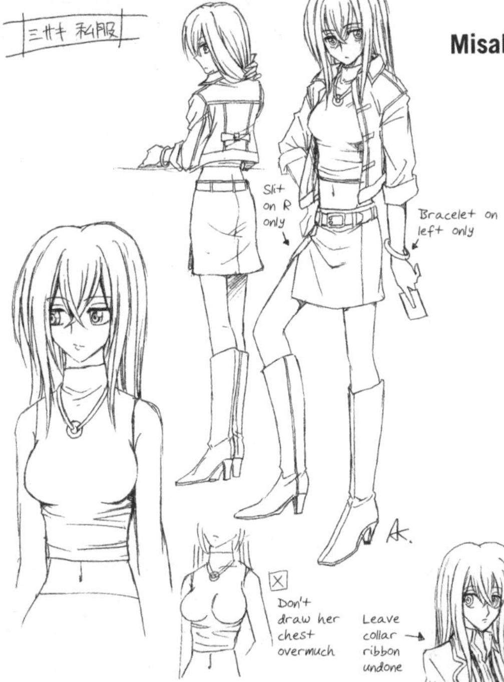

ミサキ 私服
Slit on R only
Bracelet on left only
Don't draw her chest overmuch

Misaki: School Uniform

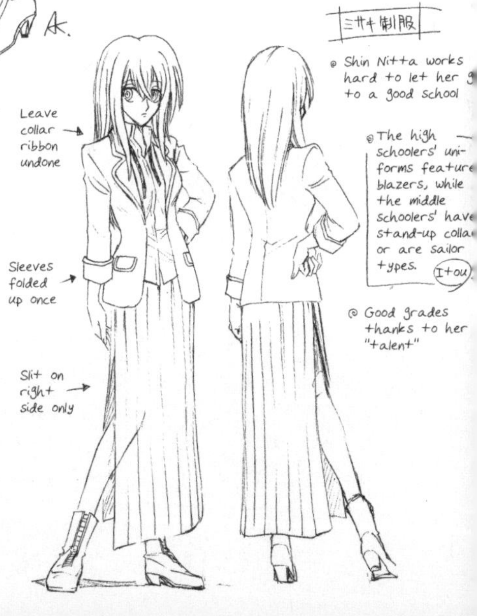

ミサキ制服
Shin Nitta works hard to let her go to a good school
The high schoolers' uniforms feature blazers, while the middle schoolers' have stand-up collars or are sailor types.
Itou
Leave collar ribbon undone
Sleeves folded up once
Good grades thanks to her "talent"
Slit on right side only

BONUS! CARDFIGHT!! Vanguard NEVER-BEFORE-SEEN IMAGE BOARDS

CHARACTERS

Bathing Suits

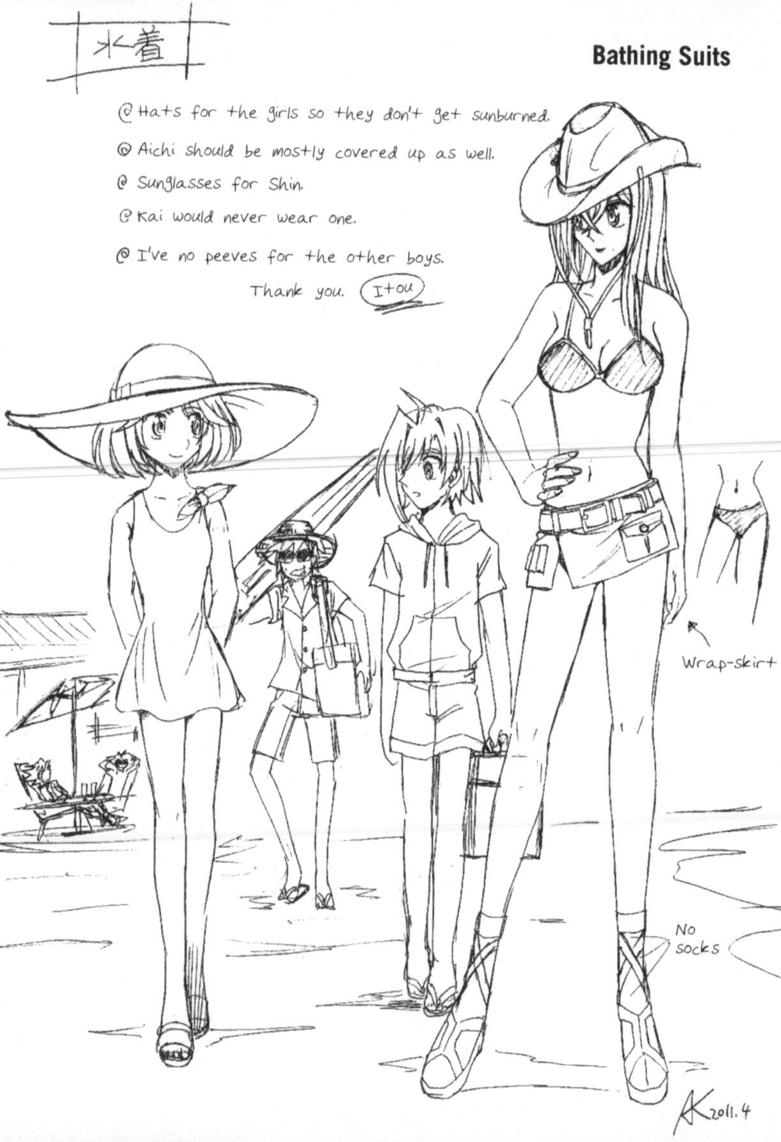

水着
@ Hats for the girls so they don't get sunburned.
@ Aichi should be mostly covered up as well.
@ Sunglasses for Shin.
@ Kai would never wear one.
@ I've no peeves for the other boys.
Thank you. Itou
Wrap-skirt
No socks
AK 2011. 4

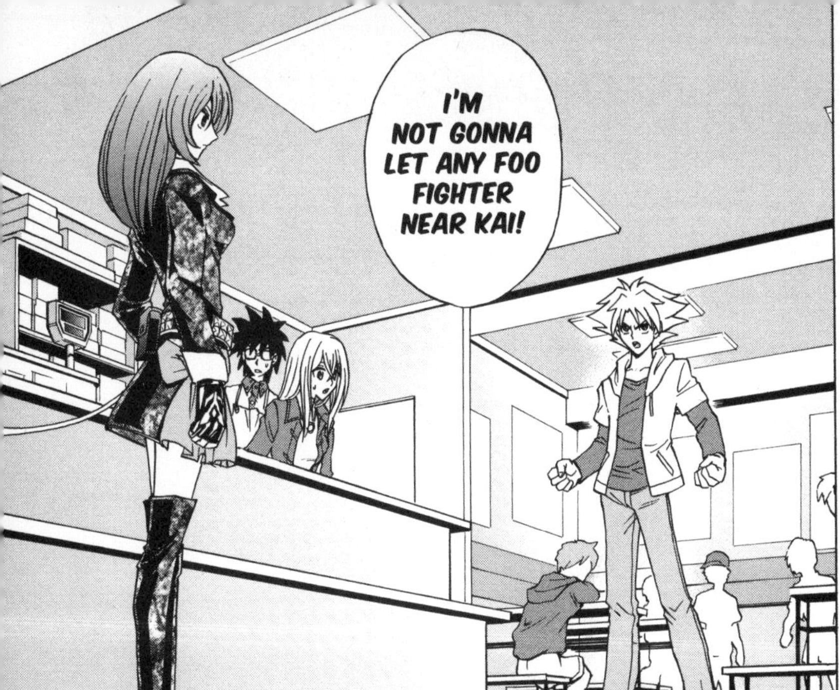
I'M NOT GONNA LET ANY FOO FIGHTER NEAR KAI!
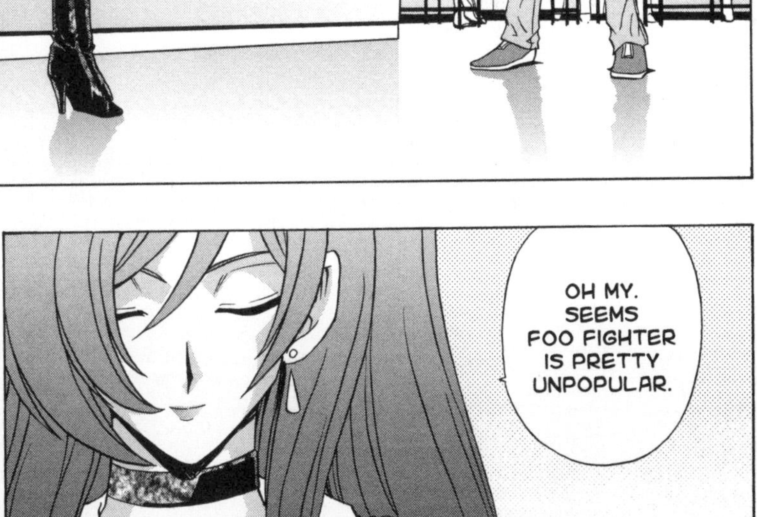
OH MY. SEEMS FOO FIGHTER IS PRETTY UNPOPULAR.

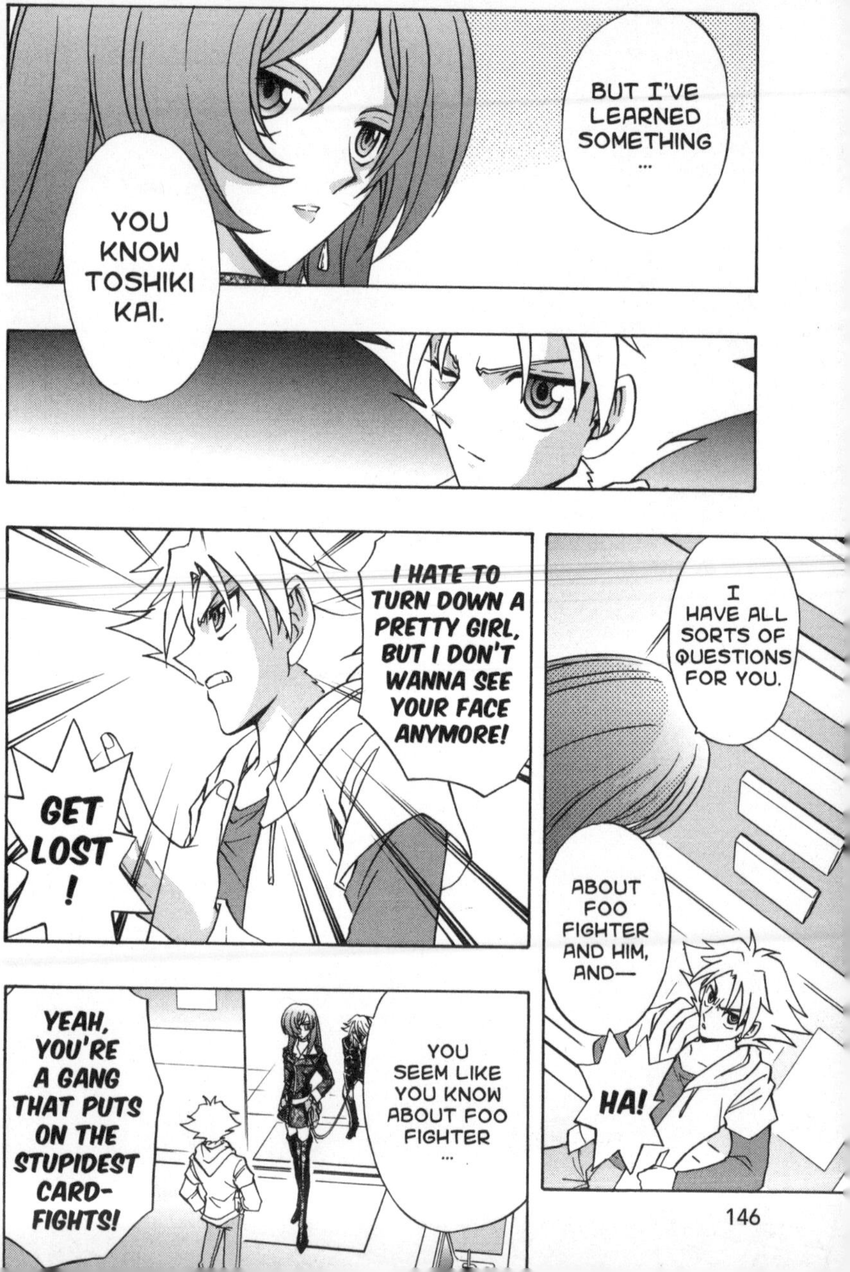
BUT I'VE LEARNED SOMETHING ...
YOU KNOW TOSHIKI KAI.
I HAVE ALL SORTS OF QUESTIONS FOR YOU.
ABOUT FOO FIGHTER AND HIM, AND—
HA!
I HATE TO TURN DOWN A PRETTY GIRL, BUT I DON'T WANNA SEE YOUR FACE ANYMORE!
GET LOST!
YOU SEEM LIKE YOU KNOW ABOUT FOO FIGHTER ...
YEAH, YOU'RE A GANG THAT PUTS ON THE STUPIDEST CARD-FIGHTS!

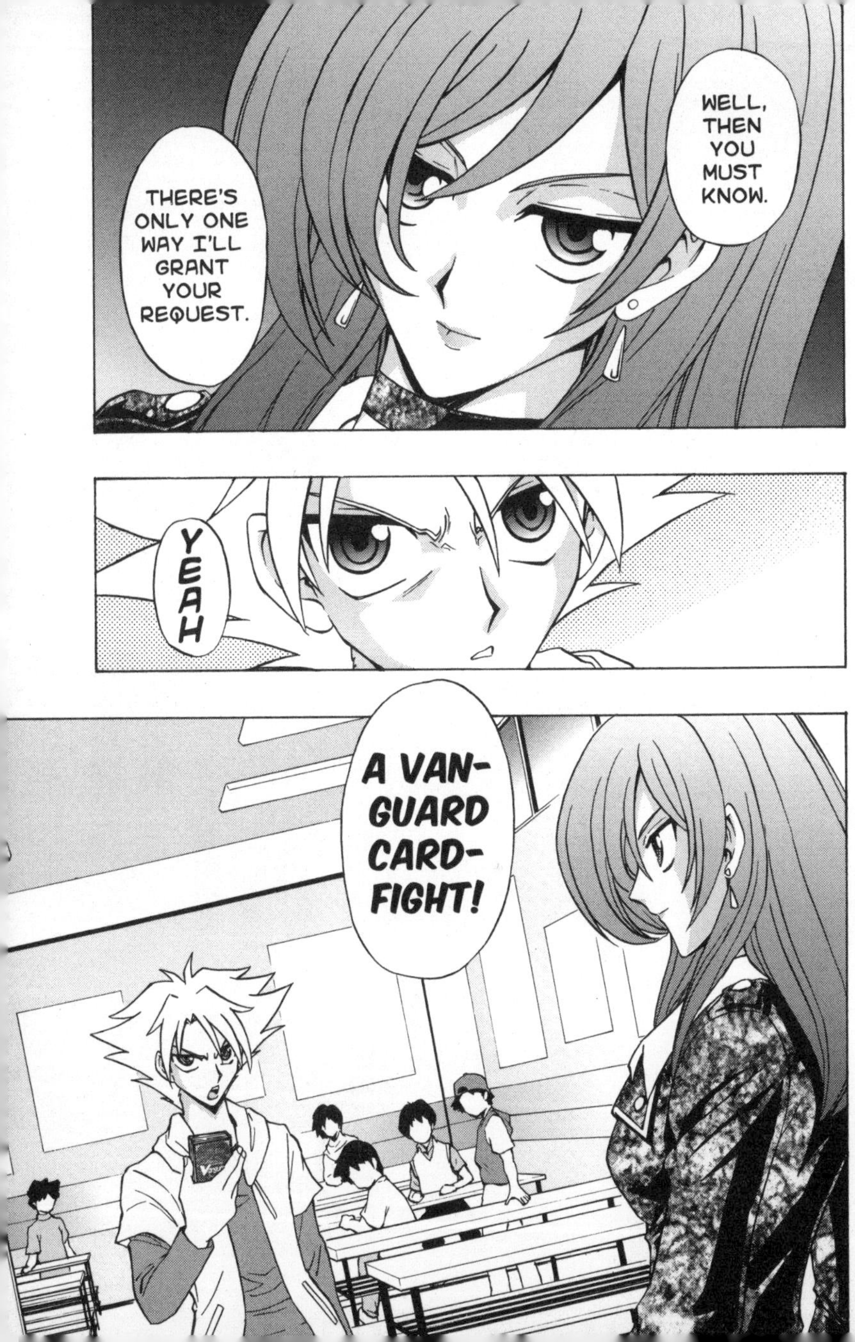
WELL, THEN YOU MUST KNOW.
THERE'S ONLY ONE WAY I'LL GRANT YOUR REQUEST.
YEAH
A VAN-GUARD CARD-FIGHT!

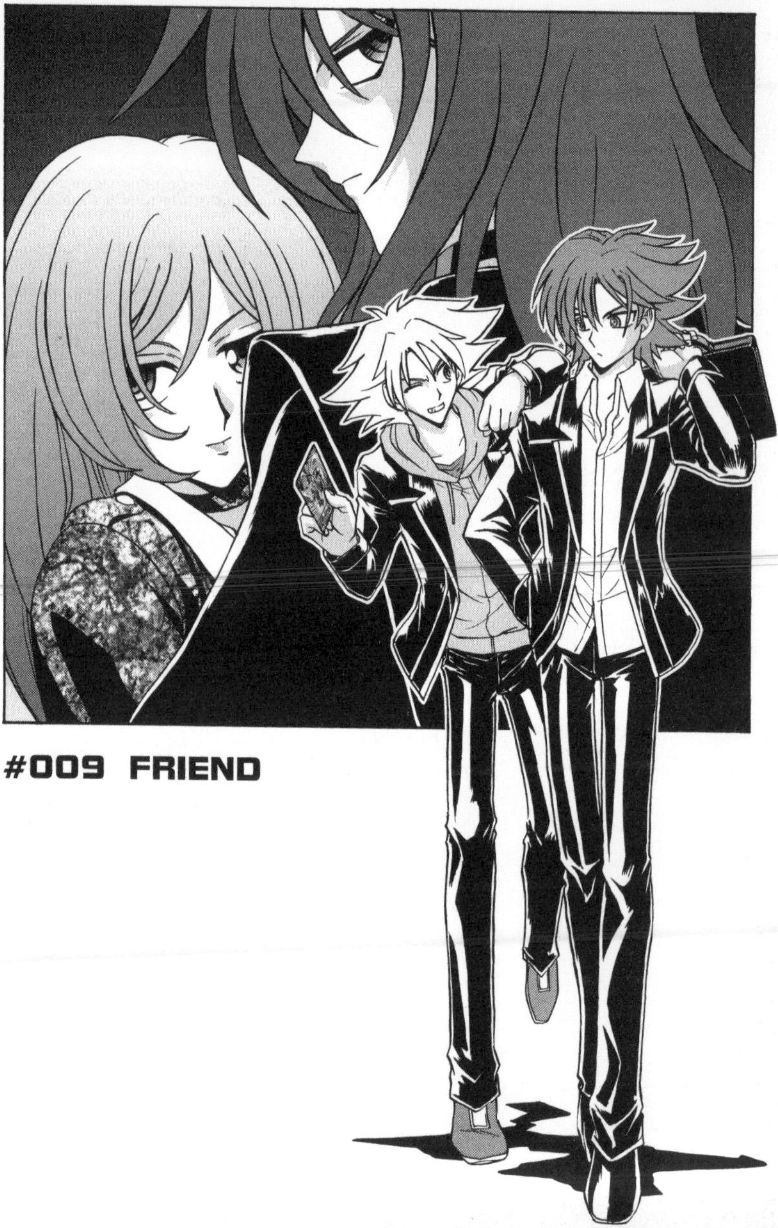

#009 FRIEND

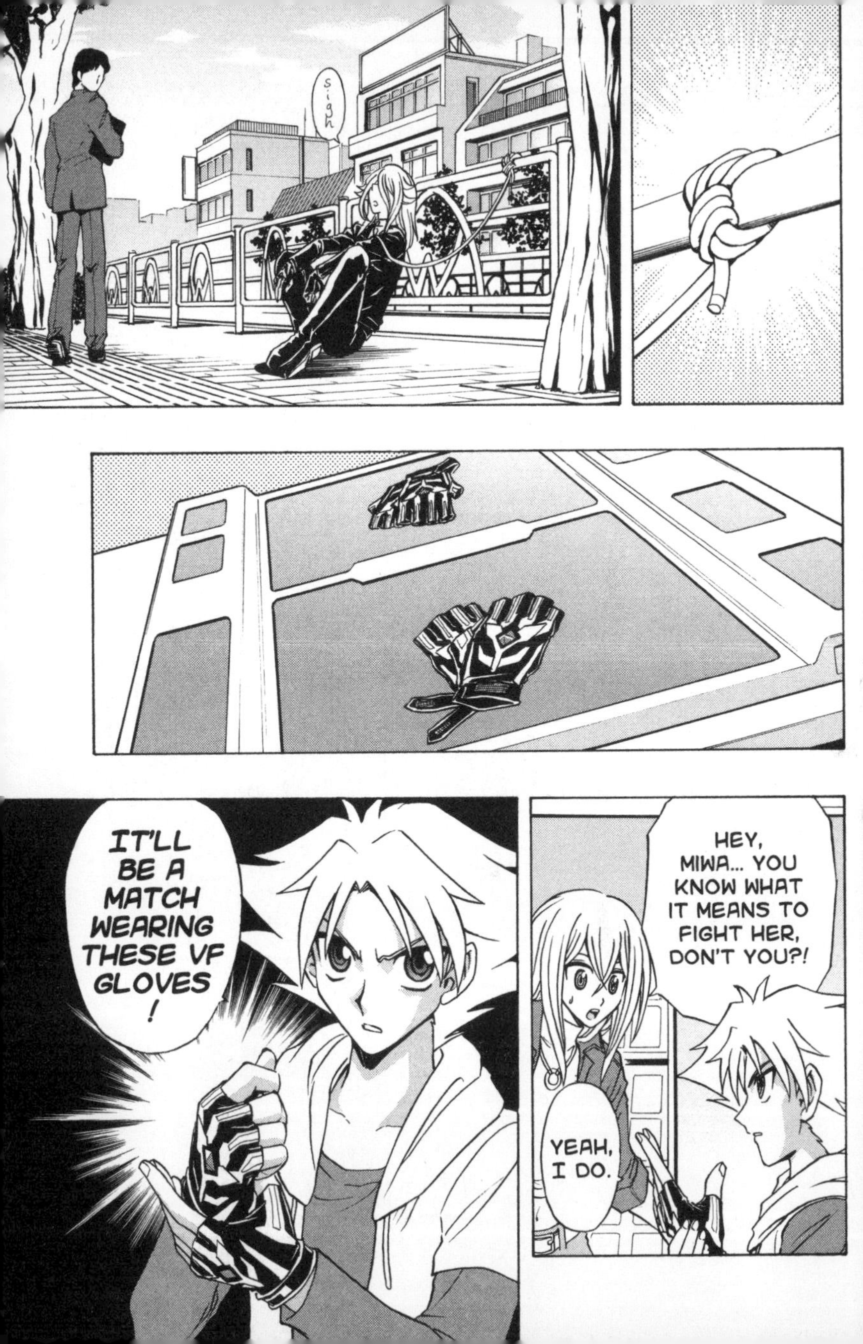
sigh
HEY, MIWA... YOU KNOW WHAT IT MEANS TO FIGHT HER, DON'T YOU?!
YEAH, I DO.
IT'LL BE A MATCH WEARING THESE VF GLOVES!

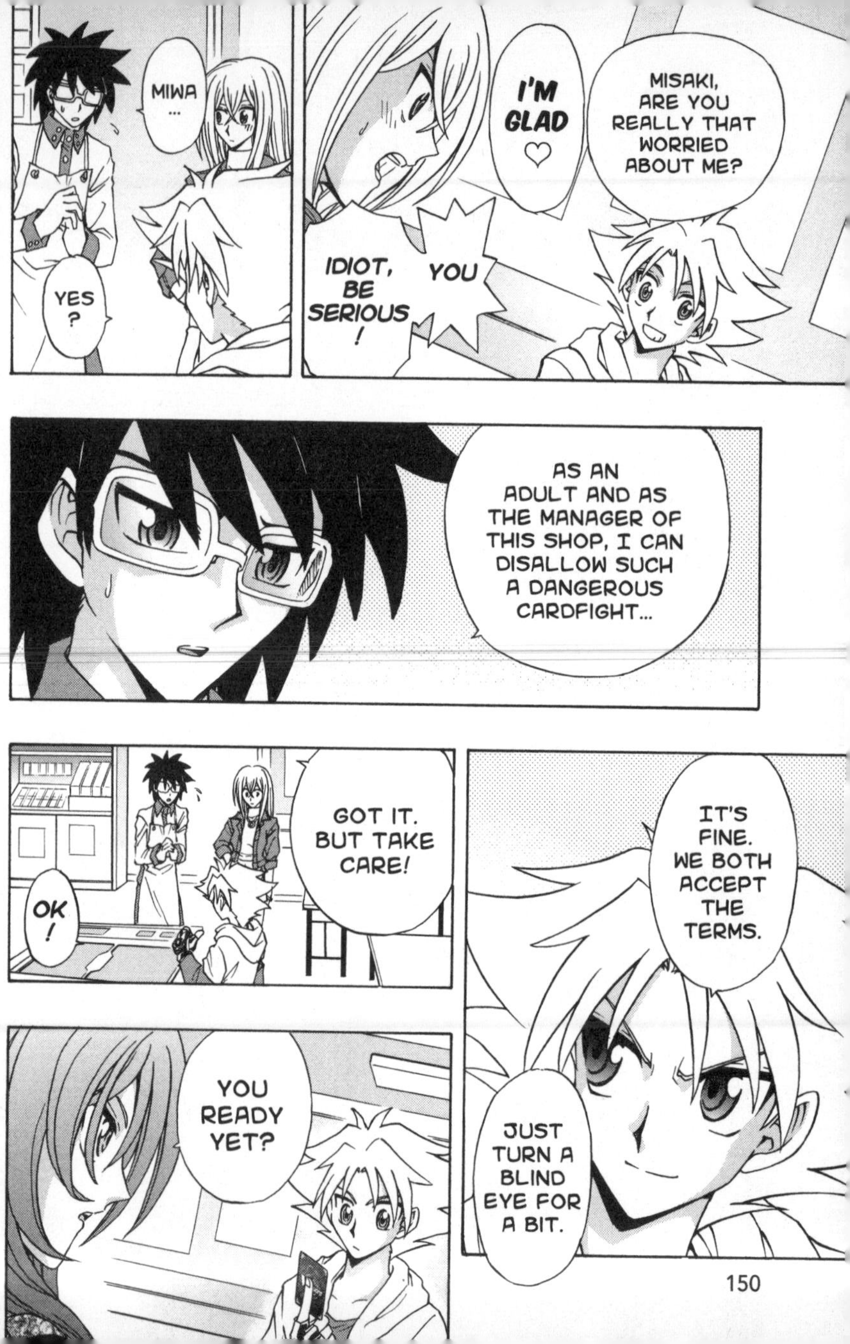
MISAKI, ARE YOU REALLY THAT WORRIED ABOUT ME?
I'M GLAD ♡
YOU
IDIOT, BE SERIOUS!
MIWA...
YES?
AS AN ADULT AND AS THE MANAGER OF THIS SHOP, I CAN DISALLOW SUCH A DANGEROUS CARDFIGHT...
IT'S FINE. WE BOTH ACCEPT THE TERMS.
JUST TURN A BLIND EYE FOR A BIT.
GOT IT. BUT TAKE CARE!
OK!
YOU READY YET?

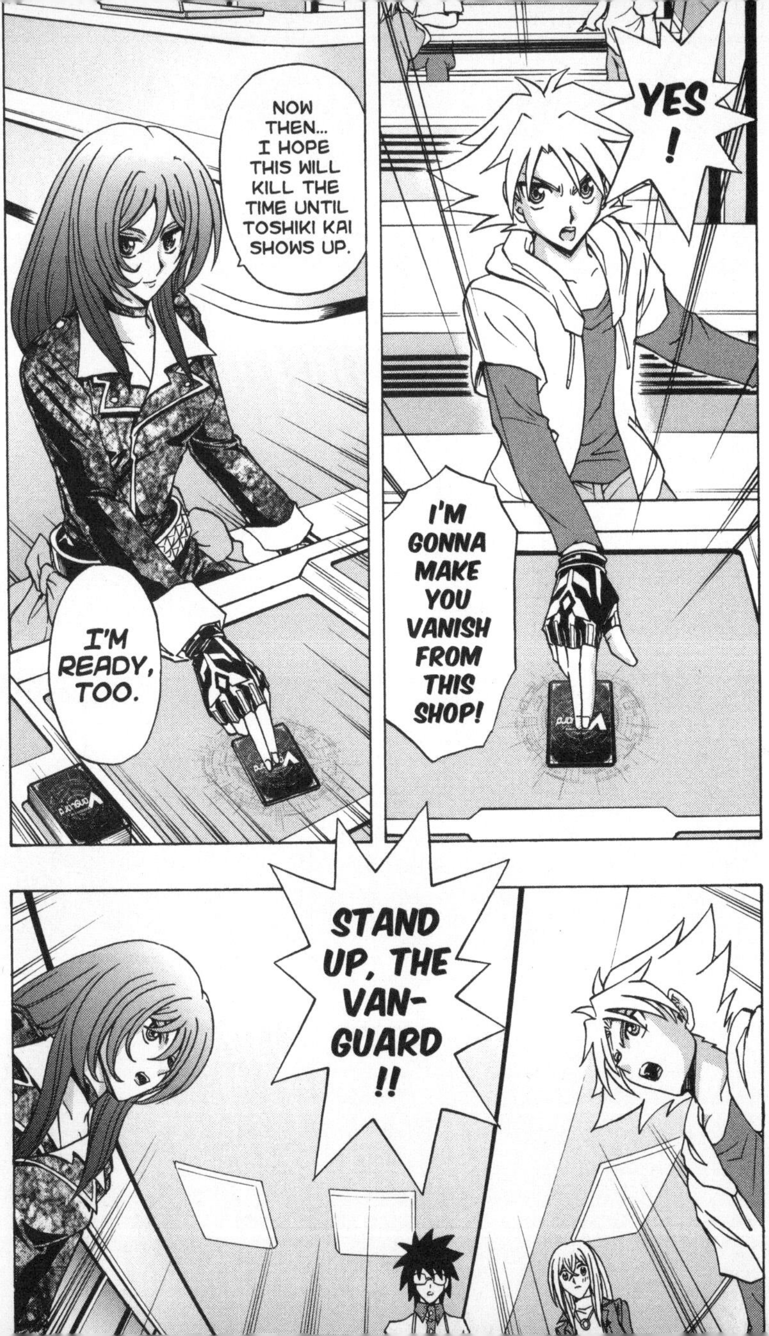
YES!
I'M GONNA MAKE YOU VANISH FROM THIS SHOP!
NOW THEN... I HOPE THIS WILL KILL THE TIME UNTIL TOSHIKI KAI SHOWS UP.
I'M READY, TOO.
STAND UP, THE VAN-GUARD!!

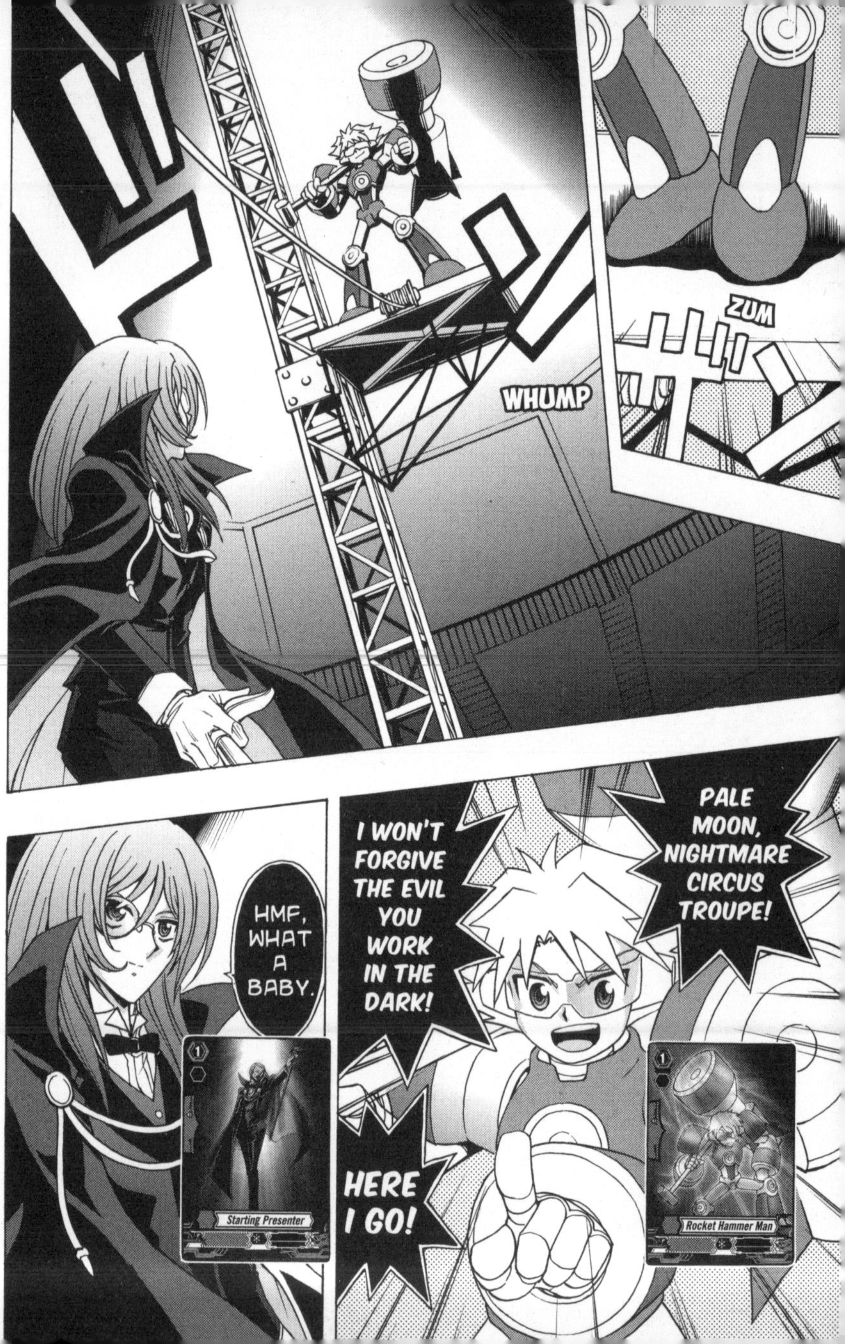
ZUM
WHUMP
PALE MOON, NIGHTMARE CIRCUS TROUPE!
I WON'T FORGIVE THE EVIL YOU WORK IN THE DARK!
HERE I GO!
Rocket Hammer Man
HMF, WHAT A BABY.
Starting Presenter

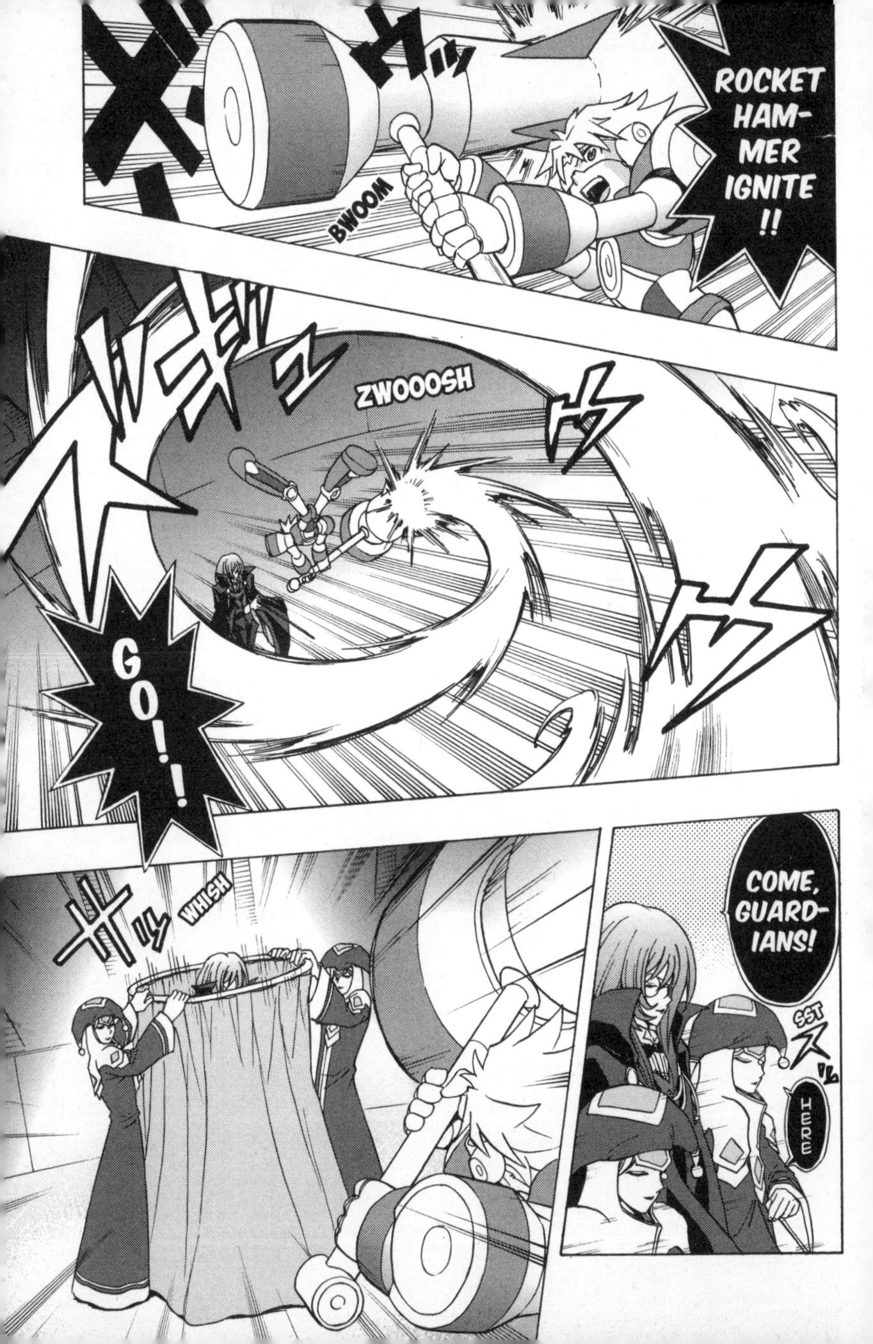
ROCKET HAMMER IGNITE!!
BWOOM
ZWOOOSH
GO!!!
COME, GUARDIANS!
SST
HERE
WHISH

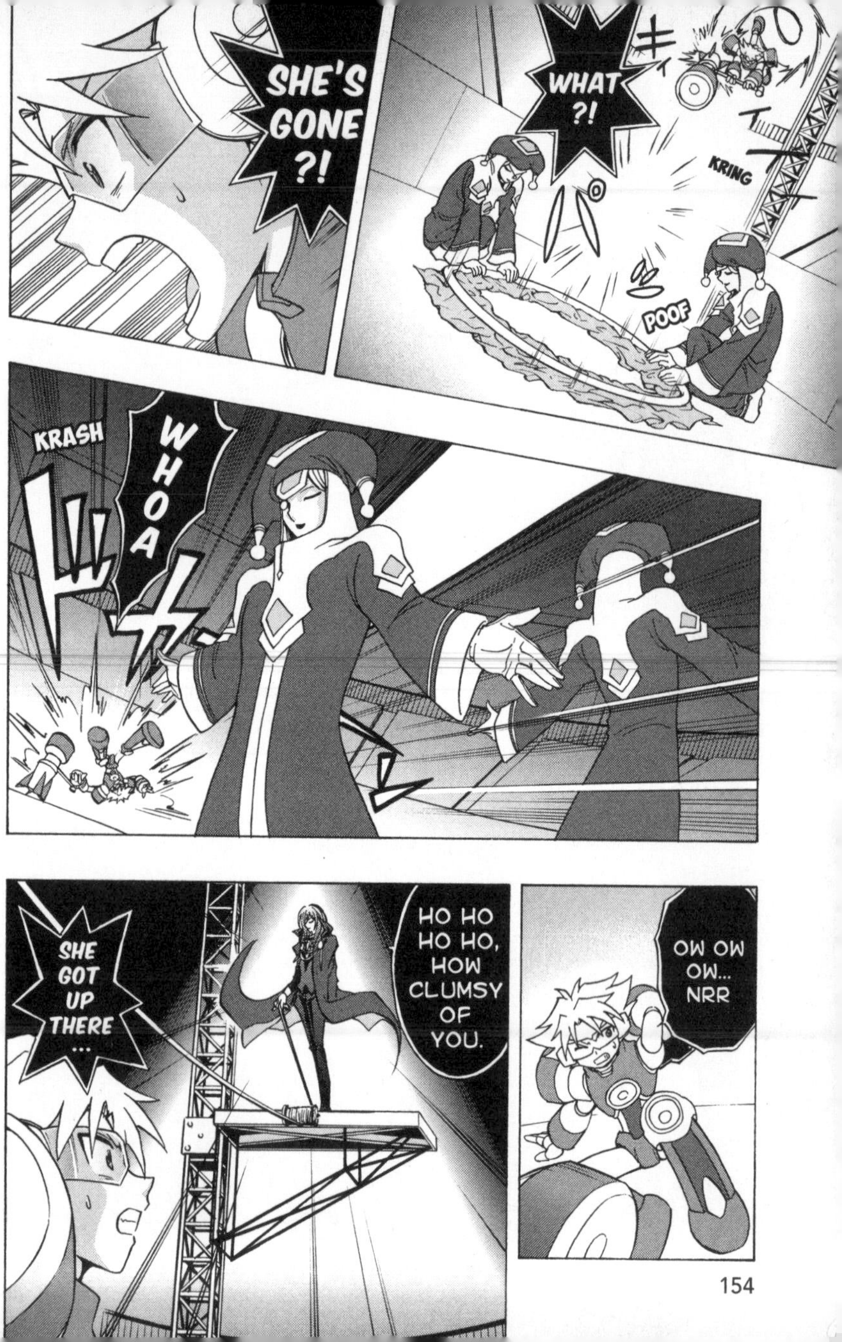
WHAT ?!
KRING
POOF
SHE'S GONE ?!
KRASH
WHOA
OW OW OW... NRR
HO HO HO HO, HOW CLUMSY OF YOU.
SHE GOT UP THERE ...

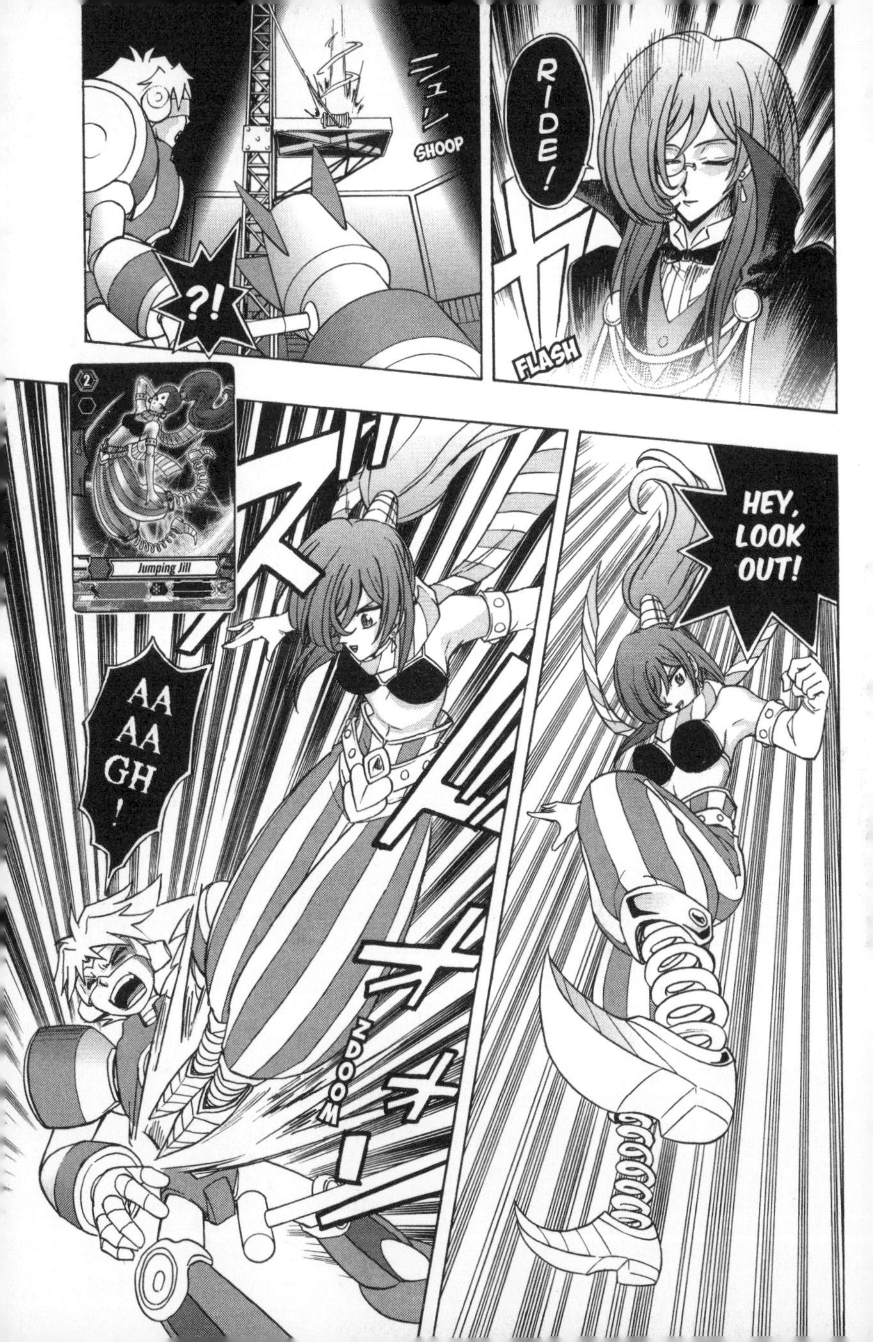
RIDE!
FLASH
SHOOP
?!
HEY, LOOK OUT!
2
Jumping Jill
AAAAGH!
ZDOOM

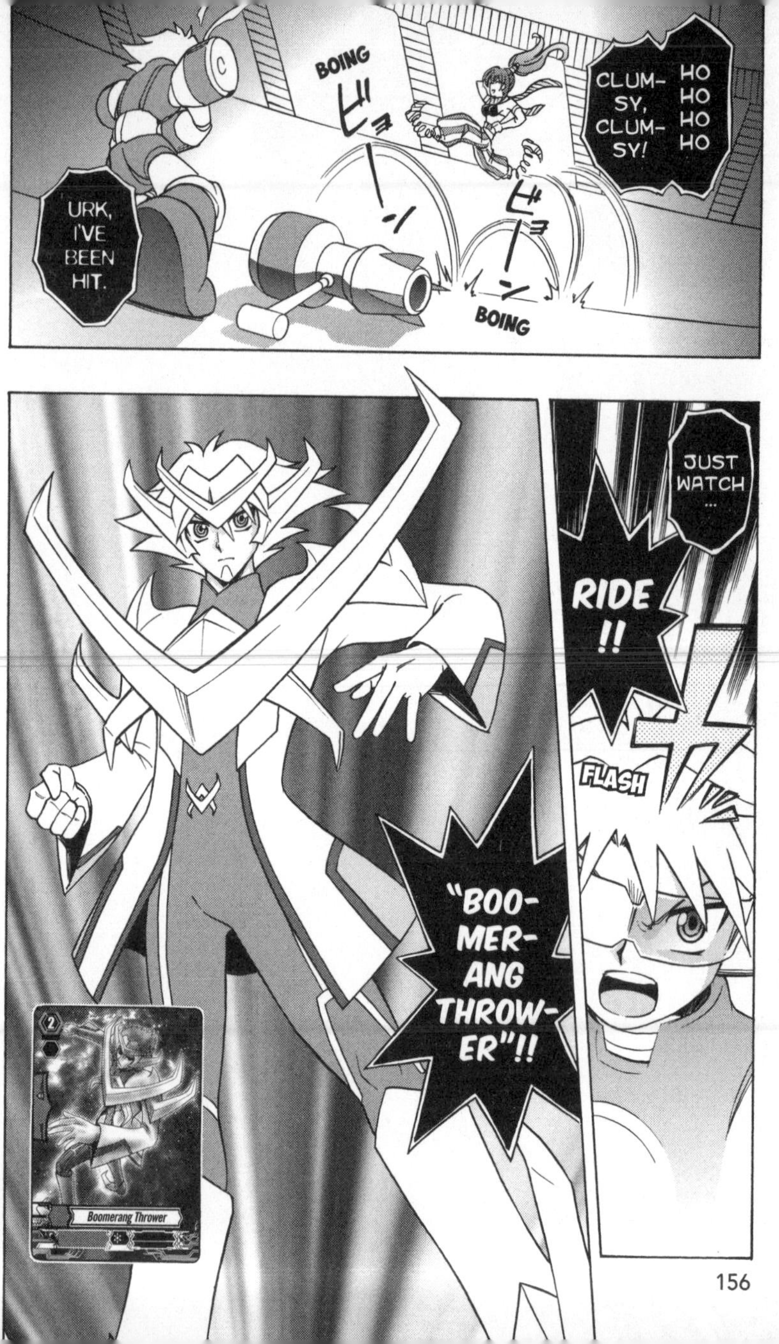
HO HO HO HO
CLUM-SY, CLUM-SY!
BOING
BOING
URK, I'VE BEEN HIT.
JUST WATCH ...
RIDE !!
FLASH
"BOO-MER-ANG THROW-ER"!!
2
Boomerang Thrower

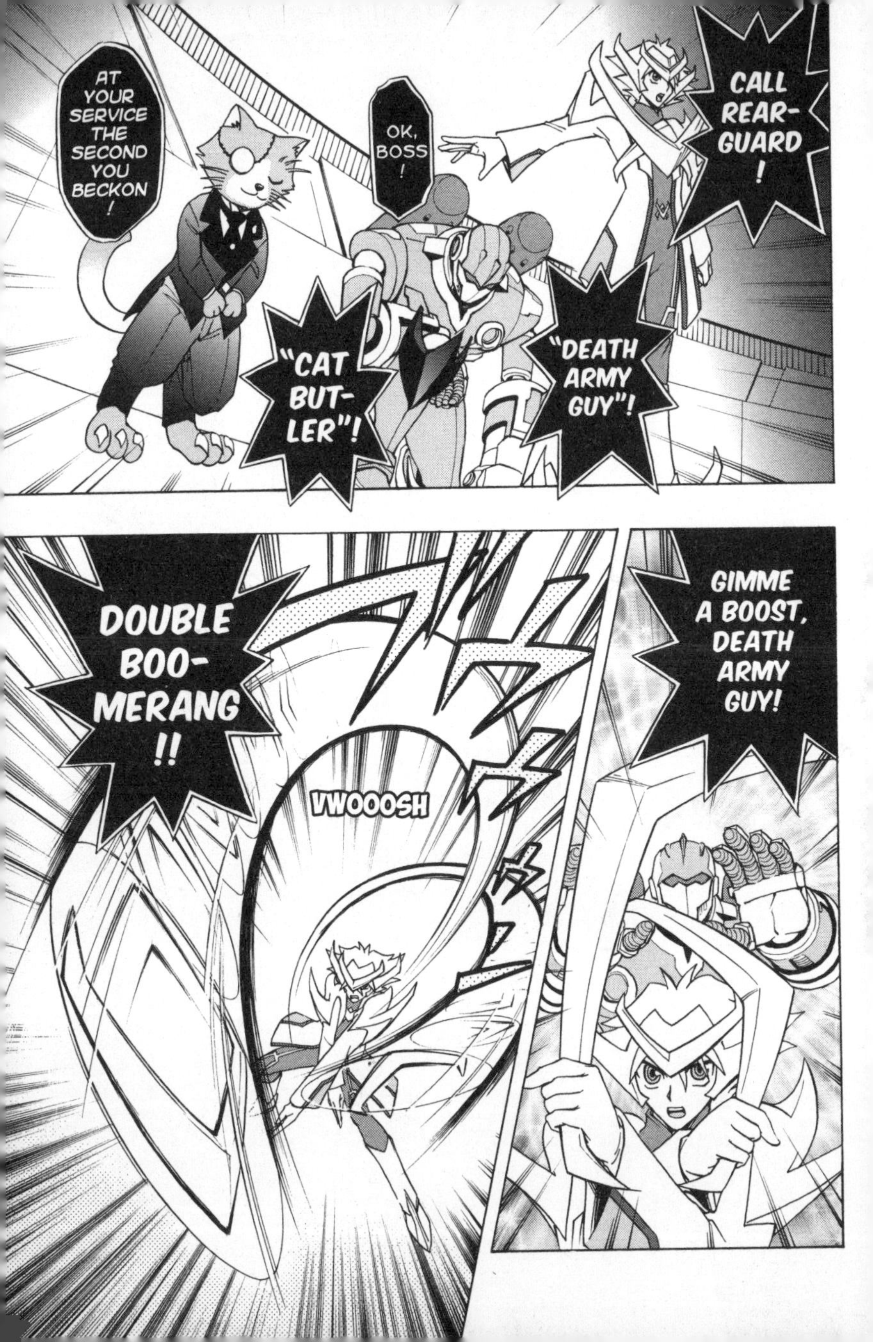
CALL REAR-GUARD!
"DEATH ARMY GUY"!
"CAT BUT-LER"!
OK, BOSS!
AT YOUR SERVICE THE SECOND YOU BECKON!
GIMME A BOOST, DEATH ARMY GUY!
DOUBLE BOO-MERANG!!
VWOOOSH

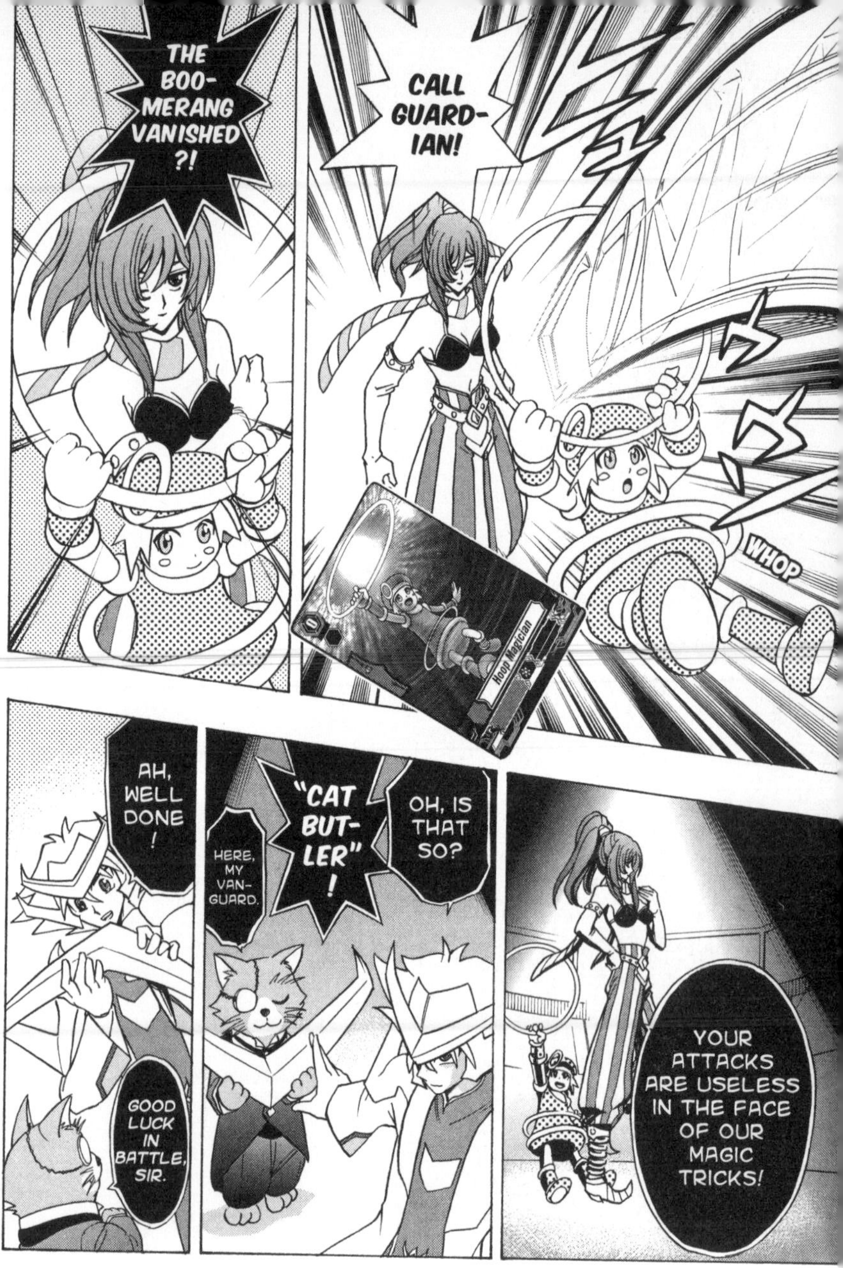
CALL GUARDIAN!
WHOP
Hoop Magician
THE BOOMERANG VANISHED?!
YOUR ATTACKS ARE USELESS IN THE FACE OF OUR MAGIC TRICKS!
OH, IS THAT SO?
"CAT BUTLER"!
HERE, MY VANGUARD.
AH, WELL DONE!
GOOD LUCK IN BATTLE, SIR.

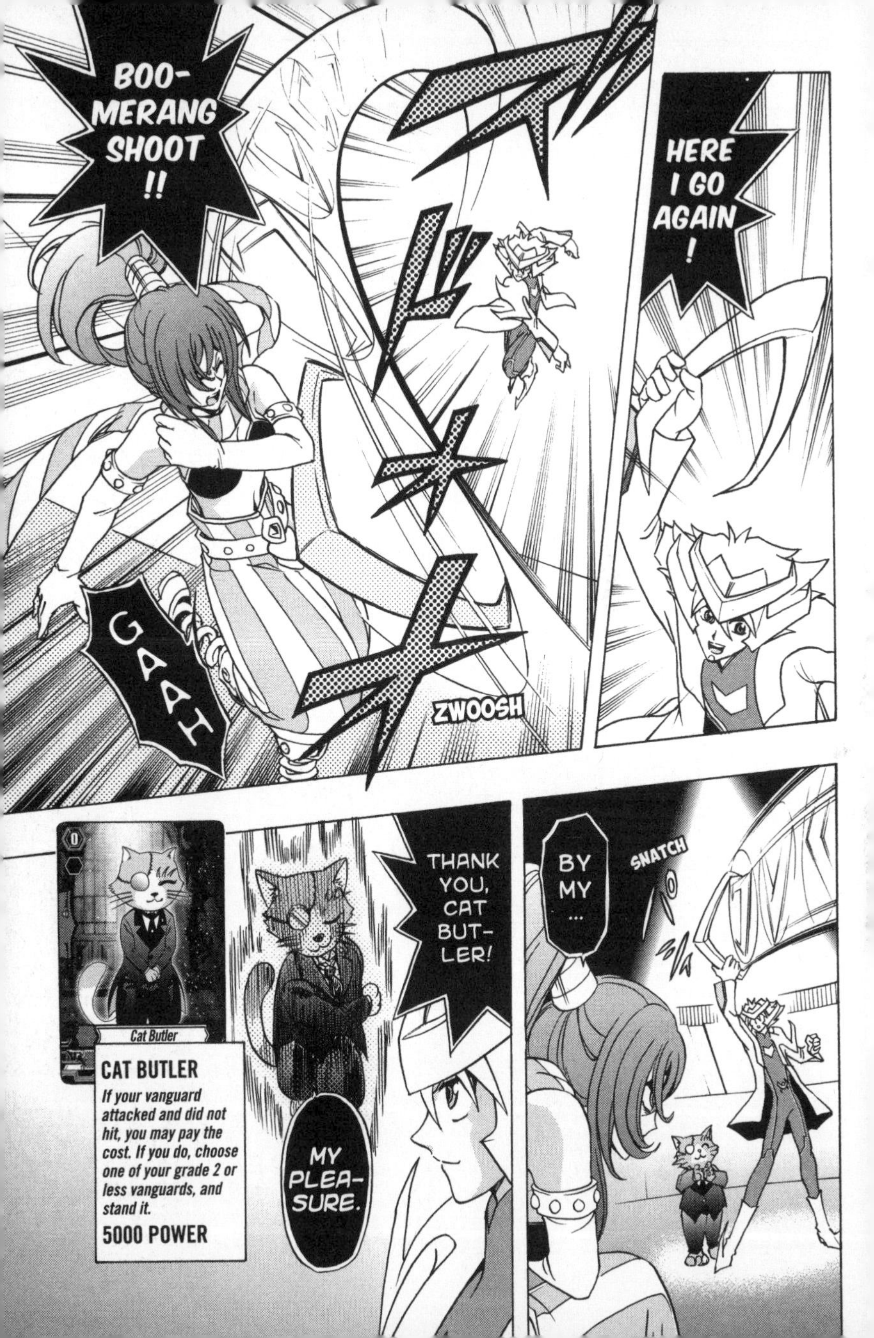
HERE I GO AGAIN!
BOO-MERANG SHOOT!!
GAAH
ZWOOSH
BY MY ...
SNATCH
THANK YOU, CAT BUTLER!
MY PLEASURE.
Cat Butler
CAT BUTLER
If your vanguard attacked and did not hit, you may pay the cost. If you do, choose one of your grade 2 or less vanguards, and stand it.
5000 POWER

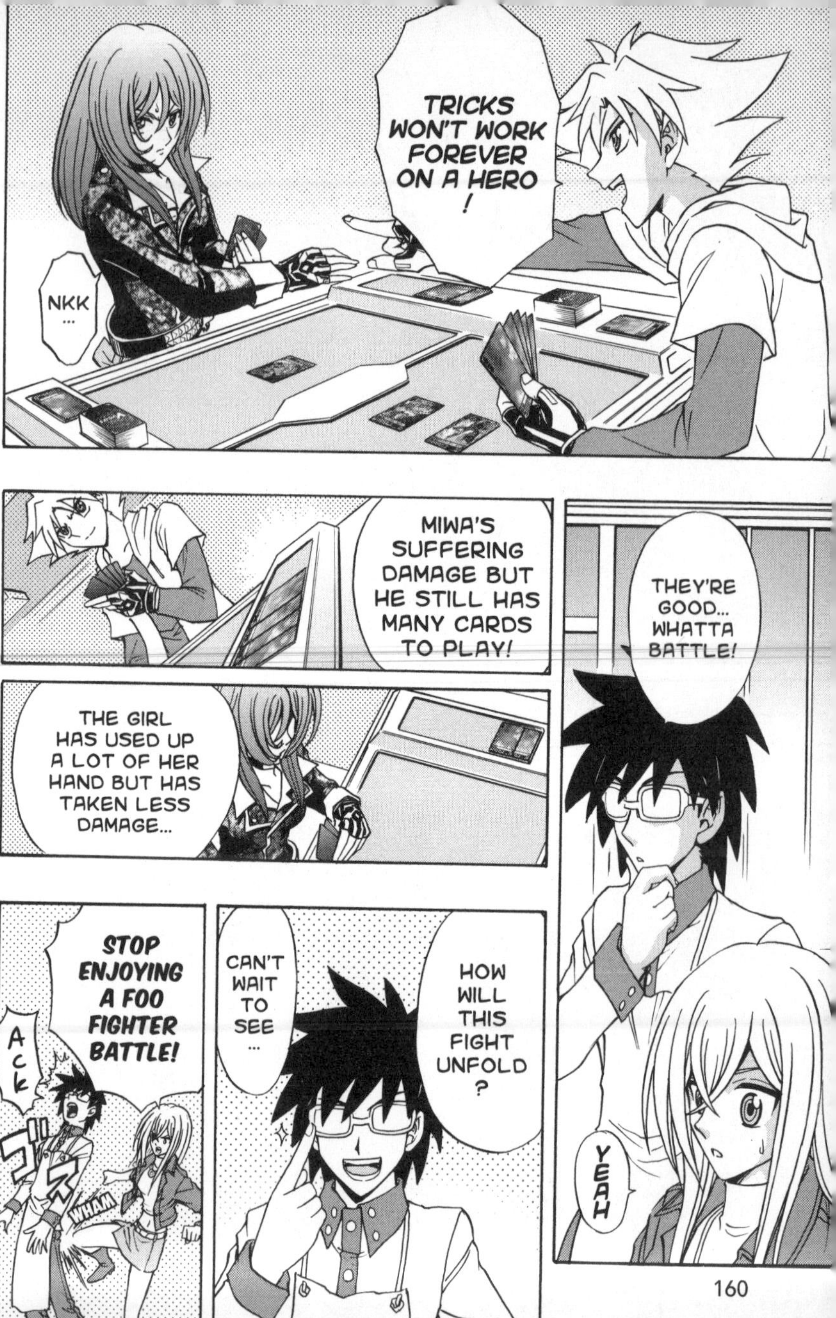
TRICKS WON'T WORK FOREVER ON A HERO!
NKK...
THEY'RE GOOD... WHATTA BATTLE!
YEAH
MIWA'S SUFFERING DAMAGE BUT HE STILL HAS MANY CARDS TO PLAY!
THE GIRL HAS USED UP A LOT OF HER HAND BUT HAS TAKEN LESS DAMAGE...
HOW WILL THIS FIGHT UNFOLD?
CAN'T WAIT TO SEE...
STOP ENJOYING A FOO FIGHTER BATTLE!
ACK
WHAM

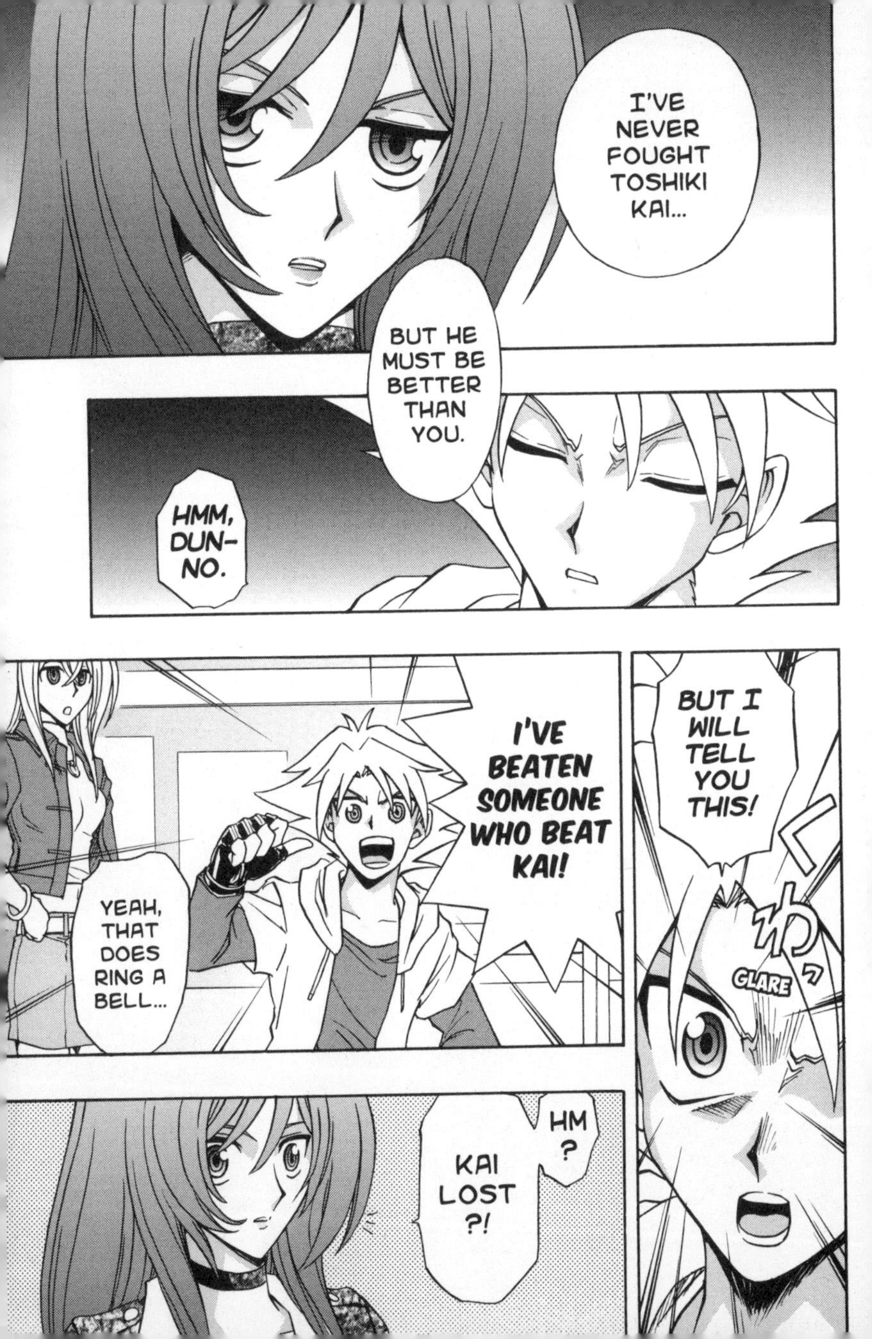
I'VE NEVER FOUGHT TOSHIKI KAI...
BUT HE MUST BE BETTER THAN YOU.
HMM, DUN-NO.
BUT I WILL TELL YOU THIS!
GLARE
I'VE BEATEN SOMEONE WHO BEAT KAI!
YEAH, THAT DOES RING A BELL...
HM?
KAI LOST?!

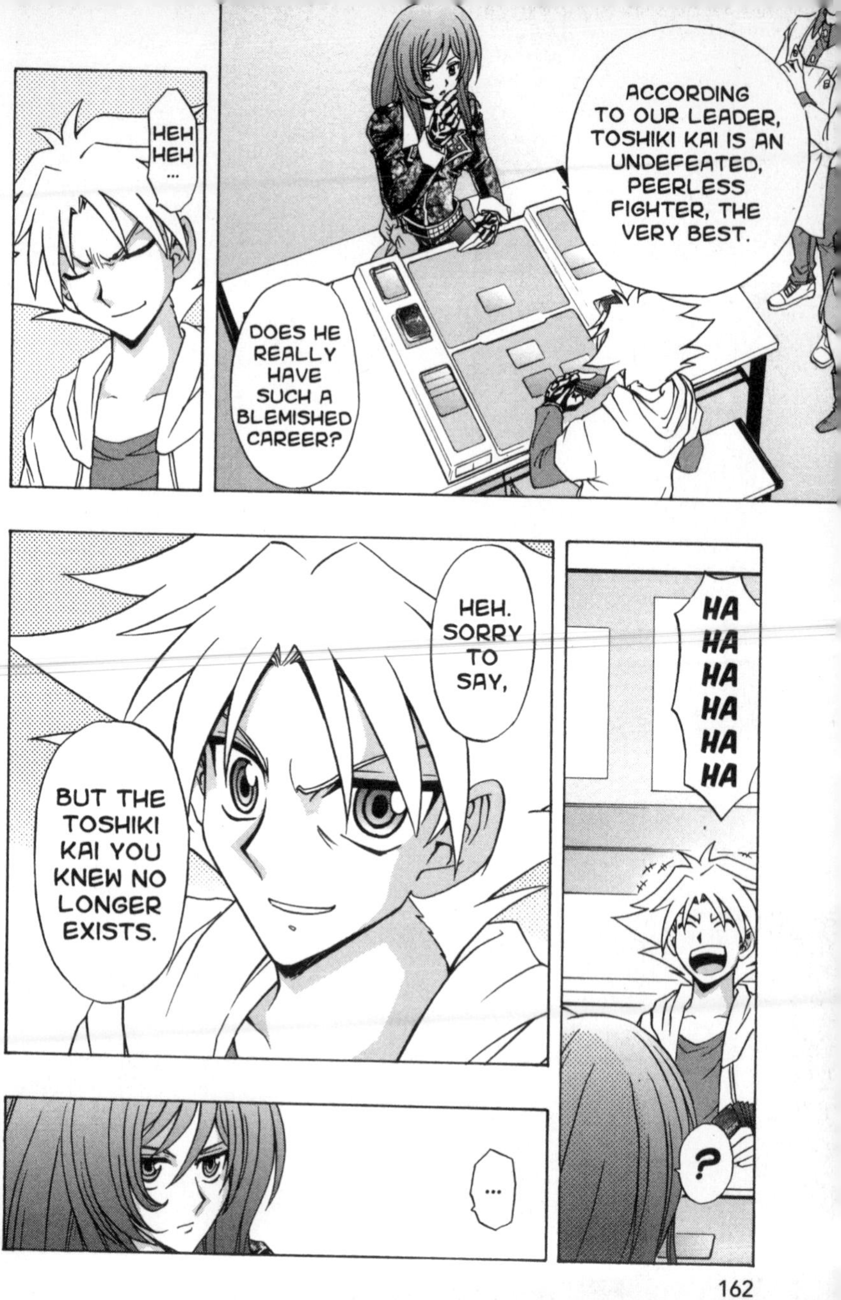

ACCORDING TO OUR LEADER, TOSHIKI KAI IS AN UNDEFEATED, PEERLESS FIGHTER, THE VERY BEST.
DOES HE REALLY HAVE SUCH A BLEMISHED CAREER?
HEH HEH ...
HA HA HA HA HA HA
?
HEH. SORRY TO SAY,
BUT THE TOSHIKI KAI YOU KNEW NO LONGER EXISTS.
...

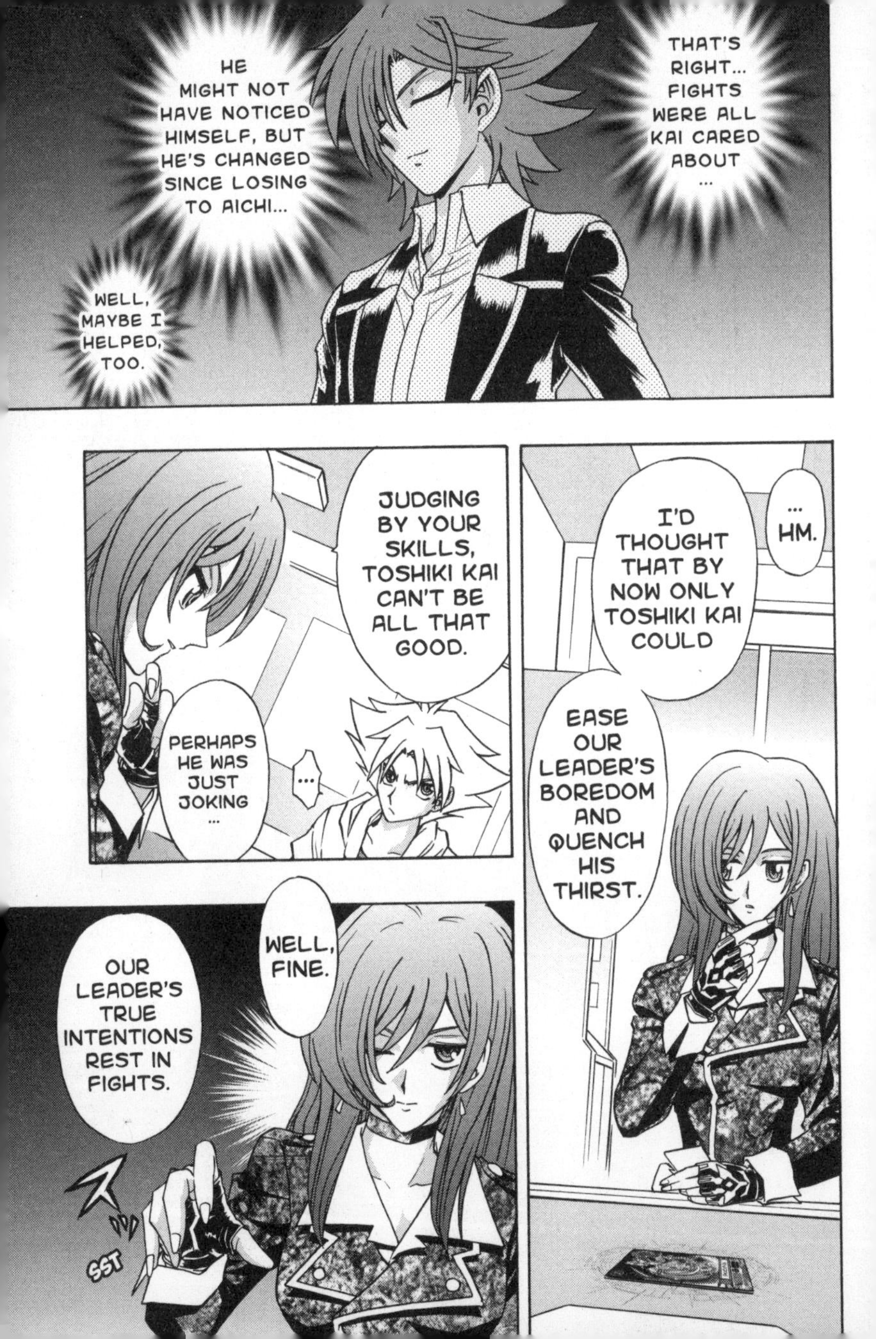
THAT'S RIGHT... FIGHTS WERE ALL KAI CARED ABOUT ...
HE MIGHT NOT HAVE NOTICED HIMSELF, BUT HE'S CHANGED SINCE LOSING TO AICHI...
WELL, MAYBE I HELPED, TOO.
... HM.
I'D THOUGHT THAT BY NOW ONLY TOSHIKI KAI COULD
EASE OUR LEADER'S BOREDOM AND QUENCH HIS THIRST.
JUDGING BY YOUR SKILLS, TOSHIKI KAI CAN'T BE ALL THAT GOOD.
...
PERHAPS HE WAS JUST JOKING ...
WELL, FINE.
OUR LEADER'S TRUE INTENTIONS REST IN FIGHTS.
SST

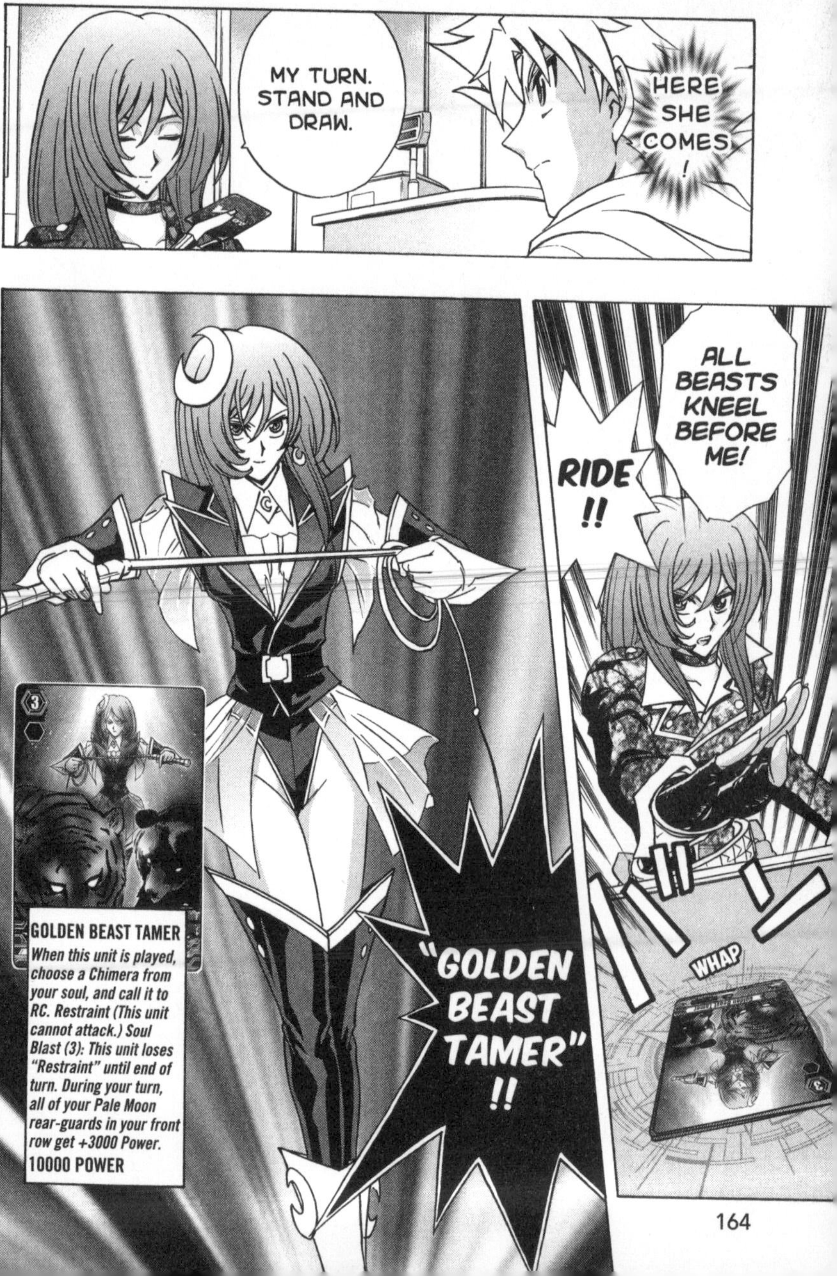

HERE SHE COMES!
MY TURN. STAND AND DRAW.
ALL BEASTS KNEEL BEFORE ME!
RIDE!!
WHAP
3
GOLDEN BEAST TAMER
When this unit is played, choose a Chimera from your soul, and call it to RC. Restraint (This unit cannot attack.) Soul Blast (3): This unit loses "Restraint" until end of turn. During your turn, all of your Pale Moon rear-guards in your front row get +3000 Power.
10000 POWER
"GOLDEN BEAST TAMER"!!

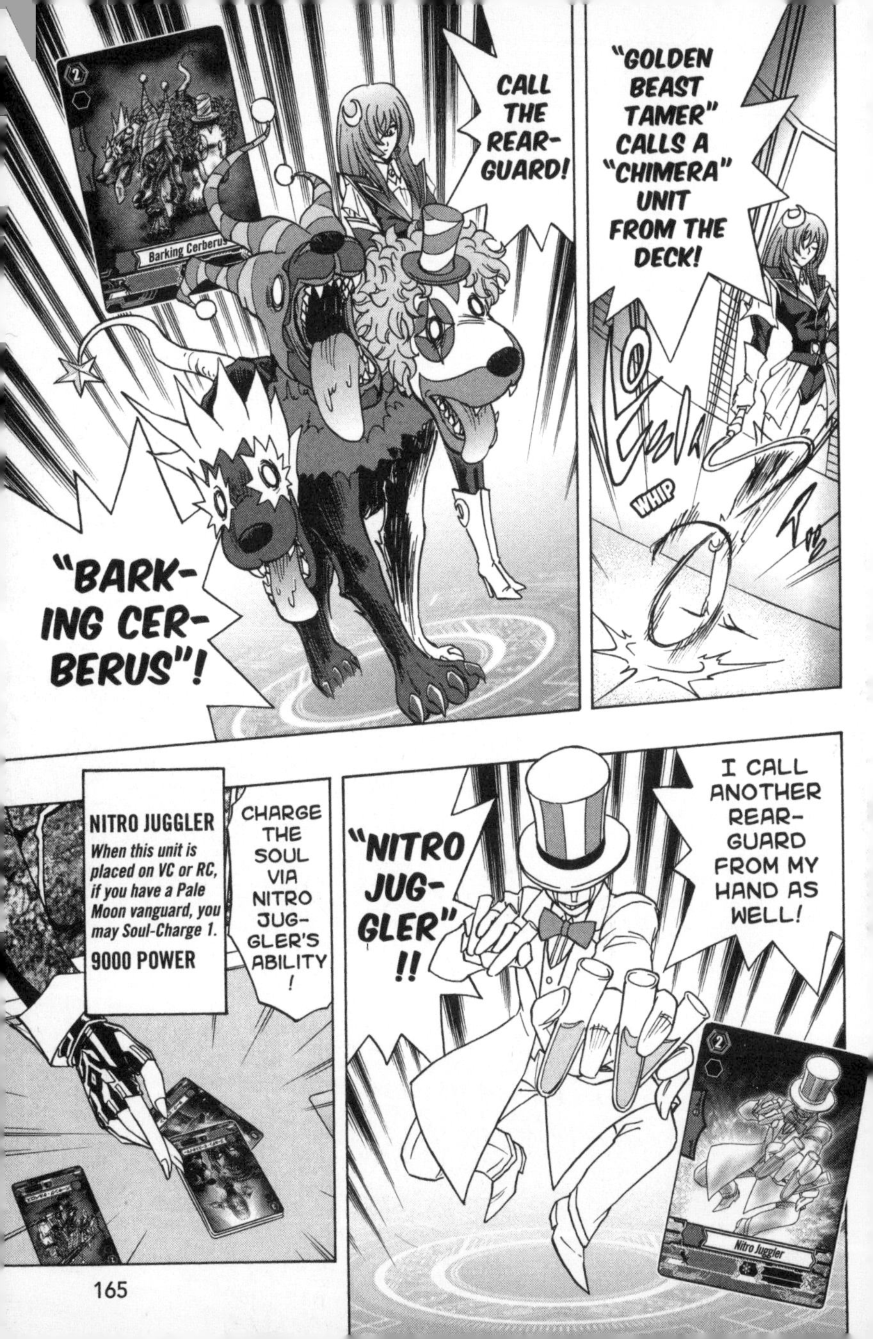
"GOLDEN BEAST TAMER" CALLS A "CHIMERA" UNIT FROM THE DECK!
WHIP
CALL THE REAR-GUARD!
"BARK-ING CER-BERUS"!
Barking Cerberus
I CALL ANOTHER REAR-GUARD FROM MY HAND AS WELL!
"NITRO JUG-GLER"!!
Nitro Juggler
CHARGE THE SOUL VIA NITRO JUG-GLER'S ABILITY!
NITRO JUGGLER
When this unit is placed on VC or RC, if you have a Pale Moon vanguard, you may Soul-Charge 1.
9000 POWER

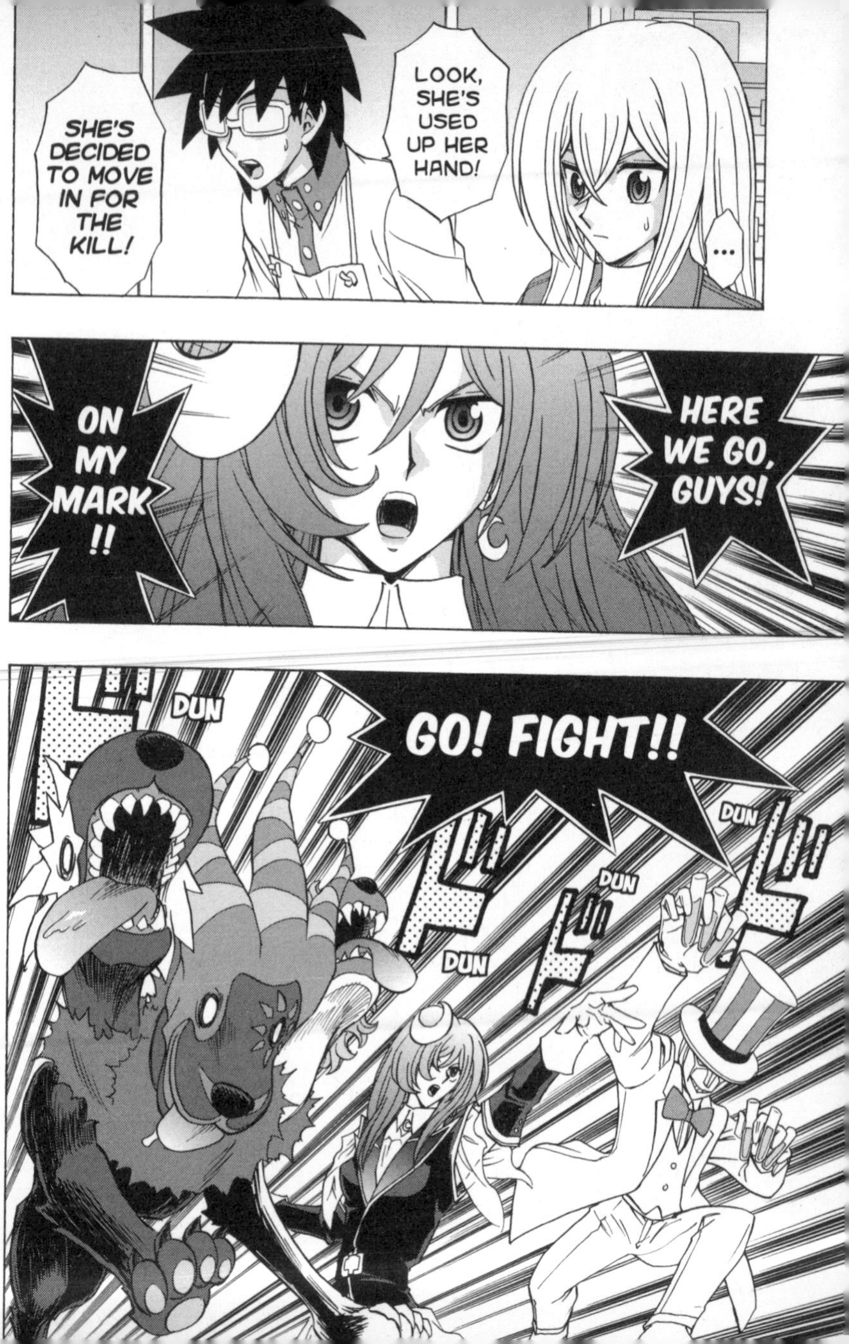
...
LOOK, SHE'S USED UP HER HAND!
SHE'S DECIDED TO MOVE IN FOR THE KILL!
HERE WE GO, GUYS!
ON MY MARK!!
GO! FIGHT!!
DUN
DUN
DUN
DUN

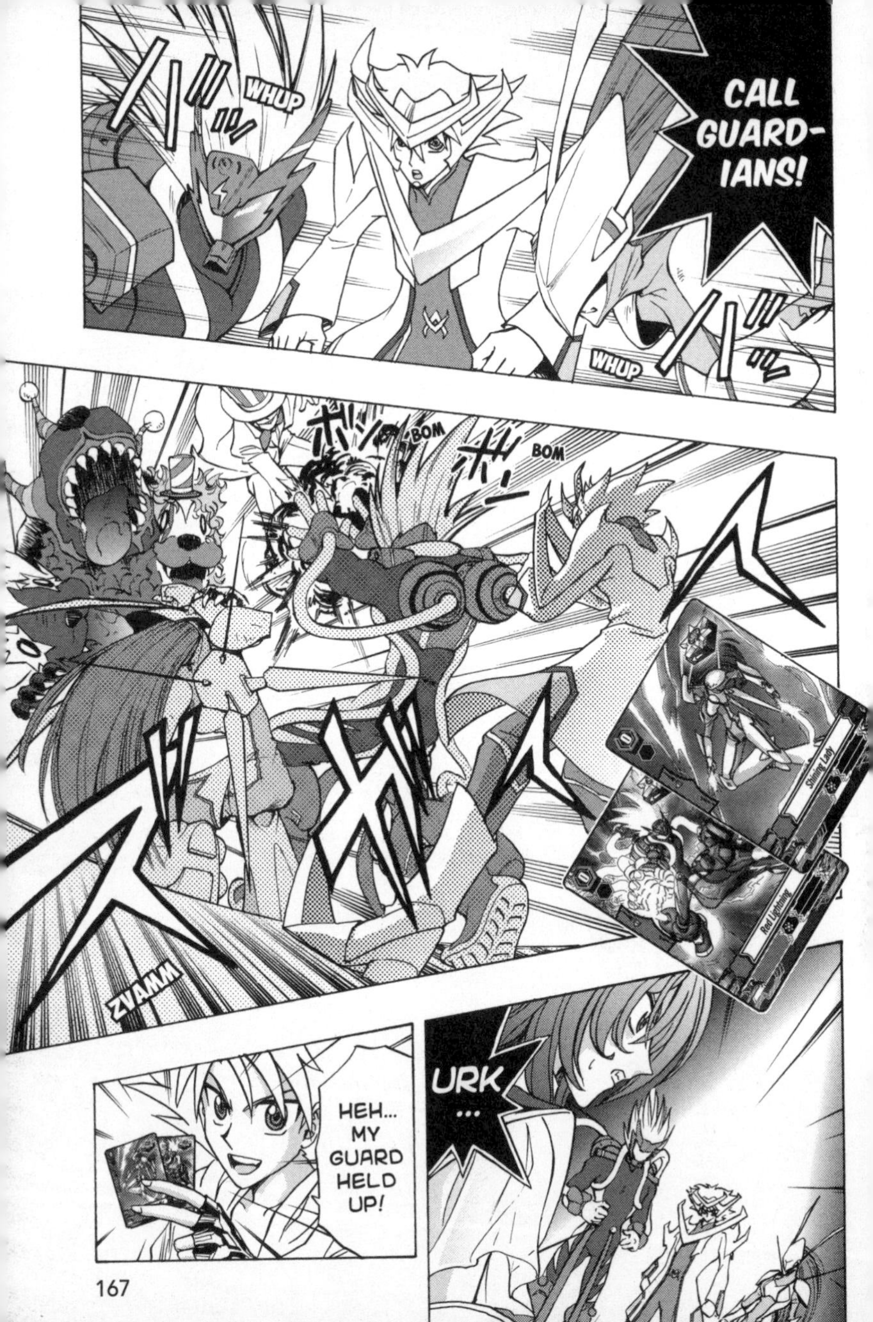
CALL GUARD-IANS!
WHUP
WHUP
BOM
BOM
Shining Lady
Red Lightning
ZVAMM
URK...
HEH... MY GUARD HELD UP!

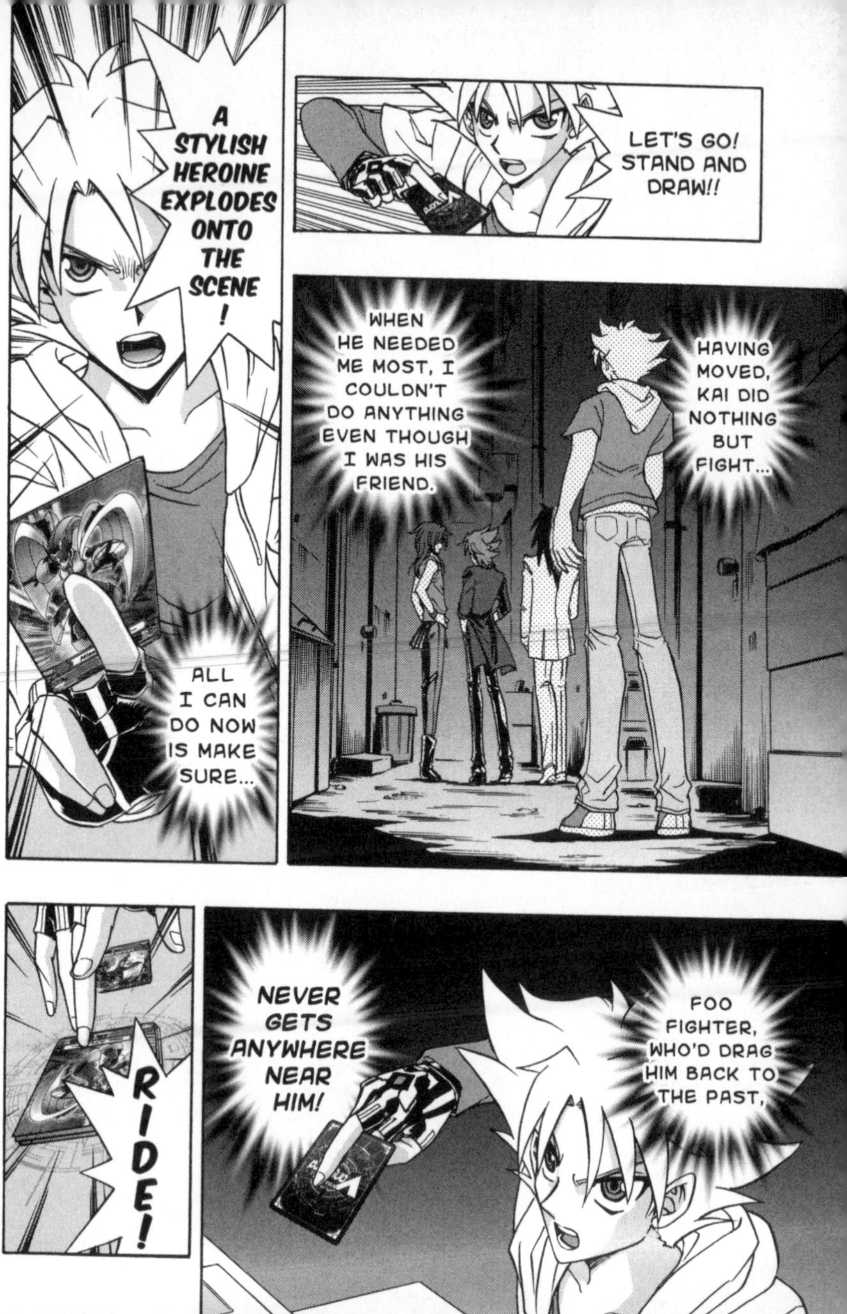

LET'S GO! STAND AND DRAW!!
HAVING MOVED, KAI DID NOTHING BUT FIGHT...
WHEN HE NEEDED ME MOST, I COULDN'T DO ANYTHING EVEN THOUGH I WAS HIS FRIEND.
A STYLISH HEROINE EXPLODES ONTO THE SCENE!
ALL I CAN DO NOW IS MAKE SURE...
FOO FIGHTER, WHO'D DRAG HIM BACK TO THE PAST,
NEVER GETS ANYWHERE NEAR HIM!
RIDE!

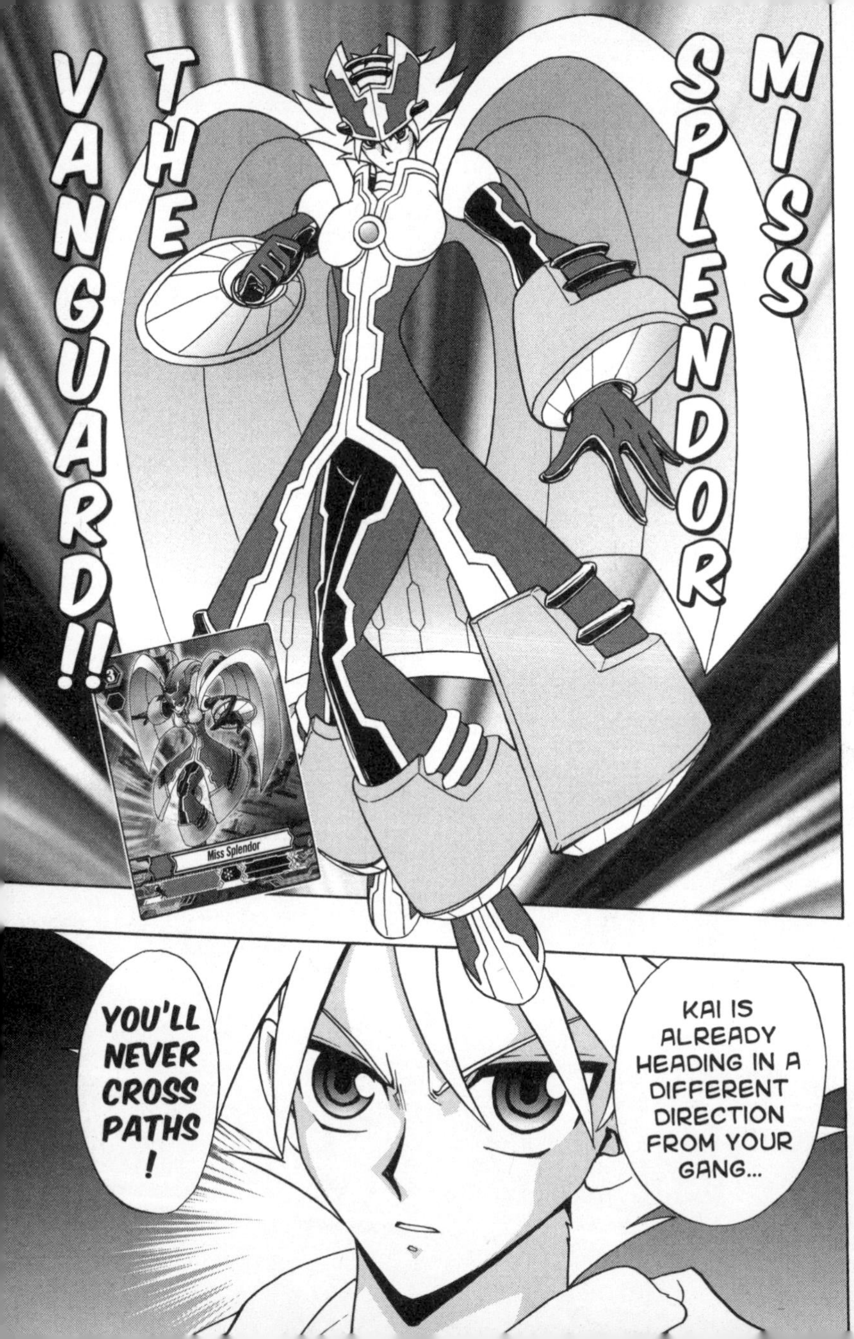
MISS SPLENDOR
THE VANGUARD!!
3
Miss Splendor
KAI IS ALREADY HEADING IN A DIFFERENT DIRECTION FROM YOUR GANG...
YOU'LL NEVER CROSS PATHS!

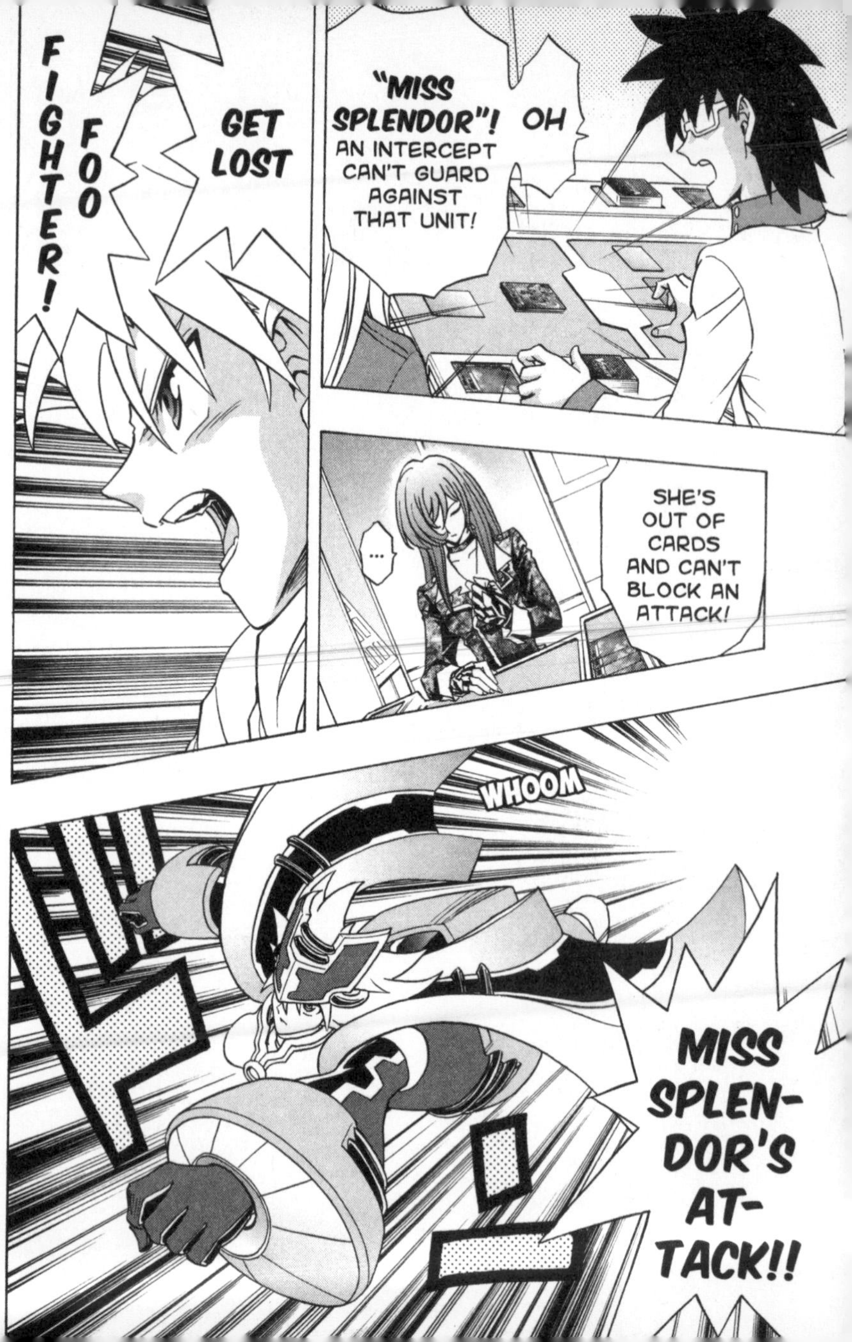
OH
"MISS SPLENDOR"! AN INTERCEPT CAN'T GUARD AGAINST THAT UNIT!
SHE'S OUT OF CARDS AND CAN'T BLOCK AN ATTACK!
...
GET LOST
FOO FIGHTER!
WHOOM
MISS SPLEN-DOR'S AT-TACK!!

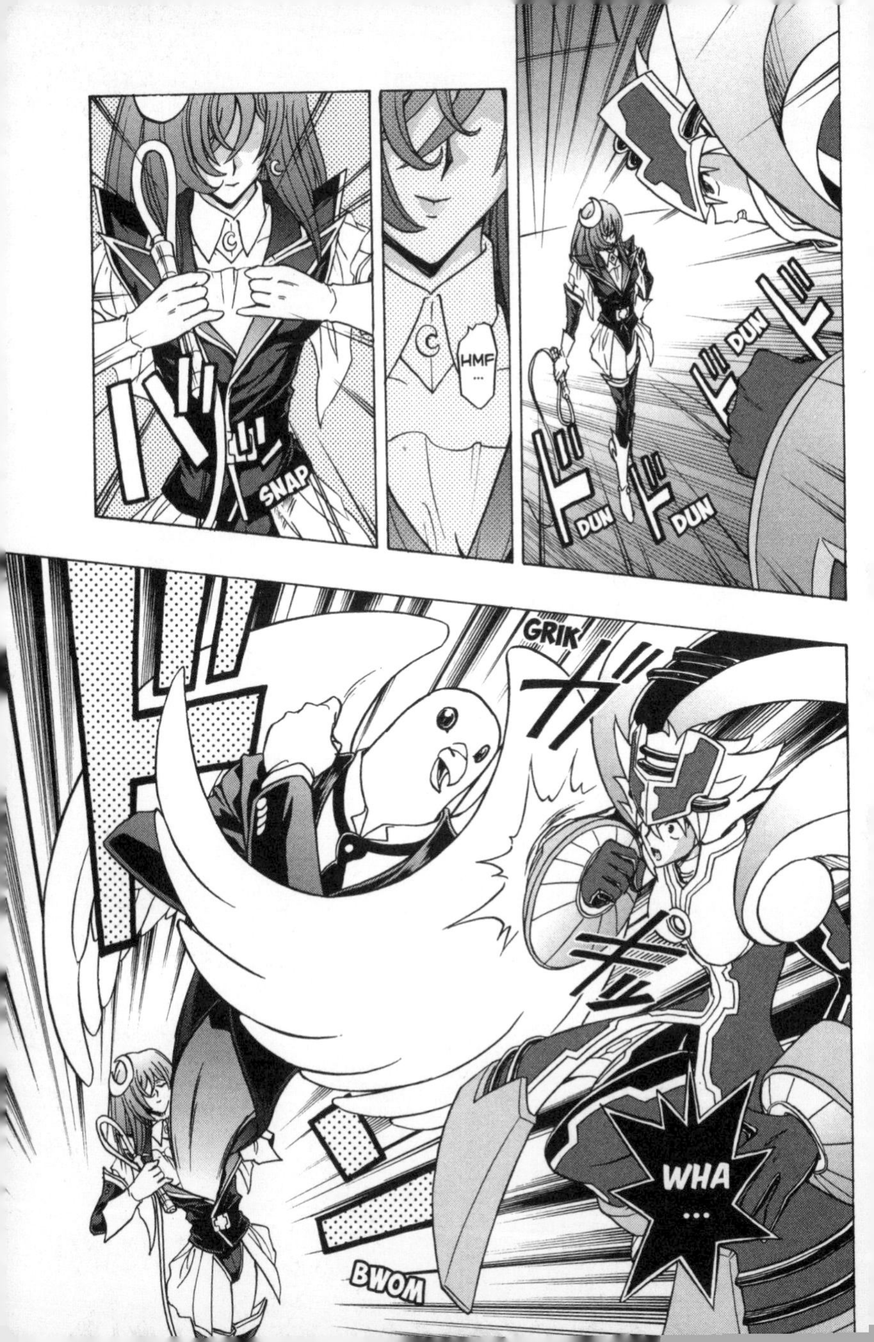
DUN
DUN
DUN
DUN
HMF...
SNAP
GRIK
WHA...
BWOM

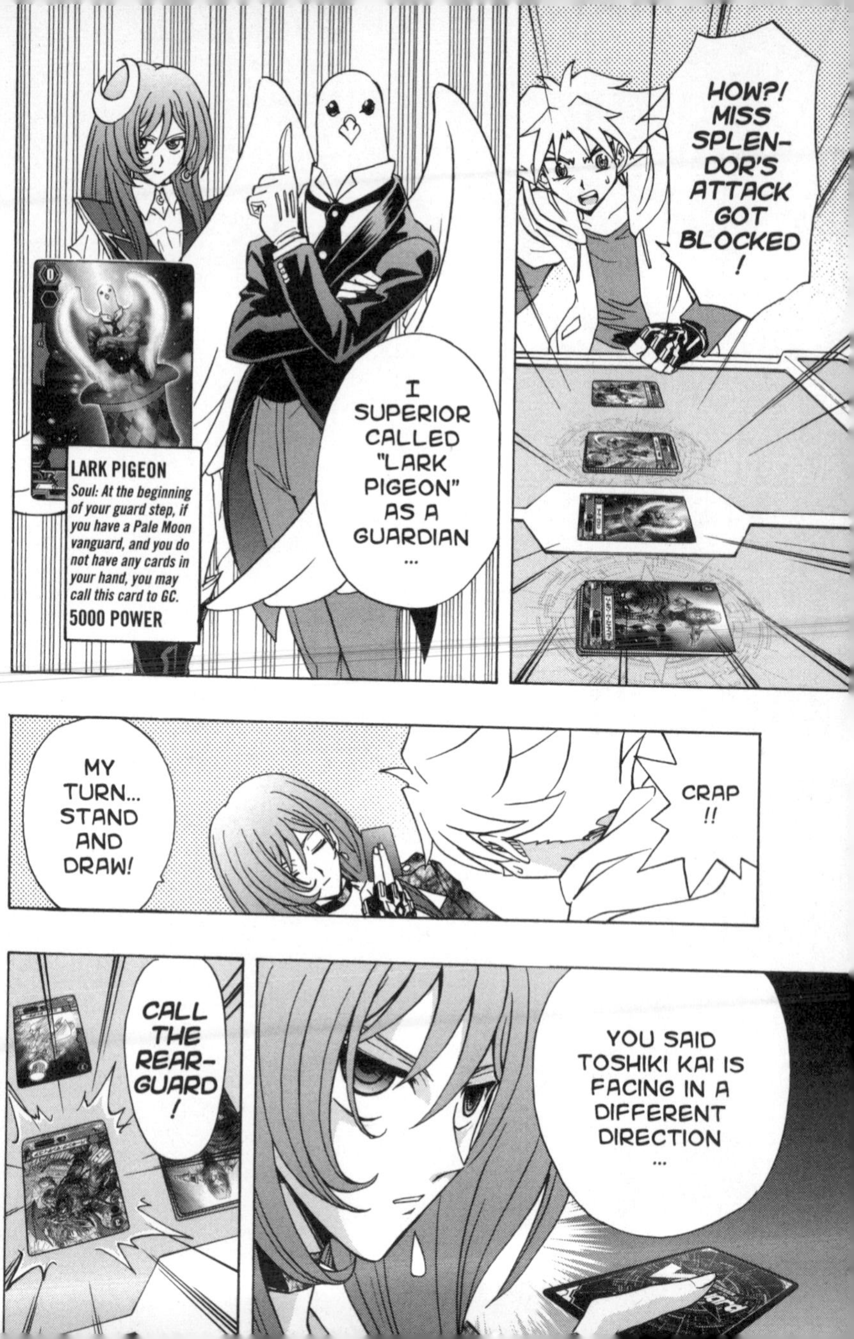
HOW?! MISS SPLENDOR'S ATTACK GOT BLOCKED!
I SUPERIOR CALLED "LARK PIGEON" AS A GUARDIAN...
LARK PIGEON
Soul: At the beginning of your guard step, if you have a Pale Moon vanguard, and you do not have any cards in your hand, you may call this card to GC.
5000 POWER
CRAP!!
MY TURN... STAND AND DRAW!
YOU SAID TOSHIKI KAI IS FACING IN A DIFFERENT DIRECTION...
CALL THE REAR-GUARD!

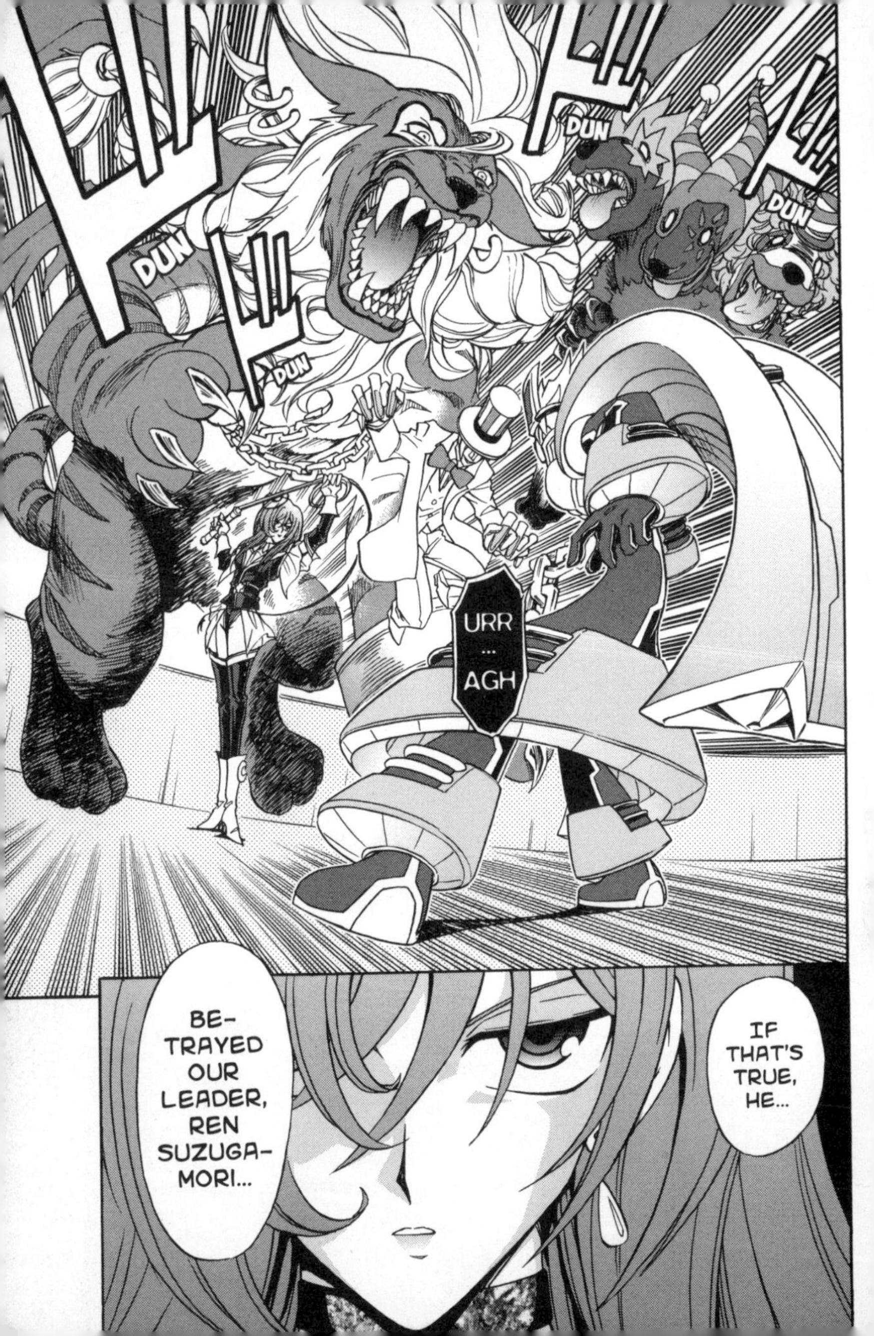
DUN
DUN
DUN
DUN
URR ... AGH
IF THAT'S TRUE, HE...
BE-TRAYED OUR LEADER, REN SUZUGA-MORI...

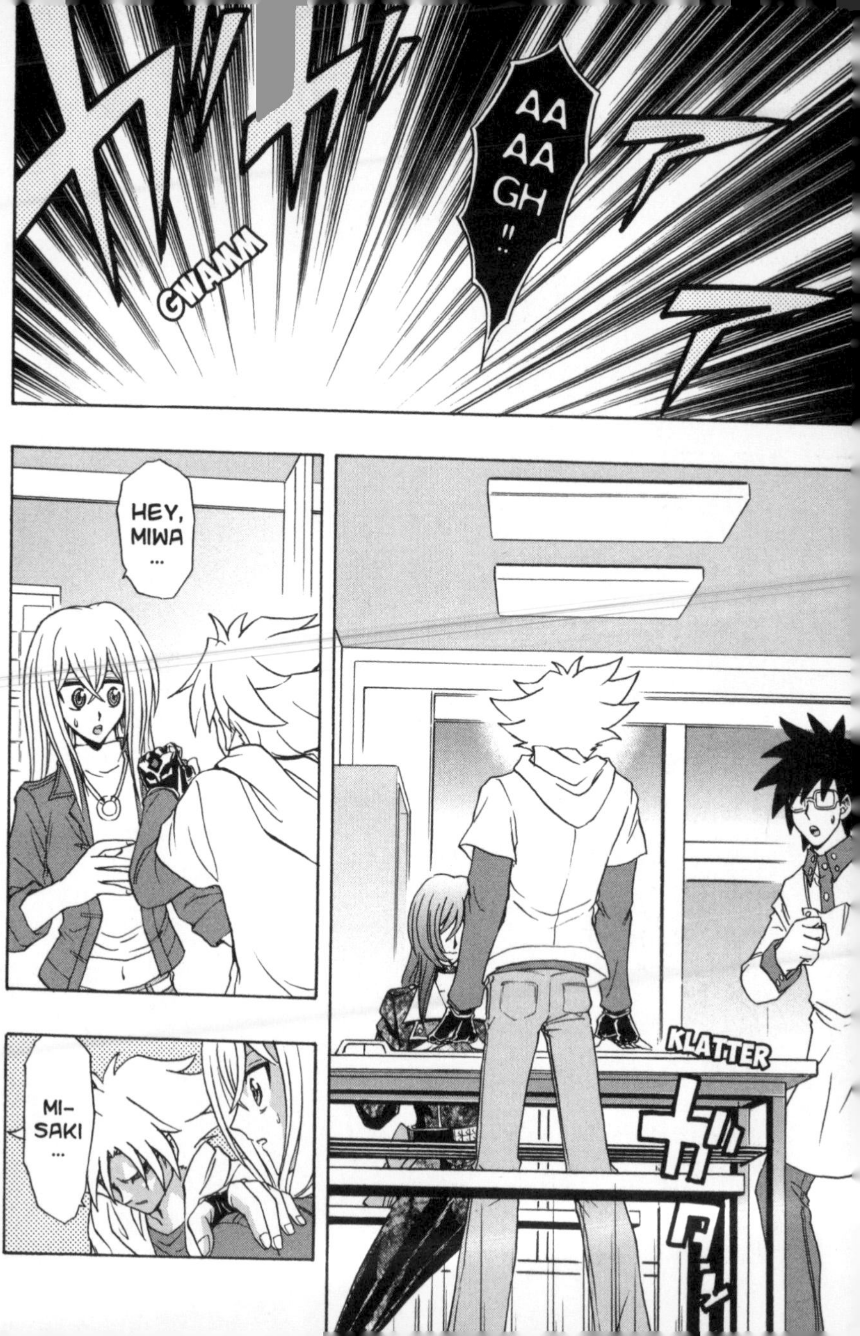
AAAAGH!!
GWAMM
KLATTER
HEY, MIWA...
MI-SAKI...

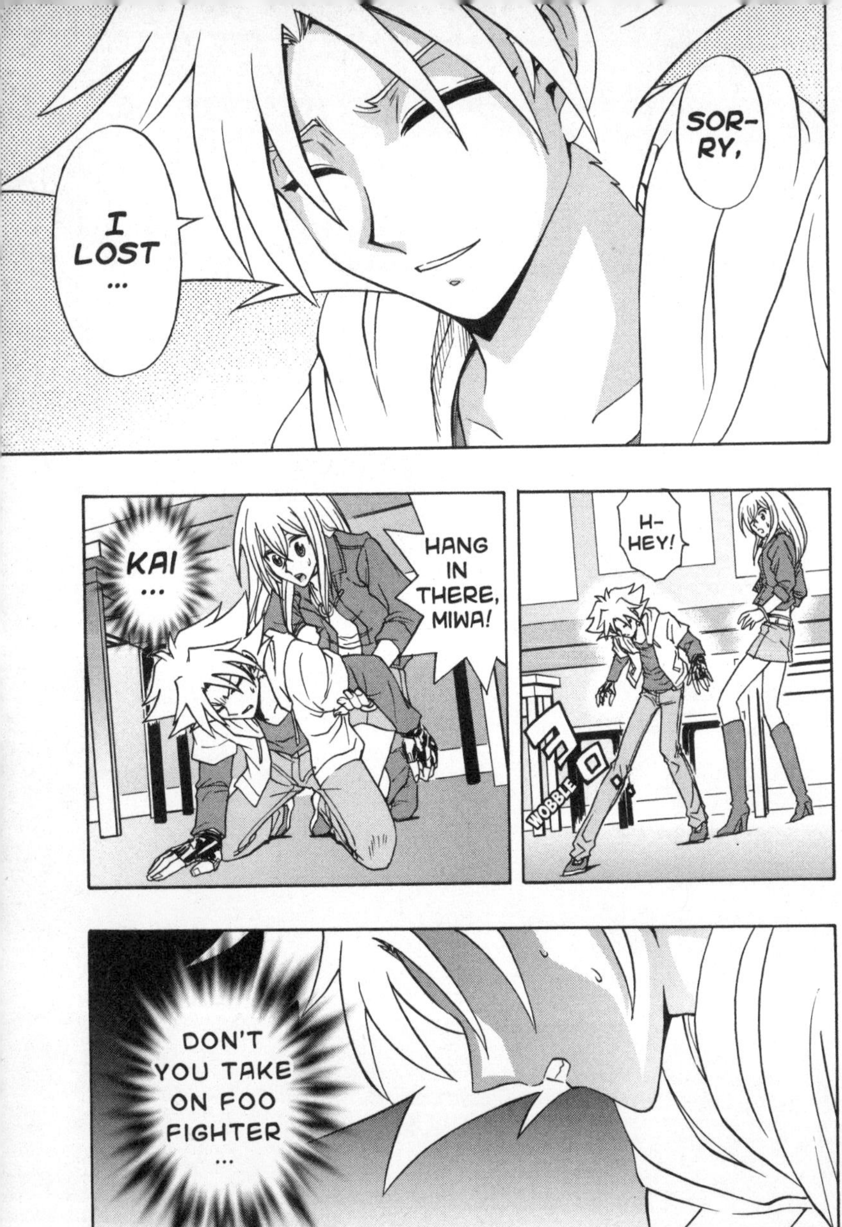
SOR-RY,
I LOST ...
H-HEY!
WOBBLE
HANG IN THERE, MIWA!
KAI ...
DON'T YOU TAKE ON FOO FIGHTER ...

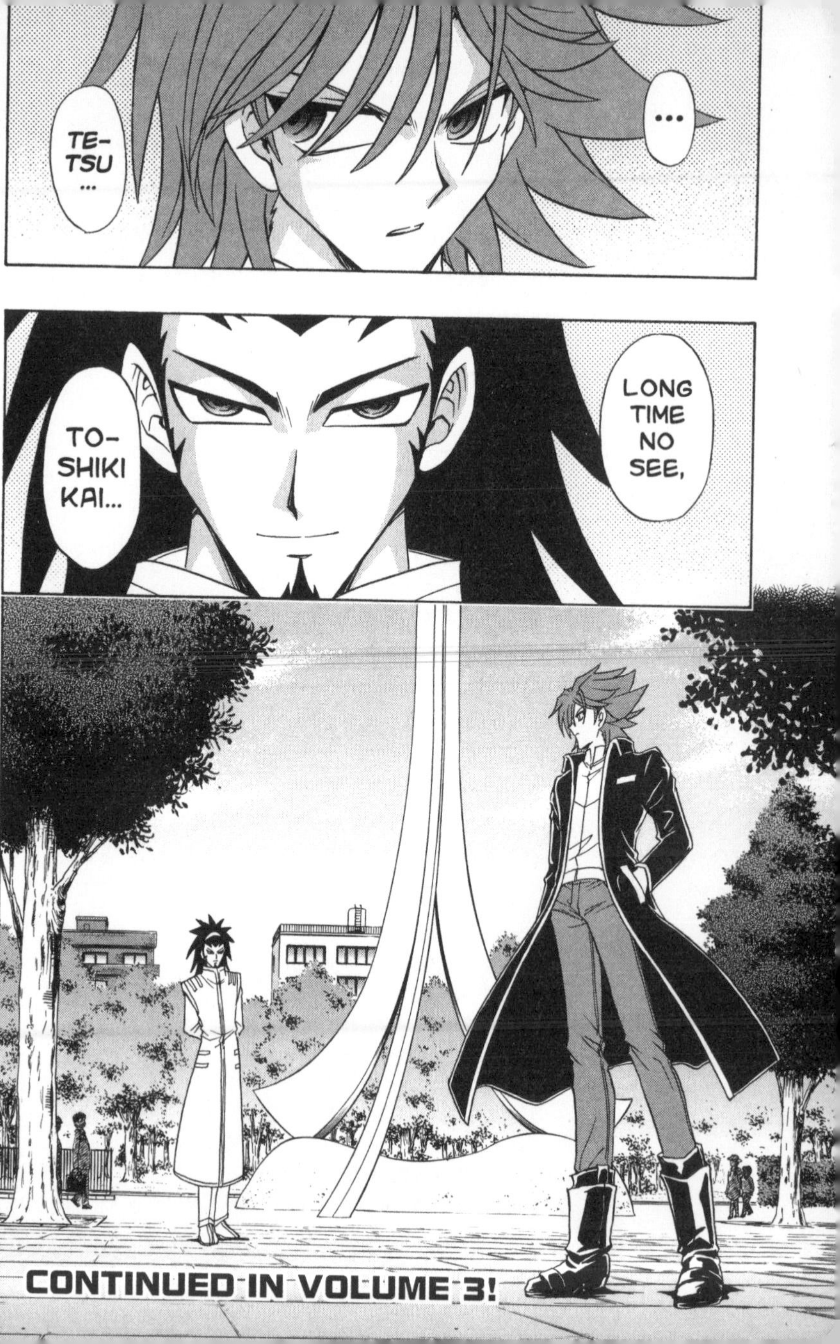
...
TE-TSU ...
LONG TIME NO SEE,
TO-SHIKI KAI...
CONTINUED IN VOLUME 3!

Concept art for Alfred Early / Akira Itou

CARDFIGHT!! VANGUARD VOL. 2
ORIGINAL DESIGNS OF THE FEATURED UNITS

CHAPTER 5
Lizard Runner, Undeux / 安達洋介 (Yosuke Adachi)
Embodiment of Armor, Bahr / Hirokorin
Embodiment of Spear, Tahr / 松島一夫 (Kazuo Matsushima)
Demonic Dragon Mage, Rakshasa / NINNIN

CHAPTER 6
Stealth Beast, Chigasumi / Goro Suzuki
King of Sword / ToMo
Stealth Beast, Hagakure / KyokaShingata-yutori

CHAPTER 7
Wingal / TMS

CHAPTER 8
Margal / Teppei Tadokoro

CHAPTER 9
Death Army Guy / Hirokorin
Barking Cerberus / Mori Chack
Red Lightning / Rintaro Murase
Shining Lady / TMS
Barking Manticore / Toshiaki Takayama

All Other Units / Akira Itou

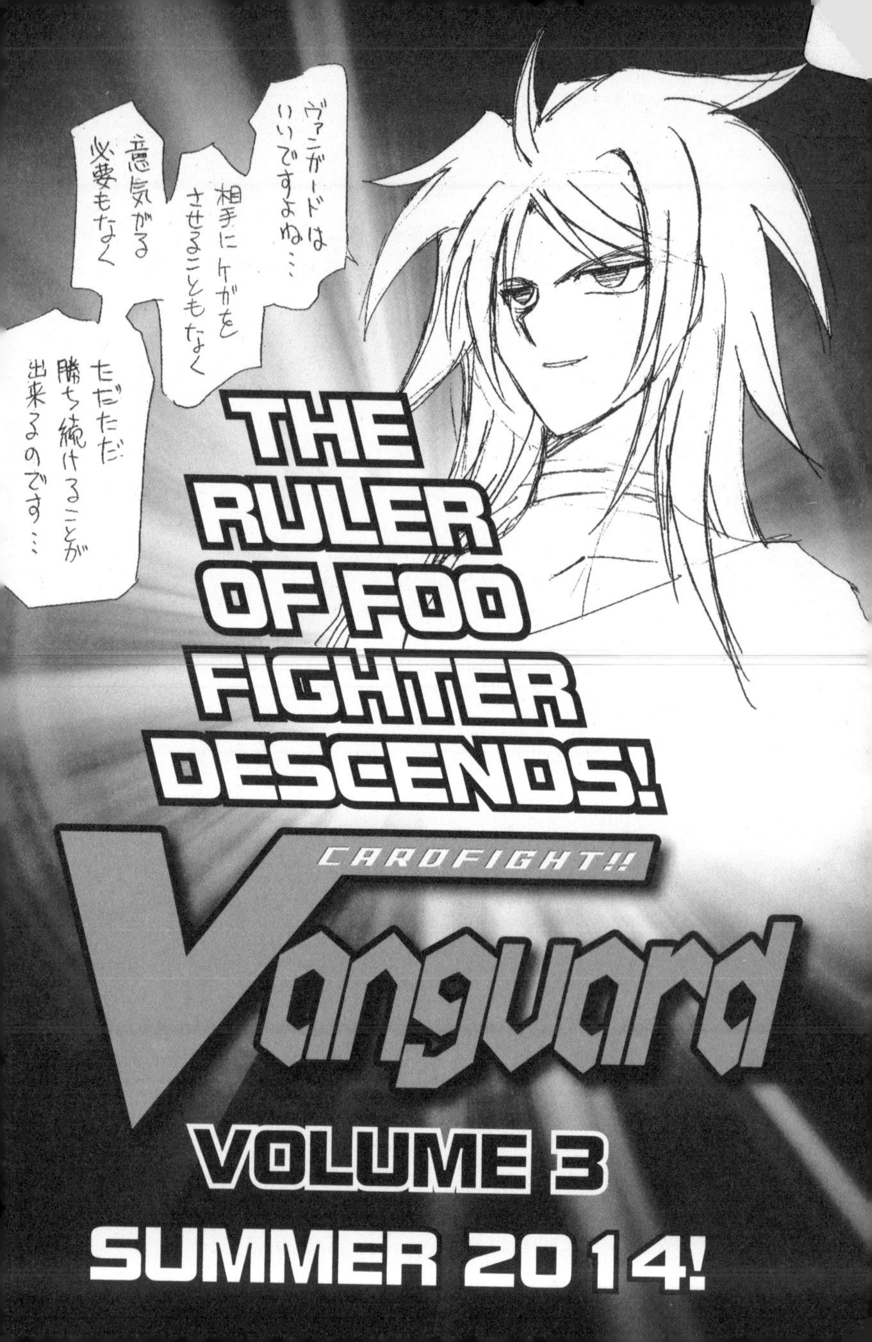
ヴァンガードはいいですよねぇ…相手にケガをさせることもなく
意気がる必要もなく
ただただ勝ち続けることが出来るのです…
THE RULER OF FOO FIGHTER DESCENDS!
CARDFIGHT!! Vanguard
VOLUME 3
SUMMER 2014!

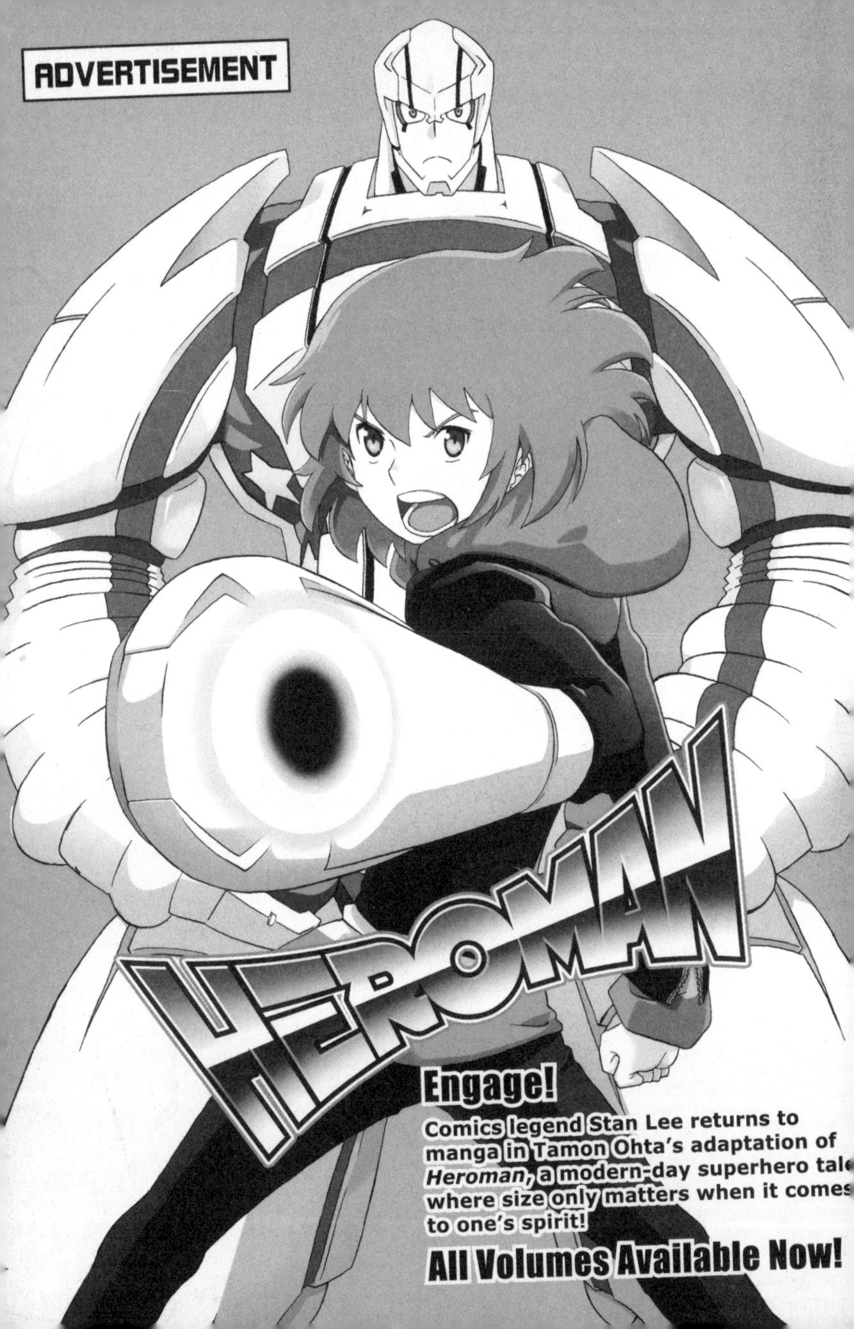
ADVERTISEMENT
HEROMAN
Engage!
Comics legend Stan Lee returns to manga in Tamon Ohta's adaptation of *Heroman*, a modern-day superhero tale where size only matters when it comes to one's spirit!
All Volumes Available Now!

CARDFIGHT! VANGUARD
VOLUME 2

Production: Grace Lu
    Anthony Quintessenza

Copyright © Akira ITOU 2011
    © bushiroad All Rights Reserved.
Edited by KADOKAWA SHOTEN
First published in Japan in 2011 by KADOKAWA CORPORATION, Tokyo.
English translation rights arranged with KADOKAWA CORPORATION, Tokyo
through TUTTLE-MORI AGENCY, INC., Tokyo.
English language version produced by Vertical, Inc.

Translation provided by Vertical, Inc., 2014
Published by Vertical, Inc., New York

Originally published in Japanese as *Kaadofaito!! Vangaado 2* by KADOKAWA
CORPORATION
Kaadofaito!! Vangaado first serialized in *Young Ace*, 2011-

This is a work of fiction.

ISBN: 978-1-939130-42-6

Manufactured in Canada

First Edition

Vertical, Inc.
451 Park Avenue South
7th Floor
New York, NY 10016
www.vertical-inc.com